The Foreign Policy of

C000130971

This book studies how smaller Gulf states managed to increase their influence in the Middle East, oftentimes capitalising on their smallness as a foreign policy tool. By establishing a novel theoretical framework (the complex model of size), this study identifies specific ways in which material and perceptual smallness affect power, identity, regime stability, and leverage in international politics.

The small states of the Gulf (Bahrain, Kuwait, Oman, Qatar, and the United Arab Emirates) managed to build up considerable influence in regional politics over the last decade, although their size is still considered an essential, irresolvable weakness, which makes them secondary actors to great powers such as Saudi Arabia or Iran. Breaking down explicit and implicit biases towards largeness, the book examines specific case studies related to foreign and security policy behaviour, including the Gulf wars, the Arab Uprisings, the Gulf rift, and the Abraham Accords.

Analysing the often-neglected small Gulf states, the volume is an important contribution to international relations theory, making it a key resource for students and academics interested in Small State Studies, Gulf studies and the political science of the Middle East.

Máté Szalai is a senior lecturer at Corvinus University of Budapest and a senior research fellow at the Institute for Foreign Affairs and Trade, Hungary. He was a visiting scholar at the Harriman Institute at Columbia University. Besides the general political, economic, and social developments of the Middle Eastern and North African region, his primary fields of research include Small State Studies, the Persian Gulf, and the Syrian and Iraqi conflicts. He is co-author of the book entitled *The Caliphate of the Islamic State*, published in 2016.

UCLA Center for Middle East Development (CMED)

Series Editors

Steven Spiegel, *UCLA*
Elizabeth Matthews, *California State University, San Marcos*

The UCLA Center for Middle East Development (CMED) series on Middle East security and cooperation is designed to present a variety of perspectives on a specific topic, such as democracy in the Middle East, dynamics of Israeli–Palestinian relations, Gulf security, and the gender factor in the Middle East. The uniqueness of the series is that the authors write from the viewpoint of a variety of countries so that no matter what the issue, articles appear from many different states, both within and beyond the region. No existing series provides a comparable, multinational collection of authors. Thus, the series presents a combination of writers from countries who, for political reasons, do not always publish in the same volume. The series features a number of sub-themes under a single heading, covering security, social, political, and economic factors affecting the Middle East.

14. Contested Sites in Jerusalem
The Jerusalem Old City Initiative
Edited by Tom Najem, Michael J. Molloy, Michael Bell and John Bell

15. The Arab Gulf States and the West
Perceptions and Realities – Opportunities and Perils
Edited by Dania Koleilat Khatib and Marwa Maziad

16. Winners and Losers in the 'Arab Spring'
Profiles in Chaos
Yossi Alpher

17. Law and the Arab-Israeli Conflict
The Trials of Palestine
Steven Zipperstein

18. Women and Resistance in the Maghreb
Remembering Kahina
Edited by Nabil Boudraa and Joseph Ohmann Krause

19. The Foreign Policy of Smaller Gulf States
Size, Power, and Regime Stability in the Middle East
Máté Szalai

For more information about this series, please visit: https://www.routledge.com/UCLA-Center-for-Middle-East-Development-CMED-series/book-series/CMED

The Foreign Policy of Smaller Gulf States

Size, Power, and Regime Stability in the Middle East

Máté Szalai

Routledge
Taylor & Francis Group

LONDON AND NEW YORK

First published 2022
by Routledge
2 Park Square, Milton Park, Abingdon, Oxon OX14 4RN

and by Routledge
605 Third Avenue, New York, NY 10158

Routledge is an imprint of the Taylor & Francis Group, an informa business

© 2022 Máté Szalai

British Library Cataloguing-in-Publication Data
A catalogue record for this book is available from the British Library

Library of Congress Cataloging-in-Publication Data
Names: Szalai, Máté, author.
Title: The foreign policy of smaller Gulf states : size, power, and regime stability in the Middle East / Máté Szalai.
Other titles: UCLA Center for Middle East Development (CMED) series ; 19.
Description: Abingdon, Oxon ; New York, NY : Routledge, 2021. | Series: UCLA Center for Middle East Development (CMED) ; 19 | Includes bibliographical references and index.
Identifiers: LCCN 2021023619 (print) | LCCN 2021023620 (ebook) |
Subjects: LCSH: National security--Persian Gulf States--History--20th century. | National security--Persian Gulf States--History--21st century. | Persian Gulf States--Foreign relations--20th century. | Persian Gulf States--Foreign relations--21st century. | Persian Gulf States--Foreign relations--Middle East. | Middle East--Foreign relations--Persian Gulf Region. | Persian Gulf States--Military relations.
Classification: LCC DS247.A13 S93 2021 (print) | LCC DS247.A13 (ebook) | DDC 953.6--dc23
LC record available at https://lccn.loc.gov/2021023619
LC ebook record available at https://lccn.loc.gov/2021023620

ISBN: 978-0-367-74520-2 (hbk)
ISBN: 978-0-367-74525-7 (pbk)
ISBN: 978-1-003-15828-8 (ebk)

DOI: 10.4324/9781003158288

Typeset in Times New Roman
by SPi Technologies India Pvt Ltd (Straive)

For Annamária

Contents

Figures

Tables

Abbreviations

ADIA	Abu Dhabi Investment Authority
CMS	complex model of size
GCC	Gulf Cooperation Council
IFLB	The Islamic Front for the Liberation of Bahrain
IR	International Relations
JCPOA	Joint Comprehensive Plan of Action
KIA	Kuwait Investment Authority
LNG	liquid natural gas
NGO	non-governmental organisation
NSA	non-state actor
PLO	Palestinian Liberation Organisation
SWF	sovereign wealth fund
UAE	United Arab Emirates
UNSC	United Nation's Security Council
WTO	World Trade Organization

Acknowledgements

This book is an updated version of my doctoral dissertation, defended in 2019 at Corvinus University of Budapest. It is the product of seven years of research conducted in Europe, the Middle East, North Africa, and the United States.

Along the way many friends, family members, and colleagues helped me in the process, starting with my supervisor, László Csicsmann, and my other professional mentor, Erzsébet N. Rózsa. I received invaluable help from around the world, including from Péter Marton, Omar Sayfo, Richard Burchill, Ahmed al-Ahmed, Silvia Colombo, Dania Khatib, Péter Marton, Omar Sayfo, Nikolett Garai, Marwa Maziad, Emma Soubrier, Dániel Vékony, Zoltán Kelemen, Jessie Moritz, Tyler Parker, Luíza Cerioli, Joshua Yaphe, Luciano Zaccara, Júlia Koncz-Kiss, Matteo Legrenzi, Gergely Romsics, Péter Tálas, Anita Szűcs, Ervin Szalai, Margit Harsányi, Csenge Ágoston, and Péter Wagner. I am really grateful to the staff at Routledge and the Taylor & Francis Group; they have done an excellent job throughout the publication process. I would like to thank the entire staff of Corvinus University of Budapest and the Institute for Foreign Affairs and Trade, who believed that my research was worth the struggle, especially my superiors who were flexible with me during the writing process. I am also thankful to all the people I managed to interview during my research trips in Qatar, Bahrain, the United Arab Emirates, Oman, Saudi Arabia, Iran, Iraq, Syria, Israel, Morocco, Egypt, as well as in the United States and the European Union, all of whom contributed to my work. Last, but not least, I would like to thank all my students at Corvinus University and of the College of Advanced Studies of Diplomacy in Practice, whose questions and comments were among the most inspiring feedback I have received.

Introduction

In Isaac Asimov's *The Foundation*, the science fiction author presents a world in which social sciences are so developed that they can predict the future. Foreseeing the inevitable fall of the "Empire", the protagonist creates a small political community called the "Foundation" which would, according to plans, replace the Empire as the new hegemon. The two entities inevitably drift into a conflict, which turns into a war *"between two systems ... between the big and the little"*. [1] Contrary to conventional logic, the smallness of the Foundation (described as *"a world the size of a handkerchief, of a fingernail; with resources so minute, a population so microscopic as would never suffice the most backward worlds"*) is not a coincidence; it is created purposefully with limited resources, based on the idea that smallness would eventually incentivise ingenuity and innovation, an asset much more valuable than tangible materials. The Foundation eventually succeeds, not in spite of its smallness, but because of it, using its size in different situations cleverly. *"There is no one to stop them."*

Surprisingly, such thoughts predominantly contradict the basic notions of the mainstream schools of International Relations (IR). Scholars of the discipline consider the importance of material size and the benefits of bigness as almost axiomatic, unintentionally equating "power" with "size". Kenneth Waltz, one of the most influential theorists in IR, built the neorealist framework based on the different capabilities (i.e. size) of functionally identical actors in the anarchic environment, which led to almost complete neglect (and even contempt) of small states. Waltz (1979, pp. 72–73) himself even jokes about those who would build theories on smaller states – according to him:

> it would be as ridiculous to construct a theory of international politics based on Malaysia and Costa Rica as it would be to construct an economic theory of oligopolistic competition based on the minor firms in a sector of an economy.

By viewing small states as negligible, weak entities, scholars of International Relations create a blind spot for themselves in many ways. Both theoretical and empirical research focuses on large states, despite the fact that the

DOI: 10.4324/9781003158288-1

majority in interstate society comprises smaller, resource-scarce entities. If scholars choose to analyse them, they often lack the proper analytical tools to circumvent existing biases towards largeness.

Even if the bias of mainstream IR towards larger states is easily understood historically, exaggerating the importance of material size in world politics became obsolete by the 21st century (Neumann and Gstöhl, 2006). Due to the systemic processes of globalisation, the institutionalisation of world politics, and the emergence of complex interdependences, small states' traditional constraints have been significantly eased. The study of world politics ceased to be dominated solely by great powers and their researchers, paving the way for scholars of smaller countries to contribute to the discussion. In parallel, there have been several attempts in contemporary academia to revise the fundamentals of IR and to revisit history with a greater emphasis on small states (e.g. Smith, 2000; Armstrong, 2013), nevertheless, the required fundamental reassessment is yet to be conducted.

Correlating size with relative importance affected Middle Eastern Studies, despite numerous contradictory observations. Contemporary studies of the regional order usually point out the diffusion of power and the rising role of small- and medium-sized countries: competitive multipolarity or heteropolarity (Kausch, 2014; Malmvig et al., 2016), the rise of swing states (Kausch, 2016), the Gulf moment (Abdulhalik, 2018), the phenomenon of spoilers (Golan and Sher, 2019) and other descriptions all refer to the growing role of smaller and weaker entities. Nevertheless, researchers remain focused on larger states and the literature available on small Middle Eastern states remains relatively scarce. To confirm my conjecture, I calculated the Pearson correlation coefficient between the number of mentions of states in the broader Middle Eastern and North African region[2] in abstracts or keywords of journal articles and the different aspects of state size in three academic online databases (see Table 0.1). What we can see is a very strong correlation between the intensity of academic inquiry and population, the economic

Table 0.1 The Pearson correlation coefficient between the number of mentions of states in the broader MENA region in journal article abstracts and different aspects of state size

	Population	Economic output (GDP)	Size of armed forces
EBSCO (all)	0.75	0.75	0.72
EBSCO (2010–2020)	0.72	0.79	0.71
JSTOR (all)	0.86	0.58	0.84
JSTOR (2010–2020)	0.85	0.61	0.84
Taylor & Francis (all)	0.79	0.68	0.74
Taylor & Francis (2010–2020)	0.82	0.67	0.77

Source: Compiled by author using data provided by the World Bank Database (2021) for population, GDP, and the size of armed forces. The number of mentions was calculated with the in-built search engines of the three databases. In the case of Taylor & Francis, keywords were used instead of abstracts.

output, and the size of armed forces, especially if we exclude Israel and Palestine (which proved to enjoy widespread interest independent of their size). Moreover, conventional wisdom would suggest that this tendency should have weakened in the last ten years but, empirically, we can only see minimal changes, and not necessarily in the expected direction. Naturally, these data are not conclusive and serve merely as illustrations to show the research bias towards larger states.

The discrepancy between the intensity of general inquiry and potential power is especially crucial for *smaller Gulf states*;[3] namely, Bahrain, Kuwait, Oman, Qatar, and the United Arab Emirates (UAE). Despite the general observations concerning their rising importance in the 21st century, the attention of scholars and observers is usually focused on Iranian–Saudi rivalry; other small states are solely considered as battlegrounds for great powers without proper agency. Analytically, they are seen as the little brothers of Saudi Arabia showing very similar political, economic, and social traits. They are usually described as autocratic oil monarchies with a Sunni (or, rather, non-Shia) political and cultural dominance with the same interests, security needs, and behavioural patterns, no mention being made of the profound differences in their polities and policies.

That being said, in the last two decades academics have started to notice the more intensive policies of, primarily, Qatar and the UAE (e.g. Ulrichsen, 2012; Abdulhalik, 2018; Saouli, 2020). When these researchers began to dig deep into their uniqueness, they usually juxtaposed their small size with their active presence as contradictory factors. Several articles described their activities as "pushing above their weight", suggesting implicitly that small states "should" act small and, if they do not, they may take a knock. Due to such explicit and implicit biases, a comprehensive and systematic analysis of smaller Gulf states without the cumbersome shadow of their neighbours is painfully missing from the literature. Lacking theoretical advancements and the wide gap between IR theory and Middle Eastern Studies both contribute to this unfortunate phenomenon.

This is not to suggest that smaller Gulf states are victims in this situation, sometimes quite the contrary. If we refuse to consider smallness as an essential weakness, we can realise how it is used oftentimes as a foreign policy tool. As one interviewee told me in Cairo in 2015, countries such Qatar use their smallness as a "cloak of invisibility", hiding behind their perceived weakness. Small states can use this cloak for various aims – to achieve a status of moral respect, to influence international developments, to interfere in other states' affairs, or, simply, to be left alone. That is why I am far from arguing that smallness is not an important factor in understanding smaller Gulf states – it does, but not in the way in which it is usually seen or understood. It can simultaneously be a source of weakness and strength; a deficiency and an opportunity; a burden and a tool.

The aim of the book is to take a fresh look at smaller Gulf states and to identify the role played by smallness in their foreign and security policy. The endeavour is both theoretical and empirical: I would like to contribute to the general discussion in IR about how small states should be analysed; to Middle Eastern studies by interpreting the role of smaller Gulf states in the region; and to the literature on their foreign policy analysis since their independence until the present day, by comparing their motives and behaviour, and the role played by their size in all this.

To achieve this aim and to circumvent the above-described biases in the IR literature regarding smallness, a new theoretical model will be used for the study. This framework, namely the *complex model of size* (CMS), is built on 3+1 observations. The first three observations refer to the proper way in which we can analyse state size, while the fourth focuses on state behaviour. First, when IR scholars talk about state size, they usually refer to four different concepts, depending on whether the viewpoint is individual/systemic or material/immaterial. The traditional criticism of Small State Studies – the lack of common conceptualisation and definition (Maas, 2009) – can be attributed to this phenomenon. In order to understand a state's behaviour, one has to differentiate between the concepts and analyse all four of them simultaneously.

Second, state size should not be understood as a state-level variable but, through the distribution of various resources and inter-state perception, a consequence of system-level developments, as well. Depending on time and space, regional systems can alter how we should interpret smallness and largeness, both in material and immaterial terms. Therefore, studying the role of small states without the systemic level is an inherently flawed initiative.

Third, following the steps of Peter Katzenstein (1985, pp. 136–137), I argue that smallness should not be seen as a "master variable" that triumphs over other aspects of political communities; it affects state behaviour in interaction with other variables. For example, territorial smallness cannot be understood without the geopolitical context, and demographic smallness exerts its effect only relative to the needs of the economy. Analysing the way in which smallness works should be done through these interactions.

Last, but not least, foreign policy behaviour is shaped by smallness in a variety of ways. On the one hand, as conventional IR would suggest, it deprives governments of various options and actions. On the other, there are at least two additional and, especially in the Gulf, more widespread phenomena that need to be taken into account. Small states learned to circumvent the direct deficiencies of smallness with what I call *compensatory policies*. In most situations, small states do not struggle with smallness per se but, rather, with the unintended consequences of such policies. Lastly, small size can be advantageous and can create opportunities for small states if they use it wisely, not just as a cloak of invisibility but also as a soft power tool.

The structure of the book builds on these four observations. In Chapter 1, I will separate the four types of size through a short literature review, pointing out the main findings of Small State Studies. I will reorganize the thoughts of scholars based on the differentiation between absolute, relative, perceptual, and normative size and smallness, building up four separate narratives focusing on the most frequently recurring questions, main debates, and expectations regarding state behaviour. In Chapter 2, I will conduct the systemic level analysis for the MENA region, focusing on regional particularities that effect how smallness works in practice.

Chapters 3 and 4 will be devoted to investigating the five smaller Gulf states in terms of their relative, normative, absolute, and perceptual size using various methodological tools, including quantitative comparison, discourse analysis, and descriptive research. The discussion will include most attributes of smaller Gulf states that effect their behaviour, which is why particular regime security considerations will also be noted.

Chapters 5 and 6 will focus on the foreign and security policy of smaller Gulf states since their independence until early 2021. The inquiry will be structured on the basis of case studies, each revolving around a particular policy issue or historical development. In Chapter 5, three strategic situations will be analysed in the history of the Gulf between 1971 and 2011; namely, the reasons why most local leaders decided to be independent as small states rather than part of a bigger federation; the effects of the Iranian revolution and the Iranian–Iraqi war on the security perception of smaller Gulf states; and the evolution of superpower relations, especially in light of the second (1990–1991) and the third (2003) Gulf wars. Lastly, Chapter 6 will include the most interesting security policy dilemmas facing the smaller Gulf states in the last decade, including those connected to maintaining regime stability during the Arab Uprisings, the various strategies in connection with Saudi–Iranian rivalry, and the spread of political Islam between 2011 and 2013, the Gulf rift between Qatar and its neighbours (2017–2021), as well as the motivations behind the Abraham Accords of 2020 and building relations with Israel.

Before starting the inquiry, I would like to make two additional clarifications. First, my aim is not to build up a general theory of small states. The CMS merely functions as an interpretative framework, which was of great help to me in understanding smaller Gulf states' behaviour, and hopefully will work the same way for the reader, too. I hope my study contributes to the general understanding of small state behaviour, but it is not conducted with the purpose of generalising observations. Second, my quest to urge scholars to pay more attention to small states is not a moral one, at least not consciously. I do not want to right a wrong, I do not think that small states are in any way better or worse than any other actor. I only want to raise awareness of a wide-ranging flaw in mainstream IR that prevents us from conducting a precise analysis, and to interpret and foresee present and future developments taking place in world politics.

Notes

1 Quote from Asimov, 1982.
2 Defined here as the members of the League of Arab Nations, Israel, Iran, and Turkey.
3 The term "smaller Gulf states" will refer to all five states as will be described in Chapter 3; not all of them can be described as a small state.

Bibliography

Abdulhalik, A. (2018) *Lahza al-Khaleej fee al-Taareeh al-Arab al-Mu'aseer*. Beirut: Dar al-Farabi.

Armstrong, C.K. (2013) *Tyranny of the Weak. North Korea and the World, 1950–1992*. Ithaca & London: Cornell University Press.

Asimov, I. (1982) *The Foundation*. Doubleday, E-book format [Online].

Golan, G. and Sher, G. (eds.) (2019) *Spoiling and Coping with Spoilers*. Bloomington: Indiana University Press. DOI:10.2307/j.ctvj7wnz6.

Katzenstein, P.J. (1985) *Small States in World Markets. Industrial Policy in Europe*. Ithaca & London: Cornell University Press. DOI:10.7591/9781501700361.

Kausch, K. (2014) Competitive Multipolarity in the Middle East, *Istituto Affari Internazionali*, [Online]. Available at: https://www.ciaonet.org/attachments/26875/uploads (Accessed 31 January 2021).

Kausch, K. (2016) The Promise of Middle Eastern Swing States. *Carnegie Europe*, [Online]. Available at: http://carnegieeurope.eu/2016/05/12/promise-of-middle-eastern-swing-states/iy77?mkt_tok=eyJpIjoiWm1ZME1tVTJNVEl4WVddaaiIsInQiOiJBNTZUYzBsN1czN0RYXC9DR1VEM0l4c3JQcTJzVDYwKzBTNktcL28rMGN3eG52azZBaWhGZU5mRWs3anhOaG0l1jMkJSWU9hSXkza-kRIVXg0TFVUUlVUdHplQXl0cVddrS0l6Z2Z0TGNUOVRwQjdvPSJ9 (Accessed 31 January 2021).

Malmvig, H. et al. (2016) The Contemporary Regional Order, in Soler, E.I.L., Colombo, S., Kamel, L. and Quero, J. (eds.) *Re-conceptualising Orders in the MENA region*. MENARA Project [Online]. Available at: http://www.menaraproject.eu/wp-content/uploads/2017/01/menara_cp_1.pdf (Accessed 31 January 2021), pp. 33–55.

Maas, M. (2009) The Elusive Definition of the Small State. *International Politics*, 46(1), pp. 65–83. DOI:10.1057/ip.2008.37.

Neumann, I.B. and Gstöhl, S. (2006) Introduction. Lilliputians in Gulliver's World?, in Igebritsen, C., Neumann, I.B., Gstöhl, S. and Beyer, J. (eds.) *Small States in International Relations*. Reykjavik: University of Iceland Press, pp. 3–39.

Saouli, A. (2020) Introduction, in Saouli, A. (ed.) *Unfulfilled Aspirations*. Oxford: Oxford University Press, pp. 1–10. DOI:10.1093/oso/9780197521885.001.0001.

Smith, T. (2000) New Bottles for New Wine: A Pericentric Framework for the Study of the Cold War. *Diplomatic History*, 24(4), pp. 567–591. DOI:10.1111/0145-2096.00237.

Ulrichsen, K.C. (2012) Small States with a Big Role: Qatar and the United Arab Emirates in the Wake of the Arab Spring. HH Sheikh Nasser Al-Mohammad Al-Sabah Publications, *Durham University* [Online]. Available at: www.dur.ac.uk/resources/alsabah/SmallStateswithaBigRole.pdf (Accessed 15 September 2018).

Waltz, K.N. (1979) *Theory of International Politics*. Reading: Addison-Wesley Publishing Company.

World Bank (2021). *World Bank Database*, [Online]. Available at: http://data.worldbank.org (Accessed 31 January 2021).

1 The four types of state size and the foreign policy of small states

The size of political communities – let them be states, city-states, empires, and so on – has always been a widely discussed topic in social sciences. Since the notion is unavoidable in several disciplines – including political science, International Relations (IR), sociology, and economics – the exact meaning and the conceptualisation of size has varied to a surprisingly great extent. In consequence, one cannot provide a complete, exhaustive overview of all literature related to the size of states, only a general framework in which the major traditions of thought can be included. This framework will be called complex model of size (CMS), and it includes the most relevant conceptualisations of smallness and the contours of behavioural patterns built on them.

Most of the ways in which scholars of IR have interpreted state size can be grouped into four distinct categories; these follow the four sociologies of IR, a framework put forward by Alexander Wendt (1999, pp. 22–39). These four schools of thought differ in their answer to two major IR questions – whether they deal with material or immaterial variables, and whether they focus on the state-level or the systemic-level. When it comes to state size, these two questions can be translated thus: Is size a purely material phenomenon that can be measured through identifying the available specific resources, or it is a construct that is shaped by norms and perceptions? Should we investigate state size in the context of a single state, or should we interpret it in an international comparative context? Based on these questions, the CMS recognises four different types of state size (see Figure 1.1):

- absolute size is the quantity of specific resources solely in the context of the state itself;
- relative size is the relative quantity of specific resources and a state's share in the distribution of such resources in a system;
- perceptual size is the perception of one's own size by the state or its society;
- normative size is the perception of one's size by the international community.

The four different kinds of size affect decision-making, power, and independence in various ways, and are connected to different traditions of

DOI: 10.4324/9781003158288-2

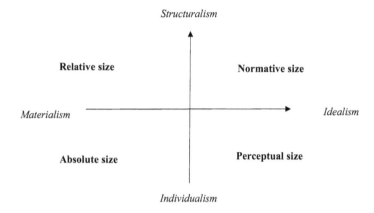

Figure 1.1 The basic framework of the complex model of size.

Source: Compiled by author, using Wendt, 1999, pp. 22–39.

political science. Researchers focusing on absolute size usually focus on questions of self-sufficiency, (dis)economics of scale, the proportional size of various resources, and so on. Relative size, which is the mainstream concept of IR, allows us to compare a state's role in a regional or global system. Perceptual size, a constructivist notion, affects how a state's identity is shaped by its own size and how the elite or the society interprets its own role. Normative size, which is also taken into account by constructivist researchers and a few representatives of the English school, determines the leverage of a state and its ability to build relations with other actors of international society.

I now offer a non-exhaustive literature review with the aim of separating the different ideas related to the four distinct traditions, setting up their research agenda and identifying their main conclusions on the definition and behaviour of small states.

Absolute size and absolute small states

In search for the optimal size

Analysing the absolute size – the available quantity of specific resources and the effect of such resources on the political community – can be regarded as the first endeavour in the study of smallness. Greek and Arab philosophers, among others, expressed the idea quite early that bigger is not necessarily better and that there are (or should be) some limits to the growth of a political entity. Searching for the "optimal size", they set the scale differently: Plato argued that 5,040 heads of families is enough, whereas Aristotle was a little more permissive with accuracy, claiming that citizens in the ideal political community should be able to maintain face-to-face relationships with each other (Beer, 1993, pp. 88–89).

Naturally, their argumentation was more interesting than the actual number they proclaimed. In Plato's *The Republic*, state size is connected with morality and self-sustainability. Socrates argues that the size of a state is healthy if it provides the "bare necessities" for its population and nothing more. If it remains as such, its smallness encourages "intimacy and friend-ship", "sobriety and moderation" (Owen Arthur cited by Henrikson, 2007, p. 50). Nevertheless, if a state overstretches, it will turn into the immoral entity of the "luxurious state" that starts wars with others in its "pursute of unlimited wealth" (Plato, 2004, pp. 55–57).

Besides Plato, Arab philosophers also differentiated between the two cate-gories. In al-Muqaddima, Ibn Khaldoun (1967) makes the distinction between the Bedouins (*al-Badw*) who "restrict themselves to what is necessary in their conditions (of life)" and sedentary people (*al-hadar*), who "concern themselves with conveniences and luxuries in their conditions". [1] Al-Farabi also describes the "necessary city" (*al-madina al-darariyya*) as a type of city in which "the people's aim is restricted to what is necessary for the subsistence of the body in (the way of) food, drink, habitation and sexual intercourse and to cooperation in obtaining these (things)" (Pines, 1971, p. 128), but he does not connect it with moral superiority (Pines, 1971, pp. 134–135).

Aristotle also favoured smaller entities; however, he did not build his argumentation on morality of self-sufficiency but, rather, on governability. In *Politics*, he argued that if a state is too large (both in terms of population and territory), it can only be governed badly. He echoes Plato's argument about the importance of satisfying the needs of the population, but he goes further and proclaims the importance of defence (Aristotle, 1998, p. 44):

> there should not be so much property on hand that more powerful neigh-bours will covet it, and the owners will be unable to repel the attackers, nor so little that they cannot sustain a war even against equal or similar people.

His argument translates into a premodern security dilemma, according to which growing is necessary to protect oneself but growing too large can actually provoke others to attack the community. While, generally, Aristotle accepted that wealth has beneficial effects, he set the "best limit" for the optimal size as the state in which "those who are stronger will not profit if they go to war because of the excess, but as they would if the property were not so great" (ibid.).

The aforementioned classic philosophers set the tone for modern understanding of smallness for millennia. Political theorists of the last centuries built upon their ideas, constructing five main research programmes related to absolute smallness.

First, the questions of self-sufficiency and morality were reborn in the literature on sustainability, degrowth and the criticism of over-consumption (DeWesse-Boyd and DeWesse-Boyd, 2007). Acclaimed authors such as Ezra Mishan (1967) and Nicholas Georgescu-Roegen (1977) criticised the "growth mania" of mainstream economic thought –the belief in the possi-bility and the necessity of "continuous material growth", embedded in what

E.F. Schumacher (2011, p. 51) calls the "idolatry of giantism", the implicit assumption that bigger is always better. From their perspective, being small is not a negative fact of life; a "non-problem" (Schumacher, 2011, p. 54).

Second, historians tried to undertake empirical investigation of the developments that shaped the size of modern states (Alesina, 2003, p. 303). They were somewhat critical of classic philosophers' admiration of smallness, arguing that their ideas "were not realistic. History did not follow [their] advice" (Gottmann, 1980, p. 220). Accordingly, in history, small states have not been morally superior communities but, rather, "economic jokes" (Hobsbawm, 1994, p. 286). To understand states' size, one has to follow historical developments such as nationalism or modernisation, and not moral dimensions. "Nation-statehood", argues Thomas Nairn (1997, p. 144) "was configured by the pressures and constraints of development [...], and these ensured that only entities above a certain threshold of scale had any chance of surviving, or of attaining independence – or indeed, the right to do so".

This brings us back to the question of the necessary size for self-sufficiency, or "viability" as Nairn puts it. The bar for this was set by the emerging competitive capitalism as the "first-wave industrialisation had to emancipate itself both from the confines of the city-state (where capitalism had always been at home) and from the bureaucratic hierarchies of the ancient empire-state" (Nairn, 1997, p. 147). Thus, the model for the ideal size of a nation state was set by France, a "medium-to-large nation state, capable of constructing a distinguishable political economy of its own, the range of cultural and administrative institutions needed for managing this, and an army capable of defending it" (Nairn, 1997, p. 133).

Third, debate surfaced in political science regarding the connection between governability and size (Beer, 1993; Anckar, 1999; Alesina, 2003; Posner, 2012). While many writers, including Niccoló Macchiavelli, Montesquieu, James Madison, Robert Dahl and Edward Tufte, agreed with Aristotle that large size contribute to ineffective governance due to growing diversity, others defied this correlation. According to the critics, there is no empirical evidence that ethnic or religious diversity is larger in bigger states but, even if it is, that cannot be directly translated into hostility or conflict.

Fourth, some economists also tried to calculate the optimal size of states. In one of the most comprehensive attempts, Alberto Alesina and Enrico Spolaore (2005) argued that the size of states is "due to trade-offs between the benefits of size and the costs of heterogeneity of preferences over public goods and policies provided by government" (Alesina and Spolaore, 2005, p. 3). Growth produces advantages and disadvantages (e.g. growing costs of governability, the multitude of interests and preferences) simultaneously, which balance themselves out. Alesina and Spolaore (2005) presupposed the existence of an "equilibrium size", in which the costs of largeness are minimal and the benefits arising from it are maximal.

The exact equilibrium size of a state is determined by international economic conditions, especially the country's integration into the world economy and the prevailing trade regime. In a completely autarchic and protectionist environment, the size of the population is the same as the market for national companies, which enlarges the disadvantages of smallness. On the other hand, in a completely liberalised environment in which all states are equally and fully integrated, the size of the market is (at least, theoretically) the same for everyone. Therefore, the "benefits from country size are smaller the larger the degree of international openness, and, conversely, [...] the benefits from openness are smaller the larger the size of the country" (Alesina and Spolaore, 2005, p. 87). This is why the more liberated the international trade, the lower the trade-off for countries, which is why (according to the authors) the rise in the number of small states and the liberalisation of the world economy went hand-in-hand after World War II.

The concept of absolute small states

Based on these ideas, we can define absolute small states as political communities that are materially below their optimal/equilibrium size, a status that creates a specific set of challenges. Scholars using the absolute size approach usually define small states in two steps: first, they identify the main resources that they consider the most determinative (e.g. population, economic capabilities) and, second, they set an objective limit for the size of smallness. Most quantitative definitions use population, territory, and economic or military capacities in different constellations and with different limits (East, 1973): 1 million inhabitants (Maas, 2009, p. 75), 1.5 million (World Bank and Commonwealth, 2000, p. i), 5 million (Bailes, 2009) or 10–15 million (Maas, 2009, p. 76). David Vital (1967) differentiated between economically developed (10–15 million inhabitants) and underdeveloped (20–30 million inhabitants) countries.

The inherent weakness of these concepts is their arbitrary nature, given the highly theoretical nature of optimal size or absolute smallness. Nevertheless, their clear advantage is their easily applicable nature and the apparent relevance of the four general resources, their unquestionable effect on foreign policy, and the easily understandable consequences we can attach to their size (see Table 1.1).

Table 1.1 The usually perceived positive and negative effects of smallness

	Positive effects of smallness	*Negative effects of smallness*
Territory	More defensible, cheaper infrastructure development	Smaller amount of resources, lacking prestige
Population	Social policies are less expensive	Smaller pool of human resources
Economy	More flexibility, specialisation, innovation	Dependence on external markets, lower-level production
Military	More resources are available for other policies, more peaceful society	Weaker defence capabilities

Source: Compiled by author based on the literature review.

Theoretical expectations regarding the behaviour of absolute small states

Not surprisingly, the literature built on absolute size is quite pessimistic about small states, and only a handful of writers attach positive attributes to absolute smallness, most frequently in connection with a bigger incentive for innovation (e.g. Cooper and Shaw, 2009). According to Ibn Khaldoun (1967, p. 274), the citizens of small cities are doomed to be poor and indigent due to the smallness of the internal market, which is why "their labour [...] does not yield them a surplus which they can accumulate as profit". Regarding domestic politics, Aristotle argued that small cities tend to be less stable than larger ones. This is due to the observation that the strongest political communities are based on the middle class (and not the rich or the poor), which is more numerous in greater communities. In contrast, "in small city-states, [...] it is easy to divide all the citizens into two, so that no middle is left and pretty well everyone is either poor or rich" (Aristotle, 1998, p. 120). Surprisingly, Aristotle (1998, p. 129) also talks about administrative consequences of small size. He states that in smaller countries the state has to have fewer offices or combine them in fewer hands.

The first comprehensive list of the consequences of smallness was created in the era of modern realism after World War II by David Vital (1967). In his book entitled *The Inequality of States*, he divided the challenges of small states into four different categories, which provides a useful framework for the overview of the literature.

First, mental and administrative capacities manifest themselves in the smaller size and number of diplomatic missions, and the lower quality of the work provided by diplomats. The literature therefore predicts lower levels of human and material resources available to the foreign and security policy apparatus (East, 1973, p. 558). As a result, they have to face severe informational discrepancy vis-á-vis greater states (at least, outside of their direct environment). On the other hand, because of the smaller bureaucracy, the competition between the different institutions is presumably less intense than in larger states (Handel, 2006, p. 150). Moreover, less hierarchy and the lower level of formality and strictness in decision-making processes make the diplomacy of small states more flexible, especially in the policy areas in which they do not have vital interests (Thorhallson, 2006, pp. 221–223).

Second, economic disabilities rise from the small size of the internal market, which translates into diseconomies of scale, less competition (Handel, 2006, pp. 164–165), a greater need for either constant aid from abroad or, more commonly, extensive foreign trade. Dependence on the foreign markets and actors is therefore a common feature among small states, which, in practice, is enlarged by the concentration in terms of goods and partner countries (Michaley, 1962; Vital, 1967; Wiberg, 1987). On the other hand, this necessary openness urges specialisation, which could be beneficial for their competitiveness, while also making them vulnerable to external shocks. In this regard, the constant need for accommodation (Moses, 2000) is not necessarily a disadvantage; contrary to the pessimists (such as Handel, 2006, pp. 154–164), Peter Katzenstein (1985) argued that this constraint contributes to greater flexibility and an ability to react more quickly and efficiently to external crises.

Third, small states are not able to spend much on national defence and do not dispose over a substantive military industry. They have to buy their equipment from larger states, which creates a dependence in national security matters (Handel, 2006, pp. 180–181). Moreover, increasing the defence budget would mean the extraction of money from other sectors, a dilemma that is especially problematic for smaller states, since the costs of governance on a per capita basis are, in general, higher (East, 1973, p. 558).

Fourth, because of all these factors, small states will be more vulnerable to coercion. They have a deficit in both influential capacity and resilience to external pressure (McGowan and Gottwald, 1975). In such circumstances, the classic tools of foreign policy are not all available to them, therefore their international behaviour is limited to specific strategies (Lee and Smith, 2010).

In the small state literature, special attention has been drawn to the investigation of small island states (Lockhart, Drakakis-Smith and Schembri, 2002; Barnett and Campbell 2010; King and Tennant 2014). These works usually investigate the challenges of small island states in connection with environmental change and degradation, remote geopolitical position and sustainable development. The small island state literature is perhaps the most clear-cut example of analysing the effects of smallness paired up with another variable (island statehood, environmental challenges, and so forth).

As we can see, without the thorough investigation of the position of small states in the international system, scholars were able to make predictions (and even draw up guidelines) for the foreign policy of small states, solely based on their absolute size. Naturally, there is no consensus over which courses are preferable for small states on the global stage, especially between the realist and liberal scholars,[2] but a general picture can be drawn about the limitations of small state foreign policy by having the following characteristics:

- survival as the utmost priority and many times the maximal aim of foreign policy, subordinating domestic political needs to tackle international challenges (Hey, 2003a, p. 5; Handel, 2006, pp. 151–152; Keohane, 2006, pp. 58–59);
- limited foreign policy activity both in terms of geography and policy areas, concentrating on the state's imminent region, and those questions in which it has vital interests (East, 1973, p. 557; Hey, 2003a, p. 5);
- preference of international institutions offering formal equality, multilateral diplomacy (Hey, 2003a, p. 5; Keohane, 2006, p. 58; Neumann and Gstöhl, 2006, pp. 20–21; Jazbec, 2010, p. 79);
- refraining from the use of force (Fox, 1959; East, 1973, p. 557; Hey, 2003a, p. 5);
- a tendency of neutrality in armed conflicts (Fox, 1959; Hey, 2003a, p. 5);

- due to their dependence in terms of economy and defence, they focus on international stability on the financial markets and international peace (East, 1973, pp. 573–575);
- priority of alliance-making as the most important decision of security policy (Vital, 1967, pp. 186–187; Wiberg, 1987, pp. 343–345; Tetreault, 1991; Hey, 2003a, p. 5; Keohane, 2006, 64–68; Neumann and Gstöhl, 2006, p. 18);
- inability to formulate strategically viable answers to unforeseen events, which results in either slow responses or high-risk behaviour (East, 1973, pp. 567–573);
- the need to focus on foreign trade and economic policy, to capitalise on globalisation and to create circumstances that avoid protectionism as well as hurtful liberalisation (Dommen and Hein, 1985; Moses, 2000);
- the possibility of refraining from even having a foreign policy due to the lack of effective agency and influential capacity (Vital, 1967, pp. 121–122; McGowan and Gottwald, 1975, pp. 473–476; Hey, 2003a, p. 5).

As we can see, a complete theory of small state foreign policy can be built solely on absolute size. Nonetheless, as many scholars expressed, such descriptions, which lack the investigation of the international environment, are insufficient to describe the situation of small states (Duval and Thompson, 1980; Hey, 2003a). That is why the turn towards the system in the study of international relations in the 1970s affected Small State Studies to a great extent, creating new ways, analytical tools, and methodologies to analyse resource-scarce entities.

Relative size and relative small states

Changing viewpoints and the concept of relative small states

Starting from the late 1970s, systemic theories began to dominate in mainstream IR theories, foreign policy analysis, and Small State Studies. In this new era, the research programmes of various IR schools – most notably neorealism and neoliberalism – developed separately, though in connection with each other, forming the basis of our current understanding of how small states behave. Contrary to absolute size, the focus was put on the relative size of states in a given regional and global comparison or context.

The definition of relative small states is quite similar to absolute small states, though with one major difference – the limit for smallness is not set by an absolute number but, rather, a ratio of the international system or a specific subsystem. Karl Deutsch defined small states as those entities that contribute to the global GNP with a maximal share of 1% (Baehr, 1975, pp. 459–460). Others (Bailes, 2009, p. 2; Muhindo and Calenzo, 2011, pp. 158–159; Garai, Koncz-Kiss and Szalai, 2017, pp. 12–13) argue for a regional approach in which the limit of smallness is set by, for example, the average of a geographic area. The logic behind this is twofold: first, the activities of small states are very much limited to a given region, and, second, a specific size can be both small and large depending on the size of its neighbours. Besides the general understanding of interpreting states' size in a relative context, the neorealists and the neoliberals regarded their behaviour in markedly different ways.[3]

Alliance policy and bandwagoning: the neorealist narrative

The neorealist concept of state size was laid down by the father of the school, Kenneth Waltz (1979). In *Theory of International Politics*, Waltz moved away from the human nature approach of classical realism and considered the most important features of the international system as the main explanatory forces of world politics. In his model, the international system has three major attributes (Waltz, 1979, pp. 87–99): the ordering principle (anarchy), the characters of units (functionally identical states), and the distribution of capabilities. Since, theoretically, only the third attribute differentiates between actors, the share in the distribution of valuable and politically practicable resources (i.e. relative size) will be the most important variable in the analysis of state behaviour.

Using this point of view, it is not surprising that neorealism became quite pessimistic about small states. If the system "is defined as the distribution of material capabilities under anarchy" (Wendt, 1999, p. 16), small units are weak and vulnerable. The lack of relative capabilities will define power relations with other countries and, thus, the foreign policy of the small state (Handel, 2006; Neumann and Gstöhl, 2006, pp. 17–19). The primary aim of the related neorealist research programme will be to determine what role small states do, can, and should play in the international system.

The Waltzian narrative of smallness and weakness has its roots in the *Melian Dialogue* of Thucydides (Baldacchino, 2009), which basically served as a cautionary tale for small states to accept the will of great powers. "The strong do what they can and the weak suffer what they must", argue the Athenians in the dialogue, as the fate of the Melians "hang[s] on a single turn of the scale". The small island state does not listen to the words of the "masters of the sea" and, ultimately, gets what it deserves in the form of complete annihilation (Thucydides, 416 BC). Representatives of modern IR built upon the interpretation of Thucydides, picturing relatively small states as helpless incapable entities, whose chances of survival depend on specific geopolitical, mental, and economic variables that are outside of the scope of their leverage (e.g. Fox, 1959; Vital 1967).

From a methodological point of view, the main attribute of the neorealist discourse is identifying relative size with *political power*. Representatives of the literature differentiated between the two sides of the notion – influential capacity (the extent to which a state can alter its environment) and independence (the extent to which a state can withhold external interference in its internal affairs) (Goetschel, 1998, p. 14; Garai, Koncz-Kiss and Szalai, 2017, p. 17). According to McGowan and Gottwald (1975, pp. 475–476), material size mostly effects the former, while the latter (which they called "stress sensitivity") is more connected to the level of modernisation). Waltz (1979, p. 192) also differentiated between the two, nonetheless he also combined them in "power", arguing that "an agent is powerful to the extent that he affects others more than they affect him".

Due to their power deficit, the most important decision a small state has to make from a neorealist perspective is its alliance policy (Wiberg, 1987). In anarchy, "small states join an alliance", argues Erich Reiter (2001, p. 12), "because they 'take refuge' in alliances to be safe from big states". Also, they receive non-military benefits, including economic or political support (Krause and Singer, 2001, p. 21).

The main question of alliance policy is whether a small state follows a *bandwagoning* or a *balancing* strategy. Stephen M. Walt defined the former as an "alignment with the source of danger", whereas the latter is "allying with others against the prevailing threat" (Walt, 2000, p. 96). As he emphasises, this choice is not precisely translatable into the choice between the stronger or the weaker side, although the balance of power and threat-perception are the most important elements (Walt, 2000, p. 98). While Kenneth Waltz (1979, pp. 117–126) argues that weaker states are more likely to engage in balancing, several researchers (e.g. Schweller, 1994; Garai, Koncz-Kiss and Szalai, 2017) come to the conclusion that small states will prefer bandwagoning, due to their inability to change the balance of power, and the lower costs and higher rewards associated with bandwagoning. Consequently, small states aggregately do not equalise power relations but, by joining the stronger side, they contribute to the *imbalance of power* (Fox, 1959).

Naturally, the question of alliances is much more complex than making a choice between the stronger and weaker sides (Sweeney and Fritz, 2004). On the one hand, balancing and bandwagoning are just two extremes on a scale of alliance strategies that are frequently neither rational nor feasible for weaker entities (Kuik, 2016). Small states therefore prefer milder strategies (which can collectively be called "hedging"); namely, various return-maximising or risk-contingency options.

On the other, state interests and perceptions independent from power relations can affect decision-making. In Randall L. Schweller's balance of interests model, the decisive factor is state interests vis-á-vis the status quo and a state's willingness to pay the price of defending it or challenging it (Schweller, 1994). Small states can either be "lambs" (pro-status quo) or "jackals" (anti-status quo), making alliances with the hegemonic "lions" or the revisionist "foxes".

In the case of small states, making alliances is a trilemma between security, influence, and autonomy (see Figure 1.2) – three values from which they can achieve only two simultaneously (Almezaini and Rickli, 2017, pp. 12–15). In this framework, three choices are available: the offensive strategy of prioritising influence and autonomy without joining alliances; the defensive strategy of remaining neutral, giving up influence for security and autonomy; and alignment (joining a permanent alliance, which provides security and

Figure 1.2 The triangle of alliance policy in the Gulf.

Source: Based on Almezaini and Rickli, 2017, pp. 12–15.

influence). The case of smaller Gulf states proves that small states can change their strategies dynamically (see Chapter 5).

Another debate in the literature is the usefulness of small states in a multilateral alliance. It is easy to argue, from the neorealist perspective, that weak states are merely free-riders, benefiting from defence cooperation without having any added value (Vandenbosch, 1964, p. 301; Lee, 2006, p. 144). Nonetheless, many scholars provided convincing counter-arguments. Anders Ahnlid (1992) found that, contrary to general belief, small states do not take advantage of the free trade regime while refusing to abandon their protectionist policies. Péter Marton (2017) enumerated a number of public goods that small states can bring to the table in a coalition, including providing legitimacy, geopolitical access, niche capabilities, a disproportionally large contribution, or strengthening the norm of the necessity of supporting coalition efforts.

Introducing soft power and shelters – the neoliberal narrative

Among other material systemic theories, the neoliberal school also built up its separate research programme. Its representatives criticise neorealism and put emphasis on the changing nature of international relations, the phenomenon of complex interdependences, the development of international law, and technological change and interconnectivity, all of which help the situation of small states considerably (Keohane and Nye, 2012). From this point of view, relative size remains an important, though less dominant factor regarding state behaviour. In the context of globalisation, the position of each state is dependent on various factors, among which size is only one (and not necessarily the most important) variable (Kay, 2004). Moreover, due to the progressively more complex nature of international challenges, multilateral governance became the way in which issues are handled on the world stage and not anarchic power competition (O'Brian et al., 2000).

These processes question the fundamentals of the neorealist approach to small states. Robert Keohane (2006, p. 59) even defied the usage of the notions of "small", "middle" and "large" states, and proposed they be categorised as system-determining (those states that mostly determine the course of international politics), system-influencing (those states that can influence political outcomes), system-affecting (those states that cannot influence the system by themselves), or system-ineffectual states (those that have no effect on international politics whatsoever).

By focusing on the systematic role of states, the neoliberal tradition moved away from the strict perception of power as a resource and moved closer to the so-called "relational" concept of power (Nye, 2011, pp. 4–10). Focusing on the processes through which decisions are made, representatives of the school understand power not as an attribute of an actor but, rather, an ability to influence the behaviour of others. Besides coercion, they recognise and prioritise other forms of power, including agenda-setting, attraction (the ability to change others' preferences to alter their behaviour), and structural power or metapower (Lukes, 1974; Guzzini, 1993). The most influential notion has been "soft power" by Joseph Nye (2011), a broad term that can include all the ways in which political actors co-opt or persuade others without coercing them to do something.

In this new field of international relations, small states have a much better position than in traditional hard power politics, since co-optation does not require as many material resources as maintaining a competitive military. Neoliberal authors mostly focus on agenda-setting and international organisations as the primary fields where small states can pursue their interests safely (Neumann and Gstöhl, 2006, pp. 20–21; Cooper and Shaw, 2009, pp. 10–13; Garai, Koncz-Kiss and Szalai, 2017, pp. 38–44). Creating or joining international organisations serves several purposes: it can strengthen international acceptance and, thus, independence (Duursma, 2006, p. 97), serve as a forum (Vandenbosch, 1964, p. 311), enlarge their representation and say in international governance, and even effect policy outcomes.

That being said, it would be a simplistic notion to argue that small states always prefer political and economic integration. As with larger states, small states always have to evaluate advantages and disadvantages connected to a specific institutional cooperation format, a decision that can be translated into a dilemma between maintaining sovereignty by opting out or enlarging influence by participation. This "integration dilemma" is a key concept with regard to understanding small state behaviour in the interstate society (Goetschel, 1998, pp. 26–27).

Neoliberal authors also investigated the various ways in which small states can protect themselves from political, security, or economic crisis. This so-called "shelter-policy" is used to find a protective umbrella that can help foresee, manage, and mitigate threats (Thorhallson and Steinsson, 2019). Small states find shelters in bilateral or multilateral security cooperation, or in various economic integrations – but they can change them if they prove to be inadequate or inefficient (Thorhallson, 2019).

Another advancement by the neoliberal school was to put more emphasis on insta-state variables to the foreign policy analysis of small states. The realist tradition would consider domestic politics as secondary to foreign and security policy, as small states should focus on external threats at all costs. Consequently, domestic political considerations should not affect how governments ensure their survival.

Breaking with the almost complete neglect of domestic viewpoints, the related research agenda (e.g. Katzenstein, 1985; Baechler, 1998; Hey, 2003a) tried to focus more on domestic institutions, various forms of government, level of development, and the economic system, for example. Neoliberals argued that domestic political considerations can be as important as international ones, especially as the survival of small states can be maintained by international law and in other ways (i.e. shelters). In what may be the most comprehensive analysis, Jeanne Hey (2003b, pp. 186–189) edited a volume in which eight analysts had to answer whether the individual, domestic, or systemic level had the most important effect on the foreign policy of specific small states. Although the results showed that "system level is a key explanatory factor in small state foreign policy", the individual level (especially in the case of underdeveloped and less institutionalised states) cannot be ignored.

Perceptual size and perceptual small states

The concept of perceptual size

The postmodern turn in International Relations enabled the rise of new concepts in the field. In Small State Studies, one of the most important contributions has been perceptual size; namely, the perception of a state's size by its own government and people (Thorhallson, 2009, pp. 131–135). "The point is not simply to argue about whether smallness should be seen as a positive or negative attribute", argues Christopher Browning (2006, pp. 673–674), "but to step outside this positivist framework and adopt a more interpretivist methodology where it is actors' understandings that become the focus of attention". As Goetschel (1998, p. 30) argues, "a state's size […] only intervenes indirectly as a component of a state's security identity, which determines the foreign and security-policy options available". In the words of Campbell and Hill (2009, p. 554), there is nothing automatic about this process, because "a country's leaders construct these perceptions out of the objective realities available to them – realities marked by the size and cultural composition of the country".

Naturally, the idea that the size of a state determines its identity was not born as a result of the constructivist revolution. Max Weber (1946, p. 161) talked about how big political communities are more likely to pay attention to "pretensions to prestige". According to Jean Gottmann, the size and the delimitation of a community's territory affects the dynamic between different communities, but through cognitive and not necessarily material processes. "Human psychology", argued Gottmann in 1973 (p. 9), "was, of course, at the root of the matter […]. A community fences a territory off to control the access of outsiders to its land, people and resources". Therefore, focusing solely on the material dimension of politics and size leaves us unprepared to understand international relations.

Notwithstanding, methodologically matured attempts have only been made since the 1980s. In his influential book entitled *Small States in World Markets*, Peter Katzenstein (1985) argued that smallness contributed to the emergence of the culture of "democratic corporatism" in Western European small states, which helped them manoeuvre successfully in the economic storms of the 1970s. Faced with unavoidable openness and exposure to external processes, these countries "have developed corporatist structures that enhance political predictability by facilitating cooperation and compromise" (Katzenstein, 1985, p. 96) and search for "reactive and flexible policy of industrial adjustments" (Katzenstein, 1985, p. 24). In contrast, larger states were not forced to have such a culture and political elasticity, which makes them less likely to produce the necessary decisions fast enough in the face of external shocks. Katzenstein's most important contribution was that smallness, coupled with other factors (such as openness, geopolitical position, or political developments), can have severe effects on both the material and immaterial structure of the state and society. According to Katzenstein, the relationship between size and policy outcomes is not inherent but more historical (Katzenstein, 1985, p. 80).

Apart from Katzenstein, many scholars tried to connect Small State Studies with self-perception, conceptualising small states as those who perceive themselves as small (see Baehr, 1975; Maas, 2009). Rothstein argued for example that "small power is a state which recognizes that it cannot obtain security primarily by use of its own capabilities, and that it must rely fundamentally on the aid of other states" (cited by Keohane, 2006, p. 56). Some wanted to mix material and immaterial factors, saying that "small states must be small in quantitative terms but must also feel and act small" (cited by Maas, 2009, p. 80).

Identity and small state behaviour

The investigation of perceptual size has become very fruitful in understanding state behaviour; nevertheless, one has to bear in mind that self-perception and identity is elusive, always being reconstructed and shaped by various actors. Laurent Goetschel (1998, pp. 27–31) talked about "security identity", which is the "product of past behaviour and images and myths linked to it which have been internalized over long periods of time by the political elite and the population of a state". His thoughts are in perfect harmony with those of Dan Reiter (2006), who emphasizes the role of "learning" in foreign policy making, arguing that when decision makers have to face unexpected challenges, they tend to rely on personal and institutional experiences more than on sophisticated, rational calculations. As a consequence, the historical experience related to the size of a state defines and limits the decision making elite's cognitive leverage. This can result in "small state mentalities" (Goetschel, 1998, pp. 27–31), which would still affect foreign policy even in changing material circumstances. Vital (1967, pp. 21–22) also discussed certain mental consequences of smallness; for example, the lack of enthusiasm for diplomats and employees in the national security apparatus due to the insignificance of their actions.

On the other hand, we have no reason to assume that smallness goes hand-in-hand with the same pack of mentalities and behavioural patterns (Browning, 2006, pp. 673–674). Communities construct their perception of smallness in different ways and can draw quite different conclusions from it. To better understand the relationship between identity and state behaviour, Herrera R. Abdelal and his colleagues offered a new analytical framework, according to which (Abdelal et al., 2006) identity consists of four separate parts:

- *constitutive norms* (formal and informal rules to define group membership and the limits of the appropriate behaviour for the members);
- *relational comparisons* (differentiation between in-groups and out-groups, and the perceiving of oneself vis-á-vis other entities);
- *cognitive models* (frameworks for interpreting and explaining material circumstances); and
- *social purposes* (collective goals for the community).

Size can play a unique role in all elements of identity in the model (summarised in Figure 1.3). First, it will be constitutive norms that determine the size of the community by defining the "admission rules" of a given community (e.g. citizenship laws). Second, the community's perception of its own relative size will be articulated by relational comparisons. It is possible to imagine that some materially small communities do not consider themselves small, or vice versa, a big community can picture itself as small. Third, societies can assign different meanings and interpretations to their perceived size, they do not necessarily identify largeness with power (Browning, 2006, pp. 681–682). Fourth, as a result of these variations, the social purposes deriving from smallness can be quite different. It is not self-evident what neorealists assume; namely, that small states automatically accept that they are destined to pursue survival as the maximal foreign policy aim due to their size.

Lastly, as Abdelal et al. (2006, p. 696) point out, members of a community do not necessarily agree on the elements of its own group identity. They call the degree of agreement in a society about various segments of identity "contestation", and they argue that the extent of such normative debates affect domestic and foreign policy to a great extent. This is also true for

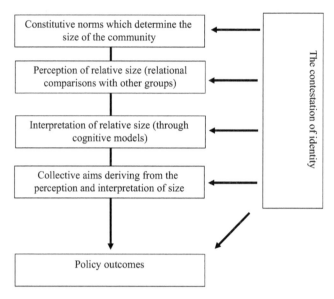

Figure 1.3 Operationalisation of perceptual size.

Source: Based on Abdelal et al., 2006.

smallness: Günther Baechler (1998, pp. 271–272) argues that the ability of small states to compensate for their smallness relies on the domestic accept-ability of the foreign policy strategies of the government, which necessitates agreement on the size of the community.

The research programme on perceptual size is quite limited, though there were several attempts to investigate its effects on foreign policy. Baldur Thorhallson (2009, pp. 131–135) argued that changes in the perception and preferences of the Icelandic elite (among other factors) led to its more active foreign and EU policy in the 2000s. He mentioned that the previous percep-tion of the state as a weak and small entity prevented the government from applying for Security Council membership in the UN. Christopher S. Browning (2006, pp. 674–681) followed the evolution of the Finnish identity after 1945, a process in which the meaning of smallness changed from a vul-nerability to an opportunity in the 1950s, and later to smartness in the 1990s. Dan Marek and Michael Baun (2010, p. 30) argued that "the notion that the Czech Republic is only a small state and thus cannot change anything within the EU [...] can lead to pessimism and a critical view of European integra-tion", which is why "Czechs are rather cautious and sceptical about attempts to deepen European integration".

In all, perceptual size opens up new perspectives for the study of small states to investigate a state's perception of its own size and its effects on for-eign policy. Nevertheless, strict operationalisation is needed as such abstract notions are quite difficult to apply or to investigate, even if many researchers refer to norms and identities. Moreover, the most traditional methods of analysing identities (Abdelal et al., 2006, pp. 702–705) are not universally applicable. Nonetheless, methodological obstacles do not mean that the observable phenomena (identity affecting foreign policy) is non-existent or not worth analysing.

Normative size and normative small states

The concept of normative size

The international normative environment represents another source of state behaviour and another way to conceptualise size. The "international structure [...] of meaning and social value" in which states are embedded shapes their self-perception, the formation of their interests, and, eventually, foreign policy (Finnemore, 1996, p. 2). Inter-state perceptions, as well as the content and distribution of the shared knowledge of international society, give meaning to material factors such as size. The relationship between norms and actors are, therefore, not casual but, rather, mutually constitutive, which undermines positivist methodologies for the full understanding of international politics (Wendt, 1999, pp. 23–50).

In the IR literature, three theoretical traditions deal with the interpretation of the normative structure of international politics: constructivism, the English School and, to some degree, institutionalism (Finnemore, 1996, pp. 14–22). In the following, I will not differentiate between their viewpoints but I will take the English School's vocabulary, which can serve as the common denominator for the related literature.

Although the number of relevant studies is quite small, the internationally perceived size and importance of states, as well as the general normative environment in which smallness and largeness is interpreted, bears huge importance in the leverage of state actors. Therefore, the *normative size* of states depends on two things: first, their perceived size in the international community, which is empirically observable through communication and actions; and, second, the context and normative environment of the investigation (e.g. a debate in the UN General Assembly or peace negotiations in 19th-century Europe or the Cold War).

In general, two separate myths have endured in the international community about smallness (Thürer, 1998). One of them – a viewpoint inspired by classic political philosophers – romanticises smallness, picturing small countries as ideal places, open for innovation and progressive thought. Many times "psychologically we attach positive things to size" (Chong, 2010, p. 385), while many observes, such as Sir Ernest Simon (cited by Katzenstein, 1985, p. 190), point out that the very existence of small states is "definite proof that when the existing tide of barbarism has subsided, men will succeed in building a new and nobler civilization". The second myth considers small states as political entities in a prison of weakness, an object of power-play between great powers without any real agency or worth; basically an "ugly neutral". Many actors "dislike and despise tiny states" (Nairn, 1997, p. 147) due to their perceived weakness.

The two narratives exist parallel with each other; nevertheless, in some periods one can dominate the other. In the post-bipolar age, it is arguable that the more optimistic narrative is winning as "small states became fashionable again" (Von Daniken, 1998, p. 48). Nevertheless, as most contemporary observers point out the return of great power politics at least in parallel with the post-bipolar neoliberal structures, it is possible that the general narrative regarding small states will become more pessimistic.

Foreign policy tools related to normative size

The way in which an actor is perceived shapes its behaviour and leverage, directly and indirectly, as self-perception and inter-social perception affect each other (Wendt, 1999, pp. 404–407). If a state is treated as small, weak, and unable to pose a threat (Baechler, 1998, p. 280), it may internalize it and renounce any kind of foreign policy activity, as predicted by David Vital. On many occasions, large states did not even tolerate their interference in important questions, which "was close to being deemed intolerable" (Baldacchino, 2009, p. 24).

According to Victor Gigleux (2016, p. 27) this is the reason why the international behaviour of small states varies widely, contrary to the expectations of both neorealists and neoliberalists. He suggested a framework that he calls "national role conceptions" (NRCs), "defined as 'policymakers' own definitions of the general kinds of decisions, commitments, rules and actions suitable to their state, and of the functions, if any, their state should perform on a continuing basis in the international system" (Gigleux, 2016, p. 28). NRCs include self-definition by "ego" and social recognition by "alter". This way, argues Gigleux, one can connect the systemic and the state levels of analysis in a subtle manner, thus connecting the notions of perceptual and normative size.

The international normative environment not only helps to understand interest-articulation and foreign policy making, but also represents a new toolkit for small states. Such strategies, which are oftentimes labelled as soft power strategies (similarly to those described by neoliberal authors) can be divided into two different categories. The first category comprises the way in which small states can alter or use the existing perception about themselves in the international community to their advantage. Such nation branding tools can be quite diverse and rich. Alan Chong (2010) called the strategy of enlarging one's importance as "virtual enlargement" and enlisted three possible methods: the promotion of national political economy potential, the articulation of a national model of good governance, and positioning oneself as a diplomatic mediator. Small states may actually have an advantage in these strategies if the optimistic narrative regarding smallness is strong in the normative environment. Using these steps, small states can persuade other actors that they are interested in their wellbeing, can make their voice heard in different social relations, and even contribute to conflict resolution or other political outcomes as the representative of moral rightness.

The second category refers to strategies of pursuing one's interest by influencing the normative environment in more general terms. Since not only size-related norms affect the leverage of (small) states, they can be interested in developing (or weakening) such implicit or explicit notions. For example, the existence of the norm of the prohibition of the use of force (even if it is not complete and imperfect) means a significant development for them. The same goes for sovereign equality, multilateralism, or global governance.

Christine Ingebritsen (2006a) described the norm entrepreneur efforts of Scandinavian countries. According to her, remote geographic position, limited material capabilities, and the unique domestic institutions made north European countries adequate for this role. Ingebritsen argued that Scandinavian states were able to strengthen norms related to sustainable development, multilateral security, and global welfare in the international sphere, thus influencing world affairs to an unexpected extent. With a much lower level of intensity (and success), the same process is taking place in some Persian Gulf states in relations with international finances, energy market coordination, and climate change (Ulrichsen, 2012, p. 4). Thus, one observes that while small states cannot lead in world politics, they can form the framework in which leadership is conducted (Ingebritsen, 2006b, pp. 289–290).

Applying the complex model of size to empirical research

Re-organising the literature based on the four kinds of size helps us conduct more precise empirical research on small states. As a first step, we should differentiate between four separate types of small states:

1. *Absolute small states*: states below their optimal size that cannot provide the desired level of welfare, security, or institutional quality for its population;
2. *Relative small states*: states whose size in terms of the resources deemed the most important in the given regional or global system is below the average of that given system;
3. *Perceptual small states*: states that are considered small by their society, or the elite, or the government;
4. *Normative small states*: states that are considered as small by other actors in the international society.

The four categories do not necessarily overlap with each other. A relative small state could have an optimal size from the perspective of its absolute size, whereas a state can be seen as a small and unimportant actor even if its identity includes a self-perception of grandeur. As has been noted in this overview, the four different kinds of smallness have different effects on foreign policy; therefore, in order to understand their behaviour, one has to analyse all four aspects and their interaction.

To translate these theoretical ideas into empirical research, one has to differentiate between the international and the state-level viewpoints. While relative and normative smallness belongs to the former, absolute and perceptual smallness can be observed from the latter.[4] That is why, before analysing small state behaviour, the regional applicability of small state theory will be analysed in Chapter 2, after which I will focus on the relative and normative size of MENA states in Chapter 3. Chapter 4 will be dedicated to individual Gulf states. The analysis will not focus solely the different types of small states but, rather, on the different attributes of the regional environment and of individual states which affect how smallness influences policies.

As has already been indicated, smallness can only be investigated if we set the scale, in this case the specific resources that will form the basis of analysis. In line with the traditional literature on relative size, I will use territory, population, economic output, and military capacities as variables, and set the regional average as the limit for relative smallness. Circumventing the debates regarding the relative importance of the four variables, I will investigate the four dimensions separately.

This approach allows us to divide the category of relative small states from two perspectives. First, we can differentiate between territorial, demographic, economic, and military small states, referring to the variable in which they have a value below the regional average. A state can be demographically small but, for example, economically large, and so on, all of which has distinct consequences on their policies and opportunities. Second, we can divide states into three categories. Large states are above the average in all four resources; medium-sized states will be small in only one, two or three dimensions; and small states will be small in all four aspects. This categorisation helps us overcome the simplistic and superficial notion of small states.

When it comes to perceptual and normative size, the methodology is much more difficult to outline, as the literature is, as yet, underdeveloped. Nevertheless, I want to conceptualise perceptions as tangibly as possible, even if it means narrowing the focus down to only a few indicators. When it comes to perceptual smallness, I will focus on the speech acts of politicians and decision makers, while in the case or normative smallness (i.e. interstate perceptions) I will focus on visible interactions. Basically, normative size can be translated to the perceived importance of a state in international society; and a state tends to interact with those actors that it deems more important.

Notes

1 Translated by Solomon Pines (1971, p. 126.).
2 Realists tend to overemphasize the role of alliances and neutrality, whereas liberals focus more on international institutions and the development of international law.
3 Besides neorealism and neoliberalism, neo-Marxism also touches upon the question of smallness, though to a much more limited degree. Although its notions can be applied in empirical research of small states' development path after

decolonisation, neo-Marxism cannot be used as a primary framework for the study of small states as it does not investigate the effects of size on centrum–periphery relations (Bernal, 2015, pp. 27–28). Among others, Immanuel Wallerstein (1989) and Giovanni Arrighi (1994) argue that dependence and interest-seeking abilities do not have a direct causal relationship with physical size. The usual measurements of state size only "define the limits of the immediate impact of state policy" (Wallerstein, 1989, pp. 68–69), which provides an outdated scope of investigation in today's globalised environment. That is why, according to neo-Marxism, the importance of size depends heavily on the context, while small and large states alike behave according to their role in the world economic system.

4 From a methodological perspective, differentiating between the different levels of analysis is more vital than differentiating between material and immaterial variables.

Bibliography

Abdelal, R., Herrera, Y.M., Johnston, A.I. and Rose, M. (2006) Identity as a Variable, *Perspectives on Politics*, 4(4), pp. 695–711. DOI:10.1017/s1537592706060440.

Alesina, A. (2003) The Size of Countries: Does it Matter? *Journal of the European Economic Association*, 1(2–3), pp. 301–316. DOI:10.2139/ssrn.343785.

Alesina, A. and Spolaore, E. (2005) *The Size of Nations*. Cambridge, MA: Massachusetts Institute of Technology. DOI:10.7551/mitpress/6261.001.0001.

Almezaini, K.S. and Rickli, J. (2017) Theories of Small States' Foreign and Security Policies and the Gulf States, in Almezaini, K.S. and Rickli, J. (eds.) *The Small Gulf States. Foreign and Security Policies before and after the Arab Spring*. London & New York: Routledge, pp. 8–30. DOI:10.4324/9781315619576-2.

Anckar, D. (1999) Homogeneity and Smallness: Dahl and Tufte Revisited. *Scandinavian Political Studies*, 22(1), pp. 29–44. DOI:10.1111/1467-9477.00002.

Ahnlid, A. (1992) Free of Forced Riders? Small States in International Political Economy: The Example of Sweden. *Cooperation and Conflict*, 27(3), pp. 241–276. DOI:10.1177/0010836792027003002.

Aristotle (1998) *Politics. Translated with Introduction and Notes by C.D.C. Reeve*. Cambridge: Hackett Publishing Company. DOI:10.5840/teachphil20194219.

Arrighi, G. (1994) *The Long Twentieth Century. Money, Power, and the Origins of our Times*. London & New York: Verso. DOI:10.1163/2468-1733_shafr_sim280020664.

Baechler, G. (1998) Conclusions: Future Relevance and Priorities of Small States, in Goetschel, L. (ed.) *Small States Inside and Outside the European Union*. Boston: Springer, pp. 267–283. DOI:10.1007/978-1-4757-2832-3_18.

Baehr, P.R. (1975) Review: Small States. A Tool for Analysis. *World Politics*, 27(3), pp. 456–466.

Bailes, A.J.K. (2009) Does a Small State Need a Strategy?. *University of Iceland* [Online] Available at: http://stofnanir.hi.is/ams/sites/files/ams/Bailes_Final_0.pdf (Accessed 15 September 2018).

Baldacchino, G. (2009) Thucydides or Kissinger? A Critical Review of Smaller State Diplomacy, in Cooper, A.F. and Shaw, T.M. (eds.) *The Diplomacies of Small States. Between Vulnerability and Resilience*. Basingstoke: Palgrave MacMillan, pp. 21–41. DOI:10.1057/9780230246911_2.

Barnett, J. and Campbell, J. (2010) *Climate Change and Small Island States. Power, Knowledge and the South Pacific.* London & New York: Earthscam. DOI:10.4324/9781849774895.

Beer, S.H. (1993) *To Make a Nation. The Rediscovery of American Federalism.* Cambridge, London: The Belknap Press. DOI:10.2307/3330868.

Bernal, R.L. (2015) *The Influence of Small States on Superpowers. Jamaica and U.S. Foreign Policy.* New York & London. Lexington Books. DOI:10.1163/2468-1733_shafr_sim150060041.

Browning, C.S. (2006) Small, Smart, Salient? Rethinking Identity in the Small States Literature. *Cambridge Review of International Affairs,* 19(4), pp. 669–684. DOI:10.1080/09557570601003536.

Campbell, J.L. and Hill, J.A. (2009) National Identity and the Political Economy of Small States. *Review of International Political Economy,* 16(4), pp. 547–572. DOI:10.1080/09692290802620378.

Chong, A. (2010) Small State Soft Power Strategies: Virtual Enlargement in the Cases of the Vatican City State and Singapore. *Cambridge Review of International Affairs,* 23(3), pp. 383–405. DOI:10.1080/09557571.2010.484048.

Cooper, A.F. and Shaw, T.M. (2009) The Diplomacies of Small States at the Start of the Twenty-first Century: How Vulnerable? How Resilient?, in Cooper, A.F. and Shaw, T.M. (eds.) *The Diplomacies of Small States. Between Vulnerability and Resilience.* Basingstoke: Palgrave MacMillan, pp. 1–18. DOI:10.1057/978023 0246911_1.

DeWesse-Boyd, I. and DeWesse-Boyd, M. (2007) The Healthy City Versus the Luxurious City in Plato's Republic: Lessons about Consumption and Sustainability for a Globalizing Economy. *Contemporary Justice Review,* 10(1), pp. 115–130. DOI:10.1080/10282580601157935.

Dommen, E. and Hein, P. (1985) Foreign Trade in Goods and Services: The Dominant Activity of Small Island Economies, in Dommen, E. and Hein, P. (eds.) *States, Microstates and Islands.* London: Croom Helm, pp. 152–184.

Duval, R.D. and Thompson, W.R. (1980) Reconsidering the Aggregate Relationship Between Size, Development and Some Types of Foreign Policy Behaviour. *American Journal of Political Science,* 24(3), pp. 511–525. DOI:10.2307/2110830.

Duursma, J. (2006) Micro-states: The Principality of Liechtenstein, in Igebritsen, C., Neumann, I.B., Gstöhl, S. and Beyer, J. (eds.) *Small States in International Relations.* Reykjavik: University of Iceland Press, pp. 89–149.

East, M.A. (1973) Size and Foreign Policy Behaviour: A Test of Two Models. *World Politics,* 25(4), pp. 556–576.

Finnemore, M. (1996) *National Interests in International Society.* Ithaca & London: Cornell University Press. DOI:10.7591/9781501707384.

Fox, A.B. (1959) *The Power of Small States.* Chicago: University of Chicago Press.

Garai, M., Koncz-Kiss, J., Szalai, M. (2017) A kisállamok lehetőségei és kihívásai a 21. Százaban, in Garai, M., Koncz-Kiss, J., Szalai, M. (eds.): *A kisállamok lehetőségei és kihívásai a 21. században.* Institute for Foreign Affairs and Trade [Online]. Available at: http://kki.hu/assets/upload/Kisellamok.pdf. (Accessed 15 September 2018), pp. 3–60.

Georgescu-Roegen, N. (1977) The Steady State and Ecological Salvation: A Thermodynamic Analysis. *BioScience,* 27(4), pp. 266–270. DOI:10.2307/1297702.

Gigleux, V. (2016) Explaining the Diversity of Small States' Foreign Policies through Role Theory. *Third World Thematics,* 1(1), pp. 27–45. DOI:10.1080/23802014.2016.1184585.

Goetschel, L. (1998) The Foreign and Security Policy Interests of Small States in Today's Europe, in Goetschel, L. (ed.) *Small States Inside and Outside the European Union*. Boston: Springer, pp. 13–32. DOI:10.1007/978-1-4757-2832-3_2.

Gottmann, J. (1973) *The Significance of Territory*. Charlottesville: University Press of Virginia.

Gottmann, J. (1980) Organizing and Reorganizing Space, in Gottmann, J. (ed.) *Centre and Periphery: Spatial Variation in Politics*. Beverly Hills: Sage, pp. 217–224.

Guzzini, S. (1993) Structural Power: The Limits of Neorealist Power Analysis. *International Organization*, 47(3), pp. 443–478. DOI:10.1017/s0020818300028022.

Handel, M. (2006): Weak States in the International System. in Igebritsen, C., Neumann, I.B., Gstöhl, S. and Beyer, J. (eds.) *Small States in International Relations*. Reykjavik: University of Iceland Press, pp. 149–193.

Henrikson, A.K. (2007) A Coming "Magnesian" Age? Small States, the Global System, and the International Community. *Geopolitics*, 6(3), pp. 49–86. DOI:10.1080/14650040108407729.

Hey, J.A.K. (2003a) Introducing Small State Foreign Policy, in Hey, J.A. K. (ed.) *Small States in World Politics: Explaining Foreign Policy Behaviour*. Boulder: Lynne Rienner Publishers, pp. 1–13.

Hey, J.A.K. (2003b) Refining Our Understanding of Small State Foreign Policy, in Hey, J.A. K. (ed.) *Small States in World Politics: Explaining Foreign Policy Behaviour*. Boulder: Lynne Rienner Publishers, pp. 185–197.

Hobsbawm, E. (1994) *The Age of Extremes: The Short Twentieth Century*. London: Abacus.

Jazbec, M. (2010) Small States and Diplomacy: An Indispensable, though Much Diversified Relation. *Holduskultuur – Administrative Culture*, 11(1), pp. 66–83.

Ibn Khaldoun (1967) *The Muqaddimah: An Introduction to History*. Princeton: Princeton University Press.

Ingebritsen, C. (2006a) Norm Entrepreneurs: Scandinavia's Role in World Politics, in Igebritsen, C., Neumann, I.B., Gstöhl, S. and Beyer, J. (eds.) *Small States in International Relations*. Reykjavik: University of Iceland Press, pp. 273–286.

Ingebritsen, Christine (2006b) Conclusion: Learning from Lilliput, in Igebritsen, C., Neumann, I.B., Gstöhl, S. and Beyer, J. (eds.) *Small States in International Relations*. Reykjavik: University of Iceland Press, pp. 286–293.

Katzenstein, P.J. (1985) *Small States in World Markets. Industrial Policy in Europe*. Ithaca & London: Cornell University Press. DOI:10.7591/9781501700361.

Keohane, R.O. (2006) Lilliputians' Dilemmas: Small States in International Politics, in Igebritsen, C., Neumann, I.B., Gstöhl, S. and Beyer, J. (eds.) *Small States in International Relations*. Reykjavik: University of Iceland Press, pp. 55–77.

Keohane, R.O. and Nye, J.S. (2012): *Power and Interdependence*. 4th Edition. United States: Longman.

Kay, S. (2004) Globalization, Power, and Security. *Security Dialogue*, 35(1), pp. 9–25. DOI:10.1177/0967010604042533.

King, D. and Tennant, D.F. (eds.) (2014) *Debt and Development in Small Island Developing States*. New York: Palgrave Macmillan. DOI:10.1057/9781137392787.0015.

Krause, V. and Singer, J.D. (2001) Minor Powers, Alliance, and Armed Conflict: Some Preliminary Patterns, in Reiter, E. and Gartner, H. (eds.) *Small States and Alliances*. Berlin: Springer, pp. 15–24. DOI:10.1007/978-3-662-13000-1_3.

Kuik, C. (2016) How do Weaker States Hedge? Unpacking ASEAN states' alignment behaviour towards China. *Journal of Contemporary China*, 25(100), pp. 500–514. DOI:10.1080/10670564.2015.1132714.

Lee, M. (2006) *How Do Small States Affect the Future Development of the E.U.* New York: Nova Science Publishers.

Lee, D. and Smith, N.J. (2010) Small State Discourses in the International Political Economy. *Third World Quarterly*, 31(7), pp. 1091–1105. DOI:10.1080/01436597.20 10.518750.

Lockhart, D.G., Drakakis-Smith, D. and Schembri, J. (eds.) (2002): *The Development Process in Small Island States.* New York: Routledge.

Lukes, S. (1974) *Power: A Radical View.* London: Palgrave MacMillan. DOI:10.1007/978-1-349-02248-9.

Maas, M. (2009) The Elusive Definition of the Small State. *International Politics*, 46(1), pp. 65–83. DOI:10.1057/ip.2008.37.

Marek, D. and Baun, M. (2010) *The Czech Republic and the European Union.* London & New York: Routledge. DOI:10.4324/9780203847398.

Marton, P. (2017) Sok kisebb megy sokra: A relative kis országok koalíciós magatartása, in Garai, N., Koncz-Kiss, J. and Szalai, M. (eds.) *A kisállamok lehetőségei és kihívásai a 21. században.* Institute for Foreign Affairs and Trade [Online]. Available at: http://kki.hu/assets/upload/Kisellamok.pdf. (Accessed 15 September 2018), pp. 63–79.

McGowan, P.J. and Gottwald, K. (1975) Small State Foreign Policies: A Comparative Study of Participation, Conflict, and Political and Economic Dependence in Black Africa" *International Studies Quarterly*, 19(4), pp. 469–500. DOI:10.2307/2600185.

Michaley, M. (1962) *Concentration in International Trade.* Amsterdam: North-Holland.

Mishan, E.J. (1967) *The Costs of Economic Growth.* Ontario: Penguin Books.

Moses, J.W. (2000) *OPEN States in the Global Economy.* Basingstoke: Palgrave Macmillan. DOI:10.1057/9780333977859.

Muhindo, M. and Calenzo, G. (2011) Neorealism and International Subsystems of Small States: Insights from Sub-Saharan African Countries' Interactions. *Interdisciplinary Political Studies*, 1(2), pp. 148–160.

Nairn, T. (1997) *Faces of Nationalism: Janus Revisited.* London & New York: Verso.

Neumann, I.B. and Gstöhl, S. (2006) Introduction. Lilliputians in Gulliver's World?, in: Igebritsen, C., Neumann, I.B., Gstöhl, S. and Beyer, J. (eds.) *Small States in International Relations.* Reykjavik: University of Iceland Press, pp. 3–39.

Nye, J.S. (2011) *The Future of Power.* New York: Public Affairs.

O'Brian, R., Goetz, A.M., Scholte, J.A. and Williams, M. (2000) *Contesting Global Governance.* Cambridge: Cambridge University Press.

Pines, S. (1971) The Societies Providing for the Bare Necessities of Life According to Ibn Khaldoun and to the Philosophers. *Studia Islamica*, 1971(34), pp. 125–138. DOI:10.2307/1595328.

Plato (2004): *The Republic. Online Edition.* Cordella Collegiate Bookshelf [Online]. Available at: http://thewritedirection.net/bookshelf/library.asp (Accessed 15 September 2018).

Posner, R. (2012) The Optimal Size of Countries. *The Becker-Posner Blog* [Online]. Available at: http://www.becker-posner-blog.com/2012/12/the-optimal-size-of-countries-posner.html (Accessed 15 September 2018).

Reiter, E. (2001) Introductory Comments on the Objective of the Small States and Alliance Workshop, in Erich, R. and Gartner, H. (eds.) *Small States and Alliances.* Berlin: Springer, pp. 11–14. DOI:10.1007/978-3-662-13000-1_2.

Reiter, D. (2006) Learning, Realism, and Alliances: The Weight of the Shadow of the Past, in Igebritsen, C., Neumann, I.B., Gstöhl, S. and Beyer, J. (eds.) *Small States in International Relations.* Reykjavik: University of Iceland Press, pp. 231–273.

Schumacher, E.F. (2011) *Small is Beautiful. A Study of Economics as if People Mattered*. London: Vintage.

Schweller, R.L. (1994) "Bandwagoning for Profit: Bringing the Revisionist State Back in". *International Security*, 19(1), pp. 72–107. DOI:10.2307/2539149.

Sweeney, K. and Fritz, P. (2004) "Jumping on the Bandwagon: An Interest-Based Explanation for Great Power Alliances". *The Journal of Politics*, 66(2), pp. 428–449. DOI:10.1111/j.1468-2508.2004.00158.x.

Tetreault, M.A. (1991) Autonomy, Necessity, and the Small State: Ruling Kuwait in the Twentieth Century. *International Organization*, 45(4), pp. 565–591. DOI:10.1017/s002081830003321x.

Thorhallson, B. (2006) The Role of Small States in the European Union, in Igebritsen, C., Neumann, I.B., Gstöhl, S. and Beyer, J. (eds.) *Small States in International Relations*. Reykjavik: University of Iceland Press, pp. 218–231.

Thorhallson, B. (2009) Can Small States Choose Their Own Size? The Case of a Nordic State – Iceland, in Cooper, A.F. and Shaw, T.M. (eds.) *The Diplomacies of Small States. Between Vulnerability and Resilience*. Basingstoke: Palgrave MacMillan, pp. 119–143. DOI:10.1057/9780230246911_7.

Thorhallson, B. (2019) Small States and the Changing Global Order. What Small States Theory Can Offer New Zealand Foreign Policymaking, in Brady, A. (ed.) *Small States and the Changing Global Order. New Zeland Faces the Future.* Switzerland: Springer, pp. 379–395.

Thorhallson, B. and Steinsson, S. (2019) A Theory of Shelter, in Thorhallson, B. (ed.) *Small States and Shelter Theory. Iceland's External Affairs*. London & New York: Routledge, pp. 24–58. DOI:10.4324/9780429463167-3.

Thucydides (416 B.C.) *The Melian Dialogue*. Warwick University [Online] Available at: http://www2.warwick.ac.uk/fac/arts/classics/students/modules/introhist/useful documents/thucydides_v.84-116.pdf (Accessed 15 September 2018).

Thürer, D. (1998) The Perception of Small States: Myth and Reality, in Goetschel, L. (ed.) *Small States Inside and Outside the European Union*. Boston: Springer, pp. 33–43. DOI:10.1007/978-1-4757-2832-3_3.

Ulrichsen, K.C. (2012) Small States with a Big Role: Qatar and the United Arab Emirates in the Wake of the Arab Spring. HH Sheikh Nasser Al-Mohammad Al-Sabah Publications, *Durham University* [Online]. Available at: www.dur.ac.uk/resources/alsabah/SmallStateswithaBigRole.pdf (Accessed 15 September 2018).

Vandenbosch, A. (1964) The Small States in International Politics and Organization. *The Journal of Politics*, 26(2), pp. 293–312. DOI:10.2307/2127598.

Vital, D. (1967) *The Inequality of States: A Study of the Small Power in International Relations*. Oxford: Oxford University Press.

Von Daniken, F. (1998) Is the Notion of Small State still Relevant? in Goetschel, L. (ed.) *Small States Inside and Outside the European Union*. Boston: Springer, pp. 43–48. DOI:10.1007/978-1-4757-2832-3_4.

Walt, S.M. (2000) Alliances: Balancing and Bandwagoning, in Art, R.J. and Jervis, R. (ed.) *International Politics: Enduring Concepts and Contemporary Issues*. Essex: Pearson Education Ltd., pp. 96–103.

Waltz, K.N. (1979) *Theory of International Politics*. Reading: Addison-Wesley Publishing Company.

Wallerstein, I. (1989) *The Modern World-System III. The Second Era of Great Expansion of the Capitalist World-Economy, 1730-1840s*. London: Academic Press. DOI:10.1525/9780520948594.

Weber, M. (1946) Structures of Power, in Gerth, H.H. and Mills, C.W. (eds.) *From Max Weber: Essays in Sociology*. New York: Oxford University Press, pp. 159–179.

Wendt, A. (1999) *Social Theory of International Politics*. Cambridge: Cambridge University Press. DOI:10.1017/cbo9780511612183.

Wiberg, H. (1987) The Security of Small Nations: Challenges and Defences. *Journal of Peace Research*, 24(4), pp. 339–363. DOI:10.1177/002234338702400403.

World Bank and Commonwealth (2000): Small States: Meeting Challenges in the Global Economy. Report of the Commonwealth Secretariat/Word Bank Joint Task Force on Small States. *World Bank* [Online]. Available at: http://siteresources. worldbank.org/PROJECTS/Resources/meetingchallengeinglobaleconomyl.pdf (Accessed 15 September 2018).

2   Applying small state theory to the MENA region

As was discussed in Chapter 1, conventional wisdom in IR theory would suggest small leverage for resource-scarce entities, especially in a region such as the Middle East and North Africa,[1] which is under-institutionalised and highly conflictual. Actually, the traditional attributes of the MENA system are exactly those usually listed among the main factors that contribute to the importance of material resources and size in international relations.

Nevertheless, a closer investigation will show these theoretical claims to be false. My main argument in this chapter is that, contrary to conventional wisdom, several aspects enable Middle Eastern and North African small states to play a more important role than their size theoretically suggests. These aspects refer to some of the main attributes of the MENA region, which, while incorporated in the global political and economic system, works a separate security complex (Kelly, 2007, p. 206) with its own institutions and norms.

Societies of the Middle East and North Africa integrated into the modern international system in the 19th and 20th centuries through modernisation. Among other strategies, the process manifested in mirroring specific political and economic institutions in order to be able to take part in interstate society, such as states, nationality, territoriality, and a market economy. Nevertheless, the actual manifestation of these institutions shows specific alterations to the textbook models (Gonzalez-Pelaez, 2009). This is not a phenomenon particular to the MENA region: local actors have always been altering norms of global politics and mixing them with local norms in specific ways (Acharya, 2011, p. 96). In the following, I will highlight four such alterations connected with state-formation, statehood, conflict, and the balance of power.

State-formation under great power protection

Becoming a state is the most profound and significant moment in the history of a political community and affects state behaviour permanently. When it comes to the smaller Gulf states, two particularities have to be pointed out. First, the process of state-building (including all efforts at creating the institutions and apparatus of management) and state-formation (the process leading to the independence of a state) did not completely overlap each other

DOI: 10.4324/9781003158288-3

(Berman and Lonsdale, 1992, p. 5), as institutions were in the process of development before and after smaller Gulf states became independent. Second, both processes took place in the context of great power protection, under the heavy influence of the British Empire.

Contrary to most states of the MENA region, the smaller Gulf states have never been integral parts of the Ottoman Empire but, rather, existed on the periphery of it (Bennison, 2009, p. 45). Due to the lack of necessary resources – i.e. relative and normative smallness – the Arabian Peninsula had not produced a regional power since the 7th century and was never sufficiently attractive for regional powers to capture it fully.[2] Consequently, it served as a buffer zone in the competition between outside actors (Commins, 2014, pp. 1–2). The most important feature of the Gulf was the trade activity between the port and trade cities (Ulrichsen, 2011a, pp. 16–17), which connected the region to the broader economic system of the Indian Ocean (Commins, 2014, pp. 4–6). None of the local centres managed to rise above the other, which resulted in a "dispersion of power" (Commins, 2014, p. 2). Therefore, any major external actor that decided to intervene was more powerful than local actors – the question was only whether there were external actors who want to intervene.

The first Europeans arriving in the Persian Gulf were the Portugese fleet, which established a permanent presence along the Southern coasts in the last years of the 16th century (Crystal, 2014, p. 158). The Ottomans actually arrived in the Gulf after the Portuguese: in 1546, Istanbul conquered Baghdad and then moved to the South, to Basrah, Qatif, and al-Hasa (Al-Qasimi, 1999, pp. 2–3; Özbaran, 2009, pp. 93–105).[3] The predominance of Portugal in Gulf trade was over by 1622, when Persian and British forces expelled them from Hormuz (Al-Qasimi, 1999, p. 17). Later came the Dutch, too, but the British Empire managed to build its monopoly by the middle of the 18th century (ibid.) as the Netherlands were forced to withdraw from the region by 1766 (Al-Qasimi, 1999, p. 188). London had the most pressing incentive to be present in the region: besides the general urge to oversee maritime trade (an aim shared by all European maritime empires), the Arabian Peninsula gained importance due to its closeness to the Indian colonies (Ismael and Ismael, 2011, p. 388).

The British forces gained the upper hand not due to the use of brute force but, rather, by understanding and manipulating the competition between the local actors (including Safavid Iran, Oman, and other Arabian tribes) (Commins, 2014, pp. 41–61). When they were able to, the British forces preferred to use indirect methods of persuasion, bribery, or negotiation. Because of the actor plurality in the region, local leaders became used to playing out empires to survive and to benefit from their struggle.[4]

Nonetheless, by the eve of the 19th century, their strategy was in jeopardy due to the intensification of piracy, escalating conflicts between the local tribes and France's attempts to gain ground in the region (Al-Qasimi, 1999, pp. 40–41). That is why the British Crown decided to change tactics and initiate a series of contracts with local tribal leaders and create formal alliances with them in the pursuit of maintaining the status quo. The leaders of the Gulf welcomed such treaties – actually, it was they who initiated them in the first place, due to their perceived weakness and small perceptual size (Onley, 2009, pp. 3–10). London – or, more precisely, the British Indian Empire and its Residents in the Gulf – was more cautious about providing perpetual protection for the tribal leaders due to the costs associated with permanent defence obligations, so the relationship grew gradually, starting with seasonal protection treaties, culminating in the late 19th and 20th centuries with the integration of the territories into the British Empire as protected states.[5]

The emerging "trucial system" (which refers to all the bilateral and multilateral agreements between the British Empire and local tribes between 1798 and 1916) was crucially important in the state-building and state-formation of the Gulf, as they represent the foundations of modern statehood. In exchange for protection and recognition, local leaders had to maintain order on a given piece of land and refrain from any kind of "foreign policy" activity unauthorised by the British government. The long-lasting effects of the trucial system can be summarised in the following points (Hazmeh, 1994; Ismael and Ismael, 2011, p. 388; Crystal, 2014, pp. 159–160):

- the monarchic structures were reinforced as the agreements were made between London and local leaders, and not communities or institutions;
- the logic of territoriality was introduced;
- the legal system became dual in nature as traditional Sharia law was mixed with British common law;
- the territory of the Eastern coast of the Arabian Peninsula was divided into smaller pieces of land that never unified completely;
- other external forces were excluded, and the British monopoly was strengthened considerably.

From the perspective of international relations, in exchange for limited autonomy the trucial system meant protection for smaller Gulf states from any kind of external threats (including Turkish, Iraqi, Iranian, or Saudi expansionism, as well as Arab nationalism). For tribal leaders, this was a welcome deal, as they were accustomed to seeking protection from outside forces. In the tribal history of the Gulf region, the tradition of paying protection money ("brotherhood fee" or *khuwa*) had been common, which represented an asymmetric power relation between a weaker and stronger actor not unlike that created by the trucial system (Onley, 2009, pp. 2–3). This relationship was very successful from the perspective of smaller Gulf states – they survived the profound developments taking place in the 20th century in the protective cage of the British Empire.

It is telling that it was mostly London that decided to end the trucial system. After World War II, the primary motive for the British Empire to stay in the Gulf (maintaining maritime security near India) was replaced by the development of the oil sector. This was manageable through other means than granting protection for smaller Gulf states. Moreover, in the 1950s, anti-imperial sentiments and pan-Arabism spread in the region, making it harder for local leaders to be part of the British Empire. Accompanied by the dominance of the British Labour Party in the 1960s, these processes led the British government to allow the smaller Gulf states to become independent by 1971 (Al-Hamad, 2002; Onley, 2009).

As an exception, Kuwait had requested independence in 1958 and been granted it by 1961 (Onley, 2009, pp. 20–21). With the country's massive oil wealth, Kuwaiti leaders were ahead of their neighbours in state-building, while Arab nationalism was especially popular in society, putting more pressure on the ruler to gain independence. The fact that, geopolitically, Kuwait was the most vulnerable to outside threats was of significant consequence when it came to domestic stability. Nonetheless, since Kuwait was instantly met with Iraqi claims, the Gulf leaders were discouraged from following the precedent for a decade.

Although state-formation materialised by the early 1970s, state-building efforts are ongoing, mostly determined by the needs and profits of the oil sector. In general, institution-building followed a bell-shaped curve, peaking in the 1980s (Hinnebusch, 2014a, p. 22). State-building has never been a one-way process, as structures can sometimes regress or disintegrate. Therefore, the analysis of the behaviour of any Middle Eastern state in various situations should include an assessment of the situation with regard to state-building at the relevant time, since state-building determines not just the leverage of a state but that of the other states as well, since "powerful states" (in the institutional sense) "are increasingly interfering in the affairs of weaker ones" (Cammack et al., 2017, p. 2). To better understand this phenomenon, one has to investigate other particularities of the Middle Eastern state model.

Statehood and state behaviour

Most theories in Small State Studies, similarly to IR in general, take statehood for granted and build their observations on the grounds of modern statehood. Nevertheless, due to the artificial nature of states in the MENA region, their functional character differs considerably from traditional models and expectations (Hinnebusch, 2014a, p. 1). The apparent reason behind this phenomenon is the altered meaning and practice of Westphalian sovereignty and territoriality (Gonzalez-Pelaez, 2009), the building blocks of our general understanding of how states operate. In practice, these amendments can be summarised in four points (Anderson, 1987, pp. 6–7):

- arbitrary boundaries that do not necessarily reflect local economic and social circumstances;
- the adaptation of modern statehood through the political dominance of European powers rather than as a result of domestic developments;

- the different effects of state-building on the dominant elites in relation to other, disenfranchised groups;
- the variation of institutional strength of state institutions both in time and space.

This process resulted in the partial rejection of these institutional frameworks, and the survival of premodern political and social structures that basically coexist with modern structures. While prima facie all modern institutions (e.g. constitutions, laws, legislative bodies, ministries, armed forces) exist in the region, the power relations between them will not only be determined by written laws, but also by other social constructions such as tribes or families. Hisham Sharabi (1988, p. 7) described this phenomenon as neopatriarchy: "the dominance of the Father (patriarch), the center around which the national as well as the natural family are organized". A neopatriarchal state, in his view, "regardless of its legal and political forms and structures, is in many ways no more than a modernized version of the traditional patriarchal sultanate".

The logic of neopatriarchy is observable in many aspects of social life. Though several countries have elections in the region, basically, "all Arab electoral systems were configured to give the ruling power elite a built-in majority" (Khouri, 2017, p. 27). In those states where the social organisation is more tribal (as in the case of the Arabian Peninsula or Jordan), the regime has to "pay" to get tribal support, which translates itself into formal governmental policies (Salzman, 2016, pp. 212–215). The logic of the Western institutional approach often fails to highlight such premodern dynamics.

The phenomenon led to a particular Middle Eastern state model that behaves differently than is theoretically expected from a "modern state" (Anderson, 1987; Brichs, 2013; Brichs and Lambridi-Kemou, 2013). During the 20th century, the process of institutionalisation took place in the framework of the competition between local power groups or elites (*differentiated accumulation of power*). This competition has usually been over natural and other resources. Thus, the state itself and the control of state institutions represented a new resource in the rivalry, which provided the necessary tools to exert dominance in the country in order to rule other social groups. The dominant elite group fundamentally merged with state institutions, thus creating a *regime* with specific formal and informal authority structures, values, and norms (Stenslie, 2012, pp. 6–7).

As a result, the regime will be the primary actor in both domestic and international politics, not the state. Its policies aim at serving the interests of the ruling elite against rival groups. Through co-optation, the regime can invite other primary or secondary elites to take part in managing state institutions, thus fragmenting the state framework (Hinnebusch, 2014a, pp. 1–2). In this multi-level competition, the support of the general public is also considered to be a specific type of resource without a great deal of agency (Brichs and Lambridi-Kemou, 2013, pp. 14–18).

This alternative state model is not uncommon in the non-Western world. The effect of such a model on state behaviour is far-reaching, but here I would like to underline two major effects. First, regimes accommodated these circumstances by directing their foreign policy behaviour to counter domestic and international challenges (frequently with an emphasis on the former). This strategy is usually conceptualised as "omni-balancing" (David, 1991; Rosman-Stollman, 2004), which is utilised by small and large states alike, especially in periods when state-building is at an early stage (Hinnebusch, 2014a, pp. 20–21). The ultimate logic for such behaviour is set by regime security, rather than national security in the form of regime-alliances with regional or global actors (Jackson, 2009, pp. 154–155). The state, arguably, lacks not only the interest, but also the ability to "deal with socio-economic grievances and disparities" (Cavatorta, 2017, p. 40), as the short-term security of the regime triumphs over any other motivation, including state-building or social progress (Jackson, 2009, pp. 154–155). The inability of governments to meet the needs of their society is closely connected to the legitimacy crisis of Middle Eastern states (Razi, 1990, p. 84), which leads to a more aggressive approach against popular demand.[6]

Second, as states are not designed to satisfy the needs of society but, rather, to maintain the ruling elite's dominance, there will always be room for non-state actors (NSAs), defined as organisations that "are at least in principle autonomous from the structure and the machinery of the state, and of the governmental and intergovernmental bodies" (Josselin and Wallace, 2001, p. 3). Such actors usually appear in situations and sectors where demands from some segments of the society are not met by the capacity or the willingness of state institutions (Wiktorowitz, 2004, p. 6). Among the various types of non-state actor, usually non-governmental organisations ("voluntary, not for profit, private and self-governing" institutions), highly empowered individuals, and violent groups using illegal violence are those mentioned in the Middle Eastern context (Valensi, 2015, pp. 61–62).

A typical form of the regional NSAs in the MENA region includes Islamic movements, which, in the name of Islam, provide services that the state cannot or will not provide. Therefore, among other factors, their activity is shaped by the nature of state repression, the institutional strength of the government, or the instability of elite alignments (Hafez and Wiktorowitz, 2004, p. 65). Such Islamic movements include the Muslim Brotherhood network, Hamas (Robinson, 2004), Hezbollah (Valensi, 2015, pp. 67–70), or even the Islamic State (Fromson and Steven, 2015; Valensi, 2015, pp. 70–74).

The relationship between state and non-state actors in the region has always been ambiguous. On the one hand, regimes can easily consider them as rivals, or merely tools in the hands of domestic or external enemies. On the other hand, due to the essential weakness of the state, governments often need the help of NSAs, for example, to maintain order and control by providing social services to the population (Gaub, 2017, pp. 57–58).[7] Moreover, NSAs operating in other countries can also be instrumentalised in foreign policy in order to use them and influence their activities in their interests. This is a common practice in the Middle East and North Africa (Kausch, 2017), especially during turbulent periods (Marchetti and Al Zahrani, 2017), due to the low costs associated with their usage, especially compared to traditional coercive measures. They are usually used as military challengers to adversaries, as future leaders, as bearers of a specific identity, as a source of legitimacy, or as leverage against other actors (Kausch, 2017, pp. 81–82).

These particularities affect small and large states alike, but are more beneficial for small states as they narrow down the security deficit between the two groups for two reasons. First, resource-scarce entities can capitalise on the strong role of NSAs as either a domestic or foreign policy tool. Their usage is quite cheap – much cheaper than engaging in traditional warfare – thus, they are available for small states. It is much easier to interfere in a large state's domestic affairs by subsidising an anti-establishment NSA than by building up traditional deterrence, bringing coercion back into the toolkit of small states. Second, the regime structure works as a counter-incentive to the waging of traditional interstate wars, which is the most depressing scenario for small and weak entities. Governing elites always have to keep an eye on domestic developments as main security threats originate from the domestic sphere, rather than the international. That is why states are incentivised to build up coercive capacities against social groups or movements, as opposed to traditional international enemies (Jackson, 2009, pp. 148–149). Therefore, traditional war is not a luxury of large states but, rather, of governments that consider their domestic status stable.

Conflict and war

The MENA region is usually (and quite correctly) described as a conflictual region. Nevertheless, after empirical investigation, one can easily see that these conflicts are usually not traditional interstate ones. Besides the Yom Kippur war of 1973, the three Gulf wars, and smaller armed clashes (e.g. in Yemen or Libya), most conflicts in the region were either domestic in nature or transnational, with the participation of both domestic and foreign actors (e.g. the Syrian, the Libyan and Yemeni civil wars). Moreover, Ana Gonzalez-Pelaez (2009) even argues that traditional war had not only been rare, but had been forbidden in inter-Arab politics until the Iraqi invasion of Kuwait.[8]

The reasons behind this phenomenon are rooted not only in Middle Eastern statehood, but also in the normative particularities of international politics in the region. In a Westphalian system, the primary institutions of conflict and war are constructed on the basis of a binary setting that differentiates between "domestic" and "foreign" affairs (Kiss, 2009, pp. 56–58). Hierarchy, peace, and order are connected to the domestic sphere, while anarchy, hostility, and instability belong to the international sphere. This distinction has its foundation in deeply rooted cultural differentiation between in-groups and out-groups, "us" and "them", and in the binary worldview of various religions (Kuhn, 2016).

In the Islamic tradition (similarly to other religions), the main differentiation is between Muslims and non-Muslims, Islamic societies and non-Islamic societies (Saeed, 2006, p. 6). This idea translated into the construction of two domains or regions (Bennison, 2009, p. 45): *dar al-Islam*, which referred to all Muslim countries and people, and *dar al-Harb*, the "house of war", which included all non-Muslim territories. This logic was not solely territorial but was, rather, normative– the former was the land of peace, while war, at least theoretically, was the order of the day in the latter.[9] In theory, this norm prohibited large-scale armed conflicts in the Muslim world.

Naturally, one can argue that this is only an old tradition that can hardly explain current international developments. On the other hand, several reasons point to indicate the validity of this interpretation. First, as already discussed, we can still observe a parallel existence of premodern and modern structures in Middle Eastern politics, which has allowed the endurance of such political traditions. The creation of nation-states did not necessarily replace Islamic norms or identity (Lewis, 1995, p. 158), and the lack of separation of religious and political affairs in Islamic thought affects how political legitimacy is constructed today and how states should behave in domestic (Mayer, 1987) and foreign affairs (Razi, 1990, pp. 75–79).

Second, the dichotomy of Islam was reproduced by different regional political developments, including the imperial tradition that dominated political communities until the 20th century (Steunebrink, 2008, p. 10), the post-independence Arab solidarity (Barnett, 1998), or even the practice of religious or Islamist movements that put great emphasis on the practice of excommunication (*takfir*). This is particularly connected to the norm of conflicts, as, often, proving that someone does not belong to the community allows an attack or prosecution against them (Lynch, 2007, pp. 73–74; Wagemakers, 2009, p. 292).

In such an environment, the power, legitimacy, and security of a leader (or a regime) at least partially derive from belonging to a specific normative group, which is highly beneficial for resource-scarce entities. Being part of a supranational community (whether Muslim, Arab, Sunni, or Shia) means protection and solidarity, which can explain why belonging to the family of Arab nations prohibits wars among its members. Such ties can be as strong as national solidarity, or even stronger due to the artificial nature of nationhood and the protracted process of state-building (Hinnebusch, 2014a, pp. 9–10).

Club membership is manifested in membership in various international organisations that represent the identity groups mentioned. The most important group from our perspective is the League of Arab States, founded in 1945 and explicitly designed to protect the norms of inter-Arab cooperation (*ta'aun*), independence (*istiklal*), and sovereignty (*siyada*) (Mithaq Jamiah al-Daul al-Arabiyah wa-Mullaqatihu, 2017, p. 2).

Built on Arab identity, the League of Arab States system worked as a normative incentive with regard to accepting sovereign equality and cooperating in the Arab region (Hinnebusch, 2014a, p. 15; Murden, 2009, p. 122).[10] This duality is especially important for small states that fear losing sovereignty and are deeply interested in interstate collaboration. It is therefore not surprising that small states played an initiating role in the creation and main-tenance of the League of Arab States (Solingen, 2008, pp. 284–285), as well as in participation in mediation efforts.

A case in point where the practical effects of such normative processes took place was the Iraqi–Kuwaiti dispute over the independence of the Kuwait in the late 1950s (Yassine-Hamdan and Pearson, 2014, pp. 117–126). Before the small Gulf state managed to achieve independence, Iraq officially claimed in June 1958 that Kuwait belonged to Iraq. The Emir of Kuwait issued a request for membership in the League, which served as normative protection of Kuwait against Iraqi aggression. While the League of Arab States did not have an army to protect the small emirate, membership expressed its sovereignty, and this put pressure on Iraq to accept Kuwait's independence.[11] The message was emphasized by the deployment of a small joint Arab force to Kuwait in 1961, which served mostly as a political and not military deterrent against any Iraqi actions. This example shows how such normative dynamics not only serve as protection for smaller states, but also create behavioural obligations for all members to respect each other and to be loyal (or, at least, seem loyal) to the Arab goals, without which they could easily lose the protection of Arab countries (Walt, 1987, p. 148).

Such an environment is beneficial for small states for several reasons, only one of which is the prohibition of traditional wars between members of each supranational group. First, the strong presence of sub- and supra-national identities poses a constant challenge to ruling elites (Milton-Edwards, 2006, pp. 222–223) and, coupled with the particularities of the regime structure, reproduces a constant deficit in legitimacy for Middle Eastern states. The usual tools with which to overcome this challenge are not necessarily con-nected to a huge surplus of resources and are frequently cheap; for example, creating the image of traditional or religious entitlements, or popular mobili-sation (Salzman, 2016, p. 211). If a small state manages to play identity poli-tics effectively, it can use these transnational networks in its own interests in relation to larger actors, which can have difficulties on their own. They even have a better chance of success if we consider the observations of several political theorists described in Chapter 1 regarding the possible correlation between heterogeneity and demographic size.

Second, these normative circumstances also incentivise political and nor-mative interventions to the detriment of classic warfare. Regimes can try to subsidise domestic groups or even tribes, which, if they are interested in fight-ing against the regime, can undermine even the hierarchic distribution of power in a country and the monopoly of the government over the legitimate use of force (Salzman, 2016, pp. 207–208).

Naturally, these normative attributes of the region can be subject to change, especially since they have never been deeply institutionalised (Hinnebusch, 2014a, p. 17). Since 1967, observers have described the process of normative fragmentation; namely, the softening of transnational Arab identity and soli-darity, and the parallel strengthening of national, regional, religious, and other identities. This normative fragmentation (Barnett, 1998, pp. 49–52;

Gause, 1999, p. 16) coincided with the crisis of the League of Arab nations (Murden, 2009, pp. 125–126; Little, 1956). The process led to the strengthening of alternative supranational identities, which manifested in the creation of sub-regional institutions (Murden, 2009, p. 131) such as the Gulf Cooperation Council (GCC) (1981), the Arab Cooperation Council, and the Arab Maghreb Union. These processes can negatively affect the situation of small states in the region; nevertheless, smaller Gulf states are in a relatively good position due to their being able to lead the sub-regionalisation process as, basically, the GCC has been the most effective organisation among these initiatives.

Balance of power

As with every regional system, the Middle East and North Africa can also be investigated through the dynamics of the balance of power between its most important states. This fluctuation affects the situation of small states to a great extent, as was described in Chapter 1.

Before I undertake this, I would like to point out two specific regional particularities that affect how we look at power relations in general. First, the MENA system has always been "penetrated" by outside actors who frequently played a greater role than their regional partners (Brown, 1984, pp. 3–5; Yurdusev, 2009, p. 79). The specific global actors changed over time – Great Britain, France, Russia, or the USA all played an important role in different periods – which complicates the measurement of power relations among regional actors. The presence of great powers downgrades the possibility of the rise of a regional hegemon, but is also beneficial for small states because they can seek the protection of extra-regional powers from their neighbours (Mason, 2018, p. 162). Second, due to the particularities of statehood, the calculation of the regional balance of power should also include non-state entities, whose role can be as significant as that of the state (Halliday, 2009, pp. 6–10).

As a result of this constellation, power is much more fractured than in a traditional Westphalian system, not necessarily horizontally but vertically, with the inclusion of actors from the domestic, regional, and supra-regional levels, too. No state managed to achieve hegemonic or system-determining status (Hinnebusch, 2014a, pp. 3–4; Lustick, 1997). Theoretically, such a system is more conflictual, but it does provide wider leverage for its members to balance each other out (Lake, 2009) on different levels.

Besides these general observations, which have been fairly constant during recent decades, the balance of power dynamics were quite mutable. Power relations changed between states, internal and external powers, as well as between ideological movements and networks. The security and status of the five smaller Gulf states was determined by power dynamics that had taken place on the regional and the sub-regional levels at the same time, especially the triangle of the three bigger Gulf states: Iraq, Iran, and Saudi Arabia (Ulrichsen, 2011b, p. 3).

Table 2.1 Periods of balance of power from the perspective of smaller Gulf states.

Period	Main threats	The regional environment in the Gulf	Participation in armed conflicts
–1971: Under British security umbrella	Pan-Arabism	Twin pillars	
1971–1979: Being independent amid relative stability	Pan-Arabism Hegemonic attempts of Kingdom of Saudi Arabia, Iraq, and Iran	Twin pillars	None
1979–1991: The post-revolutionary period	Iraq and Iran	Two Gulf wars	The Iraqi–Kuwaiti war
1991–2003: Era of American protection	Jihadi networks	American quasi-hegemony	The Iraqi war
2003–: Diverging strategies	Iraqi instability, growing Iranian influence, Jihadi and Islamist networks	Competitive hetero-polarity	The Syrian, Libyan and Yemeni civil wars, the war against Daesh, "Arab spring" revolutions, etc.

Source: Compiled by author, based on a slightly modified version of Hinnebusch, 2014b and Kamrava, 2005.

Adjusting the traditional periodisation of modern Middle Eastern and North African history to the perspective of smaller Gulf states, we can distinguish between five periods until 2021 (see Table 2.1). First, prior to their independence, smaller Gulf states were the protected states of the British Empire. Due to their late independence, the regimes of the five states witnessed the creation of Israel and the subsequent wars, hegemonic attempts by Egypt, and the rise and spread of pan-Arabism from this point of view. Among these, the most pressing for them was pan-Arabism, an ideological movement that questioned the legitimacy of monarchic regimes and wanted to unify Arab lands. The Gulf region was relatively stable, not just due to the presence of the British Empire, but to the fact that two out of the three great powers of the sub-region –Saudi Arabia and the Shah's Iran – were allied in the American cold war camp with similar political interests – the famous twin pillars policy.

The post-independence period in the 1970s was very similar; nevertheless, smaller Gulf states lost British protection. The main threat remained pan-Arabism, although a slightly weakened version of it – following the 1967 war, Nasserist Arab nationalism had seen its heyday, affecting only Iraq and Yemen in the subregion. Arab solidarity and the twin pillars policy remained intact, creating a sense of stability for smaller Gulf states. The three Gulf powers did have expansionist tendencies, but these were limited either by Arab solidarity or their Western relations.

This perception, nevertheless, radically changed after 1979 for two reasons. First, revolution in Iran resulted in the rise of a new kind of political system: the Islamic Republic, which expressed its readiness to export the revolution to the region. Second, Saddam Hussein rose to power in the same year in Iraq, and became the last symbol of Arab nationalism. The two actors both represented a threat not only to smaller Gulf states, but to each other as well, leading nine years of bloody war.

Instability led to closer ties with Saudi Arabia and the creation of the Gulf Cooperation Council in 1981. These steps aimed at countering external threats, especially the spill-over effects of the Iraqi–Iranian war; however, the Gulf Cooperation Council turned out to be ineffective as it did not prevent Iraq from attacking Kuwait in 1990 after it had finished its war with Iran and badly needed cash. That is why smaller Gulf states turned to the USA for security guarantees, which led to bilateral agreements with Washington and a privileged partnership. Smaller Gulf states experienced relative stability due to the American dual containment policy, aimed at diminishing Iraqi and Iranian influence. The smaller Gulf states used this stability to gather together as many resources as possible, and to modernise their economic and defence capabilities.

After 2003, threats started to mount once more as a result of the American intervention in Iraq, which contributed to the spread of Iranian influence, the rise of Jihadi organisations, the intensifying of Saudi–Iranian rivalry, and deepening instability. The process was exacerbated by the Arab uprisings of 2011 and the inability (or unwillingness) of the American leadership to manage these crises. In such instability, none of the internal or external actors were able to build hegemony, and power became progressively more diffused, which exacerbated international rivalry and instability. This new era – which is frequently called "competitive multipolarity" (Kausch, 2014) or, with the inclusion of non-state actors, "heteropolarity" (Malmvig, 2016, p. 38) – lead to diverging state interests and loosening alliances not only on the regional level, but also between smaller Gulf states themselves.

Throughout these five periods, the underlying tendency for smaller Gulf states has been twofold. First, their level of security fluctuated, the peaks occurring when extra-regional actors (Great Britain and the United States) managed to provide effective and cheap shelter for them. Second, on the other hand, the leverage of smaller Gulf states widened progressively in each period, which can be attributed to power becoming progressively more diffused and the lack of a single conflict or cleavage that would structure actors of the Middle East and North Africa into solidified camps. Consequently, if their status is stable, small states can pursue active and ambitious foreign policy, becoming *swing states* (Kausch, 2016).

Another interesting pattern during the five periods concerns regional armed conflicts. Between 1970 and 1990, smaller Gulf states successfully avoided participating in any conflicts (with the exception of occasional Iranian attacks on oil vessels and Omani domestic struggles); nevertheless, Iraq's aggression against Kuwait represented a game changer. The next regional conflict in which smaller Gulf states actively participated was the Iraqi intervention in 2003, when they provided support for the coalition. This cautious and reserved approach has changed drastically since 2011, when smaller Gulf states participated in one way or another in virtually all armed conflicts. This is a clear indicator of growing activity and more high-risk behaviour, which is especially interesting in the light of academic debates regarding these aspects of small state behaviour (see Chapter 1). It seems that risk-avoidance can be the result of systemic developments and not just absolute or relative size.

*

The investigation of the changing regional balance of power, supplemented by the analysis of the Middle Eastern and North African state model and norms related to conflicts, helps us understand why attributes of the MENA region are beneficial for small states. In such an environment, traditional armed conflicts are de-incentivised by the regime structure, Arab solidarity, the diffusion of power, and the presence of extra-regional and non-state actors. On the other hand, resource-scarce entities are equipped with several tools that are as available to them at a low cost as they are for larger states, such as the usage of non-state actors in domestic and international politics, capitalising on Arab or Islamic solidarity as well as exo-communication, and the norms enabling almost constant interventions in each other's domestic affairs (Halliday, 2009, pp. 15–17). The current balance of power dynamics also contribute not only to widening the leverage of smaller states, but also to a lower extent of security, deriving not from their size but from regime political dynamics and their individual attributes.

Due to the far-reaching consequences of this regional environment, regime security considerations interact with smallness, profoundly determining its role on state behaviour. That is why, in Chapter 4, I will include regime security considerations as another important variable through which to interpret the foreign and security policy of smaller Gulf states.

Notes

1 Defined as the 20 states including Turkey, Israel, and Iran, and all members of the Arab League except for Somalia, Djibouti, Sudan, Mauritania, and the Chomoros,
2 Even for the Ottomans it was only the Western coast of the Arabian Peninsula that was valuable because of its religious importance.
3 Parts of the al-Hasa *elayet* extended to territories now controlled by Kuwait, the UAE and Qatar, but Ottoman rule was rather formal.
4 See the example of Bahrain in 1559 (Özbaran, 2009, pp. 117–133).
5 Except for Oman, which was officially an independent state with "special treaty relations" with the British empire.

6 The authoritarian approach by the Arab governments can easily lead to a vicious circle very similar to the "insecurity dilemma" – repression leads to a lack of social trust, which turns into discontent (Jackson, 2009). Political frustration in society will mobilise segments of the population against the government, which will respond with more repression (UNDP, 2014). The mechanism, coupled with high military expenditures "made rulers over-confident in their ability to suppress opposition, as with the defunct Hashemite monarchy in Iraq" (Ahram and Lust, 2016, p. 12.).

7 Lebanon, for example, acknowledges the role of the institutions of religious communities in the area of personal status law (Gaub, 2017, p. 56.).

8 The author did not consider the wars between North and South Yemen as inter-state conflicts.

9 A third region is also present between the two "houses"; namely, the *dar al-'ahl*, the house (domain) of agreement or truce between Muslims and non-Muslims (Bennison, 2009, p. 49.), but only in the time of Muslim weakness (Tibi, 2001, p. 58.).

10 The Islamic Cooperation Conference/Organization serves a similar purpose, as it also strengthens the norms of sovereignty, independence, but also solidarity – the difference is that it is normatively based on Islamic and not pan-Arab identities (Hinnebusch, 2014a, p.15).

11 The bid of Kuwait to be accepted as a member of the MENA regional system by admission to the League resembles the struggle of the Principality of Liechtenstein at the same time, which also considered admission to international organisations as a way to make its statehood recognised (Duursma, 2006).

Bibliography

Acharya, A. (2011) Norm Subsidiarity and Regional Orders: Sovereignty, Regionalism and Rule-Making in the Third World. *International Studies Quarterly*, 55(1), pp. 95–123. DOI:10.1111/j.1468-2478.2010.00637.x.

Ahram, A.I. and Lust, E. (2016) The Decline and Fall of the Arab State. *Survival*, 58(2), pp. 7–34. DOI:10.1080/00396338.2016.1161897.

Anderson, L. (1987) The State in the Middle East and North Africa. *Comparative Politics*, 20(1), pp. 1–18.

Al-Hamad, T. (2002) Imperfect Alliances: Will the Gulf Monarchies Work Together?, in Rubin, B. (ed.) *Crises in Contemporary Persian Gulf*. London: Frank Cass, pp. 21–32.

Al-Qasimi, S.b. M. (1999) *Power Struggles and Trade in the Gulf. 1620–1820*. Exeter: University of Exeter Press.

Barnett, M. (1998) *Dialogues in Arab Politics: Negotiations in Regional Order*. New York: Columbia University Press.

Bennison, A.K. (2009 The Ottoman Empire and its Precedents from the Perspective of English School Theory, in Buzan, B. and Gonzalez-Pelaez, A. (eds.) *International Society and the Middle East. English School Theory at the Regional Level*. New York: Palgrave MacMillan, pp. 45–70. DOI:10.1057/9780230234352_3.

Berman, B. and Lonsdale, J. (1992) *Unhappy Valley. Book One: State & Class*. London: James Currey Ltd.

Brichs, F.I. (2013) Introduction, in Brichs, F.I. (ed.) *Political Regimes in the Arab World*. New York: Routledge, pp. 1–5. DOI:10.4324/9780203102626-6.

Brichs, F.I. and Lambridi-Kemou, A. (2013) Sociology of Power in Today's Arab World, in Brichs, F.I. (ed.) *Political Regimes in the Arab World*. New York: Routledge, pp. 6–35. DOI:10.4324/9780203102626-7.

Brown, L.C. (1984) *International Politics in the Middle East: Old Rules, Dangerous Games*. Princeton: Princeton University Press.

Cammack, P., Dunne, M., Hamzawy, A., Lynch, M., Muasher, M., Sayigh, Y. and Maha, Y. (2017) Arab Fractures. Citizens, States, and Social Contracts. *Carnegie Endowment for International Peace*, [Online]. Available at http://carnegieendowment.org/files/Arab_World_Horizons_Final.pdf (Accessed 31 January 2021).

Cavatorta, F. (2017) The Weakness of State Structures in the Arab World: Socio-Economic Challenges from Below, in Kamel, L. (ed.) *The Frailty of Authority. Borders, Non-state Actors and Power Vacuums in a Changing Middle East*. Istituto Affari Internazionali, [Online]. Available at http://www.iai.it/sites/default/files/newmed_authority.pdf (Accessed 15 September 2018), pp. 35–50.

Commins, D. (2014) *The Gulf States. A Modern History*. London: I.B. Tauris. DOI:10.5040/9780755608805.

Crystal, J. (2014) Eastern Arabian States: Kuwait, Bahrain, Qatar, United Arab Emirates, and Oman, in Gasirowski, M. (ed.) *The Government and Politics of the Middle East and North Africa*. 7th Edition. Boulder: Westview Press, pp. 157–196.

David, S.R. (1991) Third World Alignment. *World Politics*, 43(2), pp. 233–256. DOI:10.2307/2010472.

Duursma, J. (2006) Micro-states: The Principality of Liechtenstein, in Igebritsen, C., Neumann, I.B., Gstöhl, S. and Beyer, J. (eds.) *Small States in International Relations*. Reykjavik: University of Iceland Press, pp. 89–149.

Fromson, J. and Steven, S. (2015) ISIS: The Dubious Paradise of Apocalypse Now. *Survival*, 57(3), pp. 7–37. DOI:10.1080/00396338.2015.1046222.

Gaub, F. (2017) State Vacuums and Non-State Actors in the Middle East and North Africa, in Kamel, L. (ed.) *The Frailty of Authority. Borders, Non-state Actors and Power Vacuums in a Changing Middle East*. Istituto Affari Internazionali, [Online]. Available at http://www.iai.it/sites/default/files/newmed_authority.pdf (Accessed 29 January 2021), pp. 50–66.

Gause, G. (1999) Systemic Approaches to Middle East International Relations. *International Studies Review*, 1(1), pp. 11–31. DOI:10.1111/1521-9488.00139.

Gonzalez-Pelaez, A. (2009) The Primary Institutions of the Middle Eastern Regional Interstate Society, in Buzan, B. and Gonzalez-Pelaez, A. (eds.) *International Society and the Middle East. English School Theory at the Regional Level*. New York: Palgrave MacMillan, pp. 92–116. DOI:10.1057/9780230234352_5.

Hafez, M.M. and Wiktorowitz, Q. (2004) Violence as Contention in the Egyptian Islamic Movement, in Wiktorowitz, Q. (ed.) *Islamic Activism. A Social Movement Theory Approach*. Indiana: Indiana University Press, pp. 61–88.

Halliday, F. (2009) The Middle East and Conceptions of "International Society", in Buzan, B. and Gonzalez-Pelaez, A. (eds.) *International Society and the Middle East. English School Theory at the Regional Level*. New York: Palgrave MacMillan, pp. 1–23. DOI:10.1057/9780230234352_1.

Hazmeh, A.N. (1994) Qatar: The Duality of the Legal System. *Middle Eastern Studies*, 30(1), pp. 79–99. DOI:10.1080/00263209408700984.

Hinnebusch, R. (2014a) Foreign Policy in the Middle East, in Hinnebusch, R. and Ehteshami, A. (eds.) *The Foreign Policies of Middle East States*. 2nd Edition. London: Lynne Rienner Publishers, pp. 1–34.

Hinnebusch, R. (2014b) The Middle East Regional System, in Hinnebusch, R. and Ehteshami, A. (eds.) *The Foreign Policies of Middle East States.* 2nd Edition. London: Lynne Rienner Publishers, pp. 35–74.

Ismael, T.Y. and Ismael, J.S. (2011) *Government and Politics of the Contemporary Middle East. Continuity and Change.* London & New York: Routledge. DOI:10.4324/9780203847459.

Kamrava, M. (2005) *The Modern Middle East. A Political History since the First World War.* London: University of California Press. DOI:10.1525/9780520956858.

Kausch, K. (2017) Proxy Agents: State and Non-State Alliances in the Middle East, in Kamel, L. (ed.) *The Frailty of Authority. Borders, Non-state Actors and Power Vacuums in a Changing Middle East.* Istituto Affari Internazionali [Online]. Available at: http://www.iai.it/sites/default/files/newmed_authority.pdf (Accessed 31 January 2021), pp. 67–84.

Kiss, J.L. (2009) *Változó utak a külpolitika elméletében és elemzésében.* Budapest: Osiris.

Kuhn, M. (2016) The Seduction of Binary Thinking. *The Institute of Middle East Studies,* [Online]. Available at: https://imes.blog/2016/03/23/the-seduction-of-binary-thinking/ (Accessed 31 January 2021).

Jackson, R. (2009) Regime Security, in Collins, A. (ed.) *Contemporary Security Studies.* Oxford: Oxford University Press, pp. 146–164. DOI:10.1093/hepl/9780198708315.003.0014.

Josselin, D. and Wallace, W. (2001) Non-state Actors in World Politics: A Framework, in: Josselin, D. and Wallace, W. (eds.) *Non-state Actors in World Politics.* New York: Palgrave, pp. 1–20. DOI:10.1057/9781403900906_15.

Kausch, K. (2014) Competitive Multipolarity in the Middle East, *Istituto Affari Internazionali,* [Online]. Available at: https://www.ciaonet.org/attachments/26875/uploads (Accessed 31 January 2021).

Kausch, K. (2016) The Promise of Middle Eastern Swing States. *Carnegie Europe,* [Online]. Available at: http://carnegieeurope.eu/2016/05/12/promise-of-middle-eastern-swing-states/iy77?mkt_tok=eyjpijoiwm1zme1tvtjnvel4wvdaaiisinqioijbntz-uyzbsn1czn0ryxc9drlvem014c3jqctjzvdywkzbtnktcl28rmgn3eg52azzbawhgzu5mr ws3anhoag1jmkjswu9hsxkzakrivxg0tfvuulvudhplqxl0cvdrs0l6z2z0tgnuovrwqjd-vpsj9 (Accessed 31 January 2021).

Kelly, R.E. (2007) Security Theory in "New Regionalism". *International Studies Review,* 9(2), pp. 197–229. DOI:10.1111/j.1468-2486.2007.00671.x.

Khouri, R.G. (2017) Early Warning Signs in the Arab World that We Ignored – and Still Ignore, in Kamel, L. (ed.) *The Frailty of Authority. Borders, Non-state Actors and Power Vacuums in a Changing Middle East.* Istituto Affari Internazionali [Online]. Available at: http://www.iai.it/sites/default/files/newmed_authority.pdf (Accessed 31 January 2021), pp. 19–34.

Lake, D.A. (2009) Regional Hierarchy: Authority and Local International Order. *Review of International Studies,* 35(1), pp. 35–58. DOI:10.1017/s0260210509008420.

Lewis, B. (1995) Secularism in the Middle East. *Revue de Métaphysique et de Morale,* 100(2), pp. 151–164.

Little, T.R. (1956) The Arab League: A Reassessment. *Middle East Journal,* 10(2), pp. 138–150.

Lustick, I.S. (1997) The Absence of Middle Eastern Great Powers: Political "Backwardness" in Historical Perspective. *International Organization,* 51(4), pp. 653–683. DOI:10.1162/002081897550483.

Lynch, M. (2007) Brothers in Arms. *Foreign Policy*, 2007(162), pp. 70–74.

Marchetti, R. and Al Zahrani, Y. (2017) Hybrid Partnerships in Middle East Turbulence, in Kamel, L. (ed.) *The Frailty of Authority. Borders, Non-state Actors and Power Vacuums in a Changing Middle East*. Istituto Affari Internazionali [Online]. Available at: http://www.iai.it/sites/default/files/newmed_authority.pdf (Accessed 31 January 2021), pp. 107–122.

Malmvig, H. et al. (2016) The Contemporary Regional Order, in Soler, E.I.L., et al. (eds.) *Re-conceptualising Orders in the MENA region*. MENARA Project [Online]. Available at: http://www.menaraproject.eu/wp-content/uploads/2017/01/menara_cp_1.pdf (Accessed 31 January 2021), pp. 33–55.

Mason, R. (2018) Breaking the Mold of Small State Classification? The Broadening Influence of United Arab Emirates Foreign Policy through Effective Military and Bandwagoning Strategies. *Canadian Foreign Policy Journal*, 24(1), pp. 95–112. DOI :10.1080/11926422.2018.1427123.

Mayer, A.E. (1987) Law and Religion in the Muslim Middle East. *The American Journal of Comparative Law*, 35(1), pp. 127–184. DOI:10.2307/840165.

Milton-Edwards, B. (2006) *Contemporary Politics in the Middle East*. 2nd Edition. Cambridge: Polity Press.

Mithaq Jamiah al-Daul al-Arabiyah (2017) [Online]. Available at: http://www.las-portal.org/ar/aboutlas/Documents/%D9%85%D9%8A%D8%AB%D9%80%D8%A7%D9%82%20%D8%AC%D8%A7%D9%85%D8%B9%D8%A9%20%D8%A7%D9%84%D8%AF%D9%88%D9%84%20%D8%A7%D9%84%D8%B9%D8%B1%D8%A8%D9%8A%D8%A9%20%D9%88%20%D9%85%D9%84%D8%AD%D9%82%D8%A7%D8%AA%D9%87%20.pdf (Accessed 31 January 2021).

Murden, S.W. (2009) The Secondary Institutions of the Middle Eastern Regional Interstate Society, in Buzan, B. and Gonzalez-Pelaez, A. (eds.) *International Society and the Middle East. English School Theory at the Regional Level*. New York: Palgrave MacMillan, pp. 117–139. DOI:10.1057/9780230234352_6.

Onley, J. (2009) Britain and the Gulf Sheikhdoms, 1820-1971: The Politics of Protection. *Center for International and Regional Studies*, Georgetown University, [Online]. Available at: https://socialsciences.exeter.ac.uk/iais/downloads/Onley_Britain_and_Gulf_Shaikhdoms2009.pdf (Accessed 31 January 2021).

Özbaran, S. (2009) *Ottoman Expansion towards the Indian Ocean in the 16th century*. Istanbul: Istanbul Bilgi University Press.

Razi, G.H. (1990) Legitimacy, Religion, and Nationalism in the Middle East. *The American Political Science Review*, 84(1), pp. 69–91. DOI:10.2307/1963630.

Robinson, G.E. (2004) Hamas as a Social Movement, in Wiktorowitz, Q. (ed.) *Islamic Activism. A Social Movement Theory Approach*. Indiana: Indiana University Press, pp. 112–142.

Rosman-Stollman, E. (2004) Balancing Acts: The Gulf States and Israel. *Middle Eastern Studies*, 40(4), pp. 185–204. DOI:10.1080/0026320042000240401.

Saeed, A. (2006) *Islamic Thought. An Introduction*. New York: Routledge.

Salzman, P.C. (2016) Tribes and Modern States: An Alternative Approach, in Rabi, U. (ed.) *Tribes and States in the Changing Middle East*. London: Hurst & Co., pp. 207–219. DOI:10.1093/acprof:oso/9780190264925.003.0011.

Sharabi, H. (1988) *Neopatriarchy. A Theory of Distorted Change in Arab Society*. Oxford: Oxford University Press.

Solingen, E. (2008) The Genesis, Design and Effects of Regional Institutions: Lessons from East Asia and the Middle East. *International Studies Quarterly*, 52(2), pp. 261–294. DOI:10.1111/j.1468-2478.2008.00501.x.

Stenslie, S. (2012) *Regime Stability in Saudi Arabia. The Challenge of Succession*. New York: Routledge. DOI:10.4324/9780203147801.

Steunebrink, G. (2008) Sovereignty, the Nation State and Islam. *Ethical Perspectives*, 15(1), pp. 7–47. DOI:10.2143/ep.15.1.2029556.

Tibi, B. (2001) *Islam: Between Culture and Politics*. New York: Palgrave. DOI:10.1057/9780230204157.

Ulrichsen, K.C. (2011a) *Insecure Gulf. The End of Certainty and the Transition to the Post-Oil Era*. New York: Columbia University Press.

Ulrichsen, K.C. (2011b) Repositioning the GCC States in the Changing Global Order. *Journal of Arabian Studies*, 1(2), pp. 231–247. DOI:10.1080/21534764.2011.630894.

UNDP (2014) The Arab Human Development Report 2004: Towards Freedom in the Arab World. *United Nations Development Programme*, [Online]. Available at http://www.arab-hdr.org/reports/2004/english/ahdr2004e.pdf?download (Accessed 31 January 2021).

Valensi, C. (2015) Non-state Actors: A Theoretical Limitation in a Changing Middle East. *Military and Strategic Affairs*, 7(1), pp. 59–78.

Wagemakers, J. (2009) A Purist Jihadi-Salafi: The Ideology of Abu Muhammad al-Maqdisi. *British Journal of Middle Eastern Studies*, 36(2), pp. 281–297. DOI:10.1080/13530190903007327.

Walt, S.M. (1987) *The Origins of Alliance*. Ithaca: Cornell University Press. DOI:10.7591/9780801469992.

Wiktorowitz, Q. (2004) Introduction: Islamic Activism and Social Movement Theory, in Wiktorowitz, Q. (ed.) *Islamic Activism. A Social Movement Theory Approach*. Indiana: Indiana University Press, pp. 1–36.

Yurdusev, N.A. (2009) The Middle East Encounter with the Expansion of European International Society, in Buzan, B. and Gonzalez-Pelaez, A. (eds.) *International Society and the Middle East. English School Theory at the Regional Level*. New York: Palgrave MacMillan, pp. 70–92. DOI:10.1057/9780230234352_4.

Yassine-Hamdan, N. and Pearson, F.S. (2014) *Arab Approaches to Conflict Resolution. Mediation, Negotiation and Settlement of Political Disputes*. London & New York: Routledge. DOI:10.4324/9780203584224.

3 The relative and normative size of smaller Gulf states

After identifying the main particularities of the MENA region that enable small states to have a greater role than is theoretically anticipated, I turn to the analysis of the systemic sizes of regional actors: relative and normative size. Due to their fundamentally different nature, different methods will be used in the inquiry: for relative size, I will focus on the distribution of material capacities in the MENA region (territory, population, economic output, and military capacities); for normative size, I will focus on measuring interstate interactions.

Calculating relative size

According to the World Bank Database,[1] the MENA region currently possesses almost 12 million square kilometres of land, approximately 539 million people, and 4,339 billion USD of aggregate GDP. Overall governmental military spending in the region amounts to 195 billion USD, while the gross size of state armed forces is approximately 3.9 million people. As 9% of all states and state-like entities[2] belong to the region, normal distribution at the global level would indicate that the Middle East and North Africa should have roughly 9% of all resources – but this is only the case with regard to official military expenditure (10.4%) and land area (9%); however, the population amounts only to a 7% share, and the GDP to a staggering 5%. Nevertheless, when it comes to the size of the armed forces, the figure is 14%. These data in themselves suggest a highly militarised, underdeveloped region, unfitting for small states in general.

The relative size of the Gulf subregion,[3] consisting of nine states (45% of all MENA states), changed throughout the period of investigation. While its territory constituted 43% of the whole land area of the region, its population share grew from 30% to 39%, and its economic share increased from 40% to 54%. On the other hand, it seems that the states of the Maghreb[4] and Mashreq[5] developed their army at a quicker rate – the share of the Gulf in the overall size of armed forces shrank from 46% to 32% and their military budget from 70% to 64%. All these changes can partly be attributed to unofficial or unaccounted defence measures.

Using the definition outlined in Chapter 1, the Middle Eastern and North African region comprises four large states, seven complex small states, and

DOI: 10.4324/9781003158288-4

Table 3.1 The composition of the MENA region based on relative size

	Territory	Population	Economy	Military	Number
Large states	Egypt, Iran, Turkey, Saudi Arabia				4
One-dimensional	Iraq		Algeria		2
Two-dimensional	Israel, UAE				3
	Morocco*		Morocco*		
Three-dimensional	Libya				
	Yemen*		Yemen*		3
	Syria				
Complex small states	Tunisia, Bahrain, Jordan, Kuwait, Lebanon, Qatar, Oman				7
State-like entities	Palestinian Authority				1
Number	13	11	12	9	

Source: Compiled by author.

eight medium-sized states, which are small in either one, two, or three dimensions (see Table 3.1). Bahrain, Kuwait, Qatar, and Oman have had a below average value in all four variables, while the UAE has a small territory and population with relatively large economic and military capacities.

We can see stark differences between the composition of each subregion (see Table 3.2). All states of the Maghreb are medium-sized states, with the exception of Tunisia. That makes the region more competitive but, according

Table 3.2 The comparison of the three subregions of the Middle East and North Africa

	Mashreq	Maghreb	Gulf
Number of entities (share)	7 (35%)	4 (20%)	9 (45%)
Territory (share)	17%	40%	43%
Population (share)	43%	18%	39%
GDP (share)	37%	9%	54%
Armed forces (share)	52%	16%	32%
Military budget (share)	26.5%	9.5%	64%
Territory (av.)	296,483	1,185,735	572,364
Population (av.)	33,083,405	24,499,249	23,231,108
GDP (av.)	229,259,587 453	94,896,869,216	261,658,251,627
Armed forces (av.)	288,143	152,750	137,778
Military budget (av.)	8,617,426,096	4,695,290 853	13,808,823,592
Number of large states (ratio)	2 (33%) – Turkey and Egypt	0	2 (22%) – Saudi Arabia and Iran
Number of complex small states (ratio)	2 (33%) – Lebanon and Jordan	1 (25%) – Tunisia	4 (44%) – Bahrain, Kuwait, Qatar, Oman

Source: Compiled by author using data from World Bank Database, 2021.

to conventional logic, less unstable. The region has a high share in land area but none of the other resources. The Mashreq has two large states (Egypt and Turkey), three medium-sized states (Iraq, Israel, and Syria), two small states (Lebanon and Jordan), and one state-like entity (Palestine). The subregion has the largest population and the biggest armies in the Middle East and North Africa.

The Gulf region seems the most unstable, with two giants (Iran and Saudi Arabia), four small states (Bahrain, Kuwait, Qatar, and Oman), and three medium-sized states, two of which have a fairly good relative situation. Besides the status of UAE (which I have already described), Iraq is only a territorial small state, which is not necessarily worse than being a large state – one can make the argument that shrinking territorial size *ceteris paribus* makes the country more defendable. Yemen has the worst statistics as a three-dimensional small state with a relatively small territory, economy, and military capacities, but a quite large population. Overall, Gulf states have the biggest share in GDP and military budget.

The relative size of the five smaller Gulf states, the subject of this study, has not been constant in recent decades (see Figures 3.1 and 3.2) – except for their territorial size, with a cumulative 3.4% of the land area of the MENA region and 8% of the Gulf region. While they represent 25% of all MENA states and 56% of all Gulf states, they do not currently reach this percentage in any resources. Their demographic share grew both in the MENA region (from 1.2% to 4.4%) and the Gulf region (from 4% to 11%), as did their economic size – since the first year for which all four states have official data (1980), their share grew from 14% to 20% in the MENA region and 22% to

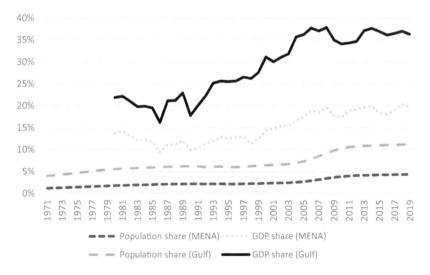

Figure 3.1 The overall share of the five smaller Gulf states in regional population and GDP (1971–2019).

Source: Compiled by author using data from World Bank Database, 2021.

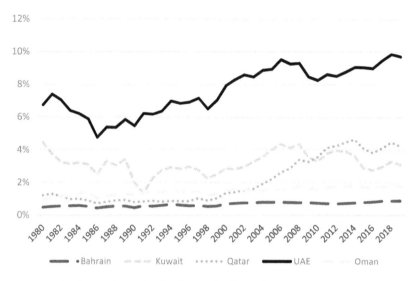

Figure 3.2 The share of smaller Gulf states in the regional economy (1980–2019).

Source: Compiled by author using data from World Bank Database, 2021.

36% in the Gulf region – but there is a stark difference between the two. While their demographic growth was relatively steady (with an accelerating rate in the late 2000s), their economic development was less stable. Due to fluctuations in the price of oil, during the 1980s their GDP did not do well in regional comparison, experiencing two weak low points in 1986 and 1990. After the first two Gulf wars, their performance bettered, and their relative size grew, except for two periods: the years following the economic crisis of 2007, and the oil price crisis of 2014–2016.

The relative size of the military of the smaller Gulf states was also highly exposed to regional developments. Following the Iraqi–Iranian war and the Iraqi–Kuwaiti war, data show a quick armament, especially from a budgetary perspective, in which their share in regional military expenditure grew from 13% to 21% in the MENA region and 19% to 33% in the Gulf region. After that, we see a decline in the second half of the 1990s, quick growth in the early 2000s (probably due to the heightened tensions around the American intervention in Iraq), after which their military expenditure remained relatively steady. The next surge took place in 2016, after which their current relative size was reached – approximately 30% in the Gulf region and 20% in the MENA region.

Increasing the size of armed forces can be especially problematic for demographically small states; nevertheless, smaller Gulf states managed to grow considerably. Their share from this perspective doubled in both regions (2.5% to 4.5% in the MENA region and 6% to 14% in the Gulf region). As these numbers are slightly above their demographic share, this is a truly important phenomenon.

The relative size of the smaller Gulf states is different in the four dimensions. Oman has far the biggest territory (309,500 km²), followed by the UAE

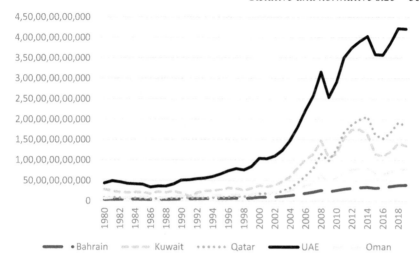

Figure 3.3 The GDP of smaller Gulf states (1980–2019).

Source: Compiled by author using data from World Bank Database, 2021.

(71,020 km²), while all other categories are led by the UAE. Regarding their demographic size, all five small states achieved independence with less than 1 million inhabitants and grew in parallel with each other, diverging extensively only in the 1990s when the UAE took off, reaching almost 10 million by the 2010s. In relation to GDP (see Figure 3.3), the primacy of the UAE was never in question, although there was a competition regarding second place between Kuwait and Qatar, the former holding onto its position until 2009 (except for the Kuwaiti–Iraqi war), after which Doha took over. Oman and Bahrain are lagging behind in this category, especially since the 2000s, when the surge in oil price benefited Kuwait and Qatar to a greater extent. Regarding military capacity, the UAE has had the advantage both in terms of armed forces and military spending. The size of armed forces and military budget is relatively large in Oman as well, while the remaining states have similar capabilities. Besides Oman, Kuwait has a tradition of having relatively greater military capacity due to its closeness to Iraq and the war of 1990–1991. In the early 1990s, it took over the first place in military spending for a while, following which it was only able to compete with Oman.

All these data suggest a relatively unfavourable distribution of material capacities for smaller Gulf states. They are located in a volatile but highly armed region, stuck between two large states and a medium-sized power that is small only in one dimension. While their relative economic size grew, so did their demographic size, while their strategic military situation did not change dramatically. Conclusively, if their power and security were in tandem with their material capacities, they should be secondary or tertiary players in regional politics. The only exception should be the one medium-sized state, the UAE, which has very similar material attributes to Israel.

The normative size of smaller Gulf states and their image in the interstate society

In the theoretical chapter, I conceptualised normative size as the interstate perception of one's importance, which is operationalised as the intensity of interstate interactions. The underlying assumption is that actors tend to interact with those states that they deem important, either in a positive (cooperative) or negative (confrontative) way. These interstate interactions are predominantly observable in international media. To measure the "normative size" of "State A", I will use the number of articles written about the expression of cooperation and/or confrontation of any governments vis-á-vis the government of "State A".

Using aggregate, long-term data, one can draw a general picture of a state's weight in the interstate system. Data for the inquiry will be provided by the database of the GDELT project, including articles about "events of confrontation/cooperation" published since 1 January 1979. In order to avoid random fluctuations, the data will be divided into decade-long periods (1979–1988, 1989–1998, 2009–2018).[6] These calculations resulted in a database of more than 700 thousand items, each reflecting an event of verbally expressed confrontation or cooperation.

Similar to relative size, normative size can be determined by comparing the values of each state, which is why I calculated the share of each state in all events in a given decade. The results tell us the relative importance of given states defined as the relative sum of expressed verbal cooperation and confrontation (see Table 3.3).

State-level data show very interesting dynamics. First, the difference between the greater states such as Saudi Arabia, Turkey, or Iran, and small states is clearly visible. The most interesting exception has been Israel, a medium-sized state that still managed to maintain the biggest normative size in the region.

Second, normative size has changed drastically in several cases, including Saudi Arabia, Turkey, and Iran, which reflects already identified processes of the more active foreign policy of these states.

Third, one can spot that armed conflict and domestic turmoil (or closeness to it) usually enlarge the importance of specific states: for example, the Lebanese civil war of 1975–1990, the Syrian conflict since 2011, or the Iraqi intervention of 2003 all boosted the normative size of Lebanon, Syria, and Iraq, respectively.

Fourth, when it comes to the smaller Gulf states, the method was able to quantify the strengthening role of Qatar, the UAE, and Bahrain over the last decade. To the contrary, Oman and Kuwait dominantly maintained their position. As we will see in the following chapters, the growth of normative size can be attributed to different causes; nevertheless, the data clearly shows intensifying diplomacy in the case of the three states. That being said, the difference in data can also show a difference in diplomatic conduct – Oman, for example, clearly conducts active foreign policy in various issues (see Chapter 5 and

Table 3.3 The normative size of Middle Eastern and North African states

	1979–1988 (%)	1989–1998 (%)	1999–2008 (%)	2009–2018 (%)	Total (%)
Qatar	0.1	0.5	0.6	1.4	1.1
Kuwait	1.2	1.4	0.9	1.0	1.0
UAE	0.2	0.3	0.6	1.5	1.2
Oman	0.2	0.4	0.2	0.4	0.4
Bahrain	0.1	0.3	0.7	1.8	1.4
KSA	6.4	6.8	10.8	13.9	12.4
Turkey	4.0	9.1	7.9	13.1	11.4
Iran	7.7	6.4	10.1	10.8	10.2
Israel	17.7	22.0	23.1	18.8	19.9
Yemen	1.2	1.7	1.4	2.0	1.8
Egypt	13.7	14.6	10.3	7.1	8.7
Syria	8.2	5.6	5.3	11.0	9.2
Iraq	5.2	9.2	11.9	4.7	6.6
Lebanon	9.3	4.2	4.7	2.6	3.4
Jordan	15.7	11.9	6.1	4.5	5.9
Algeria	2.5	1.9	1.7	1.0	1.3
Morocco	2.6	1.6	1.3	1.1	1.2
Libya	2.5	1.0	1.5%	2.4	2.1
Tunisia	1.5	1.0	0.8	0.9	0.9
Av.	5.3	5.3	5.3	5.3	5.3

Source: Compiled by author using data from GDELT Database, 2021.

Chapter 6), but it chooses to do so behind the curtains. In other words, it tries to keep its normative size small, unlike Qatar and the UAE.

Fifth, despite the meteoric rise of Doha and Abu Dhabi, Jordan and Lebanon still have a bigger relative size than any of the Gulf states. This shows, on the one hand, their embeddedness in the interstate society, as well as their preferred way of diplomacy being outspoken and more transparent than in the case of the Gulf states.

Using the country-group categories already established, we can see how the normative size of states with different relative size changed (see Table 3.4). Large states have gained importance since 1979, which reflects the trend of

Table 3.4 The average normative size of specific country-groups

	1979–1988 (%)	1989–1998 (%)	1999–2008 (%)	2009–2018 (%)	Total
Large states	8.0	9.2	9.8	11.2	10.6
Medium-sized states	5.0	5.4	5.8	5.3	5.4
Small states	4.0	2.8	2.0	1.8	2.0
Maghreb states	2.3	1.4	1.3	1.3	1.4
Mashreq states	10.6	10.9	9.9	8.8	9.3
Gulf states	2.5	3.0	4.1	4.2	4.0

Source: Compiled by author using data from GDELT Database, 2021.

growing great power rivalry in the region observed by many authors. While medium-sized states relatively maintained their position, small states lost ground, especially in the case of Jordan and Lebanon. This tendency can probably be attributed to the end of the Lebanese civil war and the decreasing importance of the Israeli–Palestinian conflict. Bearing in mind the decreasing importance of small states in general, the strengthening role of Qatar and the UAE becomes even more impressive.

Comparing the average normative size of countries belonging to the three subregions, the Mashreq comes out as the most important group (mostly due to Turkey and Israel). That being said, the decline of the international position of Maghreb states and the growing role of Gulf states can also be identified. The latter was driven not just by the growing role of smaller Gulf states, but also those of Saudi Arabia and Iran as well.

Looking at the data provided in the preceding tables in general, one can draw the conclusion that while the overall normative size of a state depends partly on its actual material size, its fluctuations can be attributed to international developments. The importance of Jordan and Lebanon is presumably the result of the Israeli–Palestinian conflict; as it lost its prominent role, both states started to lose their perceived importance. Both Syria and Iraq gained attention only due to their internal instability, while it is telling that, after 2009, the international community lost its interest in Iraq. Israel, a medium-sized state, triumphs over large states (Saudi Arabia, Iran, Turkey, and Egypt) while the UAE, another two-dimensional small state with the same attributes as Israel, has normatively been smaller than Kuwait or Bahrain, who presumably gained their importance due to their closeness to Iraq and Iran (and the subsequent internal and external pressure), respectively.

The GDELT dataset also enables us to quantify the image of states in the international system by calculating the share of confrontative interactions. According to theoretical expectations (see Chapter 1), one would expect small states to have a better image than larger states. Data (see Table 3.5) proves this trend to some extent; nevertheless, the correlation does not work with medium-sized states, which, in three out of the four decades, had a

Table 3.5 The average ratio of verbal confrontation in all interactions among specific country-groups

	1979–1988 (%)	1989–1998 (%)	1999–2008 (%)	2009–2018 (%)	Av. (%)
Large state av.	8.2	5.4	6.2	11.6	8.7
Medium-sized state av.	8.0	6.5	6.8	14.0	11.6
Small state av.	5.1	4.0	4.3	7.6	6.1
Maghreb av.	7.5	3.9	4.3	12.6	10.1
Mashreq av.	7.9	7.2	7.6	13.8	11.3
Gulf av.	6.6	5.7	5.8	8.4	7.1

Source: Compiled by author using data from GDELT Database, 2021.

worse average ratio than large states. Interestingly, states of the Gulf subregion have the best data in all decades (except for the Maghreb between 1989 and 2008), followed by the Maghreb. That being said, all categories suffer a shrink in their normative size by the last decade, which can be explained by the more conflictual nature of Middle Eastern politics.

State-level data (see Table 3.6) shows that the average ratio of verbal confrontation in all interactions has been 10.6% between 1979 and 2018, which means that only one in every ten intergovernmental actions has been categorised as negative. Nevertheless, a clear worsening is detectable after 2009, when the average ratio almost doubled which, again, proves the more conflictual nature of interstate relations in the last decade. The worse data have been produced by Syria since 2009, with more than 30% of negative interactions and a 23.5% average for all four decades. Besides, Syria, Yemen, Libya, Iraq, Israel, Tunisia, and Iran have an outstanding bad ratio.

Smaller Gulf states are on the other extreme of the scale with remarkably great values. Oman has had the best image in the Middle East, with only 1.7% of interactions being confrontative, followed by the UAE (2.8%), Qatar (4%), and Kuwait (4.3%). In spite of its neighbours' positive data, Bahrain (7.4%) is surprisingly bad, with a higher ratio than Jordan, Morocco, or Algeria. The performance of Bahrain is due to its diminishing image after 2009, probably due to the events of 2011 (see Chapter 6). The reasons behind the various ways in which smaller Gulf states managed (or failed) to better their image will be explored in the following chapters.

Table 3.6 The ratio of verbal confrontation in all interactions among MENA states

	1979–1988 (%)	1989–1998 (%)	1999–2008 (%)	2009–2018 (%)	Av. (%)
Qatar	5.9	4.0	4.7	4.4	4.0
Kuwait	7.1	5.7	4.4	6.2	4.3
UAE	7.5	3.6	3.5	3.3	2.8
Oman	0.0	0.4	2.6	2.3	1.7
Bahrain	5.4	5.3	3.5	8.4	7.4
KSA	4.0	3.3	5.2	9.3	6.8
Turkey	8.9	6.3	6.9	11.7	9.4
Iran	15.3	7.9	9.9	13.2	10.7
Israel	12.6	10.1	10.2	12.9	10.8
Yemen	2.0	4.6	5.1	17.4	13.5
Egypt	4.5	3.8	3.0	12.0	7.9
Syria	4.3	2.2	6.4	31.4	23.5
Iraq	12.1	16.5	13.5	11.0	12.4
Lebanon	6.5	5.9	9.9	11.0	9.3
Jordan	6.3	5.8	3.1	6.8	5.5
Algeria	3.0	4.9	4.8	8.3	6.6
Morocco	5.1	3.3	5.4	6.4	5.7
Libya	17.5	6.7	5.4	21.0	17.9
Tunisia	4.2	0.7	1.5	14.6	10.1
Av.	8.1	7.1	7.8	13.5	10.6

Source: Compiled by author using data from GDELT Database, 2021.

Temporal trends show that, for the five states, the 1990s were the best decade in terms of their confrontation ratio. This can be explained by the relative calm after 1991 (compared to the upheaval caused by the Iraqi–Iranian war between 1980 and 1988, as well as the American intervention in Iraq in 2003). At the same time, they also grew normatively, partly due to their changing alliance policy (see Chapter 5).

Comparing relative and normative size, we can arrive at the following conclusions. First, the perceived importance of states in the international community (i.e. their normative size) correlates with, although it is not equal to, their relative material size – at least, in the Middle Eastern and North African context. States such as Israel, Jordan, or Lebanon gained importance due to international developments and their role in specific crises. On the other hand, Saudi Arabia performed similarly to a smaller state until very recently. Second, normative size is determined greatly by transnational events, therefore it cannot be changed purely by an effective strategy. Armed conflicts enlarge the importance of states and worsen their image, while staying out of them enables some states to maintain a low ratio of verbal confrontation. Third, both material and normative investigation shows the discrepancy between the three subregions, with the Maghreb sinking in both terms, while the Gulf is enlarging its importance and gathering resources.

Fourth, despite their similar systemic position, smaller Gulf states have different relative and normative size. Being the only medium-sized state in the group, the UAE had a similar normative position to its neighbours with a really positive image. Qatar has remained under the threshold for smallness, but normatively it also performed quite well in the last decade, maintaining a relatively low confrontation ratio. Oman has the best image in the whole region, but also the smallest normative size. The relative size of Kuwait shrank while maintaining a relatively stable normative size whereas, in the case of Bahrain, enlarging importance in the last decade went hand-in-hand with a worsening image.

Naturally, using the GDELT database has its own methodological limits. The inquiry can only reflect publicly observable diplomatic interactions, leaving out secret talks. Moreover, using media coverage can be distortive due to its biases and to personally or politically driven editorial practices. Bearing in mind all these problems, the GDELT database still proved to be a valuable source of information, especially using long-term data rather than analysing yearly fluctuations. Naturally, data can be interpreted in various ways; many particularities could only be explained by the investigation of specific country-level attributes and foreign policy decisions that will be described in the following chapters.

Notes

1 The source of all data in this chapter is the World Bank Database, 2021.
2 Calculating with 217 states and state-like entities listed in the World Bank Database.

3   Besides the five smaller Gulf states, Iraq, Iran, Yemen and Saudi Arabia belong to the Gulf subregion.
4   Defined as Algeria, Morocco, Tunisia, and Libya.
5   Mashreq states include Turkey, Israel, Syria, Lebanon, Jordan, Lebanon, and the Palestinian Authority.
6   While the GDELT database is predominantly reliable, minor mistakes may have been made regarding coding, or the inability to exclude interactions between various governmental entities in the same country. A special thanks to Ervin Szalai, who helped me in accessing relevant data.

Bibliography

GDELT Database (2021) *The GDELT Project*, [Online]. Available at: https://www.gdeltproject.org/ (Accessed 31 January 2021).

World Bank (2021). *World Bank Database*, [Online]. Available at: http://data.worldbank.org (Accessed 31 January 2021).

4 Absolute size, perceptual size, and regime security in the smaller Gulf states

Scholars usually consider the absolute smallness of a state an inescapable burden, a deficit that cannot be reduced, an attribute that cannot be significantly altered. In the case of smaller Gulf states, it is seen as a limit to security, influence, and leverage. Nevertheless, a closer examination suggests that different kinds of smallness play a variety of roles in domestic and foreign policy behaviour, state identity, and regime security for Bahrain, Kuwait, Qatar, Oman, and the United Arab Emirates, which managed to tackle some of the negative consequences of size while capitalising on its advantages. Moreover, as it will be evident in this chapter, differences in absolute and perceptual size, as well as regime security – an aspect which has to be investigated due to the particularities in the regional state system described in Chapter 2 – leads to different behaviour and compensatory policies.

Absolute size[1]

As was described in Chapter 1, smallness can be investigated as a material phenomenon without comparing a state's resources with other entities, meaning a scarcity of resources that leads to various outcomes, including security leverage, instability, under-institutionalisation, military weakness, or passive foreign policy. Nevertheless, this is not an automatic process, and a relative small state is not necessarily an absolute small state. One cannot evaluate the worth of resources available for a state in the absence of context. Following the footsteps of Katzenstein outlined in Chapter 1, I will evaluate the smallness of the five states by investigating the interaction between size and other variables that determine how territorial, demographic, economic, and military smallness should be interpreted. To do this, I apply a behavioural approach, arguing that if smallness leads to substantial weaknesses, a state tries to implement specific compensatory policies to overcome these difficulties. In this way, governments can mitigate the direct consequences of the lack of resources while creating other challenges for themselves.

DOI: 10.4324/9781003158288-5

Territorial smallness

While all smaller Gulf states have a relatively small territory, there are huge differences between them. Bahrain is the smallest country in the entire region at 778 square kilometres, while the largest is Oman at almost 310 thousand km². To understand what role territorial smallness plays in their policies, we have to investigate its interaction with the climatic environment and geopolitical circumstances.

Climatic environment

Due to the intensive transformation of the climate, massive warming took place around 3000 BCE, creating a poor environment for agricultural production (Crystal, 2014, p. 157). According to David Commins (2014, p. 2), this environment can be blamed for the late state-making processes, as the difficulty of marshalling material resources "barred the development of economic foundations for empire" (Commins, 2014, p. 9). It is important to take note that serious institutional building only happened in parallel with the start of oil production in the 20th century – except for Oman, which was the first to introduce new water management technologies on the Peninsula (Commins, 2014, pp. 7–8).

In addition, climatic circumstances led to two trends. The first was a pivot to the sea, both economically and socially, which led to the prominence of pearling, fishing, and participation in maritime trade. This lasted until the 1930s, when the regional pearl market and the discovery of oil caused pearling to lose its significance (Rumaili, 1980, p. 50). Second, in parallel, the ratio of arable land has always been low, fluctuating between 0.06% and 2.9% of all lands, showing a process of degradation. Agriculture activities were limited to oases and other types of nomadic production. Since independence, the country with the smallest territory (Bahrain) has had the highest percentage (currently 2.06%), and the largest, Oman, has had the lowest (0.18%).

As a result, economic autarchy has never been an option for these states, since there have never been enough arable land to support the population (Al-Handhali and Miniaoui, 2020, p. 77). According to the World Bank, the size of arable land per person in the five states was the highest in Oman and the UAE in 1971, when it reached 0.03 and 0.025 hectares, respectively: by 2017, these figures had diminished to 0.013 and 0.005, respectively). The data for Qatar peaked in 1993 at 0.026 hectares (having diminished to 0.005 hectares by 2016), while neither Bahrain nor Kuwait have ever reached 0.01 hectares (0.001 and 0.002 in 2015, respectively). This is far from sufficient to sustain the basic food demands of the population: the global average for cultivated territory (as opposed to available arable land) is 0.65 hectares per person (Alexander et al., 2016, p. 90), which is 21 times the maximum of that in Oman. Even for low-income countries, the average is 0.17 hectares (FAO, 2018). Consequently, agriculture has always been underdeveloped in the region (amounting to 1–4% of the gross domestic product (GDP) at the GCC level), with only a minimal percentage of the workforce occupied in the sector (NCB Capital, 2010, p. 2).[2]

Apart from (but connected to) the lack of meaningful food production, there are other commodities that have only been available in very low quantities, notably potable water and wood (Potter, 2009, pp. 9–10). This has been a vital vulnerability, as it affects social wellbeing, housing, and general economic development. Historically, the lack of wood was problematic, especially in military and security terms – for centuries, regional actors were unable to build a proper fleet, while in modern times, it is primarily the construction sector that has the greatest timber requirement (TDT, 2018).

The lack of sufficient water supply is also crucial in the case of smaller GCC states (Darwish, Abdulrahim, and Mohieldeen, 2014). With less than 100 cubic meters of renewable water resources per year, all five states are at a "minimum survival level", which is characterised by compromised supply for industry and commercial purposes, and the inability to meet internal demand. When it comes to overall natural water resources, Oman has more than four times as much as the other four states combined, but Muscat still needs additional water to sustain agricultural production and everyday life, determining whether local economies are able to produce only not water-intensive corps (such as dates), fish or dairy. As a result, all five states rely on desalination which, on the other hand, is energy and capital intensive, and has a huge ecological impact. Besides importing these commodities from external partners, the lack of such vital resources has led to several technical innovations in history, including the so-called *qanat* or *falaj* system[3] of underground aqueducts in Oman or, in more modern times, sea water distillation processes (EPL, 1973, p. 539).

Consequently, smaller Gulf states have always been reliant on imported food even up to 90% of some commodities (Shahid and Mushtaque, 2014, p. 3), which evidently creates a form of dependency. This feature is common in the region due to the climatic environment and the population boom that took place in the second half of the 20th century, which caused a sixfold increase in food demand between 1961 and 2011 at the regional level (INRA, 2015, p. 2). Reliance on imported food exposes the Gulf states to "inflationary and quantity risk", as well as shocks in demand or supply on the world market (NCB Capital, 2010, p. 11); for example, the huge increase in food prices in 2007–2008, one of the top reasons behind the "Arab Spring" in the region (Zurayk and Gough, 2014). Needless to say, this dependency creates a huge political risk for the stability of the Gulf states, especially since food costs comprise approximately 20–35% of the consumer price index in these countries. The aim of keeping food prices on a stable level puts pressure on both the fiscal and monetary policy of these states.

Smaller Gulf states cannot really circumvent food dependency; nonetheless, they have tried to compensate for it in several ways. First, they all wanted to reach and maintain a healthy trade balance. Due to the fact that the oil industry developed prior to the independence of these states, the balance of trade has been predominantly positive. World Bank data shows that the amount of surplus (and the occasional deficit) has been the result of two circumstances: trends in the oil price, and armed conflict. As a result, the best period with regard to food costs was the 2000s, while the worst period was observable in the case of Kuwait, between 1990 and 1993.[4]

Another compensatory policy involved outsourcing the agricultural sector to other countries through investments in arable land (Woertz et al., 2008, NCB Capital, 2010). This strategy was more visibly put into practice in the 2000s, in spite of the fact that the question had been on the agenda since independence. The primary destination of such investments has been Central Asia and Africa (more recently the Balkans and Turkey), and, more specifically, those states that are perceived as geographically, economically, and culturally close to the GCC countries (such as Sudan or Pakistan) and that do not have economic leverage on them.

Third, smaller Gulf states try to develop their own agricultural sector by investing heavily in hydroponics, irrigation systems, desalination technologies, and greenhouse technologies (Al-Handhali and Miniaoui, 2020, p. 78). This is a clear case of how scarcity spurs innovation: the UAE, for one, tried to present itself as a leader in agricultural innovation (e.g. by organising the Global Forum for Innovations in Agriculture, a clear example of the implementation of a virtual enlargement strategy).

Geopolitical position

Four out of the five smaller Gulf states are squeezed between Iran, Iraq, and Saudi Arabia, all of which states are much bigger. Their vulnerabilities lie in a continental exposure to Saudi Arabia and a maritime proximity to Iran in the Persian Gulf. Three small states suffer special dependence on Riyadh: Qatar has no other land neighbour, while, as an island state, the Kingdom of Bahrain's only connection with the mainland is the King Fahd Bridge, leading to the Saudi city of Al-Khobar. Lastly, Kuwait shared oil and gas production with Saudi Arabia in the so-called "Divided Zone" or "Neutral Zone", a 6,200 square mile territory that was divided between the two countries in 1992 (Cordesman and Rodhan, 2007, p. 87).

Having another neighbour alleviates reliance on Saudi Arabia but, nevertheless, can create additional threats. Kuwait borders Iraq, a country that had claimed historical rights over the territory of the small Gulf state several times in modern history (Sluglett, 2002, pp. 783–784). Therefore, Kuwait is exposed to Iraqi intentions and to the Iraqi security challenges to a greater extent.[5] The UAE borders Saudi Arabia and Oman, while Oman's other neighbour is Yemen, a relatively unstable country in the Gulf.

The most valuable geopolitical asset is in the hands of Oman and the Emirates, which have a direct exit to the Indian Ocean, while the other states border the Persian Gulf. This lowers the exposure to Iran while enabling Oman and the Emirates to reach out more easily to other regions. It is not surprising that, historically, it was Oman that managed to build up a maritime empire, which incorporated African and South Asian territories, too.

This geopolitical situation helps us understand the fear of smaller Gulf states of both Saudi hegemony and Iranian influence (Martini et al., 2016, p. 10). Historically, each power centre on the two sides of the Gulf conducted an expansionist foreign policy to dominate the shores of the Gulf (Peterson, 2011, p. 26). Smaller Gulf states, whose existence is the result of British patronage, were too small to protect themselves from the two giants. Naturally, due to considerations regarding political regimes, the smaller Gulf states have a much closer relationship with Saudi Arabia; nevertheless, their relationship will always be controversial, posing a security partner and, contemporarily, a genuine threat (Wright, 2011, p. 88). Naturally, the latter perception tends "to be strongest when the external threat environment is most benign" (Martini et al., 2016, p. 10).

Demographic smallness

As was discussed in Chapter 3, the five smaller Gulf states had a similar demographic size until the 1990s, following which time we can categorise them in three groups. The UAE has the largest population with almost 10 million inhabitants, followed by Oman and Kuwait with 4–5 million people. In the third category, we have Qatar and Bahrain, two states with a combined population of 2.8 and 1.6 million. In all cases, we can see an almost constant rise in the number of inhabitants, which is mostly driven by migration, as the population boom in the national community slowed down considerably in the second half of the 20th century at varying paces of deceleration (Klitsch, 1994, pp. 79–80).

Small population size interacts with four variables: territorial smallness, the imbalance between demand and supply in the labour market, the compensatory policy of labour import, and social heterogeneity.

Territorial smallness

As their population has multiplied at least four to five times since the 1970s but their territory has remained the same (see Figure 4.1), population density has skyrocketed in the smaller Gulf states. Bahrain had always had the highest population density, which was more than six times as high as the regional average in 1971 (319 people per square kilometres compared to 51) and eight times as high as the regional average in 2018 (2017 compared to 251). This shows that the territorial constraints were more problematic for the island country than for the other smaller Gulf states. The population density of the four other countries remains much lower, below 250 people per square kilometre (especially that of Oman, at 16 people), but all have a tendency to population growth, especially Qatar. The only breaking point in this growth was the Iraqi attack on Kuwait, after which the Emirates' population density shrank and lost pace.

High population density fostered urbanisation in the Gulf. This process transformed the region into the most urbanised in the world (Ramadan,

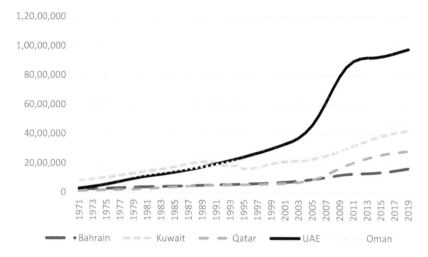

Figure 4.1 Population size in the five small Gulf states (1970–2017).

Source: Compiled by author using data from World Bank Database, 2021.

2015), with 85–100% of the population living in an urban environment.[6] Cities, especially port towns and industrial centres in the 20th century, have always played an important role in the social history of the region, a phenomenon that was only amplified by modernisation and state-building (Fuccaro, 2009, pp. 1–15). Consequently, vibrant urban spaces play an important political, economic, and social role in promoting national identity and sustaining legitimacy. On the other hand, excessive urbanisation accompanied by the rapid developments taking place over recent decades creates severe economic and social challenges, including the exacerbation of disparities, insanitary living conditions, the spread of diseases, water and electricity shortages, and air pollution (Palanivel, 2017). These challenges are being addressed by centrally planned initiatives under the label "smart cities" or "sustainable urbanism", which will certainly dominate urban policies over the next decades.[7]

The imbalance between demand and supply in the labour market

Small demographic size is, in itself, never a problem; it becomes problematic only if the available human capital does not satisfy the requirements of production or defence (McGillivray, 2016, pp. 280–281). Unfortunately, smaller Gulf states fall into the second category as, since independence, the size of their population has never been sufficiently large to meet economic demand (Brichs and Sinclair, 1980, p. 140). Consequently, GCC countries developed the compensatory policy of attracting massive amounts of foreign labour, which led to the third-largest migrant worker population in the world after the European Union and the USA (Al-Khouri, 2012, p. 1). Immigrants did not enjoy the same political, economic, or social status as citizens, which led

Table 4.1 Population statistics in 1970

Country	Total population	Migrant population	Share of the migrant population (%)
Bahrain	212,605	37,946	17.8
Kuwait	746,767	463,366	62.0
Oman	723,852	62,804	8.7
Qatar	109,514	68,339	62.4
UAE	234,514	65,827	28

Source: Compiled by author using data from World Bank Database, 2021.

to very harsh differences between the "small national population" and the "sea of expats" (Tok, Alkhater and Pal, 2016, p. 16).

This phenomenon is not new – even in the 19th century, there was a steady flow of migrant workers from the Indian subcontinent participating in pearling, trade, and fishing; so much so that the Indian rupee was a widely accepted currency (Althani, 2012, p. 39).[8] Naturally, the oil boom of the 20th century made the problem of labour force scarcity even deeper, which created a demand for skilled workers as well (Winckler, 2010). By 1970, all smaller Gulf states had a sizeable foreign community (see Table 4.1), which has continued to grow until today.

In almost all countries (except for Kuwait and Qatar, where it has always been high), the share of the migrant population has grown extensively since 1970 (see Figure 4.2). Bahrain and Oman have always had the lowest ratio in this regard, mostly due to their economic structure. While the difference between them is shrinking, it is clear that migration policies differed in these countries, partly due to their different demographic composition.

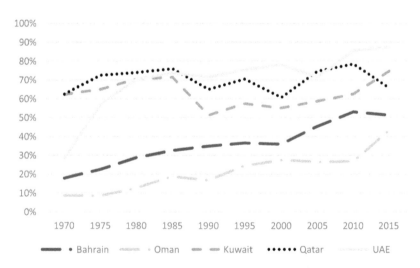

Figure 4.2 Share of migrant population (1970–2015).

Source: Compiled by author using data from World Bank Database, 2021.

Naturally, inviting a foreign population to compensate for the smallness of the national labour market also has downsides. Between the 1950s and 1990s, huge numbers of Arab migrants travelled to the smaller Gulf states for work but, due to their language knowledge and cultural closeness, they almost instantly became involved in local politics (Chalcraft, 2012, p. 69). In Bahrain, for example, migrant workers from Egypt, Palestine, and other Arab countries participated in demonstrations against the regime while, in Kuwait, Palestinian teachers politicised the curricula in the education system (ibid.). Naturally, pan-Arab ideas had a foothold in large Arab communities living in other Arab countries,[9] which also represented a danger for monarchies. To tackle these challenges, smaller Gulf states developed policies aimed at balancing the composition of the population to enable citizens to maintain their dominance.

It was due to these considerations that the migration policies of smaller Gulf states changed dramatically in the 1990s and 2000s to favour South Asians over Arab workers (who do not speak the language). Indians and Pakistanis have always been part of the labour force of the Gulf economies – even in 1975, workers of Asian origin constituted 55% of the Bahraini employee community and 63% of the Qatari employee community (Brichs and Sinclair, 1980, p. 143); however, on aggregate, the majority of workers in the region were Arab.[10] In the 1970s, the Gulf states witnessed the first governmental policies to raise the number of non-Arab migrants due to political and economic reasons; however, at that time the sending countries did not welcome the initiative. Nonetheless, due to the growing economic opportunities at the end of the 20th century, the perception of South Asian governments changed, and they also engaged in the flow of migrant workers.

As a consequence, the ratio of Arab migrants in the community of foreigners in the GCC shrank from 91% to 33% between 1975 and 2004 (Brichs and Sinclair, 1980, pp. 146–149), while the absolute number of migrant workers constantly rose due to the economic boom of the 2000s: by 2012, the overall ratio of migrants in the labour force reached 60% in Bahrain, 65.7% in Oman, 80% in Kuwait, and 89.5% in Qatar (Ulrichsen, 2011, p. 89).

The import of labour is mostly conducted in the framework of the "*kafala* system",[11] which is characterised by the dominant role of the employer (*kafeel*) and the fixed-term contract of the employee. Although specific details differ in the GCC countries, the *kafeel* has wide-ranging rights and influence over an employee's life. He controls the mobility and the visa of the migrant worker, therefore their life in general. If the contract is terminated, the migrant worker has to leave the country, or have a new contract immediately. The *kafala* system is heavily criticised from a human rights perspective since it leads to cultural and physical segregation, the lack of opportunity to gain citizenship, and complete dependence on one's employer. The only small state that has a less strict migration policy is Bahrain, which conducts a large-scale neutralisation programme to change the sectarian composition of the country (Kinninmont, 2015, p. 17).

The compensatory policy of labour import

Interestingly, in the case of the Gulf states, the compensatory policy (which aims at tackling the imbalance between demand and supply in the labour market) interacted with small population size itself, which led to severe, sometimes grotesque consequences.[12]

Due to the disenfranchised situation of migrant workers who, today, constitute the majority of the population, Anh Nga Longva (2013, p. 119) argues that the Gulf states have effectively become "ethnocracies", meaning that there is a:

> tendency for an elite to posit their own physical characteristics and cultural norms as the essence of the nation over which they rule, thus narrowing its definition and excluding all those within the polity who do not exhibit the same characteristics (…) In practical terms, ethnocracy is government by an ethnic group.

As Paul Dresch (2013a, p. 6) claims, "an appeal to exclusive culture (…), and to local values or principles (…) such as those of family, is in part an assertion of autonomy".

The narrow and nativist definition of the nation suggests that being independent and having a dominant role in shaping the community has been more important for the smaller Gulf states than the actual size of the community. These constitutive norms have become even tighter since the 1970s as a self-defence mechanism (Dresch, 2013a, p. 24) due to the fear of globalisation and the growing ratio of migrant workers (Tetreault, 2011, p. 83). When it comes to defining the "other", three circles emerged as a logic of differentiation: *Khaleeji* (Gulf) societies as the most familiar; Arabs as a middle ground; and foreigners or *Ajnabi* for everyone else (Dresch, 2013a, p. 25). In practice, this is visible in areas such as marriage rules, or granting and revoking citizenship, a tool that has been used to regulate not necessarily the size of the society but, rather, social cohesion (Kinninmont, 2013, pp. 54–56).

Opening the labour market for foreign workers has international consequences, as well, creating a form of interdependence between the country of origin and the country of residence. On the one hand, the economy of the smaller Gulf states would not be able to operate without guest workers coming from South Asia. On the other hand, sending workers to the Gulf represents a huge source of income for the sending societies in the form of remittances. Since 2015, personal remittances have mounted to more than 25% of the GDP of Nepal, the majority of which has came from Qatar and the UAE (Desilver, 2018). While the same ratio for India was only 2.8%, the absolute sum was 62.7 billion USD, more than any other country in the world (ibid.).

Social heterogeneity

Contrary to theoretical expectations presented in Chapter 1, the societies of smaller Gulf states are not more homogeneous than those of their larger neighbours and consist of diverse ethnic, religious, and tribal communities. Smallness and heterogeneity affect each other greatly, together they posed a huge challenge during the process of state-building (Salzman, 2016, pp. 207–210). Regimes in the region have ruled over tribal societies, in which building up a hierarchical power structure represented by modern statehood and defying the traditional tribal collective self-help system has been quite a challenge. To cement their rule, leaders had to choose between various tools, including forcing hierarchy top-down, redirecting loyalties towards the state, or accepting the endurance of tribal ties and decentralising decision making to include tribal leaders. In practice, Gulf states implemented a mixture of such measures, building up relatively strong state institutions but relying on tribal networks and their approval almost constantly.

Due to the lack of historical national identity and the prevalence of tribal identities, the governments of the smaller Gulf states focused heavily on national identity building (Patrick, 2012). Attempts to create civil ethnocracy, imagined and reinvented national traditions, and citizenship regulations all have a part in this endeavour. These steps practically meant that "local elites have harnessed the global discourse on 'heritage' to construct an ethnicized and gendered[13] vision of a primordial Arab homeland" (Koch, 2015, p. 522).[14] Rulers tried to connect local traditions with the ruling family, thus creating a national identity that serves the legitimacy of the rulers' power (Fromherz, 2012, p. 159). The large-scale urbanisation process taking place in the 20th century helped identity-building efforts in the smaller Gulf states to create a "unified national space" and to provide a "formative collective experience that unites Gulf citizens of different background" (AGSIW, 2016, p. 5).

Forging a national identity did not aim to disturb tribalism completely but, rather, to "disburse patronage selectively in order to maintain alliances based on family, tribe, and region" (Patrick, 2012, p. 11). In a paradoxical way, behind the disguise of a modern state and society, Gulf regimes continued to use old tribal relations to govern and to maintain "national" social cohesion. That is why the term "nation-building" may be better changed to "identity management" (Holes, 2013, p. 52). This conceptualisation has a greater explanatory value also because of the governments' reactions to the heterogeneity of the society of the small Gulf states: naturally, they want to build a unified basis for the national identity, but do not want to eliminate all tribal, linguistic, ethnic, or religious differences (Fahy, 2018; Holes, 2013).

In these efforts of identity politics, the technical side of mass communication has always played an important role for two reasons. First, by creating their own channels, smaller Gulf states were able to gain their own discursive power vis-á-vis global companies dominated by Western states or larger Arab states (Sakr, 2013). Second, fearing supra-national (Arabism, Islamism) and subnational identities, and the danger they represent for regime security, Middle Eastern states tried to monopolise the means of public communication in order to dominate identity politics (Telhami and Barnett, 2002, pp. 20–21). Nonetheless, as technology evolved and transnational and cross-border mass communication became easier, some states identified an opportunity to shape other states' domestic discourse about political issues related to identity. One successful example is the al-Jazeera satellite TV channel run by the Qatari elite.

Another important tool in identity management (and also a general compensatory policy tackling smallness) has been higher education and human capacity building. These policies are also aimed at reducing the reliance on British, American, and Western educational institutions (i.e. achieving real independence from their "formal colonial masters") (Bahgat, 1999, p. 128). Investing in the school system is also important in order to reach diversification and to move towards a knowledge-based economy (Tadros, 2015).

The cleavage that gained the most attention recently is the sectarian composition of the Gulf societies; however, there is no official data available concerning religious composition. Based on the available estimates (see Table 4.2), the ratio of the Shia community in the smaller Gulf states varies between less than 5% (Oman) and a 65% majority in Bahrain. Nonetheless, the role of the Shia community in the political, economic, and social life of the Gulf states is not solely dependent on their size; other political factors are in play.

Despite having the smallest population, Bahrain is the most socially divided country both in ethnic (Arab and Persian) and sectarian (Sunni and Shia) terms (Crystal, 2014, pp. 169–171). Another division is between the "native" and the "immigrant" families, which basically refers to the population movement of preceding centuries taking place in the Arabian Peninsula. The Sunni Bahraini government perceived these social schisms as threats and opportunities for other states (especially Iran) to intervene, therefore these divisions – primarily the sectarian – are heavily securitised, especially since the Iranian revolution of 1979 (see Chapter 5). As already mentioned, Bahrain conducted a wide-scale programme of neutralisation of Sunni migrant workers to make the society more Sunni.

Moreover, historically, the island of Bahrain has been politically unified for centuries, with some Shia territories on the mainland now belonging to the Saudi kingdom, which created many tribal and family connections between the Bahraini and Saudi Shia community (Matthiesen, 2015, pp. 24–25). These

Table 4.2 The estimated ratio of the Shia community in the small Gulf states

Country	Estimated percentage
Bahrain	60–70
Kuwait	20–30
UAE	10–15
Qatar	10
Oman	<5

Source: Compiled by author using data provided by Matthiesen, 2013.

Note: Since all numbers are estimated and not official, there is no data series available to track the changes of the Shia community since 1970; nonetheless, systematic changes did not occur during the period examined.

trans-border connections and networks are perceived as a threat not just to the Bahraini government, but also to the Saudi government.

From a demographic point of view, Oman is the odd-one-out in the GCC. First, the slight majority of the population follows Ibadi Islam, a third community that originates from the Kharijite succession in the 7th century (Al-Khalili, 2009, pp. 5–9). Lacking official data, sources debate whether the Ibadis have an absolute or relative majority in the country, due to the fact that the Sunni community comprises above 40% of the population (centred in the Dhofar region), while the Shias constitute only a small minority[15] (Valeri, 2014, p. 181). Second, the ethnic origins of the Omani society are more mixed than those of its neighbours due to the imperial history of the country: many families are considered to be of "Zanjibari" (East-African) and Baluchi (Pakistani–Iranian) origin (Kharusi, 2013, p. 429).

Third, nonetheless, the main split in society is not ethnic or religious but, rather, tribal. Historically, two political entities emerged in the territory of modern-day Oman: the Ibadi Imamate from the inner lands of the country, and the Sultanate of Muscat, in the maritime imperial capital (Rabi, 2016, pp. 80–82; Al-Khalili, 2009, pp. 3–5). The tribes of the Imamate had a more traditional, conservative, inward-looking society, with the Imam as the main mediator and arbitrator between the tribes. On the other hand, the Sultanate was the cosmopolitan centre of a huge maritime empire that dominated regional trade. The different economic interests and social tensions led to a troubled relationship between the two polities, which was reflected in the British recognition of the territory as the Sultanate of Muscat and Oman. While the society is much more integrated today than it was before, the differences between the tribes of the land and the tribes of the shore still exist.

Due to the heterogeneity in the ethnic and religious composition of Omani society, the state institutionalised a much more inclusive concept of citizenship than other Gulf states (Kharusi, 2013, p. 428). According to nationality laws, Omani citizenship is given even to those born inside or outside Oman of Omani fathers, of Omani mothers and an unknown father, and those born in Oman of unknown parents (Al-Rasheed, 2013, p. 100).[16] After the coup in 1970, Sultan Qaboos realised that the labour needs for economic development could be met through inviting (and nationalising) Zanzibari Arab families (who got to East Africa during the time when it belonged to the Omani empire), thus starting to transfer them to mainland Oman in an organised way. This was also beneficial for the regime, as these tribes of a mixed Arab-African heritage "claimed tribal links with important sections of Omani society yet were considered to be relatively far removed from Oman's internal conflicts" such as the Dhofar rebellion, or the tensions between inner Omani lands and Muscat. That is why "they were thus seen as potential supporters of the regime" (Al-Rasheed, 2013, p. 102). As a result, we can see that Sultan Qaboos treated the challenges of internal heterogeneity with imported heterogeneity, while also advocating an open and inclusive Omani identity.

Kuwaiti society is particularly heterogeneous in comparison with other smaller Gulf states (Louer, 2014; Longva, 2013). Besides the traditional

tribal cleavages and the historical tensions between the settled and the unset-
tled population,[17] there is a division in Kuwait between the *asli* (original) and
the *mutajannis* or *biltajannus* (neutralised) communities connected to the
Battle of Jahra of 1920. In national memory, this event is seen as the found-
ing moment of the country, in which the Kuwaitis managed to defeat the
conquering Saudi army of the Ikhwan. The families who participated in the
battle (in other words, those who resided in Kuwait before 1920) and their
descendants are seen as the original population of the country, whereas those
who arrived later are the neutralised. Their Kuwaiti identity has been questioned by many, and they were not even given the right to vote until 1966.

A special category in Kuwaiti society is that of the stateless people, the
bidoon.[18] They consist of those (mostly bedouin) families who, for various
reasons, were not granted citizenship; for example, those who did register to
become official citizens of the country in 1959, after the implementation of
the Law of Citizenship. In the following decades, their position constantly
deteriorated, especially after the Iraqi occupation of Kuwait, in which many
bidoon were blamed for helping the Iraqi invasion.[19] Nevertheless, several
families have received citizenship from the government since 1959 in various
waves (motivated by the regime's desire to build up a loyal base), while others
remain in a stateless political "limbo" (Abu Sulaib, 2021, p. 138; Crystal,
2014, p. 163).

Unlike the *bidoon*, the Kuwaiti Shia community is well-integrated into
society, both legally and politically, and they have frequently served as a
political ally of the emir vis-á-vis the Sunni merchant class. Shias of Kuwait
belong to three distinct communities on the basis of family origin: the *Ajam*
from Iran, the *Hasawiyyin* from Saudi Arabia (*Hasa*), and the *Baharna* from
Bahrain (Louer, 2014, p. 135). In many cases, these Shia families escaped
religious prosecution in Bahrain and Saudi Arabia, therefore they do not
have strong ties to either of these states. Nonetheless, with the arrival of Shia
networks from Iraq, the sectarian question became progressively more
complicated.

These cleavages all reflect the seriousness of debates concerning the
Kuwaiti identity and the decision as to who is Kuwaiti or not. These societal
questions, with all their political and legal dimensions, have not only created
internal divisions, but also hampered the institutionalisation of the political
community and brought about the pressure of questions related to loyalty
(Bacik, 2008, pp. 122–124). From the perspective of the Kuwaiti state, we can
see that the proper defining of who is Kuwaiti and who is not has triumphed
over concerns related to the small size of the population, as citizenship laws
in recent decades have become stricter and stricter (Longva, 2013, pp. 120–
123). The profound heterogeneity of Kuwaiti society has not only often been
mentioned as a cause for the relatively liberal public life of the emirate (especially in comparison with the smaller Gulf states), but also as a tool in the
hands of the regime to manoeuvre between various elite groups.

The Qatari national community is the most homogeneous in the region,
therefore the Thani regime had virtually no serious domestic challenges in

this regard (Fromherz, 2012, p. 26). The Qatari ruling family is the largest in ratio to the whole population, which means that the regime itself is large enough to dominate the society. Shias are present but well-integrated into the economic and political elite.

Tribal differences played a greater role than sectarian differences in the history of the United Arab Emirates, as well (Peck, 2001, pp. 145–160; Ono, 2011; Commins, 2014, pp. 152–157). After the 18th century, the main social dynamics have been characterised by the rivalry between the *Hinawi* and *Ghafili* tribal groups. Under the leadership of the *Al Bu Falah* tribe, the *Hinawi* became dominant by controlling the strategic points in the territory of today's UAE, primarily due to its ability to make alliances with external players such as the Omani sultan (due to their perceived kinship) or Great Britain. The most powerful members of the *Al Bu Falah* belonged to the *Bani Yas* tribal alliance led by the *Nahyan* family, which stuck a series of agreements with London in the 19th century. They maintained their regime in Abu Dhabi and remain the dominant regime in the country, as they control the territories that produce 90% of the oil output of the country (Peck, 2001, p. 2). Their competitors, the *Ghafilis*, did not vanish – their prominent families, which belonged to the *Qasimi* family, still rule Ras al-Khaimah and Sharjah, two of the smaller emirates in the UAE. The rivalry between the *Nahyans* and the *Qasimis* was practically decided by the British government, who considered the *Qasimis* a greater threat, as they were historically stronger on the seas.

Besides the *Nahyan* and the *Qasimis*, other prominent tribes make up Emirati society. The *Al Bu Falasah* (or *al-Falisi*) tribe, for example, belonged to the *Bani Yas* alliance, but did not want to accept the dominance of the *Nahyan* family and their relations with the British Crown, so they broke up with the *Bani Yas* and established their rule in another town: Dubai (Peck, 2001, p. 56; Rugh, 2007, p. 100). The relationship between the *Maktoum* and the *Nahyan* has always been contradictory, a truly competitive form of cooperation. Besides them, other prominent tribal groups and families include the *al-Manasir* (the primary allies of the *Nahyan*), the *al-Nu'aym* (another *Beni Yas* tribe that controls Ajman), the *Al Mu'alla* (ruling in Umm Al Quwain), the *Al Ali* or the *Sharqiyin* (the rulers of Fujairah) (Peck, 2001; Ono, 2011).

Tribal heterogeneity, connected with smallness, causes Emirati society to be highly fractured, which can be a cause for concern for regime stability. To manage tribal diversity, the Emirati ruling families established the federative structure in which the major families were given their own sovereign rule over a piece of territory while accepting the dominance of the *Nahyan* family.

As with the Qatari or the Kuwaiti Shia community, the Emirati community is marginal, highly integrated into society, and their loyalty is to the ruling family (Majidyar, 2013; Potter, 2014, p. 17; Gengler, 2014, p. 58). Though their legal status differs in the various member states, their religious organisations can work relatively freely, sometimes even with governmental subsidies. Most of the Shia live in Dubai and Sharjah, where prominent Shia families (such as the *al-Sayegh*) have close connections to the ruling class.

Economic smallness

Despite their similar position and internal structure, there are huge differences between the size and the efficiency of the economy of Bahrain, Kuwait, Oman, Qatar, and the UAE (see Figure 4.3). Similar trends show a high convergence between economic growth and the fluctuation of the oil price, making the 2000s the most profitable decade for smaller Gulf states. There have been two fractures in economic development: the economic crisis of 2008, and the oil price crisis between 2014 and 2016. Individually, the UAE has always had economic dominance, having an economic output ten times that of Bahrain. Until the second Gulf war of 1990–1990, Kuwait managed to keep up the pace as the second most-developed country but, in 1991, its output shrank to 60% of the previous year. After that, the Kuwaiti economy rebounded to some extent; nevertheless, it lost its second place to Qatar in 2010, after having experienced astonishing growth in the 2000s.

In the subregional context (see Figure 4.4), we can see the smaller Gulf states getting relatively bigger and bigger. Roughly half of the overall GDP of the GCC has been produced by Saudi Arabia with a clear downward trajectory, sinking below the 50% threshold in 2001. The output of the UAE and the four smallest Gulf states has fluctuated vis-á-vis each other; nonetheless, the overall GDP of Bahrain, Qatar, Kuwait, and Oman surpassed that of the Emirates in 2007, remaining slightly above it ever since. Again, this tendency can mostly be attributed to the quick and steady growth of the Qatari economy.

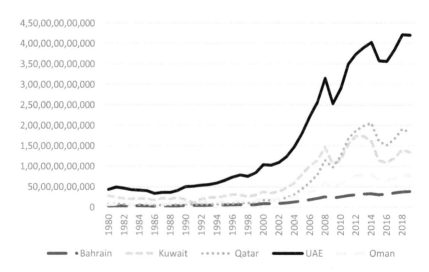

Figure 4.3 The GDP of the smaller Gulf states (1980–2018) (current USD).

Source: Compiled by author using data from World Bank Database, 2021.

Note: Statistics on Bahrain are not available between 1970 and 1980.

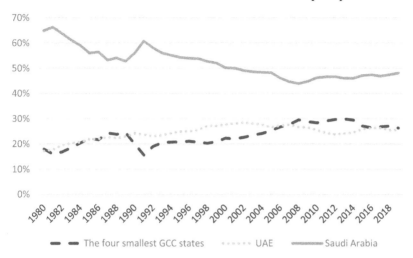

Figure 4.4 The share of the members of the GCC in economic output (1980–2019).

Source: Compiled by author using data from World Bank Database, 2021.

Note: Bahraini data is missing between 1970 and 1980, and for the UAE until 1975.

The small economic output of the Gulf states should be interpreted through its interaction with two variables: the huge amount of hydrocarbon resources, and demographic smallness.

Hydrocarbon resources

Besides their absolute small size, the most important feature of the economy of smaller Gulf states is the huge quantities of hydrocarbons to be found in their territory. Despite their limited economic output, all five states possess some reserves of oil or natural gas (see Table 4.3). In terms of oil, Kuwait and the UAE is the richest, with more than 5% of proven oil reserves on the global scale, whereas by far most natural gas is located in Qatar, which has three times more than the other four states combined. Income from natural gas is

Table 4.3 Proven oil and gas reserves in the smaller Gulf states (2019)

Country	Proven oil reserves (thousand million barrels)	Proven oil reserves (share of total) (%)	Proven gas reserves (trillion cubic metres)	Proven gas reserves (share of total) (%)
Kuwait	101.50	5.90	1.7	0.9
Oman	5.40	0.30	0.7	0.3
Qatar	25.20	1.50	24.7	12.4
UAE	97.80	5.60	5.9	3.0
Bahrain	<0.13	<0.01	0.1	<0.1

Source: Compiled by author using data from BP (2020).

important for Oman as well, where it contributes 25% of all hydrocarbon revenues (the same ratio is 75% for Qatar) (IMF, 2020, p. 20).

The utilisation of oil profit in national development happened gradually and differed for each of the Gulf states. Although the extraction and export of these commodities started between the 1930s and the 1950s,[20] for decades it remained an "external commodity", as "it was extracted by Western oil companies, sold to Western consumers, and the bulk of the profits from this process were pocketed by the oil companies" (Ehteshami, 2013, p. 51). Afterward, governments started to utilise their resources more consciously and directed them to their own needs, incentivised by increasing demand in Asia and changes in the oil market. They achieved this through the processes of bargaining with oil companies (and reaching so-called 50–50 profit agreements[21] in the 1950s), and the utilisation of the oil as a weapon in the 1970s – increasing the price of oil for political purposes. By this decade, basically, all Gulf states managed to gain full control of the fields and means of oil production (Koren and Tenreyro, 2012, p. 188). Such a huge income source enabled the states to gain a firm grasp of the national economy, building their strategy almost solely on profits from oil production. The process led to an economic system usually called a rentier economy; namely, reliance on a single unearned income, which is fixed in supply and inelastic in nature (Ehteshami, 2013, p. 57; Al Sabah, 2013, p. 17).

The effect of the rentier structure on the state and society is somewhat debated in the literature.[22] On the one hand, the higher level of economic income allows the smaller Gulf states to build and maintain well-functioning state institutions, a strong social net, and relatively high military expenditures. These advantages are particularly present in demographic small states where the per capita income is so high that governments have wide leverage. Moreover, possessing 10% of the proven global oil reserves, smaller Gulf states were able to build up relationships of interdependence with other states through commerce and other economic activities. They "have naturally taken notice of the importance attributed to oil by the major powers, and attempted to take advantage of it, acquiring guarantees for their security (…) as well as access to sophisticated weapons systems" (Luciani, 2005, p. 88). These circumstances came in handy in several foreign policy actions for the small Gulf states (e.g. during the Gulf rift; see Chapter 6).

From the perspective of the regimes, the huge income from rents represented an opportunity to make a new kind of social contract with society. According to Uzi Rabi (2016, p. 83), the "power attained through oil revenues is vested in the hands of the ruling elite and the people's rights to political participation is exchanged for social welfare". These benefits given to society include housing, distribution of available lands, financial support for the unemployed, cancelling debts, as well as free education and health care (Davidson, 2012, pp. 50–56). The primary form of delivering such benefits was hiring citizens in the public sector. This tool is especially important for smaller Gulf states with regard to maintaining stability and loyalty in their heterogeneous society.

Accompanied by demographic smallness and the growing price of oil, smaller Gulf states managed to increase savings in the 2000s, which they could turn into a domestic and foreign policy tool in the 2010s (IMF, 2020, p. 17). Details will be described in the next chapters; nevertheless, it is important to mention that the process of accumulation of wealth helped to compensate for their deficiencies in security policy vis-á-vis larger states.

On the other hand, the reliance on rents has many negative effects on economic planning and performance, as well as on international relations. First, it exposes national economies to global economic trends, something that they cannot affect individually. Growth rates have been glued to the fluctuation of the price of oil since at least the 1970s: after the oil crisis of 1973, the rising revenues of the smaller Gulf states enabled them to transform "to reformulate traditional tribal structures into modern forms of governance" (Ulrichsen, 2016, p. 26). This period lasted until the late 1980s, after which the governments had to accommodate their fiscal policies to a lower oil price. This was the time when the elites started to discuss diversification; namely, the development of other sectors of the economy independent from the energy market. The next wealthy period started in the 2000s and lasted until 2014, during which, instead of diversification, the small Gulf states started to accumulate wealth.

This reliance on hydrocarbon commodities not only translates into a form of dependency, but also into a risk of high volatility in terms of the standard deviation of annual growth rates, which, in the 1970s, reached 8.3–12.5 percentage points in the case of Kuwait, Bahrain, the UAE and Oman, and 4.7 in the case of Qatar (Koren and Tenreyro, 2012, pp. 190–191). In the following decades, volatility shrank in almost all cases, except for Kuwait (which witnessed a 40.2 percentage point volatility rate in the 1990s) and Qatar (6.2 and 5.3 percentage points in the 1990s and 2000s, respectively), largely due to global trends.

Moreover, as the academic literature on absolute size predicted, smaller Gulf states have a relatively high export market concentration ratio (see Table 4.4).[23] The five states mostly trade with the European Union, the USA, and some Eastern-Asian states (Republic of Korea, Japan, China). By 2015, Kuwait and Qatar had the highest concentration ratio of exports,

Table 4.4 Export market concentration ratio in the small Gulf states in 1995 and 2015

Country	1995	2015
Bahrain	0.3957	0.3123
Kuwait	0.6057	0.5982
Oman	0.7480	0.4467
Qatar	0.6305	0.5078
UAE	0.5657	0.2427

Source: Compiled by author using data from UNCTAD, 2016, pp.183–193.

and the UAE had the lowest in the group but, in an international comparison with other small states, the Emirati data is still relatively high (Meilak, 2008, p. 43).

Since none of the oil-producing states was big enough to alter market conditions, they stood together to form the Organization of the Petroleum Exporting Countries (OPEC) in 1960, simply to extract more favourable terms from the corporations (Citino, 2002, p. 155). This cooperative organisation managed to become the most dominant (though not hegemonic) institutional player on the global oil market. The founders of OPEC – especially Saudi Arabia – wanted to avoid an Arab oil organisation, fearing the nationalist tide. Therefore, several non-Arab states were invited to join the group (Citino, 2002, p. 145).

Second, the dominance of rents in the economy has substantial social and moral effects. The unearned nature of such revenues fosters the persistence of rent-seeking behaviour and a bias towards "unproductive activities" (Karl, 1997, p. 5) for all economic actors. This process can be seen not just in the financial world, but also in social relations, as it de-incentivises economic efficiency and self-improvement for the members of society. Another moral consequence of mixing rentierism with the Middle Eastern state structure is the constantly high level of corruption and the constantly high expectation of society to receive many benefits without having made any individual contribution (Issawi, 1982, p. 207).

As a result of this benefit-distribution system, citizens were hired in the public sector even if they had no real job to do. This put huge pressure on state budgets and led to a very inefficient public sector, which downgrades the performance of state institutions.

Third, so-called "Dutch Disease" is also observable in the Gulf in the way in which "discoveries or favourable price changes in one sector of the economy, for example, petroleum, (can) cause distress in other sectors" (Karl, 1997, p. 5). The phenomenon has been especially critical in underdeveloped economies such as those of the Gulf region during the 1950s. According to Charles Issawi (1982, p. 209), while:

> considerable advantage in infrastructure, housing, manufacturing, and social services was achieved (…), agriculture grew only slowly, a fact that aggravated inflation. Shortages and bottlenecks ensued, since neither the transport system nor the construction and other industries could cope with the huge demands made on them and the supply of nontradeable goods could not be expanded fast enough to meet demand.

As one result of Dutch Disease, smaller Gulf states are among those countries that have the highest commodity dependence[24] in the region. According to the United Nations Conference on Trade and Development (UNCTAD), only the UAE was more reliant on oil exports before the drop in the price of oil in 2015–2016 than Qatar, Oman, and Kuwait. Bahrain is in a slightly better position due to the depletion of its resources (UNCTAD, 2016, p. 182).

Fourth, oil reserves in the demographically small Gulf states and other parts of the Middle East and North Africa created a division and a constant source of tension between oil-rich and oil-poor states in the region (Luciani, 2005, pp. 96–99). Nationalist regimes such as Nasserist Egypt frequently articulated a claim to the Gulf states and others to share the income coming from oil revenues in the name of Arab solidarity. Though oil-producing states engaged in some forms of mechanism to aid their poorer neighbours – through formal financial assistance, or labour migration and remittances – these steps were frequently seen as insufficient by economically unstable regimes.

Moreover, the presence of oil reserves makes the strategy of relative deterrence unavailable for small Gulf states. As I mentioned in Chapter 1, the idea is based on raising the costs of a possible attack to a degree that outweighs the possible gains. Possessing such valuable natural resources in such a high quantity, small states are targets that are too valuable to attack, especially due to their relatively small military size. The problem manifested itself most clearly during the Iraqi invasion of Kuwait (see Chapter 5), leading to searching for security shelters provided by extra-regional actors.

These problems – coupled with the fact that resources will probably run out in the lifetime of those born today[25] (Kinninmont, 2015, p. 16) – lead to a constant political discourse about diversification. Incomes from oil dominate not just economic activity, but also fiscal governmental revenues and exports. Despite the fact that diversification has been in the public discourse in all periods since the 1970s, when the oil price declined, the Gulf states have not managed to alter their economic structure to any substantial degree. In 2018, more than 50% of fiscal revenues in the GCC came from oil revenues, except for the UAE, where that ratio is around 35% (Deloitte, 2020, p. 5); nonetheless, it is true that, by the mid-2010s, the share of the energy commodity sector in terms of GDP dropped to 24% in the case of Bahrain, 34% for the UAE, 51% for Qatar, 56% for Oman and 63% in the case of Kuwait (IMF, 2016, p. 8). Besides the rise of the service sector generally, the most notable success of the Gulf states was the diversification of the oil sector itself, with subsidising oil-based industries such as refining (Hvidt, 2013, p. 7).

In the last 20 or so years, all Gulf states have issued "national visions"; namely, mostly economic and social reform programmes aimed at diversifying the economy and making it more effective (see Table 4.5). Having the

Table 4.5 National visions in the smaller Gulf states

Country	Title	Year of publication
Oman	Oman 2020: Visions for Oman's Economy	1995
Bahrain	Economic Vision 2030	2008
Qatar	Qatar National Vision 2030	2008
Kuwait	Kuwait Vision 2035	2010
UAE	Vision 2021	2010

Source: Compiled by author using data from Ulrichsen, 2016, p.64.

lowest amount of oil reserves, Oman and Bahrain were the first to move while, due to constant political debates, Kuwait was the last to formulate its reform strategy. While all visions have a slightly similar set of tools, all of them share some commonalities, such as having more ambitions than actual results, focusing on nationalisation of the labour economy, and also emphasising human development (Ulrichsen, 2016, pp. 62–66)

A major problem with diversification is that the term itself is loosely defined, and empirical research has been limited (Alsharif, 2018, p. 23). Naturally, the share of various sectors is the primary variable by which to measure diversification, but it is very difficult to set a rate of success, or to identify additional or secondary effects (not to mention efficiency). For example, due to the structure of Gulf economies, strengthening non-hydrocarbon sectors is highly labour-intensive. According to an IMF estimate conducted in 2011, a 1% rise in the non-hydrocarbon GDP goes hand-in-hand with a 0.7–1.7% rise in total employment (IMF, 2011, p. 4). Bearing in mind demographic smallness and the compensatory policy of intensive importing of labour, this can cause serious tensions between nationals and non-nationals. In Bahrain, for example, the competition between Bahrainis and non-Bahrainis has been higher than that of its neighbours as diversification accelerated, so building up the non-hydrocarbon sectors paradoxically led to fewer employment opportunities for citizens (Kinninmont, 2011, p. 51). Similarly, in the Emirates, analysts consider diversification and the Emiratisation of the labour market as contradictory aims (Jensen, 2018, p. 71).

According to the general evaluation of the literature, the most successful smaller Gulf state in terms of diversification has been the UAE, which managed to shrink the ratio of the hydrocarbon sector from a peak of 66% to 31% between 1979 and 2007 (Flamos et al., 2013; Alsharif, 2018, pp. 33–34). Most of this can be attributed to the economic development of Dubai as a centre of international commerce, financial services, and tourism (Mishrif and Kapetanovic, 2018). The Maktoum ruling family relied on a distinctly unique model of developer state, the historical position of the city as a regional hub, as well as advantageous federal policies. Smallness also played an important role, as it made governmental programmes more efficient and incentivised integration into the global economic system.

Nevertheless, this diversification process has not been without a downside, as it caused tensions between Abu Dhabi and Dubai (most particularly between the *Nahyan* and the *Maktoum* families), the former still relying on oil exports. Moreover, it aggravated existing dissimilarities between the different emirates. Huge differences remain between the oil-exporter Abu Dhabi, the diversified Dubai, and the remaining five Northern emirates. For example, the 2008 crisis hit the more globally integrated Dubai harder than the rest. These differences reconstruct existing domestic tensions and sensibilities which make Abu Dhabi, the de-facto leader of the Emirates, focus heavily on domestic politics (a clear manifestation of the omni-balancing strategy) both in terms of attention and financial resources. That being said, such tensions would not undermine the federal structure, as the relationship between the emirates remains cooperative.

Besides the UAE, Bahrain and Oman have been able to achieve the most visible success in diversification. They managed to lower their commodity dependence on hydrocarbon exports between 1995 and 2015, while Kuwait stagnated in this regard. Data on the Qatari economy statistically even worsened in this respect; nonetheless, this is due to the huge rise in natural gas production capabilities taking place during these two decades (UNCTAD, 2016, pp. 183–189). On the other hand, they all diversified their export markets and lowered their concentration ratio, especially Oman.

Demographic smallness

Economic smallness and huge natural resources also interacted with small population size. The GDP/capita ratio shows (see Figure 4.5) that the UAE, Kuwait, and Qatar have experienced very high ratios, but even the poorer smaller Gulf states such as Bahrain and Oman surpass the Arab average to a considerable extent. Again, we can clearly see the fluctuation caused by oil prices and the effects of the growth of Qatar in the 2000s.

Demographic smallness clearly works as an advantage for smaller Gulf states, as they can redistribute wealth, and maintain social stability with relatively small absolute costs. That would theoretically create wide leverage for national budgets, but the question is slightly more complex than that. The fact that demographic changes affect the size of governmental expenditures but barely change governmental incomes (as they depend more on oil price than taxes) can easily lead to imbalances. Moreover, analysis shows that, due

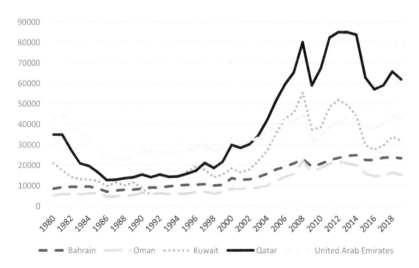

Figure 4.5 GDP/capita ratio in the smaller Gulf states (1980–2019).

Source: Compiled by author using data from World Bank Database, 2021.

Crude Oil Brent

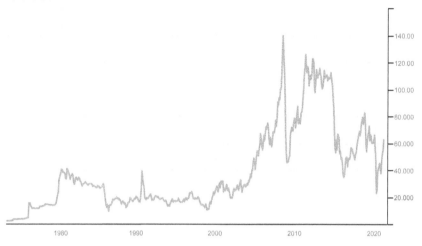

Figure 4.6 The inflation-adjusted monthly oil price (1971–2020).

Source: Trading Economics, 2020.

Note: Data show the Brent Crude Oil price per barrel on a yearly basis.

to their pro-cyclical fiscal policy, the lack of long-term fiscal planning, proper financial institutions, and regulations in place (especially in the early decades), the budgetary balance in the GCC countries has been fragile. Their fiscal room for manoeuvre has been dependent on the fluctuation of the oil price: between 1973 and the mid-1980s, as well as in the 2000s, the Gulf governments were able to pay for higher expenses, while in the late 1980s and the 1990s, they had to cut their expenses. The same is true for the period after 2016 (see Figure 4.6).

The periods with high incomes enabled Gulf states to create sovereign wealth funds (SWFs). The first SWF of the world was actually created by Kuwait in 1953 (the Kuwait Investment Authority: KIA) (Yang, 2015, pp. 16–17) followed by, among others, the Abu Dhabi Investment Authority (ADIA) in 1976, the Omani State General Reserve Fund in 1980, the Qatar Investment Authority in 2005, the Oman Investment Fund and the Bahraini Mumtakalat Holding Company in 2006 (SWFI, 2020).

The initial aim of SWFs was to eliminate the potential impacts of oil price fluctuations – basically as a counter-cyclical fiscal policy tool – but they were adjusted to conduct strategic financial investments and to help diversification attempts. While the creation of SWFs is a worldwide phenomenon, Middle Eastern SWFs dominate the market with a 75% share of global SWF capital (SWFI, 2020, p. 18). The 2000s represented an opportunity for oil-exporting states to enlarge their reserves: between 2002 and 2008, the oil price rose from 22 USD per barrel to 147 USD (Ulrichsen, 2011, 10–12). As a result, smaller Gulf states have the wealthiest SWFs: ADIA is the third largest, followed by KIA in fourth place, the Investment Corporation of Dubai in tenth place, and the QIA in eleventh place (SWFI, 2020). Among the five states' SWFs, the QIA is the least conservative and is willing to take the highest risks (Setser and Ziemba, 2009, pp. 23–24); it is also designed to make politically moti- vated investments (e.g. with regard to France and Great Britain) (Roberts, 2013, p. 3).

Similar to investments, providing aid is another tool that is enabled by the discrepancy between absolute economic size and demographic smallness (Barakat and Zyck, 2012; Davidson, 2012, pp. 81–85). Smaller Gulf states – especially Kuwait, the UAE, and, recently, Qatar – provide humanitarian and development assistance (amounting to approximately 3% of their GDP) as a form of soft power for several reasons, including enlarging their normative size, bettering their image (see Chapter 3), building influence and even financ- ing poorer Arab countries' balance-of-payments deficits when the oil price was high. The primary destination of smaller Gulf states' aid (Palestine, Lebanon, and Iraq) shows their politically motivated nature. The amount of aid provided correlates highly with the price of oil, reflecting the financial leverage of smaller Gulf states.

Specific economic attributes

Despite having similar economic systems, each Gulf state has specific attri- butes that help us understand the various effects of smallness.

Historically, Bahrain had disposal of various natural resources – espe- cially fresh water, dates, and pearls; however, since the 1930s, the economy has been based on oil production (Kinninmont, 2011, pp. 31–49). Due to the limited quantities of cheap oil[26] belonging to the island state (McLachlan, 1980, p. 89; Hvidt, 2013, p. 19), Bahrain was and is a front-runner in diversi- fication, which targets aluminium production (with the ALBA flagship com- pany), financial services, refining, and tourism. The problem with these policies is that almost all of them connect the Bahrain economy to that of Saudi Arabia, deepening its dependence on the Kingdom. From a statistical perspective, Bahraini economic policy planning has not been effective, even when compared to other GCC states, as the country-specific component of volatility is the highest it has been since the 1970s (Koren and Tenreyro, 2012, p. 197).

Bahrain is the odd-one-out regarding its SWF. First, it was the last country to establish such a fund, as its SWF (Mumtakalat) was only founded in 2006. Second, it manages non-oil assets in the country and focuses almost solely on diversification, rather than foreign investments. According to Juergen Braustein (2018), the reason behind this is the existence of a relatively strong and well-organised private sector, which did not let the government freely use the surplus in the economy and wanted it to reinvest such surplus within the country. This phenomenon deprived Bahrain of a mechanism that can create leverage in international affairs to a great extent.

Kuwait, on the other hand, has always been a "desert economy", having an "extremely poor relative endowment of natural resources" besides oil

(McLachlan, 1980, p. 188). Due to its geopolitical location, Kuwaiti businessmen have traditionally been engaged in regional and long-distance trade, making the merchant class stronger than in other states (Crystal, 1995, p. 5). After the discovery of oil, the trade elite remained united and posed a counterbalance to the emerging state institutions, forcing the emir to provide constant financial assistance to them (e.g. the land acquisition programme in the 1950s and 1960s) (ibid.). On the other hand, Kuwait had the largest exportable quantity of oil in its territory compared to its regional partners, and had higher income from oil exports than Iran, Iraq, and Saudi Arabia until the middle of the 1960s (Ehteshami, 2013, p. 53).

The main turning point in the economic history of Kuwait was the 1990–1991 war, which emptied out state reserves and caused severe instability (Crystal, 2014, p. 164). In response, the government wanted to attract foreign capital to a much greater extent than before: restrictions on foreign ownership were annulled, and Project Kuwait was announced in order to attract foreign oil companies to the country. Domestic opposition to the plan was huge since the merchant elites felt threatened by the growing foreign presence.

Historically, agriculture had been the basis of the economy of mainland Oman due to geo-economic circumstances as well as a relatively developed irrigation system called the *falaj*[27] (or *aflaj* in the plural form)/*ganat* system (Wilkinson, 1980, pp. 122–126). After the 18th century and the expansion of the Omani empire, Muscat became "the centre of a vibrant trading system in the Indian Ocean" (Hanieh, 2011, p. 8). Its dominance was based upon the control of Zanzibar, the Eastern African island that served as a link between the European, Asian, and African trade routes. Nonetheless, due to the rising British interests in the seas and the oceans, Oman had to give up Zanzibar, and it quickly fell under the influence of London.

Traditional Omani agriculture survived and still plays a role in the Omani economy. Traditional and modern techniques are mixed in order to fight the challenge of the dry climate of the country (except for the Dhofar region) (Al-Marshudi, 2001). According to the World Bank dataset, in the early 1970s, agriculture provided 10–15% of the overall Omani GDP; after that, it fell to 2–3% until 2003, after which it was set to 1.5–2%. This is still the largest share among the smaller Gulf states (since it only reaches 0.5% in the case of Kuwait, for example). Accordingly, employment in agriculture is approx. 5–6.5% in the total workforce, falling from 9% to 10% when measured in the early 1990s.

Oman, alongside Bahrain, is a front-runner in economic liberalisation and in reshaping the economy in a more market-oriented manner. As early as 1970, the government realised its human resource problem (deriving from the lack of quantity and quality of the Omani workforce), which is why the government started to involve local governments as well as central state institutions to develop the skills of society. Nonetheless, a thorough human resource strategy was only included in the Vision 2020 programme adopted in 1995 (Al-Hamadi, Budhaw, and Shipton, 2007, p. 103). By the early 2010s, it was the only small GCC state with plans to privatise major public firms (Hvidt, 2013, p. 37).

Qatar also has a unique situation compared to its neighbours. Due to its remote position, distant from major trade routes, merchants did not play a powerful role in the Qatari society until the 20th century (Crystal, 1995). Before oil production, the only major economic activity was pearling, which strengthened the rule of the emir and the men who collected tax, a dynamic that only strengthened after the discovery of oil production.

Qatar is the only GCC economy that primarily relies on natural gas production, rather than oil. Qatar has the third largest natural gas reserves in the world after Russia and Iran. The most important gas source, the North Field, was discovered in the 1970s, but the government did not decide to develop production infrastructure until 1984, the same year in which the Qatar Liquified Gas Company (Qatargas) was established (Sastry, 1994). Actual production did not start until the 1990s and comprised three phases: first, the government wanted to develop the gas industry for domestic consumption, then to provide neighbouring states via pipelines, and lastly to other states in liquid form (LNG – liquid natural gas) (Hashimoto, Elass and Eller, 2004). The reason for slow implementation was the high oil prices in the first half of the 1980s, and the lack of a proper institutional framework for economic decision making. Since then, Qatar has managed to become the largest LNG exporter in the world, being responsible for one-third of all LNG exports (Bridge and Bradshaw, 2017, p. 13).

With such a position, Qatar strengthened its role in the global economy considerably; nonetheless, gas production also creates dependency on Iran, as the North Field is shared with the Islamic Republic. Moreover, the Iranian government sporadically accuses Qatar of stealing gas from its territories in the gas field (known as South Pars field) (Dargin, 2010), which creates a constant source of tension and interdependency in bilateral relations.

Due to the large supply of natural gas, Qatar has no urge to diversify, or to implement unnecessary or risky economic reforms in the short term (Hvidt, 2013, p. 38). The current diversification plan is not innovative and includes basically the same elements as the others, with a special emphasis on tourism and, as in the case of Oman, human resource development. The establishment of the Qatar Foundation as a source of innovation can be seen from this perspective.

As is the case with its society, the economy of the UAE cannot be treated as a single entity and should be divided into three parts. Abu Dhabi has had the largest economic output in the federation, as it has controlled 90% of its oil reserves and 85% of its production (Butt, 2001, pp. 231–233). In addition to certain financial sectors and tourism, the most important player in the economy is the Abu Dhabi National Oil Company. Abu Dhabi remained the only player in the Gulf which, following the nationalisation wave of the 1970s, allowed foreign partners to participate in the oil sector on a production-sharing basis. This helped the development of corporate culture and technology transfer, making the company the most modernised and the earliest to engage in this type of activity.

Contrary to Abu Dhabi, Dubai has always had an economic culture of trade and integration into the regional economy. While some oil reserves were found in the territory of the emirate, it has never been a true rentier economy. Since the 1970s, the Maktoum family implemented a top-down development strategy with proactive and extensive fiscal and monetary policies in order to boost the competitiveness of various financial and service sectors. Besides the firm governmental control, the main attributes of this strategy have been skipping industrialisation, focusing on the service sector, quick decision-making systems, supply-driven development, international state branding activities, and the inclusion of international partners (Hvidt, 2009). While these attempts are not axiomatically contradictory to the aims of Abu Dhabi, their interests can diverge; for example, in the case of the importance of Iranian connections.

When it comes to the five Northern Emirates, barely any economic data is available, which shows the sensitive nature of domestic differences in the country. Their aggregate GDP has grown from approximately 5–10% of the federal output (Freer, 2018a, p. 63), while the per capita GDP is between half and one-quarter that of Abu Dhabi and Dubai. Unemployment and fuel shortages are observable. Despite historical tensions between the ruling families, the federal government run by Abu Dhabi and Dubai established a system of fiscal redistribution that helps out the poorer emirates to a great extent. They mostly have similar possibilities in terms of economic development, such as tourism, agriculture, or investments in science or culture. A common tool has been the creation of free zones with a more investment friendly environment in the 1980s (Fujairah, Ajman, Umm al-Qaiwain) and the 1990s (Sharjah and Ra's al-Khaimah) (Ghanem, 2001, p. 271). Nevertheless, there are differences among the five member states; for example, Sharjah has the largest relative economy with some modest oil reserves in the offshore Mubarak field, and huge manufacturing capabilities (responsible for almost half of industrial production in the country).

Military smallness

In modern history, only the UAE managed to build up a military force with more than 50,000 personnel (see Figure 4.7). Oman has been fluctuating between 29,000 and 47,900, but the others have been near or below 20,000. A process of military build-up can be seen in the 1990s, mostly due to the Iraqi invasion of Kuwait. Currently, 0.93–2.07% of the workforce in the five states is employed by the armed forces, a sign of almost constant decline since the peak of 1995, when the same ratio was 2.88–7.76%. Since that time, Bahrain has had the largest armed personnel per capita ratio, followed by Oman, both surpassing the regional average. Traditionally, the UAE also had a larage ratio (surpassing 7% in 1990), but recently witnessed an intense decline. These data suggest that, in the case of Kuwait, Qatar, and the UAE, the size of the armed forces is small in comparison with their demographic size.

According to the World Bank, military expenditures have usually had a greater share in the state budget than the regional average in Oman, the UAE,

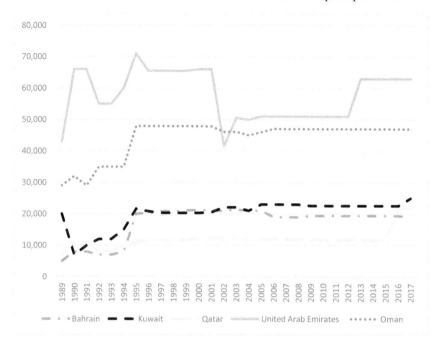

Figure 4.7 Armed personnel in the smaller Gulf states (1989–2017).

Source: Compiled by author using data from World Bank Database, 2021.

and, since 1990, Kuwait. Except for a few occasions (for example, during the Kuwaiti war, when the Kuwaiti defence budget reached 49% and 117% of the GDP), Oman has had the largest ratio with a 5–25% share, fluctuating between 8% and 12% in recent years. Other states have been below the 10% mark in the 21st century. Smallness, in general, does not make Gulf states spend less on military capacity in relation to their GDP. Other factors play a more important role.

Weak military capacity should be interpreted in connection with systemic developments, geopolitical position, and alliance-making as a compensational policy.

Systemic developments

As was discussed in Chapter 2, the Gulf region as a security architecture went through a profound transformation in the 1980s and 1990s, which manifested itself mostly in the three Gulf wars, affecting security calculations in the region (Ehteshami, 2013, pp. 195–208). Traditionally, Arab countries (small and large states alike) focus their resources on regime defence, rather than classic state defence, investing in an elite force in the army that can protect their leadership (Roberts, 2020, pp. 30–31). Nevertheless, the emergence of inter-state wars and other systemic developments changed the context of military smallness of the Gulf states in three major ways.

First, they highlighted the importance of absolute and relative military strength. If the system had remained dominated by more subtle interventions by state actors in each other's domestic affairs instead of traditional armed conflict, the importance of military smallness would have been diminished, and resources could have been allocated to block outside interference (see Chapter 5). However:

> war has had a direct and deleterious effect on interstate relations in the subregion, and domestic political pressures, coupled with pressures from the extra-regional major powers, have meant that relations between these states have been highly securitised. The result has been the sustained militarization of the subregion.
>
> (Ehteshami, 2013, p. 208)

Armed conflict and instability in the neighbourhood caused the threat of spillovers for the Gulf states (Ulrichsen, 2011). Whether that be a direct military attack (as in 1984, when a Kuwaiti tanker was attacked), terrorism (such as the spread of the Al-Qaeda network in the 2000s in the Peninsula), refugee waves (after 2003 and 2011), or other aspects, smaller Gulf states feared that the external environment may affect their polities and policies in undesirable ways. This motivation is observable in many cases.

Second, the dual threat of Iraq and Iran triggered an arms race in the Gulf, in which Saudi governmental decisions played the central role. In the wake of the Iraqi–Iranian war, Saudi military expenditure rose 164% by 1984 compared to their 1979 value, and continued to increase exponentially (Ehteshami, 2013, p. 198). In such circumstances, smaller Gulf states had to engage in armament to some extent, at least to achieve some limited form of relative deterrence.

Since smaller Gulf states also lack a significant weapons industry to meet the needs of the armament process, they rely on imports in the sector. Realising their common interests, Arab states –Egypt, Saudi Arabia, Qatar, and the UAE – founded the Arab Organisation for Industrialisation in 1975 to build up their military industry and to tackle dependence on external exporters (Gaub and Stanley-Lockman, 2017, pp. 20–21). Due to different priorities and to the deteriorating relations between Egypt and the Gulf states in the late 1970s, the initiative emptied out and, by 1993, only Egypt remained a member.

An interesting development in the Gulf recently is the successful strategy of the UAE to build up its defence and technology industrial base, and to become a net arms exporter in the region (Gaub and Stanley-Lockman, 2017, pp. 47–62). This intention can be interpreted in multiple ways: strengthening independence in the defence sector, contributing to diversification attempts, but using military-industrial capacities as a foreign policy tool to better interdependence, to enlarge its normative role, and to forge ties with stronger states have also been among the primary motivations. The initiative is conducted through centralisation (e.g. merging smaller firms into a single entity, the Emirates Defence Industries Company: EDIC), massive state subsidies through the Defence and Security Development Fund (established in 2019), cooperation with the bigger arms manufacturers of Saudi Arabia and Russia, as well as attracting companies to set up their activities in the Emirates to gather know-how (Samaan, 2019; Cohen, 2020). From the perspective of other small Gulf states, the Emirati defence industrial base can be seen as an opportunity and a threat at the same time – the UAE can be a source of diversification of arms supplies and a move to lower the level of dependency on Western partners. However, on the other hand, the development of the Emirati defence industry discourages other states from building their own production capabilities (as the UAE is a more advanced competitor).

Eventually, armament led to a classic security dilemma in the Gulf (Lawson, 2011, pp. 51–56), the intensity of which rose decade by decade. Moreover, this race included the purchase of weapons that are useful in an offensive, not just in territorial defence. As a result, despite the huge military expenditure and weapon deals, the Gulf states arguably failed to become safer.

Third, the Gulf states were vanguards in the process of normative fragmentation in the 1980s and 1990s (see Chapter 2). The aforementioned developments made smaller Gulf states realise that ethnic and religious ties will not prevent governments from attacking each other. The creation of the GCC can be seen as a result of the normative fragmentation process and a direct consequence of the perception of relative military smallness.

Fighting security deficit with alignment

As was discussed in Chapter 2, the Gulf region has traditionally been relatively weak compared to outside empires, therefore the region has served as a buffer zone between those outside entities (Commins, 2014, p. 2). As such, the military weakness of smaller Gulf states (even that of the UAE) is not a new phenomenon, as local families and tribes have always had to conduct compensatory policies to protect themselves.

To fight the security deficit arising from smallness, states have two general options: they can either build up relative deterrence capabilities, or bandwagon on a stronger actor through bilateral or multilateral cooperation. This stronger actor can be a bigger neighbour (such as Saudi Arabia or Iran), or an extra-regional force such as the USA, or Russia. Since independence, the choice of smaller Gulf states has been changing over time (see Chapter 5): at first, they tried to build up relative deterrence (especially the UAE); however, after its failure in the early 1980s, they moved to a strategy of collective bandwagoning on Saudi Arabia through the GCC. Nevertheless, in the 1990s another change can be detected, as smaller Gulf states turned to the USA to sustain their security (Martini et al., 2016, pp. 8–9). This about-turn was motivated by the painful experience of the Iraqi attack on Kuwait (in which the GCC proved to be insufficient to protect its members), but it was also rooted in the historical tradition of mistrust between the ruling families and their reliance on extra-regional partners for security, a phenomenon observable during the process of state-building, too (Ulrichsen, 2011, pp. 16–17).[28] Cooperation with the USA manifested itself in the form of bilateral defence agreements, which should therefore it not be seen as a multilateral joint endeavour but, rather, as parallel decisions made in the same direction.

While data suggests a process of armament among the smaller Gulf states, especially in the UAE, relative deterrence has never been a true option for them. First, they could have never competed with Iran or Saudi Arabia in absolute numbers and, second, their oil wealth makes the prize of conquering them more valuable, therefore relative deterrence is highly questionable.

The armed forces of the smaller Gulf states have rarely been deployed to actual combat. Even if they contribute to international coalitions or multilateral efforts, they usually play a supportive role (Davidson, 2012, p. 85).[29] Among the Gulf states, only the UAE participated in the Afghani intervention of 2001 (Harb, 2014), with Oman and Qatar offering logistical support (Katzman, 2020a; 2020b). Omani facilities were also used in the Iraqi intervention until 2004. In 2011, Qatar, alongside the UAE, contributed air and special forces to the Libyan intervention of NATO under the jurisdiction of Resolution 2011 of the United Nations Security Council.

Recently, this trend changed to some extent in two circumstances. First, all five states participated in the Global Coalition to Defeat ISIS. Nonetheless, their involvement should not be overestimated; besides occasional bombing against fix low priority targets, their role was initially somewhat symbolic (Wehrey, 2014). Later, they were more engaged in logistical support, counter-messaging, and counter-terrorism efforts in their own countries (Boghardt, 2017). Second, the smaller Gulf states also took part in the Saudi-led coalition to intervene in Yemen in 2015, except for Oman (IISS, 2017, pp. 396–397). Qatar was also kicked out of the joint efforts in 2017, as a result of the boycott against the country, while the UAE left coalition struggles in 2019 to signal a shift towards diplomatic tools and away from military ones (Harb, 2019).

Individual military strategies

Bahrain has the smallest military in the region. Due to the lack of military capacities, its compensatory policy was almost exclusively to rely on external forces for protection (Kinninmont, 2011, p. 32). Besides membership in the GCC, security is achieved by the presence of the American 5th Fleet and the official status of a major non-NATO ally since 2002. While Bahrain has frequently participated in military campaigns recently, one could argue that the state does not have the ability to defend itself and is hugely dependent in many areas; for example, to meet mobility requirements (IISS, 2017, p. 370). Bahrain relies on Saudi Arabia for the training and the development of armed forces, and also on the USA for the importing of arms (Cordesman and Rodhan, 2007, pp. 66–68). For example, the USA was the only state from whom Bahrain bought any weapons between 1993 and 2004.

Kuwait is also highly vulnerable, especially vis-á-vis Iraq. According to the official aim of the military, the armed forces should be able to withstand an external attack for 48–72 hours so that international forces can defend the country (Cordesman and Rodhan, 2007, pp. 89–90). In defence policy, the emphasis has been put on developing the army and the air force, while the navy was considered the least important defence sector. The country also followed the path of getting under the American security umbrella in the 1990s, and of achieving major non-NATO ally status in 2004. Since 1991, Kuwait has not been able to rebuild its army fully, though military expenditure and arms imports rose significantly (ibid.). Kuwait's National Guard launched a development plan for 2015–2022 to review the structure of the armed forces; nonetheless, it is yet to bear significant fruit (IISS, 2017, p. 387).

Oman has the second most powerful armed forces among the small Gulf states – except for the UAE (Cordesman and Rodhan, 2007, p. 125). Omani defence policy relied more on human resource development and not necessarily on modernising the equipment. A special emphasis has been given to protecting the country from smaller incursions from Yemen and other neighbouring territories, and also on defending the Strait of Hormuz – even if the Omani naval forces are not strong enough to withstand Iranian aggression on the sea.

Oman relies the most on British connections, but cooperation with the USA also plays an important part in modernising its army. The country was especially important for London for its the Royal Air Force facilities on the Omani Masirrah Island (Takriti, 2013, p. 157). Nonetheless, when a rebellion broke out in the Dhofar region in the 1950s, the British government was not satisfied with the way in which Sultan Said tackled the issue, which is why, in 1970, British forces supported the coup of Sultan Qaboos, who had ruled the country until 2020. London helped him to organise power and to crack down on the armed opposition in Dhofar (Gardner, 2015).[30] Therefore, the British connection was strong from the beginning.

Qatar is not much more self-reliant in terms of defence than Bahrain, with the second smallest military body in the region (Tok, Alkhater, and Pal, 2016, p. 2). According to leaked diplomatic cables, the Qatari military considers both Iran and Saudi Arabia as threats to national security (Kamrava, 2014, p. 163), so the general aim of defence policy is to develop a solid border guard on the Saudi–Qatari borders, and to maintain some form of deterrence vis-á-vis Iran (Cordesman and Rodhan, 2007, 145). That is why the Qatari regime's choice was to rely on American protection. Besides security agreements and army deals, this practically means institutionalising American military presence in the Qatari peninsula. There are two bases on Qatari soil – the al-Udeid and the al-Sayliyah – which are used by the American army (both of which bases were installed during the reign of Emir Hamad), as well as the regional forward headquarters and air operation centre of the US Central Command (IISS, 2017, p. 322). Due to the geopolitical value of these installations, there is an effective interdependence between Qatar and the USA, which is basically a compensatory policy by Qatar.

In the 21st century, the Qatari regime started to develop the army to a greater extent. Although official data is not available, academic estimates suggest that Qatar was the third-largest importer of defence items between 2007 and 2016 (behind India and Saudi Arabia) (IISS, 2018, pp. 322–323). The problem for the Qatari defence policy is not the ability to buy equipment but, rather, the ability to man it and to sustain the necessary human capital to reach their full operational capability. Despite deep cooperation with the USA, Qatar has not engaged in coalition training as frequently as its neighbours, and has not built a strong connection with foreign training academies or military advisers.

In spite of having a somewhat larger army, the UAE shares many concerns and compensatory policies with its neighbours, including maintaining close ties with American and British forces (Heller, 2019), the acquisition of state-of-the-art military equipment, and facing human resource challenges. The UAE also trusts the USA and Great Britain for its classic defence from any possible attacks, which is why the Emirates welcomed American forces in the country, especially in the military base al-Jafra and the port of Jebel Ali (Wagner, 2020). Nevertheless, unlike most of its neighbours, the Emirates experienced acute defence tension with Iran, which de facto controls three islands in the Persian Gulf (Abu Musa, Greater Tunb, and Lesser Tunb) that officially belong to the federation (Cordesman and Rodhan, 2007, p. 284). This circumstance, among others, has served as an incentive to build up one of the most impressive militaries in the region following the Iraqi–Kuwaiti war (Heller, 2019), this having been enabled by huge oil incomes.

"Little Sparta", as a former American defence secretary called the UAE, has developed the most effective and capable capacities in some areas, especially in terms of the air force. They conducted several air operations with American air support in, for example, the Horn of Africa, Syria, and Yemen, while being also capable of conducting strikes without Washington; for example, in Libya. While these capabilities are indeed impressive, Emirati defence forces have tangible deficiencies, such as lacking experience in air-to-air combat, inadequate training, small ground forces, and a weak navy.

The success of the Emirates can be attributed to a handful of strategic decisions (Roberts, 2020). The Emirates relied heavily on Great Britain in its development efforts, which manifested in the Defence Cooperation Agreement of 1998. Abu Dhabi invited British trainers and officers to give thorough assessments and recommendations. Moreover, procurement has been more focused than in the other smaller Gulf states, which has been a more cost-efficient strategy. Lastly, it is important to bear in mind that the UAE has not built an army capable of self-defence (and, arguably, has not wanted to do so); rather, it has developed small but efficient capabilities that can be used in smaller or multilateral missions so as to be a valuable partner to greater states and to promote security polity interests.

The domestic structure of the UAE affects its military capabilities. First, even if, officially, the armed forces are unified and are commanded at the federal level, in practice they are somewhat divided. Historically, three emirates had sizeable military power – Abu Dhabi, Dubai, and Ras al-Khaimah – which merged into the so-called Union Defence Forces. In the federal structure, the division between the three still exists while they were renamed as Western, Central, and Northern Command (Cordesman and Rodhan, 2007, p. 285). Second, while the leadership usually issues from Abu Dhabi and Dubai, nationals of the poorer Northern Emirates outnumber their relative population size not only among volunteers, but also among the military deaths (Pollack, 2020, pp. 4–24). Third, discrepancies remain highly visible among different factions and institutions of the armed forces – while the Presidential Guard and Air Force are exceptional, the bulk of the military has chronic problems similar to those of its neighbours.

Alliance policy as a compensational policy

As in the case of demographic smallness, military smallness has also interacted with a compensatory policy to tackle smallness and thereby caused additional problems; namely, the active alliance policy with the USA (and other actors). Engaging in security cooperation with regional and global powers led to severe consequences, which were summarised by Fred H. Lawson (2011, pp. 56–70) in three non-traditional security dilemmas:

- The *alliance dilemma* refers to the tension between focusing on one's own security threats vis-á-vis satisfying the ally by focusing on its security priorities. This is especially important for smaller states, which are reliant on a greater state, therefore they are more easily pressured to focus on the latter. For example, in the 2000s, the smaller Gulf states followed the steps taken by Saudi Arabia to reach a rapprochement with Iran, but as the Saudi–Iranian relations changed, they altered their course as well in a demonstrative manner.
- The *dilemma between external defence and internal stability* refers to the unintended consequences of the presence of American forces in the Gulf. While the U.S. can protect small Gulf states from an external, conventional threat, cooperating with Washington could undermine regime stability as the societies did not welcome American troops on their soil. This dilemma would not exist if the threat of conventional wars did not grow since the 1980s.
- *The dilemma between outside patronage and regional insularity* refers to the contradictory desires of being protected by external forces and of remaining independent. Since small Gulf states make such cooperation with stronger forces, they lost some part of autonomy by engaging in an alliance with bigger powers. A possible solution for the dilemma could be to balance great powers in the region – a strategy which is recently

becoming more and more visible – nonetheless, it risks the possibility of the Gulf turning into, once again, a buffer zone of greater powers.

These dilemmas are in line with theoretical expectations described in Chapter 1, especially regarding bandwagoning and balancing. In practice, these questions shaped the foreign and security policy of smaller Gulf states, which will be described in detail in Chapter 5.

In conclusion, the consequences of absolute smallness in the case of smaller Gulf states are summarised in Table 4.6. To better understand how size works, I investigated the interaction of territorial, demographic, economic, and military smallness with other variables (and each other), while trying to identify the related compensatory policies.

The most important conclusion of the investigation is twofold. First, smaller Gulf states coped with smallness through innovative compensatory policies, which frequently were adequate for tackling the deficit caused by smallness. It is the consequences of these policies that cause the most severe dilemmas, not smallness itself. Second, demographic and military smallness is the most pressing issue for smaller Gulf states, as there are the two dimensions that interact with the most variables, causing structural dependencies. The fewest problems are caused by economic smallness, especially due to the small demographic size of the five states.

While the UAE is considerably larger than the four other states, it behaves like a small state in many cases due to its complicated social heterogeneity, and its similar geopolitical position and weakness. The only major exception in this regard is the military capabilities of the Emirates, but the logic is very similar there: self-defence is achieved through cooperation, not by means of its own resources.

Perceptual size

So far, no thorough research has been done regarding the role of size and smallness in the social and state identity of smaller Gulf states. Naturally, undertaking interviews and surveys would be the traditional tool for analysts interested in identity elements; however, the effectiveness of such measurements would be questionable in countries where freedom of expression is limited and the governments are not representative (Pollock, 2008). That is why the argumentation will not be based on such surveys; however, I will use the 2013 Zogby Research Services survey on Iran, the World Value Survey, and the Arab Barometer. [31]

I will now investigate the perceptual size of smaller Gulf states in two steps, using the framework described in Chapter 1. First, information will be gathered regarding the relational comparison, the constitutive norms, and the level of homogeneity in the national identity of the five states. Second, to investigate the viewpoint of the political leadership, I will conduct a discourse analysis on the speeches of smaller Gulf states in the UNSC.

Table 4.6 The interaction of variables determining the absolute size of the five Gulf states

	Territorial smallness	Demographic smallness	Economic smallness	Military smallness
Climatic environment	Lack of arable lands, inability to promote self-sustainability, overdue state-building process (except for the case of Oman)			
Geopolitical situation	Vulnerability towards KSA (Bahrain, Qatar, Kuwait), Iran (Bahrain, Kuwait, UAE), Iraq (Kuwait), and Yemen (Oman)			Exposure to Iran, Iraq, and Saudi Arabia
Territorial smallness		High population density and high level of urbanisation		
Imbalance in the labour market		Need to import labour		
Importing labour (compensatory policy) Social heterogeneity		Ethnocracy, interdependence, feeling of cultural invasion Identity management, nation-building Domestic institutions		
Huge hydrocarbon resources			Rentierism	Lacking ability of relative deterrence
Demographic smallness Systemic developments			Fiscal leverage	Need to build up traditional defence capabilities
Alliance-policy (compensatory policy)				Alliance dilemmas

Source: Compiled by author.

Commonalities in terms of relational comparisons and constitutive norms

One can easily make the hypothesis that smaller Gulf states easily perceive themselves as small, for both domestic and international reasons. First, compensating for the absolute demographic smallness, they recruited workers from abroad, which led to a situation in which the national community became an "embattled minority" in its homeland (Fahy, 2018, p. 4). This status, which translates into a "cultural invasion" of foreign cultures and global trends, definitely plays a role in the self-perception of societies and states (Bacik, 2008, p. 104; Gengler, 2012, p. 71).

Several authors have observed this phenomenon. Anh Nga Longva (2013, p. 122) argues that:

> as minority in their own country, Kuwaitis live with the feeling of being permanently under siege. It is not that they fear the competition of foreigners in business, political power or social prestige. (...) What they worry about can be summed up under the vague term "cultural integrity".

John Fahy calls the connection between economic growth and cultural invasion "the dilemma of development", which is at the heart of the concept of perceptual size (Fahy, 2018). The government of the smaller Gulf states chose modernisation and economic growth (economic size), even if it led to opening up to globalisation and massive immigration. On the other hand, the societies in the Gulf feel their minority status, fear that their community and culture may evaporate, and identify economic growth as a challenge to the integrity of society (Dresch, 2013b, p. 156).

Second, at the international level, the smaller Gulf states are squeezed between three large states, which has always represented a strategic and normative challenge for them. According to a survey conducted by Zogby Research Services in 2012 (see Table 4.7), citizens of the five states consider Saudi Arabia in a much better light, except for Bahrain, where the majority of the people reject both states' regional efforts. Bahraini society seems the most divided, while Qatari society seems the most unified from this perspective. Nonetheless, public perception does not necessarily overlap with the regime's policies and identity.

Table 4.7 The percentage of respondents agreeing that Iran or Saudi Arabia contributes to peace and stability in the region

	Kuwait	*Bahrain*	*Qatar*	*UAE*	*Oman*
Iran (agree)	47	44	11	31	33
Iran (disagree)	43	50	78	60	58
Saudi Arabia (agree)	70	46	74	66	67
Saudi Arabia (disagree)	23	48	21	30	29

Source: Compiled by author using data from Zogby (2013), p. 647.

As was previously mentioned, constitutive norms – especially laws regulating citizenship – define a narrow national community in all five states, even if this creates a smaller but more cohesive national community. Exclusion based on ethnicity, family linage and gender are the main attribute of citizenship policy in the region. According to Sater (2017), defining membership so strictly serves to increase the welfare of citizens, to tackle the fear of the foreigner majority by (re)constructing hierarchy between in-groups and out-groups, and to be more efficient in protecting the national community in a cultural, economic, and physical sense.

Nevertheless, having citizenship is frequently insufficient to gain entry to the inner circles of the political community, and a stronger tie needs to be proven to obtain access to services and privileges; namely, a "family book" (Sater, 2017, p. 240). This way, naturalised citizens or children of mixed families in which the father is a foreigner can be excluded from the political community. The government thus "disenfranchises and excludes a segment of an already small population, effectively restarting a process of identity formation among a much smaller, technically proximate imagined community" (Abdulkarim, 2017, p. 47). This practice shows an interesting dynamic between different kinds of smallness: due to economic smallness and the constant urge of governments to homogenise society, regimes promote constitutive norms, which makes the community progressively smaller. From this perspective, absolute demographic smallness is clearly a challenge that is managed by shrinking perceptual size accordingly.

Normative particularities of the smaller Gulf states

Particular geopolitical and social attributes reinforce existing dynamics regarding the identity and perceptual size of smaller Gulf states. Due to its island statehood, Bahrain developed a national identity relatively independent of other GCC states (Kinninmont, 2011, p. 31). The island was previously held by many empires, including the Portuguese, the Omani, and the Persian; while the Portuguese and Omani Empires did not affect national identity to a large extent, the Persian Empire did; especially since "Iranian politicians still sporadically express nostalgia for Bahrain's former role as Iran's 'fourteenth province'" (Kinninmont, 2011, p. 32).

The social heterogeneity of the Bahraini society translates into a less unified national identity, observed by several surveys and polls. The Arab Barometer survey undertaken in 2006–2009 (Arab Barometer, 2021), for example, shows that national identity building was not decisively successful. Of the respondents, fewer than 31.5% identified as Bahraini "above all," while 48.3% referred to themselves as Muslim; 41.8% said that family and/or tribe is the most important social and geographical affiliation in the first place, compared to 29.2% who picked the country.[32]

Accordingly, loyalty to the government was questionable: 58.4% of the respondents chose the "disagree" or "strongly disagree" options to the statement that "people should always support the decisions of the government even if they disagree with these decisions" (compared to 34.7% who chose "agree" or "strongly agreed"); 50.8% disagreed or strongly disagreed with the statement that government officials seriously consider citizens' opinions, with only 39.5% agreeing.

Moreover, the Arab Barometer (2021) also shows that smallness and foreign interference was not the primary fear of Bahraini society. There was one question in the questionnaire that actually referred to insufficient financial resources and capabilities (i.e. economic smallness) as a possible reason for the inability of the government to provide all services to the people, but only 2.3% chose this option, compared to the 18.2% who voted for corruption, and 16.8% who simply stated that the government did not care. Bahraini society was divided in evaluating the cultural exposure to the West (41% thinking that it is harmful, while 48% disagreed). All these results suggest that, in the early 21st century, domestic tensions were more important for Bahraini society than external developments or dangers. This contradicts theoretical expectations of neorealism, according to which the society of small states concentrates on threats coming from the international level.

The Zogby research shows huge cleavages regarding the perception of Bahraini Sunni and Shia people. For example, 65% of Bahraini Shia see Iran as a role model, compared to only 4% of Sunnis. The USA is perceived positively by more Sunnis (79%) than Shias (43%), as well as Saudi Arabia (61% and 32%, respectively) (Zogby, 2013, p. 647). Moreover, only 30% of Shia Bahrainis think that their national culture is superior to that of Iran, compared to 80% of Sunni Bahrainis (Zogby, 2013, p. 780). An even bigger challenge for the Bahraini government is that 58% of Bahraini Shias would be comfortable with Iran playing a dominant role in the Gulf region, compared to only 2% of Sunni Bahrainis.

The threat posed by Iran to Bahrain is similar to that posed by Iraq to Kuwait.[33] Both states have constructed their nationality laws (introduced in 1962 and 1959, respectively) in order to create strictly separation of their population from their larger neighbours (Beaugrand, 2016, pp. 3–7). It is due to this security reason (deriving from the transnational nature of Gulf society) that the citizenship rules in almost all Gulf states are generally very restrictive and do not favour neutralisation in order to protect the Arab Sunni identity as well as the tribal balance of power.

Nevertheless, national identity is much more unified for Kuwaitis than for Bahrainis. The Arab Barometer's 2013 survey showed that 57% of the respondents agreed that citizens should support the government's decisions, with 41% disagreed or strongly disagreed – a ratio that is almost the exact opposite of the Bahraini numbers (Arab Barometer, 2021). On the other hand, 73% agreed to some extent that foreign interference is an obstacle in the country's development; however, in 2019, only 5% of respondents named it as the most important challenge. The 2010–2014 wave of the World Value Survey also shows that 75.7% are "very proud" of being Kuwaiti, with 87% feeling that they are part of the Kuwaiti nation (WVS, 2021).

The Zogby poll shows that the values of Kuwaiti Shias are much closer to their Sunni counterparts than in the case of Bahrain, though differences in perceptions still exist. Of Kuwaiti Shias, 80% view Iran's contribution to the region as positive (compared to 28% of Sunnis), but the absolute majority of both groups would not be comfortable with Iranian dominance in the Gulf (93% and 61%, respectively). They also view the Saudi contribution (75% and 64%, respectively) and the American contribution (78% and 51%, respectively) positively.

The very small size of the Qatari nation (not more than 300,000) and the geopolitical exposure to Saudi Arabia can easily cause a sense of smallness in the case of the Qatari regime, as well as a major challenge to differentiate itself from the neighbouring national communities of Bahrain, the UAE, Kuwait or, especially, Saudi Arabia, which was always seen as an "expansionist force" in the region (Peterson, 2011, p. 26). The primary tools to be independent of other, larger communities have always been alliance-making and foreign policy by the Thani regime; for example, cooperation with the British empire (Fromherz, 2012, pp. 45–46), even during the state-building process.

This is where the foundation of the cooperation between the Muslim Brotherhood and the State of Qatar lies. Due to the fact that the founders of the country – the Thani family and others connected to it – were staunch followers of Wahabism,[34] which is "indelibly linked to Saudi Arabia", the perception of Saudi interference in cultural affairs was there from the first day of institution-building. This explains why the Qatari state gave more room to the teachers and leaders of the Muslim Brotherhood network – a group that is free from Saudi state influence –and also utilised them in state-building (Roberts, 2013).[35]

Possibly due to its homogeneity and smallness, the Qatari national identity is much stronger and more unified than those of the other smaller Gulf states. The World Value Survey (2010–2014) shows that, in essence, 100% of the population see themselves as being part of the Qatari nation, and 98.3% are very proud of it. These are all higher numbers than in the case of Kuwait. Moreover, 97.8% of Qataris said that they were willing to fight for their country, compared to 74.7% of Kuwaitis, while the ratio of those who said no was 1.9% and 17%, respectively (WVS, 2021).

While the unique Ibadi nature of the Omani identity made it easier for the state to limit external societal dangers, it was always suspicious of Saudi interventions in its domestic affairs. This also contributes to the possibility of the emergence of smallness in the national identity, although to a lesser extent than in the previous cases. Data shows that differences in the Sunni, Shia, and Ibadi communities are not that substantive, but the latter two are closer to each other in terms of the perception of Iran, while the Sunnis and Shias are more similar to each other when it comes to the role of the US. The Ibadi community was much less afraid of growing sectarian tensions (62% compared to 77% and 80%), and they are more likely to see their culture as equal to the Iranian, or the Arab equal to the Persian (Zogby, 2013, p. 647, 780, 781, 795).

Despite having the largest population, the Emirati identity is also framed by "cultural invasion", and the fear of foreign and international interference. This phenomenon is exacerbated by two factors. On the one hand, many prominent Emirati families trace back their origins to Oman, a historically sensitive issue that questions the independence of the national community (Patrick, 2012, p. 11). In 1970, Sultan Qaboos of Oman even proclaimed that he did not wish to send an ambassador to the UAE due to the brotherly ties of the two nations (Valeri, 2017). The lack of physical, social, and normative separation was considered to be a threat to the independence of the Emirates, which became evident in managing borders between the two nations. As Valeri argues, "for a small state like the UAE (…), the fenced wall with Oman has played a critical role in justifying its existence as a nation" (Valeri, 2017, p. 604).

On the other hand, the Emirati identity is also particular due to the co-existence of national-level and emirate-level identities (Freer, 2018b). These identity elements can not only compete with each other, but also supplement and reinforce each other, depending on the context. Federal structures were designed to acknowledge the separate identities of the seven emirates (Al Abed, 2001, p. 126), many of which share common attributes such as tribalism, or a Bedouin historical narrative. But, as Paul Dresch (2013b, p. 141) notes, the leaders of each emirate can have widely different concepts of national belonging. The first President of the UAE and the Emir of Abu Dhabi between 1966 and 2004, Zayid bin Sultan Al Nahyan considered genealogy (*nasab*) as a basis of national identity, while his peer, the Emir of Dubai and the first Vice-president of the federation, Rashid bin Saeed Al Maktoum, put the emphasis of common struggles and shared experiences.

Such trends in identity politics have not undermined the federal structure so far, but have hampered the creation of a unified national identity. Jane Bristol-Rhys (2009) identified and analysed five vivid narratives regarding the past and the creation of the UAE, and she came to the conclusion that only one of these five narratives (that of the Qasimi tribes) contradicts the national project of building a unified state. Due to this fragmentation, the Emirati state (and Abu Dhabi) has been very eager to forge a national identity with (re)invented traditions (such as falconry). Arguably, this led to greater success than in other smaller Gulf states (e.g. Bahrain) (Patrick, 2012, p. 18).

Possibly due to the sensitive nature of national identities, reliable and independent surveys have not been done in Emirati society, but the Zogby (2013) research points out that differences between sectarian communities are strained, with a more enthusiastic Sunni response. The major differences between the Sunnis and Shias lie in the ratio of positive perception of Saudi Arabia (71% and 17%), Russia (34% and 87%), but not in the case of Iran (23% and 30%) or the USA (82% and 82%). Approximately 65% of both groups were concerned by growing sectarian tensions, and consider their culture superior to that of Iran. Their majority considers the Arab culture more positively, and they would overwhelmingly not be comfortable with Iranian dominance in the region (89% and 85%).

Given these differences, one can identify interesting dynamics regarding perceptual size and identity among the smaller Gulf states. Perceived smallness is simultaneously a threat and the desired status, which helps to make the society more homogeneous and more resistant to domestic or external threats, including migrant workers, larger neighbours, and the effects of modernisation and globalisation. Coherence has greater value than size. Smaller Gulf states are not equally effective in this regard; one can see a high level of heterogeneity, especially in the case of Bahrain. This observation would suggest overlapping but, to some extent, different self-perception for the regimes – it is another question of what image they actually promote.

The role of smallness in self-perception – state discourse in the United Nations Security Council

It is quite difficult to identify how states see themselves and the role that smallness plays in their self-perception. In the European context, the investigation of national security strategies could be a good source, but such documents are not systematically available for the Gulf states (except for short summaries on ministerial websites).

That is why, for the sake of comparison, I turned to the discourse of representatives of states in the highest forum of international society: the UNSC. In these speech acts, diplomats talk about their interpretation of international affairs, the international system, and, most importantly for this investigation, themselves. Based on the theories described in Chapter 1 related to state identity, the investigation of such speech acts should show states' conceptions of their national role, their relational comparisons, and the attached cognitive models. In other words, UNSC speeches should tell us whether the representatives of smaller Gulf states describe themselves small or large, whether they attach substantive meaning to state size, and whether they interpret international events through the lenses of size differences. Moreover, from a theoretical point of view, speeches in the UNSC constitute a comprehensive database capable of state-level comparisons.

Altogether, the five smaller Gulf states delivered 1,175 speeches by the end of 2020, almost half of which were made by Kuwait (see Table 4.8). It was the only state that has won non-permanent membership twice, while the others were members on only one occasion. With these numbers, Kuwait has been the most active Gulf state, as even Iran had only 316 speeches, Iraq had 311, and Saudi Arabia gave less than Qatar (only 240). These numbers only partly support the liberal idea that smaller states should be more active in international organisations – some of them have been, but not all. The UAE, Bahrain, and Oman fell short of using the UNSC as a forum.

There is also a difference between the usage of the UNSC when a state is and is not an elected member. The UAE (and, to some extent, Bahrain and Qatar) has been especially active as a guest, while Oman and Kuwait delivered two-thirds of their speeches during their tenure. Looking through the

Table 4.8 The basic data on the behaviour of the small Gulf states in the United
        Nations Security Council

	Bahrain	Kuwait	Oman	Qatar	UAE
Year of non-perma- nent membership	1998– 1999	1978–1979 2018–2019	1994– 1995	2006– 2007	1986– 1987
Number of indexed speeches in the Security Council	143	528	86	280	138
Percentage of speeches delivered during membership	42.7%	73.5%	67.5%	41.4%	13.8%

Source: Compiled by author using data provided by UNSC (2020a) and UNDL (2020).

transcripts, it is obvious that the two activities differ in their scope: while being an elected member, diplomats of small states try to demonstrate their competence and their abilities in taking part in international diplomacy, and multilateral decision making in the maintenance of international peace and security. As the agenda is shaped by occurring events, small states comment on a wide range of topics, even if they are not directly involved in the given crisis. The analysis of such speeches is useful in indicating how diplomats of a given country interpret international developments.

On the other hand, when small states chose to contribute to the UNSC's work as a guest, they can pick the topics with which they want to be associated, whether that be a given region or policy area. These are better occasions for small states to shape their perception in the international society, and to brand and virtually enlarge themselves. Besides issues related to Gulf security, smaller Gulf states favoured contributing to debates surrounding the Israeli–Palestinian conflict, the Apartheid system of South Africa (especially the UAE), the protection of women and children in armed conflicts, as well as the fight against terrorism. Nevertheless, the way in which diplomats of the five states talked about themselves differed to a great extent.

Kuwait

Smallness plays the clearest role in the self-identification of Kuwait, as the representatives of the Emirate referred to the country as being small several times. In a debate about the situation in Lebanon, the permanent representative criticised the resolution draft as "representative of a small country" (UNSC, 1978, p. 5). Referring to the year 1908, he also proclaimed that Kuwaitis "were in the depths of poverty. Deprivation was our lot. (…) We were poor" (UNSC, 1979, p. 4). Discussing the Iraqi–Iranian war, a Kuwaiti diplomat said in 1984 that his state turned to the UNSC "not out of weakness or fear, but rather out of faith in the need to settle international disputes in accordance with the principles embodied in the Charter"; nonetheless, he added that these are the principles that "will obviate the resort to force, with all its devastating effects on national construction, which we developing nations need so badly" (UNSC, 1984b, p. 4).[36]

During the discussion of the Iraqi invasion of the country in 1990, Kuwait referred to itself as a small state many times, framing the attack by Saddam Hussein in the context of a large power attacking a weak one, and thus declaring it the responsibility of the United Nations and the international community to defend the weak. In the first debate about the Iraqi aggression in which Kuwait participated (UNSC, 1990a, pp. 3–10), Ambassador Abulhassan argued that:

> The Council's quick response is in keeping with the principle of justice and righteousness, the Council is responding to the provisions of the Charter, whose authors wanted it to provide security not only to big nations, but – primarily – to small nations. (...) Kuwait, a small country, draws its strength and support in international legitimacy, represented by the Security Council and its role in implementing the provisions of the Chart. This is a test for the responsibility of the Council vis-á-vis peace and security in that vital area of the world and towards all small nations that are defenceless and helpless.

Kuwaiti diplomats repeated this notion several times. At the next meeting, Ambassador Abulhasan declared that, after the Iraqi attack, "no small nation anywhere in the world can feel safe or immune from such aggression" (UNSC, 1990b, p. 6), but that, nonetheless, Resolution 660 "was an expression of the fact that the Council defends international peace and security, represents the conscience of the world and indeed protects small nations" (UNSC, 1990b, pp. 4–5). At another meeting, he said that:

> The [Security] Council is aware of what Kuwait, a small and peaceful country does to serve its citizens, to provide them with a welfare system and to make optimal use of Kuwait's God-given natural resources.
>
> (UNSC, 1990c, p. 5)

> Sheikh Sabah Al-Ahmad al-Jabir, the minister of foreign affairs of Kuwait, cited the Secretary-General of the UN, Javier Peres du Cuellar, with an agreement that the due to the Iraqi invasion, "an injustice has been done to a small country that has been one of the states most attached to the United Nations and its objectives.
>
> (UNSC, 1990d, p. 83)

The narrative remained after the intervention of the international coalition in Kuwait. According to these quotes, the Kuwaiti state learned from the case that the small states could rely on the UN and that the institution strengthens their security. "It is true that Kuwait is a small country, both in size and population", said the foreign minister in another meeting, "but thanks to the massive and overwhelming international support which is being extended to us on the basis that justice is a true shield of peace, we find that Kuwait is indeed a Power that carries significant weight" (UNSC, 1990f, p. 13). As a result of the acts of the UN, "people may rest assured that the stronger will not prey on the weaker" (UNSC, 1990f, p. 11).

The narrative of being small resurfaced in the Kuwaiti discourse, primarily in connection with the memory of the Iraqi invasion, after which "it has been proven that the first line of defence of small countries such as the State of Kuwait is a global multilateral system based on law and justice that guarantees the rights, safety and security of small countries" (UNSC, 2018g, p. 17). In 2020, Kuwait identified the connection again between being small and supporting the UN: "The Charter, its purposes and principles represent the first line of defence for small countries. We in the State of Kuwait recognize that very well" (UNSC, 2020b, p. 3). Moreover, in a debate about the reform of the UNSC, the Kuwaiti representative proclaimed that the UN "must take into account the representation of small states, which account for more than half of the membership of United Nations" (UNSC, 2015, p. 97).

Discussing other developments, Kuwaiti representatives have not called their country small, but the framing of world events in the binary setting of small and large, weak or small states has occasionally returned. While these quotes are not direct evidence of the presence of smallness, they imply that the logic of size continued to influence Kuwaiti decision makers in the long term. Talking about a possible American intervention in Iraq, the Kuwaiti ambassador stood up for multilateral action:

> This should be done only within the framework of the United Nations system, because unilateral actions taken as a result of being in a position of power could prove, down the road, as ineffective as a reluctance to pitch in due to weakness
>
> (UNSC, 2002c, p. 10)

> In a debate about climate change, Ambassador Alotaibi claimed that "developing countries – particularly the least developed countries, African countries, landlocked countries and the small island developing States – are most harmed by the negative effects of climate change.
>
> (UNSC, 2011, p. 20)

Talking about the reasons why the UN needs to step up against the Israeli occupation in Palestine, Kuwait referred to the UN Charter's values, including the equal rights of "nations large and small" (UNSC, 2018f, p. 18). Kuwait interpreted the end of a cold war as "a new dawn in the world that emanates from international legitimacy, and it will become the shield of all states, large and small" (UNSC, 1991, pp. 11–12). "The members of the Council", said the Kuwaiti ambassador in 1994:

> have just demonstrated a very strong stand on the side of right and strong determination to uphold the law. These expressions assure every

small State that it is safe from the law of the jungle and make every small State much more attached to the United Nations.

(UNSC, 1994c, p. 12)

Kuwaiti interpretations of international conflict frequently included references to material capacities and development. According to Kuwaiti diplomats, it is the mismanagement of natural resources that leads to fights and wars:

> My country has been blessed with natural resources, and we know well that they can be linked to conflict (...). History is full of examples of armed conflicts and civil wars resulting from the legal and illegal exploitation of natural resources, which fuelled them and were a reason for prolonging them. We preserve our natural resources and exploit them in the right way, while maintaining the security of our State and its national economy in accordance with the Constitution.

(UNSC, 2018e, p. 18)

In parallel, development, or lack of it, played a significant role in the conflicts of Yemen, the Sahel, and Libya. When it comes to conflict resolution, Kuwaiti diplomats referred to mediation several times,[37] a tool often cited by the theoretical literature as a tool preferred by small states.

United Arab Emirates

Representatives of the Emirates frequently referred to themselves as small, and they connected smallness with weakness and reliance on international organisations for security. "For small States, the multilateral rules-based system and international law are vital because they ensure us equal rights as part of the community of nations and protect us all from the abuse of power and hegemony of a few" (UNSC, 2018a, p. 85) Also, small states "rely on the power of international law to protect their sovereignty and security" (UNSC, 2020b, p. 16). Criticising the inactivity of the UNSC after the American attack on Libya in 1986, Ambassador Al-Shaali said that:

> small countries, the militarily weak countries, will continue to pay the price (...). If this situation continues, we shall all one day forced to pay the price. We do not have a deterrent military force, and we shall be victims of force.

(UNSC, 1986c, p. 4)

The same connection between being small and militarily weak, or being victims of aggression, was made explicit in another meeting concerning Libya (UNSC, 1986b), Israel (UNSC, 1986a), and Serbia (UNSC, 1994b). The UAE also interpreted the call of Lebanon for help in the 1980s as "a small country pinning all its hopes on" the UNSC (UNSC, 1984d, p. 4), driven by their belief that "the fate of small nations is tied to seeking help from the international community to protect their sovereignty and peoples" (UNSC,

1986a, pp. 38–40). Talking about South African "aggression" against Angola, the Emirati representative called for action so as "not to cause small states of the world to lose their faith" in the Security Council (UNSC, 1985b, p. 12).

Related to this, Emirati diplomats also connected size and power to different extents of responsibility and abilities. World powers, such as the USA, have the "responsibility for the maintenance of peace" in the Middle East, not smaller ones (UNSC, 1983a, p. 10). In another debate, Emiratis referred to superpowers as having "responsibilities regarding the maintenance of international peace and security" (UNSC, 1989, p. 21). When it comes to the protection of women in armed conflict, the Emirates "try and help in its small way" (UNSC, 2019b, p. 97).

This notion is often translated into a critical voice against great powers, which try to impose "hegemony over countries" (UNSC, 1985a, p. 9). "Nations, large and small, are equal", and major powers should respect sovereignty and independence "so that small nations may build their independent system" (UNSC, 1986d, pp. 34–38). Implicitly, they also criticised "influential members of the Security Council" and the secretariat itself "to fully shoulder their responsibilities in line with the Charter, free from a policy of double standards and bias in favour of the more powerful side and against the weaker, injured party in this equation" (UNSC, 2002a, p. 11).

Other elements of classic Middle Eastern small state foreign policy appear in the Emirati discourse, including an implicit reference to having an unstable geographical position (UNSC, 1973a), supporting mediation (UNSC, 2018d), focusing on social coherence and institution-building (UNSC, 2018b), humanitarian diplomacy (UNSC, 2020b), and the promotion of tolerance and dialogue (UNSC, 2019f). On the other hand, they also consider themselves as a "trade and financial services hub in the Gulf" (UNSC, 2019a, p. 64).

While there is a clear parallel between the role of smallness played in the identities of both Kuwaiti and the Emirates, a sharp difference is that, contrary to the Iraqi–Kuwaiti war of 1990, the losses of Abu Musa and the Tunb islands were not framed by the UAE as aggression of a great power against a smaller one. In the first debate about the issue, the diplomat only described its country as "new and young" (UNSC, 1971, p. 23), framing the conflicts in an international legal narrative regarding independence and sovereignty, and in a normative narrative focusing on Arab–Persian neighbourly relations. Interestingly, other participants of the debate (Iraq, Kuwait, and even Great Britain) used the smallness narrative to varying degrees. Even in other debates, Emirati diplomats refrained from using this interpretation.[38]

Qatar

Qatar did not refer to itself as small in any debates, which indicates that smallness does not constitute a part of the self-description of Qatari diplomacy. During a debate in 2009 about the reform of the UNSC, several ambassadors (including those from Australia, Costa Rica, India, Uruguay, Malta, Singapore, Germany, and Pakistan) stood up for the broader inclusion of small states in multilateral decision making – the Qatari ambassador was not one of them, despite his presence and lengthy intervention (UNSC, 2010, 25–26).

Qatar did not even frame the Gulf rift and the punitive measures implemented against it by Saudi Arabia and its neighbours (see Chapter 6) as aggressive steps towards small states. In most speeches related to the conflict,[39] Qatari diplomats have mostly argued that it is against international law and the values of the UN Charter, and aimed at undermining Qatar's positive image in the international system.

Another interesting observation is that diplomats from Qatar barely framed[40] international events in the dichotomy of small and large, weak or strong, poor or rich states. Most of the argumentation by Qatar relied basically on moral and legal reasons. For example, in the only speech of a Qatari diplomat about the Iraqi–Kuwaiti war (UNSC, 1990e, pp. 23–30), the ambassador did not refer to the differences in size or state power, but focused more on the Fourth Geneva Convention, referring to "evil and wrongful acts", to a "situation" that "runs counter to justice," in which "good will prevail over evil". He also added that "great nations are made by great pains", which shows how morality dominates the Qatari perception of greatness, rather than material size.

In a few cases, Qatar emphasised the different responsibilities of large and small, developed and developing states, with a bleak indication about the position of Qatar in this categorisation. In 2006, Ambassador al-Nasser said that "the effectiveness of the international legal system depends on the degree of commitment shown, in particular, by the powerful States that play a primary role in the system". He added that "we have all come to realize that the more effective and robust international law is, the more it irritates such Powers", which could suggest that Qatar does not think of itself as a "such Power" (UNSC, 2006, p. 20). In the field of climate change, ambassador Al-Nasser talked about "differentiated responsibilities of all states"; namely, that "rich, developed and industrialized countries are assigned responsibilities different from those of poor and developing countries" (UNSC, 2007a, p. 10).

These examples represent only a fraction of the verbal contributions of Qatar to the UNSC but, on the vast majority of occasions, its representatives did not refer to size or the discrepancy of resources as being a factor in international relations. Interestingly, two extracts from speeches delivered by Qatari diplomats explain the reason behind this phenomenon. In 2007, there was a debate in the UNSC about the role of natural resources in armed conflicts. Ambassador al-Bader, the representative of Qatar, commented at length, and his main point was the irrelevance of the topic of natural resources in the work of the UNSC (UNSC, 2007b, pp. 9–10), as "the root causes of most conflict situations today are due, not to natural resources, but rather to various international and domestic political reasons". Therefore, such questions should be discussed in the General Assembly or other bodies of the UN. In another debate in 2013, the representative of Qatar repeated exactly the same idea, saying that

the presence of natural resources such as extractive materials is not per se a source or cause of, or an environment conducive to, the outbreak of conflict, threats to international peace and security, or the spread of corruption and human rights violations.

(UNSC, 2013, p. 10)

He also emphasised that natural resources have greater domestic implications than international implications, adding that:

> it is clear from our concrete experience that natural resources can be a boon to the countries that enjoy them if they are harnessed the right way to drive economic growth, progress, development and job creation, to develop indicators of social, cultural and human develop- ment and human rights, to support good governance, reinforce the rule of law and the fight against corruption, to strengthen political and economic stability, and to improve the livelihoods and well-being of citizens.

(ibid.)

These quotes suggest two conclusions regarding the perceptual size of Qatar. First, differences in size are not considered an important factor in interna- tional relations by the state, which explains why it has not frequently con- structed questions of international peace and security in this framework and has not designated itself as "small" in the UNSC. Second, as with Kuwait,[41] Qatar concentrates more on the absolute notion of size, rather than the rela- tive, as resources are constructed in having a role in domestic affairs, rather than international affairs. However, these quotes do not tell us whether Qatar perceives itself as small vis-á-vis other states; nonetheless, it does not con- sider this a question of utmost importance.

Bahrain

It is worth comparing the case of Bahrain primarily to that of Qatar. Similarly, Bahrain has never referred to itself as small in the UNSC, and has made only a few comments on the basis of which one can assume that it does not consider itself a great power. In 1983, during a discussion of the Palestinian question, a representative of Bahrain emphasised the special responsibilities of Great Powers "for safeguarding peace and security in the region" (UNSC, 1983b, p. 11). Sixteen years later, in 1999, Ambassador Buallay referred to "developed states" in a context that definitely suggests that Bahrain does not list itself among them (UNSC, 1999c, p. 18). Regarding regional security, in 2014 a Bahraini diplomat proclaimed that the country "has always assumed its fair share of burden", which can be an implicit refer- ence to the limited size of the country (UNSC, 2014b, p. 30).[42]

Despite their similarity in neglecting size both as a determinant of identity and as a framing tool, there are three major differences in the state discourses of Bahrain compared to those of Qatar. First, Bahraini diplomats do not agree with their Qatari colleagues about disconnecting the topics of

international peace and stability and natural resources, and national economic growth. In a different debate taking place years earlier, Bahraini
Ambassador Saleh contradicted the speech of Qatari Ambassador al-Bader
almost word-for-word (UNSC, 2002b, p. 25):

> We can draw a similarity in the relations between the Security Council
> and the Economic and Social Council and those between development
> and peace. The relationship between these two terms is quite close and
> a lot can be said in this respect. (...). Development cannot be achieved
> unless there is peace; peace is endangered if there is a problem with
> development. Consequently, we believe that the roles of the Economic
> and Social Council and the Security Council are complementary.

At another time, the Ambassador of Bahrain claimed that "the root causes
of many African problems and issues are economic", which is why "it may be
necessary to intensify consultation and cooperation between the Security
Council, on the one hand, and the Economic and Social Council and the
United Nations specialized agencies, on the other." In this speech, the lack of
development was due to the misuse of natural resources: "we must recall the
vast resources and wealth that are available in Africa, but which, for many
reasons, are poorly and improperly exploited" (UNSC, 1999d, p. 14).

Second, a recurring theme in which Bahrain interprets international events
and political developments is the values of social heterogeneity and the dangers of mismanaging it. "Post-cold-war conflicts", goes the argument, "are
of an internal, ethnic or religious nature" (UNSC, 1999b, p. 18). Consequently,
"it is essential to emphasize the importance of national reconciliation in the
peaceful settlements of conflicts" (UNSC, 2019f, p. 25). Bahraini diplomats
advised working for national reconciliation and unity in various cases, including that of East Timor (UNSC, 1999e); of protecting civilians (UNSC, 2000);
Iraq (UNSC, 2014b); and post-conflict peace-building in general (UNSC,
1998).[43]

On the other hand, multiculturalism plays a role in the Bahraini state
identity:

> Bahrain is an oasis of multiculturalism and multiracialism in the region
> that was the cradle of civilization. We have woven a social fabric that is
> open and welcoming to all, no matter what religion or doctrine they may
> belong to. The mosque, the synagogue and the church sit close together
> in our capital Manama, within less than one square kilometre.
>
> (UNSC, 2015, p. 74)

At other times, the Bahraini diplomats stood by the value of "coexistence"
(in the sense of ethnic and religious groups in a society) (e.g. UNSC, 2014a
and 2014c).

This sensitivity of social cohesion is probably the consequence of the heterogeneous nature of Bahraini society. It seems that the government perceives

the potential threat and tries to picture itself as a good example of the proper management of multiculturalism. It is also important to take note of the fact that such speeches were most observable during the 2010s – prior to that, Bahrain barely spoke about its own identity.

The third particularity of the verbal communication of Bahrain comprises several references to Iran as a power interfering in its affairs. The very first speech delivered by a Bahraini diplomat in the UNSC included a reference to the Persian country, dated in 1973, six years before the revolution. According to Ambassador al-Saffar, the independence of Bahrain (which, according to him, was due to the efforts of the UN and, specifically, the Secretary-General) settled a historical dispute with Iran, "a dispute which had lasted for so long. By this solution, foreign influence, which had lasted a century and a half in Bahrain, also ended" (UNSC, 1973b, p. 13). Connecting the idea of Bahraini independence to the UN, on the one hand, and to vanishing Iranian influence, on the other, is an obvious sign. References to illegal Iranian activities and interference remained constant in the Bahraini discourse, but have been becoming progressively more intense since 2017.[44]

Oman

The Omani diplomatic discourse was the hardest to analyse, due to the limited number of speeches and the overall general style of the comments. Its representatives have not referred to the country small in the UNSC, except for one occasion. In a discussion regarding the Iraqi–Iranian war taking place in 1984 (UNSC, 1984c, p. 8), the ambassador of the Sultanate declared that the wish to maintain friendly relations with Iran, stating that the Omani position:

> does not stem from weakness or from fear of a stronger and more populous neighbour, because our national capabilities and our relations with friendly countries are enough to deter any attack on our territory or national interests; rather our position is based on a sincere belief in respect for the rights of national sovereignty and in the principles of non-interference in the internal affairs of other States and the settlement of all disputes by peaceful means.

In this quote, Ambassador Ali stated the differences between Oman and Iran in relation to their demographic and military size as a relational comparison, but did not interpret this fact as a matter of weakness. The diplomat even explained the reason behind this: the natural resources of Oman and the friendly countries "are enough to deter any attack". This statement clearly chimes with the concept of relative deterrence previously outlined.[45]

After that, Ambassador Ali concluded that Omanis "believe in the inadmissibility of major-Power hegemony over smaller States; we believe that the power of smaller States derives from their adherence to and respect for the Charter" (ibid.). Contrary to the previous quotes, this statement is more inclined towards a liberal-institutionalist interpretation than a realist interpretation.

Oman barely interpreted events in a binary framework of small and large states, except for a reference to the Yugoslavian civil war in 1995 (UNSC, 1995a, p. 8) and a general notion about "diverse issues with global impact" effecting "all states, big and small" (UNSC, 2018g, p. 75). The primary approach through which Omani diplomats interpret conflicts is cultural, primarily ethnic and religious at various times. Such discussions include the American bombing of Libya in 1986 (UNSC, 1986e, p. 28), when Oman argued that the Arab nation and Arabs are against terrorism in all its forms; speaking about its neutrality in the Iraqi–Iranian war, because they are both "fraternal, Muslim countries" (UNSC, 1986e, p. 21). Religion served as an important designation when Omani diplomats talked about Muslim nations' "rightful orientation" in supporting Bosnians' right to defend themselves (UNSC, 1994a, p. 63), or the moral and political obligation to say no to "ethnic cleansing" and "to rape of Muslim women" (UNSC, 1995b, p. 5).

Naturally, the other small Gulf states also use religious or ethnic rhetoric to interpret conflicts, but there are two major differences. First, most of the time, the other four states usually use such words in relation to the Israeli–Palestinian conflict. Second, Oman used this kind of language much more often, on the basis of which we can assume that, besides a general legal perspective, the cultural dimension is the one through which Omani diplomats describe international conflict.

Summarising commonalities and differences in perceptual size

The analysis of UNSC speeches shows that, despite their similar social and geopolitical attributes, smaller states see themselves in different party ways (see Table 4.9). Kuwait and the UAE proved to be the clearest example of a rhetorically observable self-perception as a small state while, for the other three countries, size did not bear that much relevance in interpreting themselves and international politics. Smallness plays (or played) a role in the self-perception of Oman –not necessarily as a limitation, but more as a fact of life – which does not necessarily weaken the security of the country, as greater importance is given to cultural, moral, and ethical questions. These discrepancies clearly show that relative size does not go hand-in-hand with perceptual size, especially in the case of the UAE.

The most obvious interpretation of these results is that the role of smallness enlarges if there is a history of direct military confrontation with a bigger state. This clearly separates Kuwait and the UAE from the remaining three countries, and can explain why they connected smallness to an imperative to turn to international bodies and partners. If this is true, it is nonetheless difficult to explain why Emirati diplomats did not frame the losses of Abu Musa and the Tunb islands in this narrative. A factor that plays a role in this regard is that the UAE became a member of the UN only a few days after the loss of the islands without any experience or socialisation in a multilateral

Table 4.9 Commonalities and particularities in the perceptual size of the small Gulf states

	Bahrain	Kuwait	UAE	Qatar	Oman
Commonalities			"Cultural invasion" Identity management		
Particularities	Geopolitical threat from Iran as a part of the identity Multiculturalism and heterogeneity as a source of self-perception and threat	Geopolitical threat from Iraq Strong role of smallness	Territorial debate with Iran Strong role of smallness Smallness and weakness are connected to each other	Homogeneous society The amount of resources is not connected to international politics to a significant extent	Treating heterogeneity with heterogeneity More inclusive national identity Emphasis on cultural questions Smallness does not make Oman vulnerable

Source: Compiled by author.

organisation whereas, by 1990, Kuwait had been through a UNSC elected membership. One can make the hypothesis that small states are socialised into framing their struggles as small states' struggles.

It is interesting to compare the normative and the perceptual size of the smaller Gulf states. The most important conclusion we can draw regarding these data is that changes in the normative size of states can easily coincide with the time when states proclaimed their identity more clearly; for example, Kuwait in the 1990s, or Bahrain in the 2010s. This revelation leads to the assumption that growth in normative size does not translate into a growth in perceptual size, but more as an opportunity to articulate one's identity the most clearly.

Regime security in the smaller Gulf states

As has been established, all four kinds of smallness affect regime security, not necessarily in a bad way, sometimes they help balance out the consequences of other variables. For example, social heterogeneity is a cause for concern due to the Middle Eastern state structure, which is helped to some extent by demographic smallness. On the other hand, military or economic smallness can also be problematic for smaller Gulf states in relation to maintaining their stability. Nevertheless, in order to assess the situation of the five regimes, one should include political variables other than size.

All small Gulf states are traditional monarchies that are autocratic in nature, with a regime consisting of the ruling family and its tribal allies. Due to their similar historical and economic background, the political system of the four states shares many commonalities, many of which are affected by the attributes described in the previous sections. These features include:[46]

- the concentration of legislative, executive, and juridical powers;
- centralised and personalised decision making, which usually include the monarch, the crown prince, the prime minister, and/or specific ministers;
- consultative bodies of tribal origin, usually called *Majlis al-Shura* or *Majlis al-Umma*, with limited autonomy;
- stable institutions with minimal changes;
- creating a social pact with society to exclude them from political decision making in exchange for welfare and social net maintained by oil revenues;
- the problematic question of handling the Shia minority and the Islamist movements as the two main opposition forces (in varying degrees); and
- the constant fear from ideologies that question the traditional legitimacy of the monarchies, especially Arab nationalism, and republican Islamism.

The stability of the Gulf regimes is highly debated in the literature.[47] These discourses usually focus on three questions (Lucas, Demmelhuber and Derichs, 2014): whether there are any meaningful and provable differences between the resilience of monarchies and republics in the region; if so, how can this be explained theoretically; and, lastly, how do these factors affect political outcomes in the Persian Gulf monarchies.

While such questions are interesting for academic inquiries, it is a better and more efficient approach to investigate the case of the regimes separately. Besides the general attributes of the leadership of the smaller Gulf states, the following overview will focus on three kinds of domestic/transnational threats: identity movements that defy the official state identity discourse (e.g. sectarian Shia identity), representatives of hostile political ideologies, and intra-regime competition.

Bahrain

In the case of Bahrain, the ruling Sunni **Khalifa** family originates from mainland Arabia. Their tribe[48] arrived on the island in the 18th century and managed to gain political power by 1783 by forcing the Persian Empire out. Two contradicting historical narratives exist regarding their arrival (Kinninmont, 2011, p. 32; Louer, 2014, pp. 118–119): according to the "official" version, the *Al Khalifa* brought peace and stability to a society in which Shias have always constituted the majority. Those who oppose their rule are seen as the "fifth columnists" for Iran. Others, nonetheless, consider the ruling family an outside force ruling over the *Baharna* (the indigenous population of the island). Besides sectarian mistrust, the hostility towards the dynasty is rooted in the social memory of destruction as a result of the conquest of Bahrain by the *Khalifa* from Persian rule. Warfare, depopulation, and mismanagement of agriculture led to an economic downfall in the early *Khalifa* years, affecting the perception of generations of the Shia middle class of the new elite (Fuccaro, 2009, pp. 16–42).

Therefore, the main challenge for Bahraini regime security has been the historical opposition to both the monarchic structure and the rule of the Sunni *Al Khalifa* by large parts of society, especially Shia groups. Between the 1920s and the 1970s, seven organised and long-standing series of anti-establishment protests took place in the country (Ulrichsen, 2014, pp. 334–335). These protests were dangerous because the organisers managed to mobilise in both the Sunni and the Shia communities, therefore the usual narrative of a Shia revolution was not applicable. From this perspective, the Iranian revolution of 1979 helped out the Bahraini regime in the sense that the Sunni communities in the Gulf became more suspicious of any kind of Shia activism (see Chapter 5). The strengthening sectarian narrative, which has been used in foreign policy in the form of supporting anti-Iranian initiatives sectarianism, hampered the organisation of large-scale protests until 1994 (Diwan, 2014, p. 144) but has been in use ever since.

To tackle this challenge, the regime used a mixed toolkit that included slight attempts at liberalisation, as well as different forms of oppression. In 1973, the National Assembly was created only to be suspended two years later (Crystal, 2014, p. 172). In 1975, the State Security Law was introduced, which gave the government a wide-ranging authority to implement harsh measures against the opposition. In the 1990s, as most of the anti-government protestors were Shias, the government easily conducted a severe response and arrested several hundreds of protesters (ibid.). Nonetheless, in the 2000s, a series of political reforms began, which included the introduction of the constitution (adopted after a referendum), the creation of a bicameral National Assembly with elected members, and slightly enlarged legislative powers, while the State Security Law was abolished. Elections have been held since 2002; nonetheless, tensions have remained a substantial obstacle, and meaningful liberalisation is yet to be conducted.[49]

Islamist movements in Bahrain did not evolve as an anti-regime political force (Hedges and Cafiero, 2017, pp. 143–145). The Islamic al-*Minbar* Society (the local affiliate of the Muslim Brotherhood network) served as a counterweight to Shia political forces. It was only after the growing security dependence of Bahrain on Saudi Arabia after 2011 (outlined in Chapter 6) that the Bahraini regime was put under pressure to push back against the Muslim Brotherhood, which it did to some extent (Freer and Cafiero, 2017).

The Bahraini regime has traditionally been stable from the inside. Since gaining independence, two rulers led Bahrain: Isa bin Salman Al Khalifa (1971–1999) and Hamad bin Isa Al Khalifa (1999).[50] Succession was due to the natural death of Isa bin Salman and had been planned for quite some time, as Hamad had been the designated heir since 1964. The personality of the monarch has had a strong effect on state policies; for example, the timing of the liberalisation process in the 2000s was mainly caused by Hamad's personal views, rather than by structural developments.

Besides the king and the crown prince, the position of the prime minister is also crucial in the Bahraini political system (Kinninmont, 2011, p. 40). While the international focus is usually on the king and the crown prince, the prime minister has been the most stable centre of power: since the independence of Bahrain until 2020, only one person (Khalifa bin Salman Al Khalifa) had occupied the position. Nevertheless, Khalifa bin Salman died in November 2020, paving the way for the crown prince, Salman bin Hamad, to take his position and cement his power (Diwan, 2020).

Dynamics inside the regime have recently been shaped by the rise of the *Khawalid* branch of the *Khalifa* family (Diwan, 2014, p. 162). The descendants of Khalid bin Ali Al Khalifa, the governor of al-Riffa in the late 19th and early 20th centuries, who was a staunch opponent to the evolving British–Bahraini alliance, have been known as having a "worldview steeped in Sunni chauvinism, amplified due to the growing Shi'a empowerment within the Persian Gulf region" (Diwan, 2014, p. 163). The *Khawalids* were persona non grata for decades in the high circles of the Bahraini regime but, after 1999 – primarily due to the family policies of King Hamad, whose mother also is a member of the *Khawalids* – they managed to create a powerful centre of gravity in the regime. Their position strengthened even further after the events of 2011, when the sectarian narrative was used extensively to tackle political opposition (Diwan, 2020) (see Chapter 6).

Kuwait

Due to the dispersion of economic and political power in Kuwait, the ruling dynasty – the *Al Sabah* – was chosen by the powerful families in the 18th century. The deal was basically a "functional division of power" (Ismael, 1982, p. 28) between the maritime merchant elite and the *Sabahs* (who themselves were engaged in caravan trade, therefore they were able to exert influence over nomadic tribes) (Louer, 2014, p. 134). Two developments changed this dynamic between the ruler and the merchant elite: first, in 1899, the British Empire promised protection to Emir Mubarak the Great, and also provided a regular fiscal source to the *Sabah* family; second, the discovery and rise of oil resources (Roberts, 2011, pp. 92–93).

These processes granted broader leverage for the ruler but, ultimately, the merchant elite did not lose its influence completely and managed to institutionalise their power. It is due to this division of power that Kuwait has the longest constitutional tradition among the GCC states. The first consultative council was established as early as 1921, while the constitution of the country was adopted in 1962, following which the National Assembly was created in 1963 (Roberts, 2011; Crystal, 2014). This body, as in the case of the country's neighbours, is more consultative than legislative, but all of its members are elected and have power to shape or to voice concerns about governmental policies. While decision making remains autocratic in nature, the institutional break represented by the National Assembly slows down the process, leading to a competitive disadvantage vis-á-vis other smaller Gulf states.

This feature is quite unique in the Gulf region, which is why the Kuwaiti political system has been labelled in very distinct ways, such as "hegemonic electoral authoritarianism" (Diamond, 2002, p. 31), or "quasi competitive and a quasi-free plural authoritarianism" (Zaccara, 2013, p. 82).

Neither Islamist nor Shia political movements evolved systematically as an anti-establishment political force (Crystal, 2014). Like many other groups, the Islamists are also divided in Kuwait into followers of the local Muslim Brotherhood branch, *Salafis*, and independents. In the 1960s and 1970s, Islamists served as a counter-weight to Arab nationalist forces, as well as to the merchant elite (Roberts, 2011, p. 94); recently, they have been successful in representing the poorer, mainly *bidoon* population in the National Assembly.

The Iraqi invasion affected political dynamics, too (Roberts, 2011, p. 95). Many families and tribes, including the Emir, left the country when the Iraqi army arrived, but many others stayed. Between these two groups – the *al-Samidoon* (those staying) and the *al-Hariboon* (those leaving) – the tension remains. Since social anger also focused on the fleeing Emir, the elections organised in 1992 led to a two-thirds majority of the opposition in the *Majlis* (which only lasted until the 1997 elections). The first decade of the 21st century once more brought heavy parliamentary debates, which caused the Emir to dissolve the institution several times (in 2006, 2008, and 2009). A huge change took place in 2003 when the appointment of a new prime minister (Sabah Al Sabah) ended the tradition that the direct heir should be the prime minister, a change that endowed the parliament with a tool to criticise the prime minister more fiercely.

In 2008, the Islamist tribal opposition profited greatly from the elections, which resulted in a policy change from the government (Beaugrand, 2016, p. 10). While previously the regime gave citizenship to many *bidoon* families, they reversed the policy and, in 2014, they actually denaturalised some people, accusing them of forgery in the neutralisation process. As the tribal–Islamist alliance was seen as a growing domestic threat, the balancing strategy of the *Sabah* family led to more cooperation with Shia factions. These processes prove the constantly changing nature of domestic alliances in Kuwait, which is the primary feature of the country's political system.

Tensions inside the regime and in domestic political life started to surface during the 2000s (Gharba, 2014; Alnajjar and Selvik, 2016). The main reason behind this phenomenon – besides the decreasing importance of the Iraqi threat, which traditionally had unified Kuwaiti elites to some extent – was the rise of Sabah al-Ahmad al-Haber al-Sabah to the throne in 2006. Although he had been playing a dominant role in Kuwaiti politics since the 1960s,[51] he disregarded the balance of power between the two main branches of the family, the *al-Jaber* and the *al-Salim*, in favour of the former. Instead of appointing a crown prince from the *al-Salims*, the new emir appointed his own half-brother, Nawaf al-Ahmad al-Jaber al-Ahmad.

He ascended to the throne in 2020, after the death of Sheikh Sabah, which fostered the dominance of the *al-Jaber* clan in the family (as well as his choice for the crown prince, Mishal al-Jaber Al Sabah) (Anderson and DeLozier, 2020). In this case, succession itself does not undermine regime stability (especially since Sheikh Nawaf represents the same kind of politics as his brother) (Freer, 2020), but exchanging one of the most emblematic figures of Kuwaiti politics for a low-profile family member and could weaken the position of the government both domestically and internationally (Haverty, 2020).

Learning from the Iraqi war, the Kuwaiti leadership has known that, due to the geopolitical position of the country, international developments can severely undermine the position of the regime. Therefore, to achieve stability, Kuwaiti foreign policy has been somewhat conciliatory, being engaged in mediation to avoid major armed confrontation in the region.

Oman

The Omani ruling family originates from Sa'id bin Sultan, who ruled the country between 1806 and 1856 (Valeri, 2011, p. 135). Between independence and his death in 2020, Sultan Qaboos had ruled over the country. The previous Sultan, Said bin Taimur, had ruled the country since 1932 and had kept Oman in relative isolation from its neighbours, due to the identity of

distinctness and the intention of keeping foreign influence out of the country (Winckler, 2000).

Owing to the heterogeneous nature and the tribal structure of the Omani
society, the main aim of the Omani Sultan has always been to stabilise internal relations and to avoid foreign interference. In the second half of the 20th
century, the Omani government had to fight two successive movements, both
with geopolitical and ideological reasons: one based on the Ibadi Imamate
originating from the inner, more conservative territories surrounding the city
of Nizwa, and another movement in the Western Sunni parts of the country
with communist ideology (Al-Khalili, 2009, pp. 65–73). After a coup against
his father in 1970, Sultan Qaboos managed to pacify both movements in the
1970s and has managed to hold the country together ever since.

Oman does not have a very clear anti-regime opposition – due to the Ibadi
nature of society and the regime, neither the Sunni Muslim Brotherhood nor
the Shia networks are able to form meaningful political resistance. Even if
some movements start to grow, the Omani state cracks down on them with
force, as they did in 1994 and 2004 (Hedges and Cafiero, 2017, p. 139).

The Omani political system is slightly more personalised due to the strong
personal role of Sultan Qaboos in the institutionalisation of power and his
long reign. Therefore, many had expected a political crisis in event of his
death (Davidson, 2012; Said 2015), especially since Sultan Qaboos had no
designated heir or son and the rules on succession have never been put into
practice, in addition to which they are not self-evident. Coupled with the
worsening economic situation (see Chapter 6), many argued that the changing political atmosphere after the Arab Uprisings[52] and the absolute nature
of the political system could easily cause serious problems in the event of a
sudden succession (Said, 2015, pp. 50–57). Legal reforms conducted in 2011
affected succession laws, the leverage of the *Majlis*, and also the independence of the judiciary; nevertheless, it was questionable whether they were
enough to avoid destabilisation.

As in the case of Kuwait, a smooth succession process took place in 2020
after the death of Sultan Qaboos, after which his cousin, Haitham bin Tariq
Al Said, became the Sultan (Owtram, 2020). Similarities between the two
countries do not stop at the date – in both cases, members of the ruling family accepted the outcome without any strong indication of resentment,
although the real challenge comes from losing a well-respected and emblematic leader, and the subsequent rise of a less charismatic one. In Oman, the
new Sultan has been more active in his first months, introducing reforms
concerning the labour code, the rights of foreign workers, and creating the
Private Office (a governmental body reporting only to the Sultan) and the
Investment Authority to boost private sector-led development (Sievers, 2020).
Most importantly, Sultan Haitham started a power devolution process that
aims to decrease the role of the ruler in the Omani political system (Delozier,
2020). These steps support long-term regime stability, but can also serve as a
concession to other parts of the royal family.

Qatar

There are three major differences between the domestic position of Qatar compared to other Gulf state neighbours (Kamrava, 2014, p. 161). First, due to the peripheral location of the Qatari peninsula, the lack of natural resources and effective trade routes, and the relatively modest role of Islam in the state-building process, the economic and religious elites have never been true rivals to the *Thani* family. That practically means greater regime hegemony over society. Second, the community of citizens in the country is much more homogenous than in other countries, and the Shia population (constituting approximately 20% of the national population) is considered to be well-integrated and loyal to the regime. Third, nonetheless, the ruling family was numerically larger (reaching 10,000 members) and therefore more internally divided than other ruling families on the peninsula. This is shown clearly by the fact that two out of the three successions in the history of modern Qatar were forced, which is highly dissimilar to the Gulf region.

When it comes to regime and state development (Fromherz, 2012), the history of independent Qatar can be divided into two distinct periods. The first took place between 1971 and 1995, during the tenure of Khalifa bin Hamad Al Thani, who had no major ambitions in world politics and was occupied by internal strife in the ruling family. His son, Hamad bin Khalifa, organised a bloodless coup in 1995, which represents the start of the second period (which has continued until today, even though Hamad abdicated in 2013 in favour of his son, Tamim), the era of transformation and reform.[53] Hamad's rise to power meant three major shifts: increased institutional rule and forced unity in the *Thani* ruling family, more articulated affiliation to the USA, and an ambitious foreign policy trajectory aimed at putting Qatar on the map of world politics (Kamrava, 2014, pp. 160–161). These changes – accompanied by popular reforms such as the dissolution of the Ministry of Information – managed to strengthen state capacities and ensured a relatively free hand for the Emir of Qatar, both domestically and internationally.

Since 1995, Emir Hamad has shaped the foreign policy of Qatar in a distinct way vis-á-vis its small counterparts, making the country a frequently analysed case study to develop small state theories in the IR literature. Alan Chong's (2010) virtual enlargement notion fits perfectly to the case of Qatar – the small country capitalised on its normative smallness to be accepted as a mediator and a negotiating partner, while it also enlarged its importance through branding activities, as well as other diplomatic and financial tools. According to Kamrava (2014, pp. 167–181), the above-mentioned circumstances allowed Qatar to upgrade bandwagoning or omni-balancing strategies typically used by Middle Eastern small states to a strategy he calls "hedging", which means the build-up of good relations with every major player in the region.

Hedging and branding can be seen as a compensatory policy. First, they aim to develop interdependences with several major players, which can lead to relative security vis-á-vis aggressors and outside threats. Second, it also enables Qatar to exert influence outside of its borders. These achievements came in handy in both maintaining the domestic leverage of the regime (by distributing the profits arising from such activities) and in foreign relations as well. The ambitious foreign policy, which has been evident see since 1995, is a result of the political leadership's decision and not a systemic variable or smallness itself.

Moreover, the ambitious nature of the Qatari foreign policy highlighted the problems arising from smallness, especially in terms of human and institutional capacities (e.g. in the case of failed mediation affairs and the lack of ability to follow-up foreign policy actions) (Kamrava, 2014, p. 166). These problems are shared by all small states, but are more visible in the case of Qatar, which conducts such a high-profile foreign policy (see Chapter 6).

Tamim's rise to power in 2013 was the first time since independence that a Qatari ruler did not have to organise a coup to win the throne. This data shows that the most important challenges in Qatar originate more from within the regime than from society. Rival elite groups are basically non-existent, while the *Thani* family is sufficiently large to evince internal rivalry. This is why the institutional reforms implemented by Emir Hamad bin Khalifa Al Thani were crucial to stabilising the domestic politics of the country. As of today, it seems that his project was sufficiently successful, which affords the Qatari Emir wider leverage.

United Arab Emirates

As previously discussed, among the smaller Gulf states the UAE has a unique domestic political system based on the federation of seven emirates. In practice, this means that the UAE has seven regimes that formed an alliance on the basis of mutual interests of survival and prosperity. Succession in each emirate can only take place with the approval of the Supreme Council Rulers whose members (the seven emirs) have always shown solidarity with each other and hampered any attempt to oust sitting monarchs (Rugh, 2016, p. 68). The strongest regime is the *Nahyan* regime in Abu Dhabi, which did not want to use coercive tools (as in Iraq or Saudi Arabia) to unify the country and break down the rule of smaller regimes, but accepted the federal structure and the endurance of other ruling families (Rugh, 2016, pp. 65–67). Nevertheless, the *Nahyans* still dominate public policies through the federal structure and have been trying to override tribal ties with loyalty to the state. Their most important tools in this regard are the redistribution of wealth and strengthening the Emirati national identity.

The motivation behind accepting the federal structure differs for the *Nahyan* family and the others. The rulers of Abu Dhabi realised that the smaller emirates would not be viable independently, and their failure would contribute to the spread of movements, which would also endanger their survival. Besides monarchic solidarity, this is probably the most important motivation for the *Nahyan* regime to agree to a federal fiscal system in which all emirates pay into the national budget proportionately to their economic size, making them the biggest net contributors (Legrenzi, 2011, pp. 13–17). In exchange for much-needed financial help, the poorer emirates agreed to the dominance of Abu Dhabi. Due to its larger economic size and special interests, the *Maktoum* family of Dubai has had a special position with near equal political power with the *Nahyan* regime, at least historically.

Naturally, since the creation of the federation, dynamics between the seven regimes have not been stationary (Freer, 2018b, p. 39). During the early 1970s, the priority for the *Nahyan* family was to finalise the federal structure without the exact delimitation of power relations, which is why it agreed to several compromises, including the temporary nature of the constitution and the plan to establish a new capital that was independent from all emirates (both have since been annulled) (Peck, 2001, p. 131). Since 1971, the *Nahyan* regime has gradually built up its dominance in the federal structure through three major steps, two of which were conducted after a regional crisis (the Iranian revolution of 1979 and the Iraqi–Kuwaiti war in 1990–1991), capitalising on the fear of smaller emirates.[54] In the evolving structure, Abu Dhabi and Dubai delegate the president and the prime minister of the federation (as well as their deputies); have a veto right in the Supreme Council; and nominate eight representatives each to the Federal National Council (instead of the six or four representatives nominated by the smaller emirates).

Through this structure, Abu Dhabi (and, to some extent, Dubai) has dominated federal policies, including foreign and security policy (Hellyer, 2001), which they used mostly to pursue their own regime interests in the international system. This has been especially true following the economic crisis of 2008, which affected the emirates differently: due to the diversified economy of Dubai, it was more exposed to the waves of global depression than oil-dependent Abu Dhabi (Al-Yousef, 2013, pp. 573–574). The *Nahyan* family decided to bail out Dubai with a 10 billion USD deal, which practically translated into a more hierarchic relationship between the two thereafter (Sadjadpour, 2011, p. 10).

Besides cultural and social affairs, Dubai and the Northern Emirates maintained control of their economic policies, which they used to strengthen their independence and to foster foreign economic ties with other countries. Consequently, competition is ongoing between the regimes in diversification and modernisation to attract more capital and trade through various means (e.g. the creation of free investment zones). The extent of this rivalry does not undermine the regime alliance, but does give it an interesting flavour. It can also lead to different foreign policy interests, especially in the case of Iran, which has a classical oil-exporter economic structure and a focus on security policy; Abu Dhabi has no incentive to build relations with the Islamic Republic, whereas the more diversified Dubai (and, to some extent, the Northern Emirates) has always maintained trade ties with Iran (Sadjadpour, 2011).

The most important transnational security threat for the UAE has been moderate Islamist movements, especially the Muslim Brotherhood. The network reached the federation even before its independence during the 1950s and 1960s, after which they established the al-Islah (Reform) organisation in 1974 (Boghardt, 2013). Abu Dhabi has been suspicious about the movement, which they banned in 1994. The foreign and security policy of the UAE has been dominated by fighting the Muslim Brotherhood in various countries, which can mostly be attributed to the antipathy of the *Nahyan* regime (and, to some extent, the *Maktoum* family) towards these movements, which they consider a destabilising force that can undermine the success achieved over recent decades. The primary tool with which to fight the Muslim Brotherhood has been military intervention and international coalitions, and harsh coercive measures coupled with state-run education in addition to economic tools.

Interestingly enough, the fear of the Muslim Brotherhood and traditional tribal competition has overlapped to some extent, as it seems that al-Islah has been more influential in the Northern Emirates, especially in Sharjah and Ras al-Khaimah (Boghardt, 2013). The Muslim Brotherhood even penetrated the ruling family of Ras al-Khaimah: Saqr al-Qasemi, the emir of the emirate until 2010, had criticised the vilification of the Muslim Brotherhood (Salisbury, 2020, p. 11), while his cousin, Saud al-Kasimi, was convicted in 2012 as a member of the group.

The UAE has had two presidents since independence, both the emirs of Abu Dhabi. Zayed bin Sultan Al Nahyan is widely considered to be the father of the federation, having ruled Abu Dhabi since 1966 and presided over the federal government from 1971 until his death in 2004. He was succeeded by his son, Khalifa bin Zayed Al Nahyan. De facto power currently lies in the hands of the Crown Prince of Abu Dhabi, the ruler's brother, Mohamed bin Zayed Al Nahyan. He serves as the Deputy Supreme Commander of the UAE military and dominates foreign and security policy, especially in the last decade. Mohamed bin Zayed Al Nahyan – who is frequently compared to Saudi Arabia's de facto ruler Mohamed bin Salman – is known to be personally committed to fighting the Muslim Brotherhood and, to some extent, Iranian influence, which he also perceives as a destabilising force (Freer, 2018a). He cemented his power by appointing his five full brothers to key positions – collectively, they are known as the *Bani Fatima* (referring to their mother, the third wife of Emir Zayed, Fatima) (Salisbury, 2020, p. 10).

Among the six other rulers, Mohamed bin Rashid Al Maktoum, the Emir of Dubai, has the largest leverage as the Vice-president and Prime Minister of the UAE (Al Ketbi, 2020). As Dubai's economic weight grew, he tried to pursue a more independent foreign policy during the 2000s, especially using the opportunity presented by the change of leadership in 2004. His attempts have been halted by two developments: the previously mentioned effects of the economic crisis of 2008 and the rise of Mohamed bin Zayed Al Nahyan, who tried to make Emirati foreign policy more coherent (Salisbury, 2020, p. 9). The Northern Emirates have no distinct foreign policy, except for their relations with Saudi Arabia and Iran. The two emirates led by *Qasimi* rulers (Sharjah and Ras al-Khaimah) have closer ties to Saudi Arabia, while the rest are more connected to Iran. Besides social relations, the reason behind this cleavage is the geopolitical tension with the Islamic Republic concerning the

Iranian conquest of three islands in 1971 (Abu Musa, Greater Tunb, and Lesser Tunb), which belonged to Sharjah and Ras al-Khaimah (Freer, 2018a; Salisbury, 2020).

*

What has been clear from this analysis is that, despite what structuralist analysis suggests, smaller Gulf states show alterations in absolute and perceptual size, as well as in regime security. These differences urge them to tackle smallness in different ways, using a variety of compensatory policies and maintaining their security with various strategies. Absolute smallness, perceptual smallness, and specific regime security considerations are major reasons behind the differing foreign policy behaviour of smaller Gulf states, which will be discussed in the next chapters.

Notes

1 All statistical data in this chapter without a specific reference was extracted from the World Bank Database, 2020.
2 Except for Oman, due to a low level of urbanization and some specific policies.
3 Known also as *aflaj*, the plural form of *falaj* in Arabic.
4 Nonetheless, data is not available for the full period.
5 Moreover, some parts of Kuwaiti society (especially economic elites) exerted influence over the ruling family by threatening to support Iraqi territorial claims (Louer, 2014, p. 134).
6 While the regional average is at 66%, and the global average is 56%.
7 See, for example, Samad and Azar, 2019; Zaidan and Abulibdeh, 2020.
8 Besides the Indian rupee, the most popular currencies at that time included British sterling, Iranian rials, and the Austro-Hungarian Maria Theresa thaler.
9 Besides organizing demonstrations and strikes, the ideology was present in the media; for example, in the Bahraini *Saout al-Bahrain* (*The Voice of Bahrain*) daily newspaper, which also spread Communist and Leftist ideas (Kinninmont, 2011, pp. 32–35).
10 Oman was an exception in this regard, where the majority of migrant workers have always been of South Asian origin due to the unique history of the country (Winckler, 2000, p. 33).
11 For more details about the system, see Damir-Geilsdorf and Pelican, 2018; Longva, 1997; and Rahman 2010.
12 In Qatar, the foreign population outnumbers citizens 10 times over and, according to some estimates, the Indian and Nepalese community outgrew the Qatari community (Babar, 2015, p. 132).
13 Discourses on identity are predominantly shaped by and for men in Gulf societies. For a counter-narrative, see Driss, 2005.
14 Initiatives include using falconry (Krawietz, 2014), Islamic art (Gierlichs, 2014), sports (Baabood, 2008), state institutions (Eggeling, 2017), and even national companies.
15 The Shia tribes of Oman belong to two distinct groups: the *Lawatiya* community, which is a merchant community probably of mixed Arab-Indian origin, and the Bahranis of Iraqi descent (Kharusi, 2013, p. 429).

16 Though there have been changes to the law since the source was published, these amendments did not alter these regulations.

17 Which is present in other states; for example, in Qatar (Fromherz, 2012, pp. 36–37).

18 The Arabic word means "without", a term used as an abbreviation of "without citizenship" (*bidoon jinsiyyah*). See Abu Sulaib (2021).

19 Due to the fact that many *bidoon* tribes, primarily the *Shammar* and the *Anayzah*, have Iraqi relatives (Crystal, 2014, p. 163).

20 In Bahrain and Kuwait, this began in the 1930s, and in Qatar and Oman in the 1940s (Koren and Tenreyro, 2012, 188).

21 The main idea of the 50–50 agreements was that the host government received half of the profits deriving from oil commerce in two portions: first, through a royalty amounting to the 12.5% of the value of the oil at the "posted" price (minus the cost of production) and, second, through an "income tax" of 37.5% (EPL, 1973, p. 432). Since the posted price was designated by the oil companies, the host governments did not trust that they truly received 50% of the profit, which led to further changes in the distribution of the income and, eventually, to the partial nationalisation of the oil sector.

22 See, for example, Hanieh 2011, Ismael and Ismael, 2011, Crystal, 2014, Kamrava, 2016, and Ulrichsen 2016.

23 The Herfindahl-Hirschmann Index (HHI) was used to determine export market concentration ratio, which is "calculated by taking the square of export shares of all export categories in the market" (Meilak, 2008, p. 37). The HHI is widely considered to be the "simplest and most affordable indices due to (its) ease of comprehension and availability of data" (Meilak, 2008, p. 46).

24 Commodity dependence is a concept used to measure the reliance of a national economy on the export of a single commodity. It is usually measured by the share of export earnings of the top single commodity (or the top three commodities), the percentage of people engaged in the production of the given commodity (or commodities), or the share of the income from the given commodity (or commodities) in all government revenues (UNDP, 2011, pp. 56–64).

25 The oil reserves to production (R/P) ratio (which shows the years of production remaining at the current extraction levels) is only 15.2 years for Oman, 36.7 years for Qatar, 92.8 years for Kuwait, and 67 years for the UAE, 15.2 years for Omani oil, 36.1 years for Qatari oil, and 91.9 for Kuwaiti oil (Bahraini data is missing). The same numbers for natural gas are much higher (18.3 years for Oman, 92.1 years for Kuwait, 138.6 years for Qatar, and 4.6 years for Bahrain), but mostly due to much smaller production ratios (except for Qatar) (BP, 2020, pp. 14–32).

26 The break-even price for Bahrain was estimated to be 100 USD per barrel in 2011, compared to 80 USD in the case of Saudi Arabia, Oman, and the UAE, and 40–50 USD in the case of Kuwait and Qatar (Hvidt, 2013, p. 34).

27 "A *falaj* consists of a tunnel to tap groundwater and bring it to the surface for distribution to crops and housing. It is designed to transport groundwater to the surface without any mechanical device or costly expenditure of fuel" (Al-Marshudi, 2001, p. 262).

28 The centuries-long experience of competition is also responsible for the "anomalies" of the behaviour of the smaller Gulf states (especially Oman and Qatar) in their reluctance to opt to maintain wider freedom without deepening integration with Saudi Arabia, as they have been more fearful of Saudi hegemony than other security concerns (Martini et al., 2016, pp. 16–41).

29 The contrast is really sharp with the UAE, which has employed its forces in almost all regional armed conflicts since the 1970s (Davidson, 2012, pp. 85–87).

30 Nonetheless, British influence should not be over-emphasized in the early period of Sultan Qaboos, as many pieces of evidence indicate that the Omani government had an independent strategy and was able to say no to London in domestic and foreign affairs (Gardner, 2015).

31 Polls made by state authorities were excluded due to the lack of their reliability and comparability.

32 Nonetheless, in second place, the relative majority (32%) picked Bahrain.

33 Kinninmont (2011, p. 32) argues that the Iraqi invasion of Kuwait is connected to Bahraini fears of a similar action on the part of Iran, since both actions were/ would be accompanied by historical claims.

34 In 1902, Jasim Al Thani officially became *Wahabi* (Fromherz, 2012, p. 62), and others followed.

35 Besides an active alliance policy, recently national branding became an empathetic tool in keeping Qatar away from of the direct influence of Saudi Arabia (Kamrava, 2014).

36 Actually, the diplomat liked this thought so much that he repeated it at another discussion in the same year, citing himself word-for-word (UNSC, 1984c, p. 14).

37 For example, UNSC, 2019d, p. 11; UNSC, 2018d, p. 18.

38 For example, UNSC, 1974 and 2020b.

39 For example, UNSC, 2018a, 2018b, 2018c, 2018f, 2019c and 2019e.

40 Exemptions include the war between Serbia and Bosnia (UNSC, 1992, pp. 18–20) and a general notion about the spread of violence in small developing countries (UNSC, 2005, p. 11).

41 Another similarity with Kuwait includes bragging about mediation experience (UNSC, 2018d).

42 In a single remark about Bosnia, the Bahraini ambassador differentiated between the "material and moral force" of the country (UNSC, 1999a, p. 23). However, he did not specify what he meant, therefore we cannot draw conclusions regarding the perception of the connection between size and power.

43 Naturally, other states raised the question as well, although the occurrence of such reasoning was more evident in the case of Bahrain.

44 For example, UNSC, 2017, UNSC, 2018b and, in general, a plea against interference, UNSC, 2020b.

45 The idea of deterrence came up in a speech by Sultan Qaboos, as well on the national day celebration in 1975. He said that "we are able, with the help of Allah, to deter aggression, whatever its size. Because our men are protectors of faith. We carry weapons in defence of our religion, our nation and our dignity" (Sultan Qaboos, 1975). He spoke of the importance of moral aspects in strength and defence on other occasions, too (e.g. Sultan Qaboos, 1976, 1981).

46 A summary based on Byman and Green, 1999, Csicsmann, 2007; Ismael and Ismael, 2011, Wright, 2011; Davidson, 2012; Crystal, 2014.

47 For example, Herb, 1999, Lucas, 2004, 2014, Davidson, 2012, Bank, Richter and Sunik, 2014.

48 *Al Khalifa* is part of *Bani Utub*, the same tribe as the Kuwaiti *Al Sabah* (Kinninmont, 2011, p. 32).

49 The protests of 2011 should be mentioned in this context, too, (and not just in the context of the Arab Uprisings; see Chapter 5). The first gatherings were organized on the ten-year anniversary of the constitutional referendum, showing that

society wanted the reforms to continue (Kinninmont, 2011, p. 1). While at first the government seemed to be open to negotiations, they later turned to violent means to oppress the protestors. As government response became progressively more aggressive, so did the opposition's claims – after one month, some started to demand the creation of a republic. Eventually, the regime managed to suppress opposition voices; however, it was only able to do so with the help of Saudi and Emirati police and military forces (Crystal, 2014, p. 173). Since then, the domestic political situation remains unstable, as violence occasionally intensifies.

50 The ruler of Bahrain used to be called "emir" but the constitution of 2002 changed the title to "king".

51 Previously, Sabah al-Ahmad al-Sabah served as Foreign Minister between 1963 and 2003, and as Prime Minister between 2003 and 2006 (Cafier and Karasik, 2017), and he is accorded great respect by society and other regional leaders.

52 Although the Omani regime managed to tackle the Arab Spring protests, there is growing interest within society about taking part in politics. The number of registered voters in the 2011 *Majlis* elections was 52.94% higher than in the 2007 elections (Zaccara, 2013, p. 88).

53 Some call this the "transformative state project" (Al-Malki, 2016, p. 255).

54 The first step was conducted in 1976, after the first term of Emir Zayid serving as a President of the UAE.

Bibliography

Abu Sulaib, F.M. (2021) Stateless 'bidoon' in Kuwait: A Crisis of Political Alienation. *Middle Eastern Studies*, 57(1), pp. 134–150. DOI:10.1080/00263206.2020.1820992.

Abdulkarim, K.A. (2017) Crystallizing a Discourse on "Khalijiness": Exclusion and Citizenship in the Arab Gulf States. University of Pennsylvania, [Online]. Available at: https://core.ac.uk/download/pdf/129586839.pdf, (Accessed 31 January 2021).

AGSIW (2016) Gulf Societies in Transition: National Identity and National Projects in the Arab Gulf States. The Arab Gulf States Institute in Washington, [Online]. Available at: http://www.agsiw.org/wp-content/uploads/2016/06/National-Identity_Web-1.pdf. (Accessed 31 January 2021).

Al Abed, I. (2001) The Historical Background and Constitutional Basis to the Federation, in Al Abed, I. (ed.) *United Arab Emirates: A New Perspective*. London: Trident Press, pp. 121–144.

Al Sabah, M.J.A. (2013) *Resource Course Reduction through Innovation. A Blessing for All. The Case of Kuwait*. Newcastle: Cambridge Scholars Publishing.

Al-Hamadi, A.B., Budhaw, P. S. and Shipton, H. (2007) Management of Human Resources in Oman. *The International Journal of Human Resource Management*, 18(1), pp. 100–113. DOI:10.1080/09585190601068383.

Al-Handhali, K.Y. and Miniaoui, H. (2020) Food Security in the GCC countries: Towards a More Diversified and Sustainable Economic Development, in Miniaoui, H. (ed.) *Economic Development in the Gulf Cooperation Council Countries*. Doha: Springer, pp. 75–88. DOI:10.1007/978-981-15-6058-3_4.

Al Ketbi, E. (2020) Contemporary Shifts in UAE Foreign Policy: From the Liberation of Kuwait to the Abraham Accords. *Israel Journal of Foreign Affairs*, 14(3), pp. 391–398. DOI:10.1080/23739770.2020.1845067.

Al-Khalili, M. (2009) *Oman's Foreign Policy. Foundations and Practice*. London: Praeger Security International. DOI:10.25148/etd.fi13101580.

Al-Khouri, A.M. (2012) Population Growth and Government Modernisation Efforts: The Case of the GCC Countries. *International Journal of Research in Management & Technology*, 2(1), pp. 1–8.

Al-Malki, A.M. (2016) Public Policy and Identity, in Tok, M.E., Alkhater, L. and Pal, L.A. (eds.) *Policy-Making in a Transformative State. The Case of Qatar*. London: Palgrave MacMillan, pp. 241–270.

Al-Marshudi, A.S. (2001) Traditional Irrigated Agriculture in Oman. *Water International*, 26(2), pp. 259–264. DOI:10.1080/02508060108686912.

Al-Rasheed, M. (2013) Transnational Connections and National Identity: Zanzibari Omanis in Muscat, in Dresch, P. and Piscatori, J. (eds.) *Monarchies and Nations: Globalisation and Identity in the Arab States of the Gulf*. New York: I. B. Tauris, pp. 96–113. DOI:10.5040/9780755611645.ch-004.

Al-Yousef, Y.K. (2013) The United Arab Emirates at a Crossroads. *Contemporary Arab Affairs*, 6(4), pp. 567–581. DOI:10.1080/17550912.2013.837337.

Alexander, P., Calum, B., Almut, A., Finnigan, J. and Rounsevell, M.D.A. (2016) Human Appropriation of Land for Food: The Role of Diet. *Global Environmental Change*, 41(6), pp. 88–98. DOI:10.1016/j.gloenvcha.2016.09.005.

Alnajjar, G. and Selvik, K. (2016) Kuwait – The Politics of Crisis, in Kjetil, S. and Bjorn, O.U. (eds.) *Oil States in the New Middle East. Uprisings and Stability*. London & New York: Routledge, pp. 113–131.

Alsharif, N.N. (2018) Natural Resources and Diversification: Evidence from the GCC Countries, in Mishrif, A. and Al Balushi, Y. (eds.) *Economic Diversification in the Gulf Region, Volume 2*. Cambridge: Palgrave MacMillan & Gulf Research Centre, pp. 21–50. DOI:10.1007/978-981-10-5786-1_2.

Althani, M.A.J. (2012) *Jassim the Leader. Founder of Qatar*. London: Profile Books.

Anderson, S. and DeLozier, E. (2020) Emir's Death Leaves Kuwait Vulnerable to Gulf Rivals. The Washington Institute for Near East Policy, [Online]. Available at: https://www.washingtoninstitute.org/pdf/view/10703/en (Accessed 31 January 2021).

Arab Barometer (2021) Data Analysing Tool. Arab Barometer, [Online]. Available at: http://www.arabbarometer.org/survey-data/data-analysis-tool/ (Accessed 31 January 2021).

Baabood, A. (2008) Sports and Identity in the Gulf, in Alsharekh, A., Springborg, R. and Stewart, S. (eds.) *Popular Culture and Political Identity in the Arab Gulf States*. London: Saqi Books, pp. 97–121.

Babar, Z. (2015) Population, Power and Distribution Politics in Qatar. *Journal of Arabian Studies*, 5(2), pp. 138–155. DOI:10.1080/21534764.2015.1113680.

Bacik, G. (2008) *Hybrid Sovereignty in the Arab Middle East*. New York: Palgrave MacMillan. DOI:10.1057/9780230610347.

Bahgat, G. (1999) Education in the Gulf Monarchies: Retrospect and Prospect. *International Review of Education*, 45(2), pp. 127–136.

Bank, A., Richter, T. and Sunik, A. (2014) Durable, Yet Different: Monarchies in the Arab Spring. *Journal of Arabian Studies*, 4(2), pp. 163–179. DOI:10.1080/21534764.2014.971647.

Barakat, S. and Zyck, S.A. (2012) Trends in Gulf State Assistance to Crisis-affected Contexts, in Held, D. and Ulrichsen, K.C. (eds.) *The Transformation of the Gulf*. London & New York: Routledge, pp. 313–332.

Beaugrand, C. (2016) Deconstructing Minorities/Majorities in Parlamentary Gulf States (Kuwait and Bahrain). *British Journal of Middle Eastern Studies*, 43(2), pp. 234–249. DOI:10.1080/13530194.2016.1138645.

Boghardt, L.P. (2013) The Muslim Brotherhood on Trial in the UAE. The Washington Institute for Near East Policy, [Online]. Available at: https://www.washingtoninstitute.org/policy-analysis/muslim-brotherhood-trial-uae (Accessed 31 January 2021).

Boghardt, L.P. (2017) Gulf Support to the Counter-ISIS Campaign. Washington Institute for Near East Policy, [Online]. Available at: https://www.washingtoninstitute.org/policy-analysis/view/gulf-support-to-the-counter-isis-campaign (Accessed 31 January 2021).

BP (2020) Statistical Review of World Energy, 69th edition. British Patrol, [Online]. Available at: https://www.bp.com/content/dam/bp/business-sites/en/global/corporate/pdfs/energy-economics/statistical-review/bp-stats-review-2020-full-report.pdf. (Accessed 31 January 2021).

Braustein, J. (2018) Domestic Sources of Twenty-first-century Geopolitics: Domestic Politics and Sovereign Wealth Funds in GCC Economics. *New Political Economy*, 23(1), pp. 1–21. DOI:10.1080/13563467.2018.1431619.

Brichs, J.S. and Sinclair, C.A. (1980) Economic and Social Implications of Current Development in the Arab Gulf: The Oriental Connection, in Niblock, T. (ed.) *Social and Economic Development in the Arab Gulf*. New York: St. Martin's Press, pp. 135–160.

Bridge, G. and Bradshaw, M. (2017) Making a Global Gas Market: Territoriality and Production Networks in Liquified Natural Gas. *Economic Geography*, 93(3), pp. 215–240. DOI:10.1080/00130095.2017.1283212.

Bristol-Rhys, J. (2009) Emirati Historical Narratives. *History and Anthropology*, 20(2), pp. 107–121. DOI:10.1080/02757200902875407.

Butt, G. (2001) Oil and Gas in the UAE, in Al Abed, I. and Hellyer, P. (eds) *United Arab Emirates: A New Perspective*. London: Trident Press, pp. 231–248.

Byman, D.L. and Green, J.D. (1999) The Enigma of Political Stability in the Persian Gulf Monarchies. *Middle East Review of International Affairs*, 3(3), pp. 1–20.

Cafier, G. and Karasik, T. (2017) Kuwait, Oman, and the Qatar Crisis. Middle East Institute, [Online]. Available at: http://www.mei.edu/content/article/kuwait-oman-and-qatar-crisis (Accessed 31 January 2021).

Chalcraft, J. (2012) Migration policies in the Arabian Peninsula, in Held, D. and Ulrichsen, K.C. (eds.) *The Transformation of the Gulf*. London & New York: Routledge, pp. 66–85.

Chong, A. (2010) Small State Soft Power Strategies: Virtual Enlargement in the Cases of the Vatican City State and Singapore. *Cambridge Review of International Affairs*, 23(3), pp. 383–405. DOI:10.1080/09557571.2010.484048.

Citino, N.J. (2002) *From Arab Nationalism to OPEC. Eisenhower, King Saud, and the Making of U.S.–Saudi Relations*. Bloomington & Indianapolis: Indiana University Press.

Cohen, N. (2020) The UAE is Turning into the World Capital for Weapons Makers. *Foreign Policy*, [Online]. Available at: https://foreignpolicy.com/2020/10/20/the-uae-is-turning-into-the-world-capital-for-weapons-makers/ (Accessed 31 January 2021).

Commins, D. (2014) *The Gulf States. A Modern History*. London: I.B. Tauris. DOI:10.5040/9780755608805.

Cordesman, A.H. and Rodhan, K.R. (2007) *Gulf Military Forces in an Era of Asymmetric Wars. Volume 1*. Washington, DC: Center for Strategic and International Studies.

Crystal, J. (1995) *Oil and Politics in the Gulf. Rulers and Merchants in Kuwait and Qatar*. Cambridge: Cambridge University Press. DOI:10.1017/cbo9780511558818.

Crystal, J. (2014) Eastern Arabian States: Kuwait, Bahrain, Qatar, United Arab Emirates, and Oman, in Gasirowski, M. (ed.) *The Government and Politics of the Middle East and North Africa*. 7th Edition. Boulder: Westview Press, pp. 157–196.

Csicsmann, L. (2007) *Iszlám és demokrácia a Közel-Keleten és Észak-Afrikában*. Budapest & Pécs: Dialóg Campus Kiadó.

Damir-Geilsdorf, S. and Pelican, M. (2018) Between Regular and Irregular Employment: Subverting the Kafala System in the GCC Countries. *Migration and Development*, 7(4), pp. 1–22. DOI:10.1080/21632324.2018.1479215.

Dargin, J. (2010) Qatar's Gas Revolution. Belfer Center, [Online]. Available at: https://www.belfercenter.org/sites/default/files/files/publication/Qatars_Gas_Revolution.pdf. (Accessed 31 January 2021).

Darwish, M.A., Abdulrahim, H.K. and Mohieldeen, Y. (2014) Qatar and GCC Water Security. *Desalination and Water Treatment*, 55(9), pp. 2302–2325. DOI:10.1080/19443994.2014.947782.

Davidson, C.M. (2012) *After the Sheikhs. The Coming Collapse of the Gulf Monarchies*. London: Hurst & Co.

Deloitte (2020) Impact of the oil industry crisis on the GCC and potential responses. *Monitor Deloitte*, [Online]. Available at: https://www2.deloitte.com/content/dam/Deloitte/xe/Documents/energy-resources/me_eri-impact%20of%20oil%20on%20GCC.pdf (Accessed 31 January 2021).

DeLozier, E. (2020) Oman's Sultan Devolves Some of His Powers to New Cabinet. The Washington Institute for Near East Policy, [Online]. Available at: https://www.washingtoninstitute.org/policy-analysis/omans-sultan-devolves-some-his-powers-new-cabinet (Accessed 31 January 2021).

Desilver, D. (2018) Remittances from Abroad Are Major Economic Assets for Some Developing Countries. Pew Research Center, [Online]. Available at http://www.pewresearch.org/fact-tank/2018/01/29/remittances-from-abroad-are-major-economic-assets-for-some-developing-countries/ (Accessed 31 January 2021).

Diamond, L.J. (2002) Thinking about Hybrid Regimes. *Journal of Democracy*, 13(2), pp. 21–35. DOI:10.1353/jod.2002.0025.

Diwan, K.S. (2014) Royal Factions, Ruling Strategies, and Sectarianism in Bahrain, in Potter, L.G. (ed.) *Sectarian Politics in the Persian Gulf*. Oxford: Oxford University Press, pp. 143–178.

Diwan, K.S. (2020) Death of Bahrain's Prime Minister Promotes Reformer, But Perhaps not Reforms. *The Arab Gulf States Institute in Washington*, [Online]. Available at: https://agsiw.org/death-of-bahrains-prime-minister-promotes-reformer-but-perhaps-not-reforms/ (Accessed 31 January 2021).

Dresch, P. (2013a) Societies, Identities and Local Issues, in Dresch, P. and Piscatori, J. (eds.) *Monarchies and Nations: Globalisation and Identity in the Arab States of the Gulf*. New York: I. B. Tauris, pp. 1–33. DOI:10.5040/9780755611645.0005.

Dresch, P. (2013b) Debates on Marriage and Nationality in the United Arab Emirates, in Dresch, P. and Piscatori, J. (eds.) *Monarchies and Nations: Globalisation and Identity in the Arab States of the Gulf*. New York: I. B. Tauris, pp. 136–157. DOI:10.5040/9780755611645.ch-006.

Driss, H.B. (2005) Women Narrating the Gulf: A Gulf of Their Own. *Journal of Arabic Literature*, 36(2), pp. 151–171. DOI:10.1163/1570064054909145.

Eggeling, K.A. (2017) Cultural Diplomacy in Qatar: Between "Virtual Enalrgement", National Identity Construction and Elite Legitimation. *International Journal of Cultural Policy*, 23(6), pp. 717–731. DOI:10.4324/9780429199714-6.

Ehteshami, A. (2013) *Dynamics of Change in the Persian Gulf. Political Economy, War and Revolution*. New York: Routledge. DOI:10.4324/9780203066256.

EPL (1973) *The Middle East and North Africa 1973–74. A Survey and Reference Book*. 20th Edition. London: Europa Publications Limited.

Fahy, J. (2018) Out of Sight, Out of Mind: Managing Religious Diversity in Qatar. *British Journal of Middle Eastern Studies*, 45(5), pp. 1–23. DOI:10.1080/13530194. 2018.1450138.

FAO (2018) Fast Facts: The State of the World's Land and Water Resources. United Nations Food and Agriculture Organization, [Online]. Available at: http://www.fao. org/fileadmin/user_upload/newsroom/docs/en-solaw-facts_1.pdf. (Accessed 31 January 2021).

Flamos, A., Roupas, C.V. and Psarras, J. (2013) GCC Economies Diversification: Still a Myth? *Energy Sources, Part B: Economics, Planning, and Policy*, 8(4), pp. 360–368. DOI:10.1080/15567240903515000.

Freer, C.J. (2018a) *Rentier Islamism. The Influence of the Muslim Brotherhood in the Gulf Monarchies*. Oxford: Oxford University Press. DOI:10.1093/oso/978019086 1995.001.0001.

Freer, C. (2018b) National identity and the Emirati State. LSE Blog, [Online]. Available at: https://blogs.lse.ac.uk/mec/2018/12/11/national-identity-and-the-emir-ati-state/ (Accessed 31 January 2021).

Freer, C. (2020) The Post-Sabah era in Kuwait. Brookings, [Online]. Available at: https://www.brookings.edu/blog/order-from-chaos/2020/09/30/the-post-sabah-era-in-kuwait/ (Accessed 31 January 2021).

Freer, C. and Cafiero, G. (2017) Is the Muslim Brotherhood's "Special Status" Over? *The New Arab*, [Online]. Available at: https://www.alaraby.co.uk/english/com-ment/2017/8/7/is-the-bahraini-muslim-brotherhoods-special-status-over (Accessed 31 January 2021).

Fromherz, A.J. (2012) *Qatar. A Modern History*. Washington, DC: Georgetown University Press.

Fuccaro, N. (2009) *Histories of City and State in the Persian Gulf. Manama since 1800*. Cambridge: Cambridge University Press. DOI:10.1017/cbo9780511605420.

Gardner, N. (2015) The Limits of the Sandhurst Connection: The Evolution of Oman's Foreign and Defense Policy, 1970–1977. *Journal of Middle East and Africa*, 6(6), pp. 45–58. DOI:10.1080/21520844.2015.1028850.

Gaub, F. and Stanley-Lockman, Z. (2017) Defence Industries in Arab States: Players and Strategies. Instute for Security Studies, [Online]. Available at: https://www.iss. europa.eu/sites/default/files/EUISSFiles/CP_141_Arab_Defence.pdf. (Accessed 31 January 2021).

Gengler, J.J. (2012) The Political Costs of Qatar's Western Orientation. *Middle East Policy*, 19(4), pp. 68–76. DOI:10.1111/j.1475-4967.2012.00560.x.

Gengler, J.J. (2014) Understanding Sectarianism in the Persian Gulf, in Potter, L.G. (ed.) *Sectarian Politics in the Persian Gulf*. Oxford: Oxford University Press, pp. 31–66.

Ghanem, S.M. (2001) Industrialization in the UAE, in Al Abed, I. and Hellyer, P. (eds) *United Arab Emirates: A New Perspective*. London: Trident Press, pp. 260–277.

Gharba, S. (2014) Kuwait: At the Crossroads of Change or Political Stagnation. Middle East Institute, [Online]. Available at: https://www.mei.edu/sites/default/ files/publications/Ghabra%20Policy%20Paper_0.pdf. (Accessed 31 January 2021).

Gierlichs, J. (2014) A Vision Becomes an Institution: The Museum of Islamic Art (MIA) in Doha, Qatar, in Wippel, S., Bromber, K., Steiner, C. and Krawietz, B. (eds.) *Under Construction: Logics of Urbanism in the Gulf Region*. Farnham: Ashgate, pp. 199–210.

Hanieh, A. (2011) *Capitalism and Class in the Gulf Arab States*. New York: Palgrave MacMillan. DOI:10.1057/9781137495105.

Harb, I.K. (2014) The Return of Strong GCC–U.S. Strategic Relations. National Council on U.S.-Arab Relations, [Online]. Available at: https://ncusar.org/publications/Publications/2014-11-26-return-gcc-us-relations.pdf. (Accessed 31 January 2021).

Harb, I.K. (2019) Why the United Arab Emirates is Abandoning Saudi Arabia in Yemen. *Foreign Policy*, [Online]. Available at: https://foreignpolicy.com/2019/08/01/why-the-united-arab-emirates-is-abandoning-saudi-arabia-in-yemen/ (Accessed 31 January 2021).

Hashimoto, K., Elass, J., and Eller, S. (2004) Liquified Natural Gas from Qatar: The Qatargas Project. Baker Institute, [Online]. Available at: https://www.bakerinstitute.org/media/files/Research/36c4f094/liquefied-natural-gas-from-qatar-the-qatargas-project.pdf (Accessed 31 January 2021).

Haverty, D. (2020) The Death of Kuwaiti Emir Sheikh Sabah Could Diminish the Country's International Standing. *Foreign Policy*, [Online]. Available at: https://foreignpolicy.com/2020/09/30/the-death-of-kuwaiti-emir-sheikh-sabah-could-diminish-the-countrys-international-standing/ (Accessed 31 January 2021).

Hedges, M. and Cafiero, G. (2017) The GCC and the Muslim Brotherhood: What Does the Future Hold? *Middle East Policy*, 24(1), pp. 129–153.

Heller, C.H. (2019) Little Sparta's Big Ambitions: The Emirati Military Comes of Age. *Real Clear Defence*, [Online]. Available at: https://www.realcleardefense.com/articles/2019/09/17/little_spartas_big_ambitions_the_emirati_military_comes_of_age_114748.html (Accessed 31 January 2021).

Hellyer, P. (2001) Evolution of UAE Foreign Policy, in Al Abed, I. (eds.) *United Arab Emirates: A New Perspective*. London: Trident Press, pp. 161–178.

Herb, M. (1999) *All in the Family: Absolutism, Revolution, and Democracy in the Middle Eastern Monarchies*. Albany: State University of New York Press.

Holes, C. (2013) Dialect and National Identity: The Cultural Politics of Self-Representation in Bahraini Musalsalat, in Dresch, P. and Piscatori, J. (eds.) *Monarchies and Nations: Globalisation and Identity in the Arab States of the Gulf*. New York: I.B. Tauris, pp. 52–72. DOI:10.5040/9780755611645.ch-002.

Hvidt, M. (2009) The Dubai Model: An Outline of Key Development-Process Elements in Dubai. *International Journal of Middle East Studies*, 41(3), pp. 398–401. DOI: 10.1017/s0020743809091120.

Hvidt, M. (2013) Economic Diversification in GCC Countries: Past Record and Future Trends. London School of Economics, [Online]. Available at: https://core.ac.uk/download/pdf/19578014.pdf (Accessed 31 January 2021).

IISS (2017) *The Military Balance 2017*. London: International Institute for Strategic Studies.

IISS (2018) *The Military Balance 2018*. London: International Institute for Strategic Studies.

IMF (2011) Gulf Cooperation Council Countries: Enhancing Economic Outcomes in an Uncertain Global Economy. International Monetary Fund, [Online]. Available at: https://www.imf.org/external/pubs/ft/dp/2011/1101mcd.pdf. (Accessed 31 January 2021).

IMF (2016) Economic Diversification in Oil-Exporting Arab Countries. International Monetary Fund, [Online]. Available at: https://www.imf.org/external/np/pp/eng/2016/042916.pdf (Accessed 31 January 2021).

IMF (2020) The Future of Oil and Fiscal Sustainability in the GCC region. International Monetary Fund, [Online]. Available at: https://www.imf.org/en/Publications/Departmental-Papers-Policy-Papers/Issues/2020/01/31/The-Future-of-Oil-and-Fiscal-Sustainability-in-the-GCC-Region-48934 (Accessed 31 January 2021).

INRA (2015) Addressing Agricultural Import Dependence in the Middle East–North Africa Region Through the Year 2050. INRA, [Online]. Available at: https://inra-dam-front-resources-cdn.brainsonic.com/ressources/afile/308329-e5409-resource-addressing-agricultural-import-dependence-in-the-middle-east-north-africa-region-through-to-the-year-2050.html (Accessed 31 January 2021).

Ismael, J.S. (1982) *Kuwait: Social Change in Historical Perspective*. Syracuse: Syracuse University Press.

Ismael, T.Y. and Ismael, J.S. (2011) *Government and Politics of the Contemporary Middle East. Continuity and Change*. London & New York: Routledge. DOI:10.4324/978020 3847459.

Issawi, C. (1982) *An Economic History of the Middle East and North Africa*. New York: Columbia University Press. DOI:10.4324/9781315888972.

Jensen, S. (2018) Policy Implications of the UAE's Economic Diversification Strategy: Prioritizing National Objectives, in Mishrif, A. and Al Balushi, Y. (eds.) *Economic Diversification in the Gulf Region, Volume 2*. Cambridge: Palgrave MacMillan & Gulf Research Centre, pp. 67–88. DOI:10.1007/978-981-10-5786-1_4.

Kamrava, M. (2014) The Foreign Policy of Qatar, in Hinnebusch, R. and Ehteshami, A. (eds.) *The Foreign Policies of Middle East States*. 2nd Edition. London: Lynne Rienner Publishers, pp. 157–184.

Kamrava, M. (2016) Weak States in the Middle East, in Kamrava, M. (ed.) *Fragile Politics. Weak States in the Greater Middle East*. Oxford: Oxford University Press, pp. 1–28. DOI:10.1093/acprof:oso/9780190246211.003.0001.

Karl, T.L. (1997) *The Paradox of Plenty. Oil Booms and Petro-States*. Berkely: University of California Press.

Katzman, K. (2020a) Oman: Reform, Security, and U.S. Policy. Congressional Research Service, [Online]. Available at: https://fas.org/sgp/crs/mideast/RS21534.pdf (Accessed 31 January 2021).

Katzman, K. (2020b) Qatar: Governance, Security, and U.S. Policy. Congressional Research Service, [Online]. Available at: https://fas.org/sgp/crs/mideast/R44533.pdf. (Accessed 31 January 2021).

Kharusi, N.S. (2013) Identity and Belonging among Ethnic Return Migrants of Oman. *Nationalism and Ethnic Politics*, 19(4), pp. 424–446. DOI:10.1080/13537113.2013.847600.

Kinninmont, J. (2011) Bahrain, in Davidson, C. (ed.) *Power and Politics in the Persian Gulf Monarchies*. London: Hurst & Company, pp. 31–62.

Kinninmont, Jane (2013) Citizenship in the Gulf, in Echague, A. (ed.) *The Gulf Arab States and the Arab Uprisings*. Spain: Fride & Gulf Research Centre, pp. 47–58.

Kinninmont, J. (2015) Future Trends in the Gulf. Chatham House Report, [Online]. Available at: https://www.chathamhouse.org/sites/default/files/field/field_document/20150218FutureTrendsGCCKinninmont.pdf (Accessed 31 January 2021).

Klitsch, M. (1994) Six Arab Gulf Nations Show Considerable Variation in Current Fertility Levels and Infant Mortality Rates. *International Family Planning Perspectives*, 20(2) pp.79-81. DOI:10.2307/2133444.

Koch, N. (2015) Gulf Nationalism and the Geopolitics of Constructing Falconry as a "Heritage Sport". *Studies in Ethnicity and Nationalism*, 15(3), pp. 522–539. DOI:10.1111/sena.12160.

Koren, M. and Tenreyro, S. (2012) Volatility, Diversification and Development in the Gulf Cooperation Council Countries, in Held, D. and Ulrichsen, K.C. (eds.) *The Transformation of the Gulf*. New York: Routledge, pp. 188–217.

Krawietz, B. (2014 Falconry as a Cultural Icon of the Arab Gulf Region, in Wippel, S., Bromber, K., Steiner, C., and Krawietz, B. (eds.) *Under Construction: Logics of Urbanism in the Gulf Region*. Farnham: Ashgate, pp. 131–146.

Lawson, F.J. (2011) Security Dilemmas in the Contemporary Persian Gulf, in Kamrava, M. (ed.) *International Politics of the Persian Gulf*. New York: Syracuse University Press, pp. 50–71.

Legrenzi, M. (2011) *The GCC and the International Relations of the Gulf. Diplomacy, Security and Economic Coordination in a Changing Middle East*. London & New York: I.B. Tauris. DOI:10.5040/9780755609086.

Longva, A.N. (1997) *Walls Built on Sand: Migration, Exclusion and Society in Kuwait*. Boulder: Westview Pres. DOI:10.4324/9780429503177.

Longva, A.N. (2013) Neither Autocracy Nor Democracy but Ethnocracy: Citizens, Expatriates and the Socio-Political System in Kuwait, in Dresch, P. and Piscatori, J. (eds.) *Monarchies and Nations: Globalisation and Identity in the Arab States of the Gulf*. New York: I.B. Tauris, pp. 114–135. DOI:10.5040/9780755611645. ch-005.

Louer, L. (2014) The State and Sectarian Identities in the Persian Gulf Monarchies. Bahrain, Saudi Arabia, and Kuwait in Comparative Perspectives, in Potter, L.G. (ed.) *Sectarian Politics in the Persian Gulf*. Oxford: Oxford University Press, pp. 117–142.

Luciani, G. (2005) Oil and Political Economy in the International Relations of the Middle East, in Fawcett, L. (ed.) *International Relations of the Middle East*. New York: Oxford University Press, pp. 79–104.

Lucas, R.E. (2004) Monarchical Authoritarianism: Survival and Political Liberalization in a Middle Eastern Regime Type. *International Journal of Middle East Studies*, 36(1), pp. 103–119. DOI:10.1017/s0020743804361064.

Lucas, R.E. (2014) Monarchies and Protests in the Arab Uprisings: Path Dependencies or Political Opportunities. *Journal of Arabian Studies*, 4(2), pp. 195–213.

Lucas, R.E., Demmelhuber, T. and Derichs, C. (2014) Introduction. *Journal of Arabian Studies*, 4(2), pp. 161–162.

Majidyar, A.K. (2013) Is Sectarian Balance in the United Arab Emirates, Oman and Qatar at Risk? American Enterprise Institute, [Online]. Available at: https://www.aei.org/research-products/report/is-sectarian-balance-in-the-united-arab-emirates-oman-and-qatar-at-risk/ (Accessed 31 January 2021).

Martini, J., Wasser, B., Kaye, D.D., Egel, D. and Ogletree, C. (2016) The Outlook for Arab Gulf Cooperation. Rand Corporation, [Online]. Available at: https://www.rand.org/content/dam/rand/pubs/research_reports/RR1400/RR1429/RAND_RR1429.pdf. (Accessed 31 January 2021).

Matthiesen, T. (2013) *Sectarian Gulf. Bahrain, Saudi Arabia and the Arab Spring that Wasn't*. Stanford: Stanford University Press. DOI:10.1515/9780804787222.

Matthiesen, T. (2015) *The Other Saudis. Shiism, Dissent and Sectarianism*. Cambridge: Cambridge University Press. DOI:10.1017/cbo9781107337732.

McGillivray, M. (2016) State Capacity and Aid Effectiveness in Weak States in the Greater Middle East, in Kamrava, M. (ed.) *Fragile Politics. Weak States in the*

Greater Middle East. Oxford: Oxford University Press, pp. 275–294. DOI:10.1093/acprof:oso/9780190246211.003.0012.

McLachlan, K. (1980) Natural Resources and Development in the Gulf States, in Niblock, T. (ed.) *Social and Economic Development in the Arab Gulf*. New York: St. Martin's Press, pp. 80–94.

Meilak, C. (2008) Measuring Export Concentration: The Implications for Small States. *Bank of Valletta Review*, 2008(37), pp. 35–48.

Mishrif, A. and Kapetanovic, H. (2018) Dubai's Model of Economic Diversification. in Mishrif, A. and Al Balushi, Y. (eds.) *Economic Diversification in the Gulf Region, Volume 2*. Cambridge: Palgrave MacMillan & Gulf Research Centre, pp. 89–112. DOI:10.1007/978-981-10-5786-1_5.

NCB Capital (2010) GCC Agriculture. *NCB Capital*, [Online]. Available at: https://www.gulfbase.com/ScheduleReports/GCC_Agriculture_Sector_March2010.pdf (Accessed 31 January 2021).

Ono, M. (2011) Reconsideration of the Meanings of Tribal Ties in the United Arab Emirates. Abu Dhabi Emirate in Early '90s. *Kyoto Bulletin of Islamic Area Studies*, 4(1–2), pp. 25–34.

Owtram, F. (2020) Oman after Qaboos: Continuities, Challenges and Choices. London School of Economics, [Online]. Available at: https://blogs.lse.ac.uk/mec/2020/01/24/oman-after-qaboos-continuities-challenges-and-choices/ (Accessed 31 January 2021).

Palanivel, T. (2017) Rapid Urbanisation: Opportunities and Challenges to Improve the Well-Being of Societies. *UNDP*, [Online]. Available at: http://hdr.undp.org/en/content/rapid-urbanisation-opportunities-and-challenges-improve-well-being-societies (Accessed 31 January 2021).

Patrick, N. (2012) Nationalism in the Gulf States, in Held, D. and Ulrichsen, K.C. (eds.) *The Transformation of the Gulf*. London & New York: Routledge, pp. 47–65.

Peck, M.C. (2001) Formation and Evolution of the Federation and Its Institutions, in Al Abed, I. and Hellyer, P. (eds) *United Arab Emirates: A New Perspective*. London: Trident Press, pp. 145–160.

Peterson, J.E. (2011) Sovereignty and Boundaries in the Gulf States. Setting the Peripheries, in Kamrava, M. (ed.) *International Politics of the Persian Gulf*. New York: Syracuse University Press, pp. 21–50.

Pollock, D. (2008) Slippery Polls. Uses and Abuses of Opinion Surveys from Arab States. The Washington Institute for Near East Policy, [Online]. Available at: https://www.washingtoninstitute.org/uploads/Documents/pubs/PolicyFocus82.pdf (Accessed 31 January 2021).

Pollack, K.M. (2020) Sizing Up Little Sparta. Understanding UAE Military Effectiveness. American Enterprise Institute, [Online]. Available at: https://www.aei.org/research-products/report/sizing-up-little-sparta-understanding-uae-military-effectiveness/ (Accessed 31 January 2021).

Potter, L.G. (2009) Introduction, in Potter, L.G. (ed.) *The Persian Gulf in History*. New York: Palgrave MacMillan, pp. 1–26.

Potter, L.G. (2014) Introduction, in Potter, L.G. (ed.) *Sectarian Politics in the Persian Gulf*. Oxford: Oxford University Press, pp. 1–30.

Rabi, U. (2016) "The Sultanate of Oman: Between Tribalism and National Unity, in Rabi, U. (ed.) *Tribes and States in the Changing Middle East*. London: Hurst & Co., pp. 76–95. DOI:10.1093/acprof:oso/9780190264925.003.0005.

Rahman, A. (2010) Migration and Human Rights in the Gulf. Middle East Institute, [Online]. Available at: http://www.mei.edu/content/migration-and-human-rights-gulf (Accessed 31 January 2021).

Ramadan, E. (2015) Sustainable Urbanization in the Arabian Gulf Region: Problems and Challenges. *Arts and Social Sciences Journal*, 6(2), pp. 1–4. DOI:10.4172/2151-6200.1000109.

Roberts, D.B. (2011) Kuwait, in Davidson, C. (ed.) *Power and Politics in the Persian Gulf Monarchies*. London: Hurst & Company, pp. 89–112.

Roberts, D.B. (2013) Qatar as a financial investor. *Norwegian Peacebuilding Resource Centre*, [Online]. Available at: http://noref.no/var/ezflow_site/storage/original/application/e61db69c6eebc2326b43638fde2576a3.pdf. (Accessed 31 January 2021).

Roberts, D.B. (2020) Bucking the Trend: The UAE and the Development of Military Capabilities in the Arab World. *Security Studies*, 29(2), pp. 1–34. DOI:10.1080/09636412.2020.1722852.

Rugh, A.B. (2007) *The Political Culture of Leadership in the United Arab Emirates*. New York: Palgrave. DOI:10.1057/9780230603493_12.

Rugh, A.B. (2016) Backgammon or Chess? The State of Tribalism and Tribal Leadership in the United Arab Emirates, in Rabi, U. (ed.) *Tribes and States in the Changing Middle East*. London: Hurst & Co., pp. 57–75. DOI:10.1093/acprof:oso/9780190264925.003.0004.

Rumaili, M.G. (1980) The Mode of Production in the Arab Gulf before the Discovery of Oil, in Niblock, T. (ed.) *Social and Economic Development in the Arab Gulf*. New York: St. Martin's Press, pp. 49–60.

Sadjadpour, K. (2011) The Battle of Dubai. *Carnegie Endowment*, [Online]. Available at: https://carnegieendowment.org/files/dubai_iran.pdf (Accessed 31 January 2021).

Said, B.M. (2015) The Future of Reform in Oman. *Contemporary Arab Affairs*, 9(1), pp. 49–67.

Sakr, N. (2013) Channels of Interaction: The Role of Gulf-Owned Media Firms in Globalisation, in Dresch, P. and Piscatori, J. (eds.) *Monarchies and Nations: Globalisation and Identity in the Arab States of the Gulf*. New York: I.B. Tauris, pp. 34–51.

Salisbury, P. (2020) Risk Perception and Appetite in UAE Foreign and National Security Policy. Chatham House, [Online]. Available at: https://www.chathamhouse.org/sites/default/files/2020-07-01-risk-in-uae-salisbury.pdf (Accessed 31 January 2021).

Salzman, P.C. (2016) Tribes and Modern States: An Alternative Approach, in Rabi, U. (ed.) *Tribes and States in the Changing Middle East*. London: Hurst & Co., pp. 207–219. DOI:10.1093/acprof:oso/9780190264925.003.0011.

Samaan, J. (2019) The Rise of the Emirati Defence Industry. Carnegie Endowment, [Online]. Available at: https://carnegieendowment.org/sada/79121 (Accessed 31 January 2021).

Samad, W.A. and Azar, E. (2019) Smart Cities in the Gulf: An Overview in Wael, in Samad, A. and Elie, A. (eds.) *Smart Cities in the Gulf*. Cambridge: Palgrave MacMillan & Gulf Research Centre, pp. 3–6. DOI:10.1007/978-981-13-2011-8_1.

Sastry, G.R.N. (1994) Qatar's Economy Transition from Oil Based Economy to Gas Based Economy. Ministry of Energy & Industry of the State of Qatar, [Online]. Available at: http://www.iaea.org/inis/collection/NCLCollectionStore/_Public/24/055/24055009.pdf (Accessed 31 January 2021).

Sater, J. (2017) Migration and the Marginality of Citizenship in the Arab Gulf Region: Human Security and High Modernist Tendencies, in Meijer, R. and Butenschøn, N. (eds.) *The Crisis of Citizenship in the Arab World*. Leiden: Brill, pp. 223–245. DOI:10.1163/9789004340985_010.

Setser, B. and Ziemba, R. (2009) GCC Sovereign Funds. Reversal of Fortune. Council of Foreign Relations, [Online]. Available at: https://www.cfr.org/content/publications/attachments/CGS_WorkingPaper_5.pdf (Accessed 31 January 2021).

Shahid, A.S. and Mushtaque, A. (2014) Changing Face of Agriculture in the Gulf Cooperation Council Countries, in Shahid, S.A. and Ahmed, M. (eds.) *Environmental Cost and Face of Agriculture in the Gulf Cooperation Council Countries*. London: Springer & Gulf Research Centre Cambridge, pp. 1–26. DOI:10.1007/978-3-319-05768-2_1.

Sievers, M.J. (2020) Sultan Haitham makes a strong start by addressing economic challenges. Atlantic Council, [Online]. Available at: https://www.atlanticcouncil.org/blogs/menasource/sultan-haitham-makes-a-strong-start-by-addressing-economic-challenges/ (Accessed 31 January 2021).

Sluglett, P. (2002) The Resilience of a Frontier: Ottoman and Iraqi Claims to Kuwait, 1871–1990. *The International History Review*, 24(4), pp. 783–816. DOI:10.1080/07075332.2002.9640981.

Sultan Qaboos (1975) Khitab Jalalatuhu fee al-Eid al-Watanee al-Khamis. The Official Website of Sultan Qaboos, [Online]. Available at: http://www.sultanqaboos.net/article-action-s-id-61.htm (Accessed 31 January 2021).

Sultan Qaboos (1976) Khitab Jalalatuhu fee al-Eid al-Watanee al-Sadis. The Official Website of Sultan Qaboos, [Online]. Available at: http://www.sultanqaboos.net/article-action-s-id-60.htm (Accessed 31 January 2021).

Sultan Qaboos (1981) Khitab Jalalatuhu fee al-Eid al-Watanee al-'Asir'. The Official Website of Sultan Qaboos, [Online]. Available at: http://www.sultanqaboos.net/article-action-s-id-56.htm (Accessed 31 January 2021).

SWFI (2020) Top 92 Largest Sovereign Wealth Fund Rankings by Total Assets. Strategic Wealth Fund Institute, [Online]. Available at: https://www.swfinstitute.org/fund-rankings/sovereign-wealth-fund (Accessed 31 January 2021).

Tadros, M.E. (2015) The Arab Gulf States and the Knowledge Economy: Challenges and Opportunities. The Arab Gulf States Institute in Washington, [Online]. Available at: http://www.agsiw.org/wp-content/uploads/2015/07/Tadros_Knowledge-Economy_Rev1.pdf (Accessed 31 January 2021).

Takriti, A.R. (2013) The 1970 Coup in Oman Reconsidered. *Journal of Arabian Studies: Arabia, the Gulf, and the Red Sea*, 3(2), pp. 155–173. DOI:10.1080/21534764.2013.863682.

Telhami, S. and Barnett, M. (2002) Introduction: Identity and Foreign Policy in the Middle East, in Telhami, S. and Barnett, M. (eds.) *Identity and Foreign Policy in the Middle East*. Ithaca & London: Cornell University Press, pp. 1–25.

Tetreault, M.A. (2011) Identity and Transplant-University Education in the Gulf: The American University in Kuwait. *Journal of Arabian Studies: Arabia, the Gulf, and the Red Sea*, 1(1), pp. 81–98. DOI:10.1080/21534764.2011.576052.

TDT (2018) Construction Sector is the Biggest Consumer of Wood in the GCC. *Timber Design & Technology*, [Online]. Available at: http://www.timberdesignandtechnology.com/construction-sector-is-the-biggest-consumer-of-wood-in-the-gcc/ (Accessed 31 January 2021).

Trading Economics (2020) Brent Crude Oil. *Trading Economics*, [Online]. Available at: https://tradingeconomics.com/commodity/brent-crude-oil (Accessed 31 January 2021).

Tok, M.E. and Alkhater, L.R.M. and Pal, L.A. (2016) Policy-Making in a Transformative State: The Case of Qatar, in Tok, M.E. and Alkhater, L.R.M. and

Pal, L.A. (eds.) *Policy-Making in a Transformative State. The Case of Qatar.* London: Palgrave MacMillan, pp. 1–36. DOI:10.1057/978-1-137-46639-6_1.

Ulrichsen, C.K. (2011) *Insecure Gulf. The End of Certainty and the Transition to the Post-Oil Era.* New York: Columbia University Press.

Ulrichsen, C.K. (2014) Bahrain's Uprising: Domestic Implications and Regional and International Perspectives, in Gerges, F. (ed.) *The New Middle East. Protest and Revolution in the Arab World.* Cambridge: Cambridge University Press, pp. 332–352.

Ulrichsen, K.C. (2016) *The Gulf States in International Political Economy.* Hampshire: Palgrave MacMillan. DOI:10.1057/9781137385611.

UNCTAD (2016) State Commodity Dependence 2016. UNCTAD, [Online]. Available at: http://unctad.org/en/PublicationsLibrary/suc2017d2.pdf. (Accessed 31 January 2021).

UNDL (2020) United Nations Digital Library [Online]. Available at: https://digitallibrary.un.org/?ln=en (Accessed 31 January 2021).

UNDP (2011) Towards Human Resilience: Sustaining MDG Progress in an Age of Economic Uncertainty. UNDP, [Online]. Available at: http://www.undp.org/content/dam/undp/library/Poverty%20Reduction/Towards_SustainingMDG_Web1005.pdf (Accessed 31 January 2021).

UNSC (1971) 1610th Meeting: 9 December 1971. UN Security Council, [Online]. Available at: https://undocs.org/en/S/PV.1610(or) (Accessed 31 January 2021).

UNSC (1973a) 1719th Meeting: 8 June 1973. UN Security Council, [Online]. Available at: https://undocs.org/en/S/PV.1719(or) (Accessed 31 January 2021).

UNSC (1973b) 1726th Meeting: 14 June 1973. UN Security Council, [Online]. Available at: http://daccess-ods.un.org/access.nsf/Get?Open&DS=S/PV.1726(OR)&Lang=E (Accessed 31 January 2021).

UNSC (1974) 1764th Meeting: 28 February 1974. UN Security Council, [Online]. Available at: https://undocs.org/en/S/PV.1764(or) (Accessed 31 January 2021).

UNSC (1978) 2075th Meeting: 19 March 1978. UN Security Council, [Online]. Available at: http://daccess-ods.un.org/access.nsf/Get?Open&DS=S/PV.2075(OR)&Lang=E (Accessed 31 January 2021).

UNSC (1979) 2163rd Meeting: 24 August 1979. UN Security Council, [Online]. Available at: Records, http://daccess-ods.un.org/access.nsf/Get?Open&DS=S/PV.2163(OR)&Lang=E (Accessed 31 January 2021).

UNSC (1983a) 2414th Meeting: 16 February 1983. UN Security Council, [Online]. Available at: https://undocs.org/en/S/PV.2414(OR) (Accessed 31 January 2021).

UNSC (1983b) 2460th Meeting: 2 August 1983. UN Security Council, [Online]. Available at: http://daccess-ods.un.org/access.nsf/Get?Open&DS=S/PV.2460(OR)&Lang=E. (Accessed 31 January 2021).

UNSC (1984a) 2541st Meeting: 25 May 1984. UN Security Council, [Online]. Available at: http://daccess-ods.un.org/access.nsf/Get?Open&DS=S/PV.2541(OR)&Lang=E (Accessed 31 January 2021).

UNSC (1984b) 2543rd Meeting: 29 May 1984. UN Security Council, [Online]. Available at: http://daccess-ods.un.org/access.nsf/Get?Open&DS=S/PV.2543(OR)&Lang=E (Accessed 31 January 2021).

UNSC (1984c) 2546th Meeting: 1 June 1984. UN Security Council, [Online]. Available at: http://daccess-ods.un.org/access.nsf/Get?Open&DS=S/PV.2546(OR)&Lang=E (Accessed 31 January 2021).

UNSC (1984d) 2554th Meeting: 31 August 1984. UN Security Council, [Online]. Available at: https://undocs.org/en/S/PV.2554(OR) (Accessed 31 January 2021).

UNSC (1985a) 2594th Meeting: 17 June 1985. UN Security Council, [Online]. Available at: https://undocs.org/en/S/PV.2594(or) (Accessed 31 January 2021).

UNSC (1985b) 2616th Meeting: 7 October 1985. UN Security Council, [Online]. Available at: https://undocs.org/en/S/PV.2616(or) (Accessed 31 January 2021).

UNSC (1986a) 2650th Meeting: 30 January 1986. UN Security Council, [Online]. Available at: https://undocs.org/en/S/PV.2650 (Accessed 31 January 2021).

UNSC (1986b) 2671st Meeting: 31 March 1986. UN Security Council, [Online]. Available at: https://undocs.org/en/S/PV.2671 (Accessed *31 January 2021*).

UNSC (1986c) 2674th Meeting: 15 April 1986. UN Security Council, [Online]. Available at: https://undocs.org/en/S/PV.2674 (Accessed 31 January 2021).

UNSC (1986d) 2675th Meeting: 15 April 1986. UN Security Council, [Online]. Available at: http://daccess-ods.un.org/access.nsf/Get?Open&DS=S/PV.2675&Lang=E. (Accessed 31 January 2021).

UNSC (1986e) 2697th Meeting: 3 July 1986. UN Security Council, [Online]. Available at: https://undocs.org/en/S/PV.2697 (Accessed 31 January 2021).

UNSC (1986f) 2710th Meeting: 3 October 1986. UN Security Council, [Online]. Available at: http://daccess-ods.un.org/access.nsf/Get?Open&DS=S/PV.2710&Lang=E. (Accessed 31 January 2021).

UNSC (1989) 2840th Meeting: 12 January 1989. UN Security Council, [Online]. Available at: https://undocs.org/en/S/PV.2840 (Accessed 31 January 2021).

UNSC (1990a) 2932nd Meeting: 2 August 1990. UN Security Council, [Online]. Available at: http://daccess-ods.un.org/access.nsf/Get?Open&DS=S/PV.2932&Lang=E. (Accessed 31 January 2021).

UNSC (1990b) 2933rd Meeting: 6 August 1990. UN Security Council, [Online]. Available at: http://daccess-ods.un.org/access.nsf/Get?Open&DS=S/PV.2933&Lang=E. (Accessed 31 January 2021).

UNSC (1990c) 2938th Meeting: 25 August 1990. UN Security Council, [Online]. Available at: http://daccess-ods.un.org/access.nsf/Get?Open&DS=S/PV.2938&Lang=E. (Accessed 31 January 2021).

UNSC (1990d) 2943rd Meeting: 25 September 1990. UN Security Council, [Online]. Available at: http://daccess-ods.un.org/access.nsf/Get?Open&DS=S/PV.2943&Lang=E. (Accessed 31 January 2021).

UNSC (1990e) 2960th Meeting: 27 November 1990. UN Security Council, [Online]. Available at: http://daccess-ods.un.org/access.nsf/Get?Open&DS=S/PV.2960&Lang=E. (Accessed 31 January 2021).

UNSC (1990f) 2963rd Meeting: 29 November 1990. UN Security Council, [Online]. Available at: http://daccess-ods.un.org/access.nsf/Get?Open&DS=S/PV.2963&Lang=E. (Accessed 31 January 2021).

UNSC (1991) 2981st Meeting: 3 April 1991. UN Security Council, [Online]. Available at: http://daccess-ods.un.org/access.nsf/Get?Open&DS=S/PV.2981&Lang=E. (Accessed 31 January 2021).

UNSC (1992) 3137th Meeting: 16 November 1992. UN Security Council, [Online]. Available at: http://daccess-ods.un.org/access.nsf/Get?Open&DS=S/PV.3137&Lang=E. (Accessed 31 January 2021).

UNSC (1994a) 3336th Meeting: 14 February 1994. UN Security Council, [Online]. Available at: http://daccess-ods.un.org/access.nsf/Get?Open&DS=S/PV.3336&Lang=E. (Accessed 31 January 2021).

UNSC (1994b) 3367th Meeting: 21 April 1994. UN Security Council, [Online]. Available at: https://undocs.org/en/S/PV.3367.

UNSC (1994c) 3438th Meeting: 15 October 1994. UN Security Council, [Online]. Available at: http://daccess-ods.un.org/access.nsf/Get?Open&DS=S/PV.3438&Lang=E. (Accessed 31 January 2021).

UNSC (1995a) 3553rd Meeting: 12 July 1995. UN Security Council, [Online]. Available at: http://daccess-ods.un.org/access.nsf/Get?Open&DS=S/PV.3553&Lang=E. (Accessed 31 January 2021).

UNSC (1995b) 3564th Meeting: 10 August 1995. UN Security Council, [Online]. Available at: http://daccess-ods.un.org/access.nsf/Get?Open&DS=S/PV.3564&Lang=E. (Accessed 31 January 2021).

UNSC (1998) 3954th Meeting: 16 December 1998. UN Security Council, [Online]. Available at: http://daccess-ods.un.org/access.nsf/Get?Open&DS=S/PV.3954&Lang=E. (Accessed 31 January 2021).

UNSC (1999a) 4069th Meeting: 15 November 1999. UN Security Council, [Online]. Available at: http://daccess-ods.un.org/access.nsf/Get?Open&DS=S/PV.4069&Lang=E. (Accessed 31 January 2021).

UNSC (1999b) 4072nd Meeting: 30 November 1999. UN Security Council, [Online]. Available at: http://daccess-ods.un.org/access.nsf/Get?Open&DS=S/PV.4072 (Resumption1)&Lang=E. (Accessed 31 January 2021).

UNSC (1999c) 4078th Meeting: 10 December 1999. *UN Security Council*, [Online]. Available at: http://daccess-ods.un.org/access.nsf/Get?Open&DS=S/PV.4078&Lang=E. (Accessed 31 January 2021).

UNSC (1999d) 4081st Meeting: 15 December 1999. UN Security Council, [Online]. Available at: http://daccess-ods.un.org/access.nsf/Get?Open&DS=S/PV.4081&Lang=E. (Accessed 31 January 2021).

UNSC (1999e) 4085th Meeting: 22 December 1999. UN Security Council, [Online]. Available at: http://daccess-ods.un.org/access.nsf/Get?Open&DS=S/PV.4085&Lang=E. (Accessed 31 January 2021).

UNSC (2000) 4130th Meeting: 19 April 2000. UN Security Council, [Online]. Available at: http://daccess-ods.un.org/access.nsf/Get?Open&DS=S/PV.4130&Lang=E. (Accessed 31 January 2021).

UNSC (2002a) 4525th Meeting: 3 May 2002. UN Security Council, [Online]. Available at: https://undocs.org/en/S/PV.4525(resumption1) (Accessed 15 September 2018).

UNSC (2002b) 4538th Meeting: 22 May 2002. UN Security Council, [Online]. Available at: http://daccess-ods.un.org/access.nsf/Get?Open&DS=S/PV.4538&Lang=E. (Accessed 31 January 2021).

UNSC (2002c) 4625th Meeting: 16 October 2002. UN Security Council, [Online]. Available at: http://daccess-ods.un.org/access.nsf/Get?Open&DS=S/PV.4625(Resumption2) &Lang=E. (Accessed 31 January 2021).

UNSC (2005) 5319th Meeting: 9 December 2005. UN Security Council, [Online]. Available at: http://daccess-ods.un.org/access.nsf/Get?Open&DS=S/PV.5319&Lang=E. (Accessed 31 January 2021).

UNSC (2006) 5474th Meeting: 22 June 2006. UN Security Council, [Online]. Available at: http://daccess-ods.un.org/access.nsf/Get?Open&DS=S/PV.5474&Lang=E. (Accessed 31 January 2021).

UNSC (2007a) 5663rd Meeting: 17 April 2007. UN Security Council, [Online]. Available at: http://daccess-ods.un.org/access.nsf/Get?Open&DS=S/PV.5663&Lang=E. (Accessed 31 January 2021).

UNSC (2007b) 5705th Meeting: 25 June 2007. UN Security Council, [Online]. Available at: http://daccess-ods.un.org/access.nsf/Get?Open&DS=S/PV.5705&Lang=E. (Accessed 31 January 2021).

UNSC (2010) 6300th Meeting: 22 April 2010. UN Security Council, [Online]. Available at: http://daccess-ods.un.org/access.nsf/Get?Open&DS=S/PV.6300&Lang=E. (Accessed 31 January 2021).

UNSC (2011) 6587th Meeting: 20 July 2011. UN Security Council, [Online]. Available at: http://daccess-ods.un.org/access.nsf/Get?Open&DS=S/PV.6587&Lang=E. (Accessed 31 January 2021).

UNSC (2013) 6982nd Meeting: 19 June 2013. UN Security Council, [Online]. Available at: http://daccess-ods.un.org/access.nsf/Get?Open&DS=S/PV.6982&Lang=E. (Accessed 31 January 2021).

UNSC (2014a) 7164th Meeting: 29 April 2014. UN Security Council, [Online]. Available at: http://daccess-ods.un.org/access.nsf/Get?Open&DS=S/PV.7164&Lang=E. (Accessed 31 January 2021).

UNSC (2014b) 7271st Meeting: 19 September 2014. *UN Security Council*, [Online]. Available at: http://daccess-ods.un.org/access.nsf/Get?Open&DS=S/PV.7271&Lang=E. (Accessed 31 January 2021).

UNSC (2014c) 7281st Meeting: 21 October 2014. UN Security Council, [Online]. Available at: http://daccess-ods.un.org/access.nsf/Get?Open&DS=S/PV.7281&Lang=E. (Accessed 31 January 2021).

UNSC (2015) 7389th Meeting: 23 February 2015. UN Security Council, [Online]. Available at: http://daccess-ods.un.org/access.nsf/Get?Open&DS=S/PV.7389&Lang=E. (Accessed 31 January 2021).

UNSC (2017) 7929th Meeting: 20 April 2017. UN Security Council, [Online]. Available at: http://daccess-ods.un.org/access.nsf/Get?Open&DS=S/PV.7929&Lang=E. (Accessed 31 January 2021).

UNSC (2017b) 7419th Meeting: 27 March 2017. UN Security Council, [Online]. Available at: http://daccess-ods.un.org/access.nsf/Get?Open&DS=S/PV.7419&Lang=E. (Accessed 31 January 2021).

UNSC (2018a) 8262nd Meeting: 17 May 2018. UN Security Council, [Online]. Available at: https://undocs.org/en/S/PV.8262 (Accessed 31 January 2021).

UNSC (2018b) 8293rd Meeting: 25 June 2018. UN Security Council, [Online]. Available at: https://undocs.org/en/S/PV.8293 (Accessed 31 January 2021).

UNSC (2018c) 8316th Meeting: 24 July 2018. UN Security Council, [Online]. Available at: https://undocs.org/en/S/PV.8316 (Accessed 31 January 2021).

UNSC (2018d) 8334th Meeting: 29 August 2018. UN Security Council, [Online]. Available at: https://undocs.org/en/S/PV.8334 (Accessed 31 January 2021).

UNSC (2018e) 8372nd Meeting: 16 October 2018. UN Security Council, [Online]. Available at: https://undocs.org/en/S/PV.8372 (Accessed 31 January 2021).

UNSC (2018f) 8375th Meeting: 17 October 2018. UN Security Council, [Online]. Available at: https://undocs.org/en/S/PV.8375 (Accessed 31 January 2021).

UNSC (2018g) 8395th Meeting: 9 November 2018. UN Security Council, [Online]. Available at: https://undocs.org/en/S/PV.8395 (Accessed 31 January 2021).

UNSC (2019a) 8496th Meeting: 28 March 2019. UN Security Council, [Online]. Available at: https://undocs.org/en/S/PV.8496 (Accessed 31 January 2021).

UNSC (2019b) 8514th Meeting: 23 April 2019. UN Security Council, [Online]. Available at: https://undocs.org/en/S/PV.8514 (Accessed 31 January 2021).

UNSC (2019c) 8600th Meeting: 20 August 2019. UN Security Council, [Online]. Available at: https://undocs.org/en/S/PV.8600 (Accessed 31 January 2021).

UNSC (2019d) 8633rd Meeting: 7 October 2019. UN Security Council, [Online]. Available at: https://undocs.org/en/S/PV.8633 (Accessed 31 January 2021).

UNSC (2019e) 8648th Meeting: 28 October 2019. UN Security Council, [Online]. Available at: https://undocs.org/en/S/PV.8648 (Accessed 31 January 2021).

UNSC (2019f) 8668th Meeting: 19 November 2019. UN Security Council, [Online]. Available at: https://undocs.org/en/S/PV.8668 (Accessed 31 January 2021).

UNSC (2020a) United Nations Security Council. UN Security Council, [Online]. Available at: https://www.un.org/securitycouncil/search/member (Accessed 31 January 2021).

UNSC (2020b) 8699th Meeting: 10 January 2020. UN Security Council, [Online]. Available at: https://undocs.org/en/S/PV.8699%20(Resumption1) (Accessed 31 January 2021).

Yang, L. (2015) The Rise of the Middle East Sovereign Wealth Funds: Causes, Consequences and Policies. *Journal of Middle Eastern and Islamic Studies*, 9(2), pp. 16–37.

Valeri, M. (2011) Oman, in Davidson, C. (eds.) *Power and Politics in the Persian Gulf Monarchies*. London: Hurst & Co, pp. 135–161.

Valeri, M. (2014) Identity Politics and Nation-Building under Sultan Qaboos, in Potter, L.G. (ed.) *Sectarian Politics in the Persian Gulf*. Oxford: Oxford University Press, pp. 179–206.

Valeri, M. (2017) So Close, So Far. National Identity and Political Legitimacy in UAE–Oman Border Cities. *Geopolitics*, 23(3), pp. 587–607. DOI:10.1080/14650045 .2017.1410794.

Wagner, P. (2020) Az Egyesült Arab Emírségek biztonságpolitikájának átalakulása: az operetthadseregtől az aktív szerepvállalásig. *Biztonságpolitika.hu*, [Online]. Available at: https://biztonsagpolitika.hu/egyeb/az-egyesult-arab-emirsegek-biztonsagpolitikajanak-atalakulasa-az-operetthadseregtol-az-aktiv-szerepvallalasig (Accessed 31 January 2021).

Wehrey, F. (2014) Gulf Participation in the Anti-Islamic State Coalition: Limitations and Costs. Carnegie Middle East Centre, [Online]. Available at: http://carnegie-mec.org/diwan/56710?lang=en (Accessed 31 January 2021).

Wilkinson, J.C. (1980) Changes in the Structure of Village Life in Oman, in Niblock, T. (ed.) *Social and Economic Development in the Arab Gulf*. New York: St. Martin's Press, pp. 122–134.

Winckler, O. (2000) The Challenge of Foreign Workers in the Persian/Arabian Gulf: The Case of Oman. *Immigrants & Minorities: Historical Studies in Ethnicity, Migration and Diaspora*, 19(2), pp. 23–52. DOI:10.1080/02619288.2000.9974990.

Winckler, O. (2010) Labor Migration to the GCC States: Patterns, Scale and Policies. The Middle East Institute, [Online]. Available at: http://www.mei.edu/content/labor-migration-gcc-states-patterns-scale-and-policies (Accessed 31 January 2021).

Woertz, E., Pradhan, S., Biberovic, N. and Jingzhong, C. (2008) Potential for GCC Agro-investments in Africa and Central Asia. Gulf Research Centre, [Online]. Available at: https://www.files.ethz.ch/isn/111335/Potential_for_GCC_Agro_5729. pdf (Accessed 31 January 2021).

World Bank (2021). *World Bank Database*, [Online]. Available at: http://data.worldbank.org (Accessed 31 January 2021).

Wright, S. (2011) Foreign Policy in the GCC States, in Kamrava, M. (ed.) *International Politics of the Persian Gulf*. New York: Syracuse University Press, pp. 72–94.

WVS (2021) World Value Survey, [Online]. Available at: http://www.worldvaluessurvey.org/wvs.jsp (Accessed 31 January 2021).

Zaidan, E. and Abulibdeh, A. (2020) Master Planning and the Evolving Urban Model in the Gulf Cities: Principles, Policies, and Practices for the Transition to

Sustainable Urbanism. *Planning Practice & Research*. DOI:10.1080/02697459.2020
.1829278.

Zaccara, L. (2013) Comparing Elections in Gulf Cooperation Council Countries
after the Arab Spring: The United Arab Emirates, Oman, and Kuwait. *Journal of
Arabian Studies: Arabia, the Gulf, and the Red Sea*, 3(1), pp. 80–101. DOI:10.1080/
21534764.2013.802941.

Zogby, J. (2013) *Looking at Iran*. Zogby Research Services, E-book format [Online].

Zurayk, R. and Gough, A. (2014) Bread and Olive Oil: The Agrarian Roots of the
Arab Uprisings, in Gerges, F. (ed.) *The New Middle East. Protest and Revolution in
the Arab World*. Cambridge: Cambridge University Press, pp. 107–135. DOI:10.1017/
cbo9781139236737.006.

5 The foreign and security policy history of smaller Gulf states (1968–2011)

In this chapter, three case studies will be presented regarding some of the most pressing dilemmas and questions facing the smaller Gulf states. Instead of providing a more general foreign policy overview, this structure was chosen to reflect on some of the most important theoretical issues identified by the International Relations literature in Chapter 1. These questions involve preferring independence as a small state over belonging to a political federation (i.e. the integration dilemma); threat perception and security policy decisions in light of external threats; and tendencies of alliance policy.

Debates regarding a Gulf union (1968–1971) as a form of integration dilemma

Developments described in Chapter 2 paved the way for the independence of Kuwait (1961), Bahrain (1971), and Qatar (1971), as well as the United Arab Emirates, formally called the Trucial States (Abu Dhabi, Dubai, Sharjah, Umm al-Quwain, Ra's al-Khaimah, al-Fujairah, and Ajman). Locked between Iran, Iraq, and Saudi Arabia, the rulers of the small emirates engaged in a series of negotiations about political unity between themselves, which involved the Trucial States, Qatar, and Bahrain. Kuwait and Oman were largely excluded from the process due to their special status, Kuwait having been independent since 1961 and Oman remaining formally outside the trucial system.[1] As a result of the negotiations, the United Arab Emirates was founded in 1971 and initially comprised five members (Abu Dhabi, Dubai, Umm al-Quwain, al-Fujairah, and Ajman), being joined later by Ra's al-Khaimah.[2] Despite their geopolitical exposure to their larger neighbours, Bahrain and Qatar decided to leave the negotiations and try their independence separately.

The decision regarding participation was a form of integration dilemma between sovereignty and influence. While, in retrospect, the individual decision of each country may seem self-explanatory, in the given historical context, it was a result of severe geopolitical calculations, which were determined, among other matters, by the size of the different countries.

The British decision to withdraw from the Persian Gulf region did not come out of the blue in the late 1960s. As a mandatory power, London was a

DOI: 10.4324/9781003158288-6

primal actor in the Middle East after World War I in Iraq, Jordan, Palestine, and the Gulf; nonetheless, by the second half of the 1950s, the British focus was almost solely in the Persian Gulf (Pickering, 1998, p. 105). The changing British policy was due to structural economic and political reasons coupled with Britain's realisation that it lacked vital national interests east of the Suez, which would be worth investing in heavily (McCourt, 2009).

The British decision came as a surprise to Gulf leaders (Heard-Bey, 1999, p. 129). After the independence of Kuwait, London assured local leaders that they had no intention of pulling out the approximately 6,000 British troops, which remained the official policy until the second half of the 1960s. In a White Paper about defence policy issued in 1966, the British government announced that they would abandon the Aden base in a few years and "South Arabia [today's Yemen] is due to become independent not later than 1968" (Ministry of Defence, 1966, p. 233). Nonetheless, in this document, London proclaimed that it would increase its remaining military presence in the Persian Gulf in order to fulfil its obligations set by the treaties made with the Gulf emirates. Even in the Supplemental White Paper on Defence published in July 1967, there was "nothing to indicate that the government was planning a future withdrawal from the area" (Heard-Bey, 1999, p. 129).

The reason behind this delayed announcement was a prolonged debate within the government. The Board of Trade and the Treasury agreed that the primary British interest in the region (namely, safe access to oil) could be reached through "normal diplomatic and commercial procedures", while the Foreign Office believed that military presence was vital in the process (Dockrill, 2002, p. 52).[3] Nonetheless, after recalculating the costs and the domestic political implications, normal diplomatic and commercial procedures were chosen as the way forward (Dockrill, 2002, pp. 153–155).

It was only on 16 January 1968 that the British government announced its withdrawal from the territory by 1971 (Heard-Bey, 1999, p. 129). The declaration took the emirs by surprise: state-building was yet to be final, security capacities were lacking, and even border disputes had not been settled in a satisfying manner.[4] These debates were the causes, rather than the reasons, for the historical mistrust between smaller emirates, on the one hand, and between the smaller emirates and their larger neighbours, on the other (Okruhlik and Conge, 1999, p. 248.; Friedman, 2017, pp. 113–114).

Nevertheless, as a result of the sudden shock of the announcement, the emirs of Abu Dhabi and Dubai invited their neighbours for official negotiations on 18 February, which marked the commencement of the federalisation of the Gulf. The decision to engage in dialogue regarding a political unity "followed the gradual evolving of a consensus that their small population, their small size, (…) and their poverty (…) did not permit the emirates independently, or in smaller groupings, to establish a viable, independent, political and constitutional entity" (Al Abed, 2001, p. 121). Political leaders realised that, due to their military weakness and accompanied by huge oil resources, relative deterrence was unachievable; as Rosmarie Said Zahlan (1978, p. 194) argues, they realised that "the enormous wealth, small size and strategic location of the shaykhdoms made them especially vulnerable to any kind of threat."

Talks about possible Gulf unity were not without precedent (Smith, 2002, pp. 49–77; Al Abed, 2001, pp. 121–126). The first proposal to integrate the Trucial States Bahrain, Kuwait, and Qatar was made by Great Britain in 1937. The question remained on the agenda for a couple of years, but no implementation followed. Later, in the 1950s and 1960s, the idea resurfaced in the British government, primarily because of questions regarding the viability and sustainability of such small entities in the region. Nonetheless, official meetings organised by London among the Gulf sheiks usually took place in a formal and distanced manner, as a result of which British diplomats felt that the only reason the tribal leaders participated in the meetings was to show courtesy to London. Besides historical distrust between the ruling families, a major obstacle in any kind of serious integration dialogue was the perceived relative largeness of the emirates: Kuwait and Abu Dhabi in terms of economy, Bahrain in terms of population, and Qatar in terms of state institutional capacities. Moreover, these "larger" emirates engaged in a competition of influence over the smaller emirates. London also did not see how the integration could work independently in a way in which British influence would not vanish.

The differing sizes of the Gulf monarchies also played an important role in the negotiations that started in February 1968 (Heard-Bey, 1999, p. 29). While Abu Dhabi, Dubai, Bahrain, and Qatar wanted to maintain control over their relative wealth (Friedman, 2017, p. 113), the five smallest emirates – the Northern emirates of the UAE, or the "little five" as British diplomats called them – found themselves between a rock and a hard place. On the one hand, they wanted to restrain some form of independence, while, on the other, they sought protection and a share from their neighbours' oil incomes. Four of the five Northern emirates usually supported Abu Dhabi and the *Nahyans*, due to its perceived richness[5] and the closeness to their inner Omani identity (Friedman, 2017, pp. 119–120). Ras al-Khaimah, on the other hand, frequently stood independently and wanted to use its brotherly relations with the *Saud* family in order to put pressure on the larger emirates. In all, all five Northern emirates complained that the negotiations were dominated by the four "big monarchies" – Bahrain, Qatar, Abu Dhabi, and Dubai. At one point, the Qatari Emir even suggested that the five smaller emirates should be represented by a single ruler who should only have one vote (Smith, 2002, pp. 80–81).

The interesting notion here is not the fact that the relative size of the smaller emirates mattered but, rather, the fact that it mattered more than the threat perceived from Iran and/or Saudi Arabia. While all the political leaders were engaged in fighting with each other, both powers wanted to expend their influence. The logic of both realism and tribal political thought would suggest that, facing an external threat while losing British protection, smaller Gulf emirates should have cooperated to a much greater extent (Friedman, 2017, p. 114).[6] Nevertheless, the Gulf states "did indeed realize the risk of falling under the influence of powerful neighbours such as Saudi Arabia if they remained independently separate, they loathed even more the idea of surrendering their national prerogatives to a federal government structure" (Legrenzi, 2011, p. 18).

Talks on a merger were, therefore, rocky from the beginning. The invitation made by the leaders of Abu Dhabi and Dubai on their bilateral meeting on 18 February 1968 did not aim to create a new integration together by finding common ground but, rather, to join a union of Abu Dhabi and Dubai, the foundations of which they had already decided on at their separate meeting. According to their offering, the federation would include joint decision making in the areas of foreign affairs, defence, security, immigration, and social questions, while the remaining judicial and internal affairs would be retained by each member (Al Abed, 2001, p. 128). In spite of the already settled framework, the emirs accepted the invitation and travelled to Dubai at the end of February to discuss the details, where they reached the so-called Dubai agreement concerning the creation of a "Federation of Arab States" of the nine emirates.

While the document's 12 points served as a cornerstone for the future constitution of the UAE, the evaluation of the achievements reached at the meeting was mixed at best. According to a British diplomat, the outcome of the summit was "by no means negligible", but "no one (...) is likely to be optimistic about the prospects" (Smith, 2002, p. 79). The leaders of Bahrain, for example, admitted that they only participated in the meeting to avoid being the odd-man-out and that they had signed the Dubai agreement so that the meeting would not break up in disarray. Pressured by the Iranian claims over the islands of Bahrain, the *Khalifa* family was open to negotiations (or even to Saudi protection), but accepting the leading role of Qatar and/or Abu Dhabi was a hard pill to swallow. The *Saud* family advised Bahrain to take a back seat in the negotiation process because their larger weight in the process could have easily triggered an Iranian intervention (Friedman, 2017, p. 116).

According to the British diplomats, the Qatari presence was not sincere either: they simple wanted to hinder the deepening of the relationship between Abu Dhabi and Dubai by diluting the cooperation. The *Thani* family felt betrayed by the *Maktoums* of Dubai, as they left them out of the talks with the *Nahyans*. Due to their historical rivalry with Abu Dhabi, Qatar considered Dubai an ally, which alliance was strengthened by marriage, as the Qatari Emir Ahmed al Thani married the daughter of the Dubai Emir (Friedman, 2017, p. 115).[7] Throughout the negotiations, Qatar constantly wanted to undermine the leadership of Abu Dhabi in the process; for example, it was Qatar who initiated the meeting taking place in Dubai.

Negotiations were also hampered due to mistrust caused by the small arms race, which started in the late 1960s between the nine emirates after the announcements of the British withdrawal (Pakistan Forum, 1973; Friedman, 2017, p. 117;). As a matter of fact, Edward Kennedy said that the security dilemma originating from the arms race was not recognised even in the larger Gulf states (Kennedy, 1975, p. 26). Moreover, by late 1969, there was also a "state institution-building race", at least between Abu Dhabi, Dubai,

Bahrain, and Qatar, in order to prove that they were ready for independence if the negotiations were to collapse (Friedman, 2017, p. 120).

Talks between the nine emirates continued after the Dubai agreement in the framework of the Supreme Council, consisting of the nine rulers. The last meeting of the forum took place on 21 October 1969, which marked the failure of the negotiating format (Al Abed, 2001, p. 130). It was during these 20 months that Bahrain and Qatar practically left the conversation and focused on their individual independence. According to the records, the *Khalifa* and *Thani* families framed the negotiations as competition for political power, and they feared that, if they compromised, they would lose influence to the other or to Abu Dhabi. For example, they seemed unable to reach an agreement even on the capital: Bahrain wanted to postpone the selection of a permanent centre (while temporarily agreeing to put the seat in Abu Dhabi), as it thought that, in time, it could solve the issue of Iranian territorial claims and, later, could use its demographic size to pressure the others to let Bahrain become the capital.

On the other hand, Qatar supported the establishment of a new federal city on the borders of Abu Dhabi and Dubai (Friedman, 2017, p. 118–122), which they saw as a symbolic way to limit the influence of the *Nahyans* in the federation. The most problematic notions for the *Thani* family came when the nine parties discussed veto rights and financial contribution to the common budget. First, Qatar did not support the idea that, in the event of the lack of unanimity, the vote should be repeated within a month when only a simple majority would be sufficient. Second, being demographically small but economically large, Qatar was outraged by the idea that each member state should pay to and receive from the federal budget proportionally to their economic and demographic size. Due to these technical disagreements, among others, the Qatari leadership felt that they would not be able to balance the influence of Abu Dhabi in the formative stages of the federation, even in cooperation with Dubai (Zahlan, 1978, p. 195).

For the *Khalifa* family, the most important question was the voting system in the federation. As they were the largest state demographically, they wanted to have a weight designated to each member state based on the size of their population. As the eight other emirates did not agree on this principle – even after the acceptance of the island state in the UN, which at least temporarily eased the Iranian pressure – Bahrain announced that it would refrain from further negotiations (Al Abed, 2001, p. 120–131). It turned out that it was only due to fear of Iran and diplomatic pressure from Saudi Arabia that Bahrain had not exited the negotiations before. Eventually, Bahrain declared its independence on 14 August, 1971, followed by Qatar on 1 September.

The subsequent federation comprised seven emirates and fitted the British vision of the Gulf. Britain did not want to see a weak state that was vulnerable both domestically and internationally but, rather, a more centralised entity with a single, dominant leader. London quickly realised that this aim was unachievable with the participation of Qatar and Bahrain and therefore accepted the smaller federation to reach a higher level of unity, thanks to the domination of the *Nahyan* family of Abu Dhabi (Smith, 2002, pp. 80–82). Zayed bin Sultan Al Nahyan, the Emir of Abu Dhabi, has always preferred this option, as they wanted to have the dominant role in the federation.

Three points should be noted regarding the motivations of Qatar and Bahrain to opt out of the federation. First, it is clear that rational calculations did not dominate the strategic thinking about unity, as historical rivalry and mistrust between each them clouded the decision makers' rationale. Second, both of them "preferred weak independence to a strong union in which they would not be the first among equals" (Friedman, 2017, p. 125), even if that meant geopolitical exposure to Iran and Saudi Arabia. Third, neither of them wanted to decide about independence without the approval of the *Saud* family.

Although both Kuwait and Oman skipped the negotiation process, it is important to investigate their motives regarding and approaching possible Gulf unity. For both states, joining a federal entity was out of the question, as state-building processes were much more developed there than in their neighbours (Davidson, 2012, pp. 26–39). Therefore, for Kuwait and Oman, the issue was more of a question of foreign policy. From this perspective, they both realised that the power vacuum created by the British withdrawal enabled outside forces – especially Baathist Iraq and the Communist bloc – to intervene in regional, and even domestic, affairs; therefore, the power hiatus should be minimised. According to historical documents, the Kuwaiti Prime Minister and crown prince Jabir al-Ahmed Al Sabah even advised the British government to hand the Gulf over to the *Saudis* (Friedman, 2017, p. 114). As this idea did not come to fruition, Kuwait constantly tried to make the nine emirates compromise on as many issues as possible, as they saw parallel independence as a threat to stability.

Oman, on the other hand, only passively pledged support for the plans of the federation of the nine (Kechichian, 1995, pp. 77–78). The Sultan's attention was focused on fighting the domestic threats from the rebellion of the Dhofari Marxists, a fight in which his strategy was to gather regional support (Owen, 1973, p. 271). That is why Sultan Qaboos was among the first to welcome the creation of the UAE as a hopefully powerful neighbour with whom security cooperation was possible. Oman had no large claims over the smaller emirates and did not seek to assimilate the tiny emirates into some kind of "Greater Oman", to the surprise of many diplomats (Wright, 2011b, p. 306).

In all, we can see that, in resolving the integration dilemma, size mattered greatly for Gulf regimes regarding the perception of the security of the small emirates, although not in the way that would seem the most obvious. While, naturally, all entities feared their large neighbours – Iran, Iraq, and Saudi Arabia – to varying degrees, they focused more on the difference in size between each other and, in parallel with that, the distribution of power. Bahrain tried to use its demographic size to dominate the decision making process in the forming union, although unsuccessfully. Qatar considered its own perceptual size greater than that of Abu Dhabi, which made it impossible for Abu Dhabi to accept the dominance of *Nahyans* in the new federation.

The other most important factor that determined the outcome of the discussions was the level of state-formation:Kuwait and Oman, which had the highest level of institutionalisation, did not consider joining the union. The same logical connection was observable in the case of Bahrain and Qatar to a lesser extent.

Threat perception, the Iranian revolution, and the first Gulf war (1979–1989)

The Iranian revolution and the first Gulf war between Iraq and Iran (1980–1988) represented the first major foreign policy challenge for smaller Gulf states. In the late 1970s, state-building was far from complete, while experience was also lacking in dealing with such a huge crisis. This bring up two interesting points: first, the reasons for the different perception of external threats in the smaller Gulf states and, second, how they treat military and political threats differently.

The Iranian Islamic revolution (1979)

Iran had represented a security threat for smaller Gulf states even before the revolution of 1979 when it was a monarchy led by the Shah. The large Persian country had always tried to balance Saudi Arabia, an effort in which spreading influence in the Gulf was a primary tool (Kamrava, 2005, p. 177). The primary target of Tehran was Bahrain due to its disenfranchised Shia majority and its location (Belfer, 2014, p. 32). Both the pre- and post-revolutionary Iranian regime was determined to achieve supremacy in the Persian Gulf (Karsh, 1989, p. 26), which was perceived to be a "Persian lake", making Iran the rightful hegemon of the region (Marschall, 2003, p. 5).

Under the Shah, Iran's role in the cold war system was to act as a stabilising entity in the region, to suppress revolutionary movements, and to protect American interests (Theberge, 1973): that is why Tehran supported the Omani efforts to stabilise the Dhofar region. Nonetheless, giving the impression of being a good ally to the Americans, Tehran used the situation to act on its own regional interests. This was especially observable in the 1970s, as Iranian activities intensified in the region due to the oil crisis of 1973 and the British withdrawal, which was perceived as an opportunity to shut out all extra-regional powers in the region (Zabih, 1976). Despite being an American ally, the Shah even warned the American government in an interview conducted by *The New York Times* in 1969 that they should not replace the British Empire in the region (Marschall, 2003, p. 7).

Enjoying American sympathy, Iran acted out to achieve its interests through the seizure of the several smaller islands previously belonging to Sharjah (Abu Musa) and Ras al-Khaimah (the two Tunb islands), in the early 1970s. After that, the main interest of Tehran was to preserve the 1971 status quo; namely, to conserve these territorial gains and to keep superpowers out. The previously revisionist actor became a pro-status quo force. Consequently, by the mid-1970s, the biggest threat to this system was posed by Iraq due to its territorial claims on Iranian territories, the Shatt al-Arab debate, and the Soviet orientation of Baghdad, which showed support for the Dhofar rebellion in Oman in the 1960s.

Despite being a larger, stronger, and more powerful neighbour, the role of Iran was acceptable to the Gulf monarchies to a degree. While they were not able to balance Iran, whose behaviour was overbearing, the international situation was tolerable, and even beneficial, for the survival of smaller Gulf states as Iran was able to balance Iraq. That calculation profoundly changed following the Islamic revolution in 1979, which altered the way in which Tehran wanted to gain influence: previously, the Shah had been thinking in geopolitical and material terms, whereas the post-revolutionary regime "extended its hegemonic claims from the geopolitical to the spiritual (or ideological) domain" (Karsh, 1989, p26). This changed the game and has determined the perception of threat of smaller Gulf states, as it translated into not only an external military threat, but also a domestic political threat contemporarily (Gause, 2010, p. 50).

The Iranian revolution grew out of the most economically motivated demonstrations organised since 1976 (Kamrava, 2005, p. 140). Many different political, social, and economic power groups joined a progressively more anti-regime movement, including anti-establishment political parties, guerrilla organisations, independent intellectuals, and the clergy (Kamrava, 2005, pp. 149–151). The revolution swept away the old regime, and the Islamist faction led by Rumollah Khomeini took power. Naturally, the institutionalisation of the new system was a lasting process, so the threat posed by Tehran was not primarily perceived as a traditional military threat (Gause, 2010, p. 50; Kamrava, 2005, pp. 154–156).

The events of 1979 had lasting regional and international consequences. The leaders of Iran quickly proclaimed that they would support the spread of their values and ideology to other countries in the Middle East. In the words of Ajatollah Khomeini,[8] "We should try to export our revolution to the world." Naturally, this was quite a fearful notion for smaller Gulf states, even if there was an apparent debate among the Iranian leadership about the actual implementation of the policy. The first interim government led by Mehdi Barzargan rejected the idea of any tangible interference with neighbours' domestic affairs, even if Ajatollah Khomeini, prior to the revolution, appointed representatives to lead the Shia community in Bahrain and Kuwait (Gause, 2010, pp. 46–51). Abol-Hasan Bani-Sadr, the interim President, proclaimed that the revolution would not be victorious if it were not exported. Moreover, a few politicians threatened Bahrain outright with an intervention. In September 1979, Ibrahim Yazdi, the member of the interim government, publicly threatened the island state that "if you do not want to stop oppressing the people, and restore Islamic laws, we will call on the people to demand annexation to the Islamic government of Iran" (cited by Marschall, 2003, p. 34).[9] Sadeq Rohani, a member of the Revolutionary Council, said that Iran should invade Bahrain if the Shias did not take control. While these comments sound serious, it should be noted that Mohamed Montazeri – one of the leaders of the Islamic Revolutionary Guard Corps – almost immediately denied the claim and said that Rohani was a CIA agent who did not represent the Iranian government (Ostovar, 2016, p. 105). In 1982, Khomeini also proclaimed that Iran does not have any "intention of interfering militarily" with any country (Bill, 1984, p. 118).

The political threat posed by the Iranian revolution included three elements, none of which was connected directly to the size of smaller Gulf states. First, naturally, there was the Shia component as the export of the system was built on disenfranchised Shia communities and Shia Islamist networks throughout the region. Although the Middle Eastern Shia society is highly fragmented and is anything but unified, specific political and social networks of an "informal and highly personalistic" nature had been built up long before the revolution through *diwaniyas* (places of assembly), mosques, and other religious centres, or simply through the homes and shops of community leaders (Bill, 1984, p. 121). In the Gulf, two networks emerged by the late 1970s, both with ties to Iraqi and Iranian clerics (Matthiesen, 2013, pp. 33–49.; Wright, 2017, pp. 67–68). The *Dawa* network, which is influenced by the political-religious centre of Najaf, was the most widespread, with mostly moderate leaders emphasising the importance of dialogue with the local governments to better the socio-economic situation of the Shia communities. Their counter-balance was the *Shirazi* or *Modarrisi* network, which is more closely connected to the families of *Kerbala* and Iran. The Iranian leadership was ideologically closer to the *Shirazi* network, as it accepted the use of violence to achieve political goals.

Second, the nature of the new Iranian regime, a mixture of Islamist and democratic elements, was a threat to the monarchic-autocratic political system of the Gulf states in itself. Beyond its ethnic and religious colours, the new Iranian leadership represented an alternative model of government, one that promised more genuine participation for citizens than the highly rigid tribal system of the monarchies (Hooglund, 1992, p. 20). This could have potentially been attractive to the lower classes of the Gulf societies; "the revolution was, after all, a movement carried out by the masses" (Bill, 1984, p. 118).

The third element of the Iranian political threat is connected to the normative protection deriving from group membership for Middle Eastern states described in Chapter 2. Iran wanted to persuade Muslims around the world that Gulf monarchic systems contradict Islamic principles (Sreedhar, 1982, pp. 255–256). Ayatollah Khomeini frequently called them "enemies of Islam" (Ahrari, 1985, p. 49). Such rhetoric pressure represented the potential danger of losing their membership in the Islamic community and the protection connected with it.

The Iranian revolution was perceived differently in smaller Gulf states (Baktiari, 1993, p. 72.; Gause, 2010, pp. 46–51). Initially, two ideas were circulating in the Arab monarchies: to reject the Iranian revolution and discredit it, or to acknowledge its legitimacy and try to maintain normal and friendly relations. In the first months, the second option was stronger as

Kuwait, Oman, Qatar, and the UAE shared the same beliefs but, in a little more than a year, the tables turned.

The first sign of threat was a series of demonstrations inspired by Iranian events between 1979 and 1981. The two most exposed states were Bahrain and Kuwait, due to their large Shia community and their grievances about the unequal distribution of the fruits of modernisation, as well as the presence of Iranian nationals in the country (Marschall, 2003, p. 42). That being said, the exact extent of Iranian involvement in these events was debatable. While Iran did take some steps – for example, when the Association of Militant Clerics and the Revolutionary Guards gathered members of the *ulema* from the region to strengthen its network in March 1982 (Marschall, 2003, p. 28) – it mostly capitalised on existing social problems. Ultimately, the exportability of the revolution was dependent not on Tehran but, rather, on those willing to "import the revolution". Therefore, socio-economic grievances mattered more than Iranian rhetoric (Naruzzaman, 2012, p. 543). This encouraged Iran to deny any involvement (Pelletiere, 1992, p. 61). It is nevertheless true that Tehran was focusing more on exporting the revolution to countries where Tehran had a bigger foothold; namely, Iraq and Lebanon (Marschall, 2003, p. 25). Even so, the reception of the Iranian message was stronger in the Shia communities experiencing a worse socio-economic position, such as those of Bahrain and Saudi Arabia (ibid).

Consequently, the Iranian revolution caused the most problems in Bahrain due to its internal social problems (described in Chapter 4). Shia zealots created the Islamic Front for the Liberation of Bahrain (*al-Jabha al-Islamiyya li Tahrir al-Bahrayn* – IFLB) with the leadership of Ayatollah Mohammed Taqi al-Modarresi, under the coordination of Grand Ayatollah Hussein Ali Montazeri (Wright, 2017, pp. 67–68). Members of the organisation (which was part of the *Modarresi* network) allegedly plotted a coup against Bahrain under the leadership of Hadi al-Moderrisi but, before this could be executed, they were arrested in December 1981 (Pelletiere, 1992, p. 61). Of the 73 arrested, none was Iranian: 60 were Bahraini, 11 were Saudi Arabian, and 1 was from Kuwait and from Oman. This shows the exposure of Gulf societies to the networks (Wright, 2017, pp. 68–69). The alleged attempted coup became a symbol of Iran trying to undermine Gulf states using proxies and networks.

In Kuwait, similar network-building was going on after 1979 but to a lower intensity. Contrary to Bahrain, the *Dawa* network in Kuwait was much more influential (Hunter, 1988, p. 747) with looser ties to Iran. The authorities suspected that Abbas al-Muhri, the brother-in-law of Ajatollah Khomeini (Commins, 2014, p. 235), was appointed to a similar position as Hadi al-Modarresi in Bahrain: he was arrested in September 1979 and eventually was deported from the country with his family, all members of which were stripped of their citizenship (Boghardt, 2006, p. 33). Kuwait also kicked out people holding Iranian citizenship, as well as some Lebanese and Iraqi nationals (Hunter, 1988, pp. 747–748).

In the other smaller Gulf states, the Iranian revolution did not have such a direct effect (Marschall, 2003, pp. 42–43). Shia communities in Qatar, Oman, and the UAE were either much smaller, better integrated, or had looser connections with Iranian Shias (e.g. in the case of Omani Ismaili Shias, whose origins traced back to India). For them, the Islamic revolution did not change their perception of geopolitical or domestic threats. The Omani Sultan did feel sorry for losing the Shah as an ally against Communist rebels, but did not feel his regime's security had altered.

The first Gulf war (1990–1991)

Besides growing fear of possible Iranian interference, the Islamic revolution set another major development in motion. After becoming the President of Iraq on 16 July 1979, Saddam Hussein realised that he could use the threat posed by revolutionary Iran to push for regional dominance (and to correct unresolved territorial disputes with Iran) (Sirriyeh, 1985). He tried to build up an image similar to that of Gamel Abdal Nasser but, instead of the "Zionist enemy", he wanted to use Khomeini as the enemy against which he could defend the Arab world (Kamrava, 2005, p. 177).

To achieve this aim, Saddam wanted to start a war against the new Iranian regime, which was yet to stabilise its position, and he wanted its Gulf neighbours to provide financial and normative support. Before 1979, smaller Gulf states tried to balance between Iraq and Iran, but the success of the revolution changed their calculation to some extent. To further persuade smaller Gulf states, Saddam Hussein offered to send troops to Bahrain and Kuwait (which they reluctantly accepted on Saudi advice), and demanded the return of Abu Musa and the Tunb islands to the UAE in October 1979 (Marschall, 2003, pp. 66–67). Perceiving the Iraqi and Saudi diplomacy intensifying, Iraq also sent delegations to smaller Gulf states to persuade them to accommodate Tehran's friendly ambitions – unsuccessfully.

The role of smaller Gulf states in the decision of Iraq to attack Iran is not completely clear but, sometime between May and September 1980, they became convinced of its necessity (Gause, 2010, p. 63). According to Iranian and Kuwaiti newspaper sources, Kuwait, Bahrain, and Qatar, alongside the UAE and Saudi Arabia, agreed to lend 14 billion USD to support a military attack on 19 September 1980, three days before the start of the conflict (Baktiari, 1993, pp. 74–75).

The war between the two giants lasted for eight years, representing a constant and multi-level threat to smaller Gulf states, especially after 1982 when most of the fighting took place on Iraqi soil as a result of an Iranian counterattack (Gause, 2010, pp. 57–58). The situation was particularly crucial after February 1986, when Iranian military forces seized the Faw Peninsula, which enabled them potentially to separate Iraq from the Gulf states and to target Kuwait directly (Boghardt, 2006, p. 104). According to an Iranian politician, the conquest of Faw opened up a way to "Saddam's defenders" in the region (i.e. the Gulf states), which was "terrifying to them. They're witnessing our dominance over the Persian Gulf" (Ostovar, 2016, pp. 94–95). [10]

Spill-overs of the conflict did reach Kuwait, especially due to its geopolitical position and the support it provided to Iraq. In 1980, a Kuwaiti airliner was hijacked, and the offices of the Kuwait Oil Company in London were bombed. In the same year, two explosives went off at the office of the *al-Rai al-Amm* newspaper, which represented the first attack on Kuwaiti soil (Boghardt, 2006, pp. 42–43). In October 1981, an Iranian aircraft attacked Kuwaiti oil fields (Pelletiere, 1992, p. 61). In 1983, a series of coordinated explosions took place while, in 1985, the authorities stopped an assassination attempt on the Emir himself (Gause, 2010, p. 77). Between 1984 and 1987, a total of 28 ships with Kuwaiti flags were hit by Iranian naval forces as retaliation for the support given to Iraq (Ostovar, 2016, p. 96).[11]

In addition to direct military confrontation, the Iraqi–Iranian war had other effects. Iran's behaviour changed: contrary to inspiring massive demonstrations, Tehran started to attack ships in the Gulf sailing under flags of the Arab states, especially after 1984 (Marschall, 2003, p. 34; Wright, 2017, p. 69). Also, the region became more exposed to superpower rivalry as both the USA and the Soviet Union acquired their stakes in it. Lastly, the crisis also affected the economic security of smaller Gulf states with contradictory affects. Since 1960, the major oil producers of the region had been cooperating with each other in the OPEC structure to determine the level of oil production and to shape global oil prices. Tensions between Iran and Arab Gulf states surfaced before the revolution, in the mid-1970s when Tehran wanted to raise its production level to boost income, whereas Saudi Arabia and Algeria feared that raising production may lower prices (Halliday, 1980, p. 11). Domestic instability in Iran and the fall of the old regime in 1979 undermined any sort of coordination in OPEC, leading to a de facto "free-for-all" system, raising prices on the market (Gause, 2010, pp. 52–53). This process had a positive effect on smaller Gulf states, as their incomes rose significantly.

Different perceptions and reactions

Traditional interpretations based solely on the balance of power cannot explain the various reactions of smaller Gulf states, as they were framed by the perception of the importance of the two dimensions of the threat (Rubin, 1989, p. 121): the military (physical attacks and spill-overs) and the political (domestic and ideological movements). What shaped the strategy of the regimes is the relative perceived importance of the military threat: if they considered it to be great, as in relation to Bahrain and Kuwait, they concentrated more on the tools with which they could tackle the situation. On the other hand, Oman, the UAE, and Qatar did not feel the military threat to be that great, so they prioritised domestic stability, with Oman and the UAE trying to maintain a neutral position in the conflict, while Qatar took as passive a stance as possible (Marschall, 2003, p. 70).

Tackling the military and political implications of the crisis required different tools. The primary form of defence for the countries in military terms was to balance the Iranian threat with allying more strongly with Iraq (Gause, 2010, p. 50), especially after Iranian attacks on Gulf ships became regular (Wright, 2017, p. 69). Exact numbers are not available regarding the amount provided by the Gulf states to Baghdad, but Kuwait and Saudi Arabia gave Iraq loans and grants worth approximately 25 to 50 billion USD (Ostovar, 2016, p. 81). In addition to financial support, Gulf monarchies, primarily those of Kuwait and Saudi Arabia, gave Iraq access to ports and military facilities, and helped to sustain Iraq's foreign trade relations (Alnasrawi, 1986, p. 874; Gause, 2010, p. 76). To better relations with Iraq, smaller Gulf states (except for Oman) loosened their ties with Egypt, since Baghdad wanted to put pressure on Cairo (as its rival hegemon in the Arab region). Saddam Hussein used the Israeli–Egyptian peace treaty signed in 1979 to isolate the North African state, and Gulf states were partners in this initiative.

Another tool to achieve military security was to seek protection from a great power. In 1982 – immediately following the scandal regarding the Islamic Front for the Liberation of Bahrain (IFLB) – Bahrain, Qatar, the UAE, and Oman all signed defence agreements with Saudi Arabia (Marschall, 2003, p. 36). At one point, Oman invited the American, British and German fleets to patrol the Low Gulf seas, fearing further instability. Nevertheless, upon the proclamation of Saddam's Pan-Arab Charter, which called for an absence of superpower participation in the conflict,[12] Oman withdrew its invitation (Pelletiere, 1992, p. 30). Later, in 1986, after the shock of the Iranian capture of Faw, Kuwait invited both the Soviet Union and the USA to send naval patrols to overview security and stability offshores. The most striking point of this initiative was the fact that Kuwait asked not only the USA, but also its adversary (Pelletiere, 1992, p. 124).

Smaller Gulf states – primarily the UAE, Oman, and Kuwait – also supported and initiated mediation and facilitation efforts in the region, though mostly to limited effect.[13] The UAE and Oman were the most visible in this regard for a variety of reasons, but they also cooperated with Syria to push Iran closer to the negotiating table.

Dealing with the political implications of the crisis, the most visible common step of smaller Gulf states included promoting a sectarian narrative domestically framing political dissent as promoting Shia interests (Boghat, 2008, pp. 30–31). This strategy resurfaced later in the 2010s with greater intensity (see Chapter 6). Moreover, the crisis was the last push for the six Gulf monarchies to establish institutional cooperation, the Gulf Cooperation Council (GCC). The GCC should not be seen as the first step towards political unification but, rather, a regime alliance to tackle common threats and to establish a region independent from Iran, Iraq, and great power interference (Bill, 1984, p. 123; Legrenzi, 2011, pp. 27–33).

The exact nature and extent of cooperation, especially in the military field, was debated among the six countries. Due to its geopolitical situation, Oman focused on maritime security, while Kuwait wanted to avoid perception of the GCC as being a Western-oriented security organisation, and thus wanted to foster cultural and education cooperation. Eventually, the GCC evolved into an organisation oriented more towards political security, and which serves as a forum for regimes to coordinate actions against political threats. Besides joint exercises, the only manifestation of the military sector was the creation of the Peninsula Shield Force in 1986: even so, it was more a symbolic manifestation of solidarity than an actual and potent military force. It heavily relied on Saudi capabilities and only played a symbolic role; for example, after the Iranian conquest of Faw (Legrenzi, 2011, p. 18).

Two additional steps were taken by Bahrain and Kuwait to tackle the domestic political pressure caused by the Iranian regime (Bill, 1984, p. 123). First, governments put progressively more pressure on the Shia population, a practice that was borrowed from Saudi Arabia and Iraq. In Kuwait, high-level Shia bureaucrats were forced out of their jobs, while progressively fewer permits were given to build Shia mosques. In October 1979, a new Kuwaiti law prohibited the private meeting of more than 20 people without prior approval of the authorities, while authorities also expelled Iranian nationals from the country (Boghardt, 2006, pp. 34–38).

Second, they began to reinforce institutions that represented the establishment and mainstream Islamism vis-á-vis the populist Islamism represented by Sunni fundamentalists. Their policies aimed to appease domestic Islamist sentiment, on the one hand, and crack down on potential revolutionaries (Rubin, 1989, p. 123), on the other. In Kuwait, the parliament, which was dissolved in 1976, was reinstated in 1981 (Boghardt, 2006, pp. 34–38). While the regime officially declined to say that organising elections had anything to do with the Iranian revolution, the timing speaks volumes. The government manipulated the results (with means such as gerrymandering) to lower the votes cast to both Shias and Arab nationalists and to favour the Islamists and the *bidoon*, whom they thought would be a pillar against the anti-establishment forces. Censorship rules in local newspapers were also eased. This trend to liberalisation lasted until the mid-1980s: as a result of the growing feeling of insecurity following the Iranian capture of Faw, the Kuwaiti emir dissolved the National Assembly (Boghardt, 2006, p. 108), which was a clear sign that the government wanted to focus more on the international level of the conflict. He officially declared that institutions only divide Kuwaitis in a moment of crisis (Commins, 2014, p. 237).

These steps taken by Bahrain and Kuwait did not ease the domestic tension on the regimes, as terrorist activities and anti-establishment movements continued to be organised extensively. In Kuwait, a very worrisome development was the fact that, even in the second half of the 1980s, Kuwaiti citizens were involved in plotting terrorist attacks in the country, questioning the social contract between the ruling family and society (Boghardt, 2006, p. 103). The situation was worsened by the 1982 financial crisis, which caused the collapse of the Suq al-Manakh, the semi-official stock exchange of the country (Commins, 2014, p. 236), erasing the savings of many Kuwaiti families.

In Bahrain, no major domestic demonstrations took place between 1981 and 1994; nevertheless, it was during the early years of the Iraq–Iran war that Shia religious identity became extensively used as a symbol of protest against the regime, while the Bahraini government also embraced a sectarian concept of loyalty, picturing Shias as potential threats (Louer, 2013, p. 247). The security forces underwent a transformation as a result of which Shia members were expelled, and the army was "Sunnitized", conserving the anti-establishment attitude of Shia communities.

These measures taken by Bahrain and Kuwait were highly counter-productive. They did not solve either the political or the military threat posed by Iran and Iraq but, instead, perpetuated tensions in their own society, translating an international problem into a domestic one. Theoretically, their strategy is in line with expectations about small state behaviour, as their primary worry was being dominated by a larger power. Nevertheless, in the Middle Eastern context, undermining domestic regime security had a long-lasting effect on both countries.

The remaining three smaller Gulf states chose a different path. Under the leadership of Sultan Qaboos, Oman did not want to break up with Iran (or Egypt) as they did not perceive the Iranian threat to be that ominous due to their historical relations[14] and the necessity to maintain communication with Tehran on maritime security (Marschall, 2003, p. 42). Moreover, they feared Iraqi influence in the Gulf to a greater extent as Baghdad had previously supported the Dhofari rebels in the country.

For these reasons, Muscat actively tried to facilitate discussion between the two parties during the war (Kechichian, 1995, pp. 110–112; Valeri, 2017, pp. 156–157). Oman did not allow the Iraqi army to use its facilities, even when Iran violated its territorial integrity. According to the Sultan, "Iran, as a Muslim country, deserved similar assistance because of its Islamic credentials" (Kechichian, 1995, pp. 111–112). Omani efforts at facilitation – which were pursued even when Iran seemed much less open to dialogue – proved to be crucial to the resolution of the conflict (Valeri, 2017, p. 157; Allen and Rigsbee, 2002, p. 191). In 1987, a special representative of the Omani government, Thuwayni bin Shihab, managed to convince the Iranian leadership to accept the UN cease-fire resolution of 1988.

In addition to Oman, the UAE also tried to mediate between Iraq and Iran, refraining from breaking ties with Tehran due to their close trade relations, which were sustained during the war (especially with Dubai and Sharjah) (Marschall, 2003, p. 62). The first such attempt took place in 1981, when Emirati diplomats accompanied their Saudi colleagues to visit Tehran, but they continued their work throughout the decade, playing an important role, as did Oman, to bring the countries closer to peace.

Conventional wisdom (and theory) would suggest a more anti-Iranian policy from the UAE due to Tehran's conquest of Abu Musa and the Tunb islands; nevertheless, it seems that this territorial dispute did not affect the Emirati perception of the Iraq–Iran war, even when Tehran used the islands militarily against Iraq (Marschall, 2003, pp. 134–136). The Emirati government wanted to separate the question of the islands from the overall framework of bilateral ties completely, a stance that allowed it to pursue its economic and other interests by being more neutral in the war. The motivation behind this policy lies in the dynamics between the seven emirates: the Tunbs belonged to a poor emirate (Ras al-Khaimah had no effect on federal foreign policy) and Abu Musa was of no great value to Abu Dhabi. The question was useful for putting pressure on Tehran every now and then, but it did not shape Emirati foreign policy to any great extent.

While Qatar did perceive the Iranian revolution as a threat, it did not want to side with Iraq for two reasons (Kamrava, 2017, pp. 172–174). First, the *Thani* regime feared that, due to the military might of Iran, Tehran could easily retaliate (as it did in the case of Kuwait). Second, they feared that cooperating with Saddam Hussein may jeopardise the domestic equilibrium between Sunnis and Shias, which so far had not represented a challenge for the country. Qatar did not cease diplomatic ties with Iran – as, for example, Bahrain had done following the alleged attempted coup – and tried to remain as neutral as possible. Nonetheless, maritime strikes on oil vessels in the Gulf came very close to Qatari borders; at one point, a massive oil slick had almost reached Qatari desalination plants. This led to confusion and inconsistencies in the Qatari foreign policy, which included advocating for more sanctions on Iran, on the one hand, and simultaneously engaging in reconciliatory dialogue with the Islamic Republic, on the other.

Relative smallness is not the only – and is definitely not the most important – determinant of the threat perception of smaller Gulf states during the 1980s. Maintaining domestic stability mattered more than conventional military threats (or, in the case of the UAE, territorial integrity). From this perspective, as is argued by James Bill (1984, p. 122), demographic smallness actually played a positive role as – accompanied by oil reserves and the tribal structure – regimes perceived it easier to maintain social order in such turbulent times. With their active neutrality, Oman and the UAE managed to tackle the crisis in an optimal way, while Qatar's passive neutrality also enabled the regime to remain stable. Nevertheless, social tensions in Bahrain and Kuwait were magnified by the decision of the governments to overemphasise the military component of the situation (thus behaving more as theoretical expectations related to small states would suggest), siding with Iraq and repressing Shia minorities. Thus, it was not war but, rather, the interaction of smallness and mismanaged heterogeneity that represented the gravest danger to regime stability.

Alliance-making, superpowers, and the second and third Gulf wars (1990–2003)

The second (1990–1991) and third (2003) Gulf crises represented the most profound transformation of the regional balance of power in the post-Cold War era in the Gulf region. In 1990, Kuwait was attacked by Iraq, and an international coalition led by the United States intervened to restore the

Table 5.1 Periods of the balance of power from the perspective of smaller Gulf states

Period	Superpower shelter	Alliance policy
1971–1990	None	Defensive strategy
1990–2003	American shelter	Alignment policy
2003–	Diverging strategies	

Source: Compiled by author.

territorial integrity of the Emirate. Thirteen years later, in 2003, the regime of Saddam Hussein was overthrown by another coalition, pushing Iraq into decade-long instability, igniting a regional competition for influence in the country.

Maybe the most profound effect the two developments had was on the alliance-policy of the smaller Gulf states vis-á-vis global powers (see Table 5.1). These changes can be interpreted as the neorealist notion of picking two out of the three basic values of security, influence, and autonomy, or the more neoliberal idea of choosing a shelter provided by superpowers (see Chapter 1). From either point of view, the alliance policy of smaller Gulf states had three distinct periods. The first, starting from independence until the second Gulf war, was mostly characterised by defensive strategy, which excluded long-lasting formal alliances[15] with great powers and making efforts to avoid involvement in a conflict. The second stage, between the second and third Gulf war, witnessed a turn to alignment policy by formalising security ties with the United States, turning to American shelter. The third stage, beginning with the third Gulf war, marked a slow alteration of this alignment policy to becoming more diverse and individualised.

Superpower relations between 1971 and 1990

Smaller Gulf states are usually described as American allies in the Cold War; even so, they did not engage in deep security cooperation with the USA before 1990. Due to the three non-traditional security dilemmas described in Chapter 4, they wanted to keep Washington in sight "on the horizon" (Gause, 2010, pp. 127–128) so that they could feel safe in the event of an attack, but politically distance themselves from the USA. The lukewarm approach was also mirrored by the USA as, from the American perspective, primary interests in the Gulf were limited to maintaining stable access to hydrocarbon resources and containing Soviet expansion (Yetiv, 2008, pp. 30–64).

In the 1970s, the primary mutual interest for the two sides was the containment of Iraq, especially after the Iraqi–Soviet friendship grew stronger (which manifested itself, among other matters, in the 1972 bilateral Treaty of Friendship and Cooperation, which enabled Moscow to use the Umm Qasr base). Nevertheless, under the twin pillar policy of the USA, American priority was given to Saudi and Iranian relations, neglecting smaller states.

After 1979, security perceptions became only slightly closer: smaller Gulf states supported Iraq before the USA did after 1981 (following the policy of "benign neglect") in the form of arms, material support, and even the sharing of intelligence information. For Washington, its two priorities remained the same: when oil trade was threatened, they agreed to hold joint military manoeuvres with the GCC states, to reflag Kuwaiti tankers (but only in 1987), and also take a close look at any attempts by the Soviet Union to spread its influence. Consequently, the first Gulf war, in itself, was not a game-changer for Gulf–USA relations, as it only "reduced – but not yet eliminated – the Gulf states' reservations" about Washington (Strategic Survey, 1983, p. 79).

In parallel, the image of the Soviet Union also changed in the 1970s and 1980s, as it was perceived to be progressively less threatening (Trenin, 2018, pp. 27–34). Soviet policy in the region had previously been seen as quite dangerous due to its support for Marxist and Arab nationalist forces; for example, in Iraq, South Yemen, and Oman. Nevertheless, the events of the late 1970s showed that Soviet influence was very limited – Iraq did not ask permission from Moscow to attack Iran, while the post-revolutionary elite in Tehran was anti-Soviet. These events downgraded the sensitivity of the Soviet question, which is why several smaller Gulf states (Qatar, UAE, and Oman) established diplomatic relations with Moscow in the late 1980s or – after Moscow sided with Washington to condemn Iraq's attack on Kuwait – in 1990 (Bahrain) (Melkumyan, 2015, p. 6).

Bilateral relations with superpowers varied among the Gulf states. Bahrain had the most advanced ties with the USA before 1990 having hosted the largest naval port used by American ships in the region since 1949 (Joyce, 2012, p. 40); in 1966, this accommodated the *USS Valcour*, the flagship of the fleet of the American Middle East Force (MIDEASTFOR) (Joyce, 2012, p. 27). As with the British presence previously, the American military presence was welcomed by the Bahraini government, as they feared that Communist-inspired political networks or Arab nationalism could manifest in the country. Nonetheless, American–Bahraini relations did not intensify until the late 1980s (Gause, 2010, p. 127).

Due to the Marxist nature of the Dhofar rebellion, Oman was also very suspicious of the Soviet Union and did not establish diplomatic relations with it until 1985 (Commins, 2014, p. 165; Melkumyan, 2015, p. 5). The Sultan was open to cooperation with the USA: he signed an arms treaty with Washington in 1975 that provided TOW anti-tank missiles for Muscat to fight the Dhofar rebellion (Kechichian, 1995, p. 146). Five years later, in 1980, the two parties signed the Facilities Access Agreement, which was the most profound security agreement between a Gulf state and the USA up until that point (Baabood, 2017, p. 109). The Facilities Access Agreement allowed the USA to use Omani military installations in Salalah, Thumrayt, Masirah Island, Mutrah, Seed, and Khassab in exchange for economic and military assistance of approximately 80–100 million USD (Kechichian, 1995, pp. 147–150). At that time, the agreement represented an anomaly not just in the Gulf, but also in the Arab region as well, which trigged heavy criticism from Arab and Gulf governments (Gause, 2010, p. 127). Even during the talks preceding the creation of the GCC, Oman was seen as conducting an openly pro-American foreign policy, which hampered reaching a compromise (Strategic Survey, 1983, p. 79).

American–Qatari relations were tenser in the 1980s because, after recognising the Soviet Union in 1988, Doha immediately engaged in arms trade (Fromherz, 2012, pp. 105–106). The reason behind this step (which surprised both Saudi Arabia and the USA) was that Washington sold Stinger anti-aircraft missiles to Bahrain, which it refused to do for Qatar. The *Thani* regime decided to acquire the weapons on the black market through relations with the Soviet bloc. The following American–Qatari dispute froze economic and military cooperation between the countries; moreover, the American Congress banned arms sales to Qatar altogether (Blanchard, 2014, p. 4). Diplomatic tensions remained heightened until 1991.

Kuwait established diplomatic relations with the Soviet Union as early as 1964 (Melkumyan, 2015, pp. 3–5), only three years after having done so with the USA (Katzman, 2009, p. 4). This development was perceived as problematic in the eyes of the American government, especially since Bahrain and Qatar had so far refused to establish diplomatic ties with the Soviet Union after their independence, despite Russian offers (Joyce, 2012, p. 42). The *Sabah* regime's decision was rooted in the annoyance of Russian support for Iraq, especially in their territorial claims against Kuwait. Therefore, the government decided to open a backdoor to Moscow, a capital with arguably greater importance to it than Washington.

Nonetheless, it was only during the Iraq–Iran war that Kuwait tried to upgrade relations with the Soviet Union. Before 1980, only technical and cultural cooperation had existed between the two countries (and a low-profile military agreement in 1975) but, at that time, Soviet relations were seen as a tool with which to defend the territorial integrity of the country. Kuwait even sought Soviet approval before agreeing to the creation of the GCC (Legrenzi, 2011, p. 31). That was why Kuwait refused the Omani initiative to create fully fledged security cooperation, which, they feared, would appear to be a security alliance with the West (due to the strong connections between the USA and Saudi Arabia). On diplomatic forums, Kuwaiti representatives always tried to emphasise the neutrality of the GCC in relation to the Cold War setting. Even during the height of the tensions of the Iraq–Iran war, the Kuwaiti government tried to maintain its projected non-aligned stance, which is why it turned to both the USA and the Soviet Union to provide defence for tankers in the Persian Gulf, following which Moscow sent enough military presence to defend three vessels. Due to the special interests of Kuwait, American relations did not evolve to any appreciable degree until the second Gulf war (Katzman, 2009, p. 4).

The UAE had perhaps the most low-key connection with either country. While having diplomatic relations with the USA, they only cosied up to extra-regional military presence in the region in the second half of the 1980s

(Hellyer, 2001, p. 176). When it came to the Soviet Union, they only established ties in 1986, but relations remained formal (Melkumyan, 2015, p. 5).

Effects of the Iraqi invasion of Kuwait (1990–1991)

Regional dynamics changed considerably after the end of the first Gulf war
(Gause, 2010, pp. 88–102). Iraq did not manage to capitalise on the conflict
as much as it had hoped. The Arab Gulf states did not accept its leading role
over them and stopped giving substantial support to the Saddam regime. As
a result, Iraqi leaders concluded that domestic, regional, and global powers
worked together to undermine their rule in the country. Relations with
Kuwait started to deteriorate gradually during 1990, mainly due to existing
territorial disputes (e.g. the Bubiyan and the Failaka islands); Iraqi claims of
illegal Kuwaiti activities, including slant drilling that allegedly drained the
Iraqi Rumaili oil fields; and of overproduction of oil and disrespecting OPEC
quotas. Moreover, Iraq wanted to get rid of the debts it owed to the small
emirate.

Sources suggest that Kuwait underplayed the seriousness of the accusa-
tions (Ibrahim, 1992, pp. 10–11). The government thought that such misun-
derstandings were nothing out of the ordinary and could be solved
diplomatically. In July 1990, Kuwait agreed to reduce the level of oil production and was also open to coordinating the issue of the Rumaila. On 1 August
1990, 24 hours before the invasion began, the Kuwaiti and the Iraqi governments held a meeting in Jeddah, with the mediation of Saudi Arabia, to solve
their issues. Eventually, discussions broke off when Iraq left the table due to
the uncompromising stance of Kuwait in terms of debt-relief and territorial
disputes.

As a result of miscalculating the reactions of global and regional powers,
Iraq attacked Kuwait on 2 August 1990 (Commins, 2014, pp. 245–246). Due
to the unpreparedness of the Kuwaiti army, the Iraqi forces won quickly, and
Saddam could announce the annexation of the country. In November, the
Security Council set 15 January 1991 as the deadline by which Iraq was to
withdraw from the country and re-establish the territorial sovereignty of
Kuwait.

One day after the deadline passed, the USA and its allies began a six-week
campaign to expel Iraqi forces, which they managed to do quickly. The USA
reacted quite swiftly due to concerns regarding oil supplies, the security of
Saudi Arabia, and to set an example at the very beginning of the new, post-
bipolar global order (Gause, 2010, pp. 110–114). Smaller Gulf states welcomed
the initiative and, except for Oman, took part directly in Operation Desert
Storm (Hura et al., 2000, p. 191). Kuwaiti planes participated in 780 sorties (all
air interdictions: AIs), Bahrainis in 293 (of which 122 were AIs, 152 combat
air patrol, 14 offensive counter-air), the Emiratis in 109 (58 AIs and 45 airlifts),
and Qataris in 43 (all AIs). Qatari forces also participated in retaking the Saudi
border town of al-Khafji, which had been taken by Iraqi forces on 29 January
(Khadduri and Ghareeb, 2001, p. 174; Commins, 2014, p. 247).

The crisis had profound effects on the Gulf region. In Kuwait, the Iraqi invasion was preceded by domestic political debates regarding the reinstitution of the National Assembly (Commins, 2014, pp. 247–249). In 1989, a petition signed by several thousand people was circulating to ask the Emir to reopen the legislative institution, but Emir Jabir refused to meet with the organisers. In 1990, the monarch proposed a new "National Council", which would have taken over the function of the National Assembly with much more limited jurisdiction. While the opposition rejected the idea, elections took place two months before the Iraqi attack with a satisfactory turnout (62%).

The seven-months occupation of Kuwait paused the debate on the surface but, on the other hand, it intensified already existing tensions in society and added to their number (Al Essa, 1992; Boghardt, 2007, pp. 147–171). First, tension rose between those who left the country and those who stayed. The political leadership operated the government in exile while many remained in the country, some cooperating with the Iraqis and some working against them. This cleavage was, more importantly, connected to the Sunni–Shia divide in the country, as Shias were over-represented among those who stayed.[16] After the war, some of these military people engaged in political organisation; for example, General Muhammad Badr created the 2 August Movement, which pressed for the resignation of leading officials and for reform.

Second, doubts regarding the loyalty of two groups in the population rose significantly. One such community were the *bidoon*, who comprised approximately 75% of Kuwaiti armed forces personnel before the attack, as many *bidoon* families travelled to Iraq following the invasion – many only to find refuge with related families. The second community comprised expatriates, of whom, according to the Kuwaiti government, many supported the Iraqi forces during the seven-month occupation of Kuwait – especially Palestinians. Between April and June 1991, military courts charged 164 people with collaboration, almost all of whom were expatriates (Boghardt, 2006, pp. 161–162). Many of them were expelled in the subsequent years.

Third, the parliamentary movement, which was silenced by the war, was once again demanding political reform. They were supported by the international coalition and the general atmosphere after the armed conflict (Commins, 2014, p. 278). In order to divide the parliamentary opposition, the government announced that the National Council would convene on the 9 July 1991, with the same members as had been elected during the summer elections of 1990. Nonetheless, it narrowed its mandate further and excluded investigation of the reasons behind the dissolution of the National Assembly in 1985. On the other hand, they announced that elections of a new National Assembly would be held in October 1992, much later than the date for which the opposition would have hoped.

All these social and political effects were accompanied by the severe economic consequences of the war. The most damaging effects were attributed to the short-term activities of the puppet government established by the Iraqis (the "Kuwait Free Provisional Government"), which began to transfer public and royal financial assets; to allow the Iraqi confiscation of oil resources; and to destroy the industrial, welfare, education, and transport infrastructure, including setting oil fields on fire during the retreat, which took some eight months to extinguish (Karsh, 1989, pp. 747–755).

Regionally, the most important change was the development and institutionalisation of direct American military presence in the Gulf (Schwab, 2008, p. 67; Gause, 2010, p. 127), establishing a security umbrella for smaller Gulf states. As in the case of British shelter centuries earlier, the American umbrella was also built on the basis of mutual interests. Washington developed a dual containment policy against Iraq and Iran, in which building up deterrence on the Arab side of the Gulf played an important role. On the other hand, the security perception previously demonstrated by smaller Gulf states was altered, too. The American support provided during the Kuwaiti crisis convinced them "of the necessity to ensure that such support will be readily forthcoming in the future, if necessary" (Anthony, 1992, p. 21).

Self-defence was out of the question as the former defensive strategy of focusing on security and autonomy failed. Smaller Gulf states contributed to coalition efforts, but mostly logistically, their militaries were barely involved in military operations due to their small size and defensive capabilities (Khadduri and Ghareeb, 2001, p. 167). Importantly, neither the GCC nor other regional organisations (such as the Arab League) had any added value in crisis management (Khadduri and Ghareeb, 2001, p. 161). Nevertheless, in 1991, GCC states experimented with a regional alliance with Syria and Egypt by signing the Damascus Declaration (Whitehall Papers, 1993, pp. 35–38; Marschall, 2003, p. 117). The "six plus two" format would create a permanent Egyptian and Syrian presence in the Gulf in exchange for 10 billion USD; however, due to a lack of trust and the debates, the initiative did not yield any results.[17]

Similar to historical experiences, extra-regional actors were needed to maintain the security of smaller Gulf states against Iraq or Iran (Anthony, 1992, p. 132). The invasion of Kuwait proved that the five states were not able to do so themselves due to their inability to provide relative deterrence, a result of the interaction of military smallness and huge hydrocarbon resources (Brown, 1992, pp. 32–33). The military build-up was only a theoretical possibility due to their small demographic size (and internal socio-political problems), which made it impossible even for the UAE or Saudi Arabia to match Iraqi or Iranian forces (Al Essa, 1992, p. 180). In all, getting closer to the USA was essentially like paying "protection money" to keep away potential candidates wishing to lay hands on their oil wealth (Brown, 1992, pp. 32–33).

Smaller Gulf states in the American security shelter (1991–2003)

After the Iraqi invasion, smaller Gulf states opened their doors to American forces, changing their defensive strategy to one of alignment, which was formalised with bilateral security agreements signed with Bahrain and Kuwait in 1991, Qatar in 1992 (Katzman, 2009, 5; El-Katiri, 2014, p. 10) and the UAE in 1994 (Katzman, 2020, p. 14). Kuwait welcomed approximately 5,000 American troops and 24 aircraft, and heavy equipment. In 1995, the American naval forces stationed in Bahrain were upgraded to become the Fifth Fleet with 15 vessels, including an aircraft carrier. Qatar agreed to host a new military airbase near al-Udeid, and heavy military equipment, including approximately 100 armed vehicles. The UAE opened its Jabel Ali port to American forces, as well as the Al-Dhafra Air Port and the Fujairah Air Base. Due to the Facilities Access Agreement, Oman had already given permission to the USA to use its facilities; the military presence stationed in Oman also grew significantly (Gause, 2010, p. 127).

Direct American military presence became the norm in the Persian Gulf, which made the USA a quasi-military hegemon in the Gulf, being able to defend the status quo (Gause, 2010, p. 88; Ayoob, 2011, p. 130). Militarily, this situation was highly favourable for smaller Gulf states, especially coupled with the fall of the Soviet Union. While they still feared Iraq and Iran, they enjoyed American protection, the effectiveness of the dual containment policy, and access to American weapon systems (Ehteshami, 2013, pp. 33–34).

Naturally, the American shelter had disadvantageous consequences for smaller Gulf states, too. The non-traditional security dilemmas that had driven their policy of distancing from the USA before 1991 resurfaced in the early 1990s. The GCC states, especially Saudi Arabia and Kuwait, "emerged from the war increasingly internally divided and domestically insecure" (Ayoob, 2011, p. 129), due to the alliance of the regimes with an "infidel" government fighting against another Muslim regime (that of Saddam Hussein). Moreover, under the policy of dual containment (and later the global war on terror), smaller Gulf states practically became logistical hubs for the execution of American foreign policy. Many speculated in the Gulf media that the USA only used the Gulf crisis to capitalise on the weakness of the Gulf states so as to advance its agenda in the region (Kostiner, 2011, p. 99). In addition to foreign policy complications (e.g. criticising Israel while being allied to the USA), the Gulf states internal stability was also damaged due to strengthening anti-American sentiments in the GCC states, which paved the way for the spread of the transnational Jihadi movement (Schwab, 2008, p. 71; Ulrichsen, 2011a, p. 29). For these reasons, the small Gulf states had to keep their relations with the USA "restricted, at least in the eyes of the domestic public opinion" (Kostiner, 2011, p. 99).

The process of growing American presence coincided with falling oil prices until the 2000s, which decreased the leverage of the Gulf states, giving more room for Islamists and other opposition parties (Ulrichsen, 2011a, p. 30). The smaller Gulf states identified this trend, and they simply concluded that "the risk of internal political turmoil was lower than doing without Washington's protection" (Commins, 2014, p. 251).

To tackle these challenges, smaller Gulf states initiated a series of limited political reforms in the 1990s (Niethammer, 2011, pp. 243–249; Ulrichsen, 2011a, p. 32.; Commins, 2014, pp. 277–287; Lucas, 2014, pp. 172–173).[18] Even during the crisis, many sections of society – especially in Kuwait, Bahrain, and the UAE – began to publish articles demanding more political participation (Al Essa, 1992, p. 183). In Kuwait, the re-installed National Assembly began its work in 1992, with regular elections and the extension of voting rights to women in 2005. In Qatar, Emir Khalifa did not take social calls for more representation seriously, but his son Hamad, who overthrew his father in 1995, opened up the municipalities for popular election in 1999 and began to draft a new constitution, which came into effect in 2005. He also promised to make two-thirds of the members of the Consultative Assembly elected representatives, but elections did not follow. In Oman, Sultan Qaboos replaced the State Consultative Council with the Consultative Council, the members of which are selected by the Sultan from nominees elected by a small electorate of 500 voters per province. The electorate was gradually increased in the 1990s and 2000s, reaching universal suffrage in 2003. In 1996, Sultan Qaboos also issued a Basic Law; this served as a constitution for the country but, in contrast to the other Gulf states, it was never put on a referendum. In the same year, the Sultan made the legislation a bicameral body: to complement the work of the Consultative Council, he created the State Council, which, together, would form the Council of Oman (*Majlis al-'Oman*). Reforms were also limited in Bahrain, where the streets witnessed large demonstrations between 1992 and 1995 demanding new elections of the National Assembly, which had been dissolved in 1975. A new Constitutional Council was created in 1993, but a more substantive reform process took place after the death of Emir Isa in 1999, which led to the adoption of a new constitution in 2002 (transforming the country from an Emirate to a Kingdom). The UAE already had a constitution that created the federal structure, but it was made permanent in 1996, while limited elections took place for the Federal National Council only in 2006. Political reform in the Emirates was more limited due to the fact that domestic trends (the power balance between Abu Dhabi, Dubai, and the rest) shaped the political structure more than international trends.

In the next decade, "quite a bit happened in the Persian Gulf (...), but not that much changed" (Gause, 2010, p. 134). Besides the strengthening opposition towards Islamist movements and the creation of a sanctions regime on Iraq, the other important development of the 1990s was the slow opening of the Gulf states to Iran. By 1989, the Islamic Republic managed to stabilise relations with the five smaller Gulf states, but it was only able to re-establish diplomatic relations with Saudi Arabia in 1991 (Marschall, 2003, p. 101). In the first decade of the post-bipolar era, Iranian foreign policy seemed to return to its pragmatic pre-revolutionary past (especially after the election of President Mohammad Khatami in 1998), which was still menacing, but at least familiar and less harmful (Akbarzadeh, 2017).

Oman and Qatar proved to be the most eager to integrate Iran into the Gulf political and security system. Qatar, at the annual GCC summit in 1990, proposed closer ties with the Islamic Republic to counter the Iraqi threat in the future (Marschall, 2003, p. 110). Between 1988 and 1991, Oman played an important role as a facilitator: first, between Riyadh and Tehran, organising a secret meeting for the Iranian and Saudi foreign ministers in May 1989; and, second, between Baghdad and Tehran prior to the second Gulf crisis. Muscat saw relation-building as a way to help pragmatists in the Islamic Republic with whom Gulf states could work to advance their interests (Marschall, 2003, pp. 114–115).

Among the Gulf regimes, Kuwait changed its policy towards Iran the most significantly. While, in the late 1970s, Iran had been seen as a primary threat to the region, the Iraqi invasion redirected Kuwaiti attention to containing Iraq, in which Tehran proved to be a partner (Gause, 2010, p. 130). Re-building relations with Tehran actually started before the second Gulf crisis, as the first foreign minister-level visit from Iran since the revolution took place in July 1990 (Marschall, 2003, pp. 104–111). During the American-led counterattack on Iraqi forces, Iran secretly opened up its space and, diplomatically and with humanitarian contributions tried to support the resolution of the conflict, for which the Kuwaiti government have remained thankful. In the 1990s, Tehran offered technical services and aid for reconstruction. In the words of the Kuwaiti ambassador to the USA, Kuwait–Iran relations were "correct," but "not overly warm", with a focus on containing Iraq (Marschall, 2003, p. 115). Nevertheless, this did not create a trustful relationship, merely an interest-driven one (Akbarzadeh, 2017).

The only country that did not significantly alter its relations with Iran was Bahrain (Wright, 2017, pp. 70–75). Due to the demonstrations in the country, the government perceived internal tensions to have been provoked by Iran. Officially, the government declared that the events in the 1990s were a result of direct interference by the Islamic Republic, which wanted to organise a coup similar to that of 1981. This perception limited the extent to which Bahrain engaged in cooperation with Iran, with which it basically had formal ties, but nothing more. Bilateral relations changed only slightly after the death of Emir Isa – his successor, Hamad bin Isa, invited the Iranian president to the country in 2003, during which visit President Khatami was able to meet with Shia religious leaders, which was a surprisingly indulgent gesture from the Bahraini regime.

The UAE was the odd-man-out in this period for two reasons. First, it explicitly criticised the sanctions regime on Iraq, which it deemed counterproductive and an unnecessary burden on the Iraqi people; moreover, it reestablished ambassadorial-level diplomatic relations with Baghdad in 2000 (Hellyer, 2001, pp. 168–170). While Kuwait heavily criticised the Emirati course (which was driven by Abu Dhabi's quest for regional stability and the differentiation between regime and society), relations were not harmed to as great an extent as they had been in insensitive times (e.g. when Iraqi troops were mobilised near the Kuwaiti border in 1994); the UAE stood firmly behind Kuwait's security.

Second, the dynamics with relations with Iran were dominated by an issue that had remained dormant in the 1980s; namely, the question of the islands occupied by Iran (Hellyer, 2001, pp. 171–172; Marschall, 2003, pp. 121–147). In 1992, Tehran announced that it would strengthen its grip around Abu

Musa. Due to the political and legal pressure of the UAE (which manifested attempts to turn to the International Court of Justice), Iran backed down. After this episode, the UAE was able to involve other actors, notably the GCC (and its member states and their Arab partners), which resulted in a series of joint communiques on the issue. After the election of President Khatami, Emirati–Iranian ties slowly improved – which shows that the strategy of the UAE concerning separating bilateral relations and the question of the islands continued to work, and the question of the islands only popped up if there were no other security interest at stake, or there was a change in the status quo.

The perception of the American invasion of Iraq (2003)

The next milestone in the evolution of the alliance policy of smaller Gulf states was the American invasion of Iraq in 2003. The events of 2001 and the global war on terror did not have a substantial effect on the five states: they accommodated to the new narrative of fighting Jihadi terrorism, which they also considered a threat (Ulrichsen, 2011a, p. 34). The spotlight was more strongly on Saudi Arabia, not its neighbours, as the 15 terrorists that executed the 9/11 attacks were Saudi nationals, and only 2 of them were Emiratis (Gause, 2010, pp. 136–148; Ulrichsen, 2011a, pp. 31–32). Smaller Gulf states wanted to prove their worth by contributing multilateral efforts in Afghanistan; for example, by giving permission to use military bases for operations; contributing to the training of Afghan forces; and, in the case of the Emirates, to engaging in combat together with the ground and air forces (Kishk, 2016, p. 10; Pollack, 2020). Qatar served as a mediator between the USA and the Taliban, which also opened a representation in Doha (Barakat, 2014), the city where peace talks took place until, at least, 2021.

Smaller Gulf states had an ambivalent perception of the invasion of Iraq, torn between eliminating the threat posed by the Hussein regime and their fear of regional instability. While Kuwait publicly supported the operation (Roberts, 2011, p. 108), Bahrain and Oman actually attempted to dissuade the American government from the attack. The Bahraini King visited Washington in February 2003 and tried to convince President Bush to find a peaceful solution (Joyce, 2012, p. 112). In parallel, Sultan Qaboos tried to facilitate discussion between Saddam Hussein and President Bush (Al-Khalili, 2009, p. 118). Muscat feared that the intervention would cause "deep anti-American feeling" and strengthen the existing alliance dilemma. Sultan Qaboos famously invited the Iraqi president to Muscat on 2 October 2002, who delivered a letter that is generally suspected to include a message to Washington (Al-Khalili, 2009, p. 119).

Nevertheless, after the decision was made, the smaller Gulf states concluded that it was in their interest to make the war as short as possible to avoid regional destabilisation. Consequently, they contributed to American war efforts and the subsequent stabilisation process while trying to distance themselves publicly from Washington (Alterman, 2007; Al-Khalili, 2009,

p. 120; Kostiner, 2011, p. 100). Kuwait was the most transparent in helping Washington: it opened its borders and allowed the USA to set up a military base for the deployment of approximately 30,000 troops and 522 armed vehicles (Tucker-Jones, 2013, p. 12). Qatar provided space for the American Regional Headquarters (CENTCOM) in 2002, which has stayed in the country ever since, and when the Saudis asked the American government to leave the Daharan air force base, they volunteered to relocate the installation at the Al-Sayliyah base. These centres were highly important in the coordination of military operations, while the Saudis also stationed 3,000 troops and 175 armed vehicles (Tucker-Jones, 2013, p. 12). Bahrain welcomed the transfer of the US Marine Forces Central Command to the country (Joyce, 2012, p. 112). Oman allowed American and British forces to use air bases on its lands (Al-Khalili, 2009, p. 119), while the UAE not only allowed a surveillance aircraft at the station at Al-Dhafra, but also volunteered to host President Hussein as a political refugee if he would comply with American demands to leave Iraq (Alterman, 2007, p. 10; Mason, 2018, p. 103).

Behind the curtains, the third Gulf war profoundly altered the perception of the value of the alliance, as it felt like a "double betrayal" (Gervais, 2017). First, the neoconservative agenda, intent on spreading democracy, suggested that the USA is willing to use force against autocratic states, a notion which was aggressive and problematic for smaller Gulf states and contradicted their domestic political interests (Kostiner, 2011, p. 100). One could argue that American behaviour has become similar to that of Soviet foreign policy in the Cold War by promoting an ideology that is considered to be "dangerous, revolutionary and unstable" for their regime's stability (Sieff, 2004). Ironically, in parallel, the perception of Russian foreign policy also transformed in the 21st century as Moscow broke with its ideologically driven past and began to act like a pro-status quo superpower, usually supporting the strongest actors on the ground (Shumilin and Shumilina, 2017). Even if this policy were contrary to Gulf interests (e.g. with Iran or Syria), it was perceived as a stabilising force.

Second, American intervention was also seen as a betrayal, as it allowed Iranian influence to spread in the region, accompanied by sectarian violence (Kostiner, 2011, p. 101; Goldfischer, 2017, pp. 71–72). Smaller Gulf states blamed Washington for enabling Tehran to build up its network of state and non-state actors in Iraq, Syria, and Lebanon, constructing the "Shia Crescent" (Ulrichsen, 2011a, pp. 38–41). While the Hussein regime in Baghdad was unfavourable in many respects, it was Sunni-dominated and represented a balance to Iran, while the post-intervention Iraqi government was dominated by Shias, having close ties with Tehran (Bahgat, 2008, p. 237). The primary fear of smaller Gulf states was not a traditional war but, rather, the spread of transnational Shia networks in their societies, supported by the presidential change in Tehran with the hawkish Mahmoud Ahmadinejad being in power (Wehrey, 2014, pp. 17–18).

Moreover, smaller Gulf states also feared the potential and actual spillover effects of the intervention (Byman, 2011; Ulrichsen, 2011a, pp. 49–55).

In the 2000s, approximately four million refugees left their homes and, while the majority left for Syria or Jordan, the Gulf states also accommodated a small proportion. Due to the changing perception of Arab migrant workers, Gulf governments were totally suspicious of them. Sunni Jihadi terrorists also managed to capitalise on the disintegration of Iraq: the network of al-Qaeda and that of al-Qaeda in Iraq (later to be known as the Islamic State of Iraq) threatened the stability of Gulf states. The al-Qaeda cells in the Persian Gulf countries – later to be called Al-Qaeda in the Arabian Peninsula – had operated actively in the peninsula since 2003.

Similar to the previous Gulf crises, the two countries most exposed to the consequences of the Iraqi war were Bahrain and Kuwait (Wehrey, 2014). The Bahraini Shia opposition looked for inspiration from Iraqi developments (especially after the 2005 elections) and reactivated themselves in Bahraini politics, ending the boycott on parliamentary elections. In parallel, Sunni Bahrain was angered by the abuses suffered by the Iraqi Sunni community after 2003, contributing to the polarisation of Bahraini society. In Kuwait, Shia politicians used the events of 2003 to push for greater concessions in cultural and religious spheres but, contrary to Bahrain, their internal divisions were also visible. Shia networks competed for influence. Kuwaiti Sunnis acted similarly to the Bahrainis, but they were more critical of their government's lack of action in defending Iraqi Sunnis. Both governments faced a serious dilemma between easing sectarian tensions and remaining popular among the Sunni population.

In all, the post-2003 security environment was considerably much worse than previously. In addition to spreading Iranian influence and the spill-over effects of the war, the inability of Saudi Arabia to step up as a regional balancer contributed to the decision of smaller Gulf states to rely more on their own strategies, rather than wait for bigger states to handle the crisis.

Strategic changes in alliance policy after 2003

Due to the complexity of the new security environment, smaller Gulf states did not articulate a common, comprehensive strategy after 2003 (Bahgat, 2008, p. 239). Most of their actions were reactive, aimed at preventing undesired outcomes, rather than pushing to reach a specific goal. The Western management of the Arab Uprisings after 2011 further strengthened the reassessment of the American alliance (Rickli, 2016, p. 4) due to Washington's inconsistent "wait and see" approach, which directly contributed to the fall of Western-friendly regimes (first and foremost, in Egypt), and the proclaimed American goal to pivot to Asia, representing the threat of American disengagement from the Gulf.

This process eventually led to two strategic changes in the Gulf. First, smaller Gulf states decided to diversify their security relations and arrange security agreements with other powers such as France (Kuwait, Qatar and the UAE), Great Britain (Bahrain, Kuwait, and Oman), Turkey (Qatar), or later Israel (Bahrain and the UAE) (Rickli, 2016, pp. 8–9). These forms of cooperation did not aim at replacing American relations, merely comple-menting them. Smaller Gulf states still cooperated with the American mili-tary and participated in America-led projects; for example, the Islamic Cooperation Initiatives (ICI), which aimed at building relations between NATO and the GCC in the fields of counter-terrorism, the proliferation of weapons of mass destruction, border security, civil emergency planning, defence reform, and other fields of military cooperation (Bahgat, 2008, p. 240; Rickli, 2016, p. 9). Nevertheless, they viewed the worth of American alliance as degraded.

Second, such developments contributed to the individualisation of smaller Gulf states' foreign and security policy, and widened the gap between their security perception. Among the five countries, we can identify three patterns that they followed after 2003. Kuwait and Bahrain did not make any signifi-cant changes to the course of their security policy. Using the realist vocabu-lary, they continued their alignment policy, prioritising security and influence. Both countries signed up for the initiative, as well as for other forms of coop-eration; for example, Bahrain was the first Gulf state with which the USA made a free trade agreement (Kinninmont, 2011, p. 57). Kuwait and Bahrain continued to buy weaponry from the USA in great amounts. Between 1999 and 2006, Kuwait bought American arms to the value of 2,900 million USD – the highest expenditure among the Gulf states, while Bahrain pur-chased weaponry to the value of 1,000 million USD (Bahgat, 2008, p. 240).

Due to their perceived stability, Qatar and the UAE changed their previ-ous strategy and began to favour influence and autonomy over security, and engaged in active participation in regional affairs (Soubrier, 2017, p. 129; Mason 2018). Both countries remained allied to the USA, but they stood upon the international stage even if it was contrary to American interests, even risking good relations. In some international questions (e.g. maintain-ing political and/or economic ties with Iran, intervening in other states' domestic affairs, or pushing against each other), these states followed poli-cies even if it caused visible tension with the USA.[19] In both cases, domestic political tendencies (see Chapter 4) (mostly regarding the rise of Hamad bin Khalifa al Thani in Qatar and Crown Prince Mohamed bin Zayed in Abu Dhabi) and economic developments contributed to these changes, especially after 2008.[20]

That being said, both countries maintained military cooperation with the USA, letting American forces be present in their territory and also engage in arms trade (Saidy, 2016, p. 299). Nonetheless, this "security alignment with the (…) Western powers will coexist alongside economic (and possibly ide-ational) reorientation toward a variety of new partners in Asia, Africa and even Latin America" (Ulrichsen, 2011b, p. 244). Moreover, diversified eco-nomic relations were also used as a soft security guarantee by them (espe-cially in the case of Qatar), which made them less reliant on the hard security provided by the American military presence (Wright, 2011a, p. 130). Qatar had already managed to become more active on the international stage in the 2000s, while the UAE followed in its footsteps but with different aims and tools determined by different regime security interests (outlined in Chapter 4). These differences quickly led to tensions between Qatar and the UAE, and manifested themselves in questions such as the perception of moderate Islamism or Saudi Arabia.

Third, Oman represents a category in itself. In the triangle of alliance policy, Muscat prioritised security and autonomy, maintaining low-key behaviour and preferring behind-the-scenes activities rather than the broad political initiatives of Qatar and the UAE. In this regard, Oman acted defensively and tried to contribute only to solving international disputes through facilitation and mediation, without pursuing self-interests through various forms of intervention. This active neutrality required Oman to maintain a greater distance from the USA, which is probably the main reason why Muscat opted out from the ICI (Bahgat, 2008, p. 240; Yenigun, 2016, pp. 16–17). The Omani absence (coupled with the Saudi absence) severely limited the relevance of the NATO initiative, as they account for 70% of the defence expenditures in the region (Beshr, 2015).

That being said, Oman was still open to American military presence in the Gulf and to buying American arms (Bahgat, 2008, p. 240). It also engaged in various activities in the ICI framework without formally being a member (Rickli, 2016, p. 9). Through its facilitation activities, Muscat frequently played the role of a "go-between" (Neubauer, 2016) between Western actors (or allies) and other players; for example, in 2007, Oman helped to negotiate the release of 15 British navy personnel captured by Iran, and did the same again in 2009 for three Americans. During the Obama presidency, Oman played a crucial role in facilitating nuclear talks between the USA and Iran while, later, Oman tried to bring different factions in Yemen closer to the negotiation table (Baabood, 2017, p. 118). All these examples show that Oman has great added value to American and Western security policy precisely because it tries to keep its distance publicly.

In all, the second (1990–1991) and the third (2003) Gulf wars heavily shaped the alliance policy of smaller Gulf states. Generally speaking, in the 1970s and 1980s, they prioritised security and autonomy, pursuing a defensive strategy without any superpower shelter (arguably, except for Oman). This proved to be unsustainable after the Iraqi invasion of Kuwait, which was not necessarily the result of the relative smallness of the emirate but more due to the inability of relative deterrence. Large hydrocarbon resources contributed to growing normative size and diminishing security. This is why smaller Gulf states changed course, rushing into American shelter in the 1990s, choosing security and influence over strategic autonomy, following the lead of Washington in the 1990s and early 2000s, regardless of its negative political, economic, and social consequences.

Lastly, the American attack on Iraq and its consequences transformed the smaller Gulf states' behaviour once again due to the devaluation of the value of American alignment and to security perceptions becoming more diverse. In parallel with systemic changes, smaller Gulf states adopted different alliance policies: Bahrain and Kuwait mostly continued the alignment policy as

Qatar and the UAE tried to step up independently, pursuing an active strategy. Meanwhile, Oman considered the defensive approach most appropriate to its security needs.

Besides diverse regime security needs and domestic stability, the difference between the approach of smaller Gulf states arguably has its roots in different perceptions of what it means to be a small state. Kuwait and Bahrain see their position as the least stable, pushing the leadership to focus more on security. Even if smallness plays a role in the Emirati identity, the UAE does not consider itself weak, neither does Qatar. Omani historical experience makes its leadership cautious, refraining from overly visible political projects, but cooperating closely with the USA ever since the 1980s.

When it comes to alliance policy, a major question is whether Russia and China could capitalise on the developments to build up their presence in the Gulf. To some extent, the process is already ongoing: smaller Gulf states strengthen their ties with both Moscow (Shumilin and Shumilina, 2017) and Beijing (N. Rózsa, 2020), especially as their activities seem to stabilise the status quo (e.g. by contributing to the stability of Iraq, and fighting piracy in the Gulf of Aden). Nevertheless, Russia and China will not be able to replace the USA in the foreseeable future due to their careful balancing act between basically every major regional power (some of whom are feared by smaller Gulf states), their lack of cultural soft power, and their inability to solve the complex international crisis.

Notes

1　Which was due to the agreement between France and Britain signed in 1862, which granted independence for the "Sultanate of Muscat and the Sultan of Zanzibar" (Kieran, 1968; Onley, 2009).

2　The motivation for Ras al-Khaimah to refuse to join the federation the first time was in opposition to the passivity of the other emirs regarding the loss of the Tunb islands in 1971. A day before the announced withdrawal of British forces, Iran invaded the Greater and Lesser Tunb islands, and forced the government of Sharjah to agree to the loss of Abu Musa. The eventual accession of Ras al-Khaimah to the UAE determined the relations between Iran and the UAE to a great extent (Zahlan, 1978, pp. 195–196; Hellyer, 2001).

3　The biggest concern in this regard was the territorial integrity of Kuwait in light of its geopolitical exposure to Iraq (Dockrill, 2002, p. 127).

4　Regarding, for example, the Hawar Islands and Zubarah between Bahrain and Qatar; Khwar Al Udayd and Sabkhat Mutti between Saudi Arabia and Abu Dhabi; the Abu Musa and Tunb islands between the UAE and Iran; Qaru and Umm al-Maradim between Saudi Arabia and Kuwait; the Buraimi Oasis between Abu Dhabi, Oman, and Saudi Arabia; the borderlands between Sharjah, Dubai; and Oman (Peterson, 2011).

5　Oil production in Abu Dhabi started in 1962 and, while it was not as wealthy as Qatar or Kuwait (Sarbadhikari, 1977, pp. 143–144), the smaller emirates saw it as a primary actor in the Trucial Coast, due to its geographical closeness.

6　The leaders of the nine emirates frequently visited Riyadh or Tehran for consultation and to use them against other smaller states (Friedman, 2017, pp. 117–118).

7   Other information suggested that the activities of Qatar were attributed to Saudi Arabia, which wanted to prolong the discussions in order to regain possession of the Buraimi oasis. The main aim of Qatar, in this narrative, was to loosen up the integration, as it did not want to see a federalised entity emerging, but preferring to see a group of small states that were mostly smaller than Qatar (Smith, 2002, p. 79).

8   Cited by Kamrava, 2005, p. 176.

9   The constant references to the Bahraini government not respecting Islamic laws can be seen as an attempt to be seen as *taqfir*.

10 The territory was not retaken by Iraq until 1988, a few months before the conclusion of the war.

11 In comparison, seven Bahraini ships and only two Qatari ships and one Emirati ship were recorded as having been hit between 1984 and 1987. The Kuwaiti casualties were only outnumbered by the Saudi casualties, with 36 ships having been attacked (Ahrari, 1985, p. 143).

12 The Arab Charter was born after the refusal of deeper security cooperation with Iraq by the Gulf states (Legrenzi, 2011, p. 29).

13 In the Omani narrative, Muscat only conducts facilitation of dialogue between various political actors: Muscat does not engage in mediation.

14 As well as the Iranian help provided in the Dhofari war.

15 Except for the GCC and Saudi cooperation which, nonetheless, was more political than military in nature.

16 Partly because many Sunni officials had enough income to pay for a vacation abroad during the summer of 1990, so they were not even in the country when the attack took place.

17 It is not surprising that Sultan Qaboos, who was appointed as the head of the GCC committee for regional security arrangements, was highly sceptical of the cooperation all along.

18 After 2001, an additional motivation for further liberalisation was to fit into the Bush administration agenda to promote democracy; nevertheless, Washington did not opt for a full-blown democratisation process (Niethammer, 2011, p. 239).

19 For example, Qatari diplomats engaged in rhetoric with American Secretary of Defence Robert Gates in 2008 in Manama regarding the regional role of Iran.

20 Both countries altogether capitalised on the 2008 economic crisis to strengthen their role in the global economy with building south-to-south networks, undertaking greater participation in Western markets at the same time (Ulrichsen, 2011b). In the case of the UAE, the global economic crisis also contributed to the strengthening of Abu Dhabi in the federal structure, leading to stronger influence from the emirate and its de facto leader, Mohamed bin Zayed Al Nahyan, in foreign affairs.

Bibliography

Ahrari, M.E. (1985) Theological Insurgency: Iran in the Region. *The Washington Quarterly*, 8(2), pp. 47–60. DOI:10.1080/01636608509450268.

Akbarzadeh, S. (2017) Iran and the Gulf Cooperation Council Sheikhdoms, in Almezaini, K.S. and Rickli, J. (eds.) *The Small Gulf States. Foreign and Security Policies before and after the Arab Spring*. London & New York: Routledge, pp. 89–106. DOI:10.4324/9781315619576-6.

Allen, C. and Rigsbee, W.L. (2002) *Oman under Qaboos: From Coup to Constitution, 1970-1996*. London & Portland: Frank Cass. DOI:10.4324/9781315040097.

Alnasrawi, A. (1986) Economic Consequences of the Iraq-Iran War. *Third World Quarterly*, 8(3), pp. 869–895. DOI:10.1080/01436598608419929.

Alterman, J.B. (2007) Iraq and the Gulf States. The Balance of Fear. US Institute for Peace, [Online]. Available at: https://www.usip.org/sites/default/files/sr189.pdf (Accessed 31 January 2021).

Al Abed, I. (2001) The Historical Background and Constitutional Basis to the Federation,in Al Abed, I. (eds.) *United Arab Emirates: A New Perspective*. London: Trident Press, pp. 121–144.

Al Essa, S.Y. (1992) Political Consequences for Kuwait, in Ibrahim, I. (ed.) *The Gulf Crisis. Background and Consequences*. Washington: Georgetown University, pp. 169–185.

Al-Khalili, M. (2009) *Oman's Foreign Policy. Foundations and Practice*. London: Praeger. DOI:10.25148/etd.fi13101580.

Anthony, J.D. (1992) After the Gulf War: The GCC and the World, in Ibrahim, I. (ed.) *The Gulf Crisis. Background and Consequences*. Washington: Georgetown University, pp. 121–144.

Ayoob, M. (2011) American Policy Towards the Persian Gulf, in Kamrava, M. (ed.) *International Politics of the Persian Gulf*. New York: Syracuse University Press, pp. 120–143.

Baabood, A. (2017) Oman's Independent Foreign Policy, in Almezaini, K.S. and Rickli, J. (eds.) *The Small Gulf States. Foreign and Security Policies before and after the Arab Spring*. London & New York: Routledge, pp. 107–122. DOI:10.4324/9781315619576-7.

Bahgat, G. (2008) Security in the Persian Gulf: Two Conflicting Models. *Defense & Security Analysis*, 24(3), pp. 237–245. DOI:10.1080/14751790802321313.

Baktiari, B. (1993) Revolutionary Iran's Persian Gulf Policy: The Quest for Regional Supremacy, in Amirahmadi, H. and Entessar, N. (eds.) *Iran and the Arab World*. Macmillan Press, London, pp. 69–93. DOI:10.1007/978-1-349-22538-5_5.

Barakat, S. (2014) Qatari Mediation: Between Ambition and Achievement. Brookings Doha Center, [Online]. Available at: https://www.brookings.edu/wp-content/uploads/2016/06/Final-PDF-English.pdf (Accessed 31 January 2021)

Belfer, M.A. (2014) Iranian Claims to Bahrain: From Rhetoric to Interference. *Revista de Investigaciones Politicas y Sociologicas*, 13(2), pp. 31–51.

Beshr, H. (2015) NATO and the Gulf: What's Next? Middle East Institute, [Online]. Available at: http://www.mei.edu/content/article/nato-and-gulf-what%E2%80%99s-next. (Accessed 31 January 2021)

Bill, J.A. (1984) Resurgent Islam in the Persian Gulf. *Foreign Affairs*, 63(1), pp. 108–127. DOI:10.2307/20042088.

Blanchard, C.M. (2014) Qatar: Background and U.S. Relations. Congressional Research Service, [Online]. Available at: https://fas.org/sgp/crs/mideast/RL31718.pdf (Accessed 31 January 2021)

Boghardt, L.P. (2006) *Kuwait amid War, Peace and Revolution. 1979-1991 and New Challenges*. New York: Palgrave Macmillan. DOI:10.1057/9780230627451.

Brown, L.C. (1992) America's Middle Eastern Policy, 1945–1991, in Ibrahim, I. (ed.) *The Gulf Crisis. Background and Consequences*. Washington: Georgetown University, pp. 18–37.

Byman, D.L. (2011) Regional Consequences of Internal Turmoil in Iraq, in Kamrava, M. (ed.) *International Politics of the Persian Gulf*. New York: Syracuse University Press, pp. 144–168.

Commins, D. (2014) *The Gulf States. A Modern History*. London: I. B. Tauris. DOI:10.5040/9780755608805.

Davidson, C.M. (2012) *After the Sheikhs. The Coming Collapse of the Gulf Monarchies.* London: Hurst & Co.

Dockrill, S. (2002) *Britain's Retreat from East of Suez. The Choice between Europe and the World?* New York: Palgrave Macmillan. DOI:10.1057/9780230597785_6.

Ehteshami, A. (2013) *Dynamics of Change in the Persian Gulf. Political Economy, War and Revolution.* New York: Routledge. DOI:10.4324/9780203066256.

El-Katiri, M. (2014) United States–Gulf Cooperation Council Security Cooperation in the Multipolar World. Strategic Studies Institute, [Online]. Available at: https://www.globalsecurity.org/military/library/report/2014/ssi_el-katiri_141001.pdf (Accessed 31 January 2021).

Friedman, B. (2017) From Union (ittihad) to United (muttahida) the United Arab Emirates, a Success Born of Failure. *Middle Eastern Studies*, 53(1), pp. 112–135.

Fromherz, A.J. (2012) *Qatar. A Modern History.* Washington, DC: Georgetown University Press.

Gause, G. (2010) *The International Relations of the Persian Gulf.* Cambridge: Cambridge University Press. DOI:10.1017/cbo9780511818264.

Gervais, V. (2017) The Changing Security Dynamics in the Middle East and Its Impact on Smaller Gulf Cooperation Council States' Alliance Choices and Policies, in Almezaini, K.S. and Rickli, J. (eds.) *The Small Gulf States. Foreign and Security Policies before and after the Arab Spring.* London & New York: Routledge, pp. 31–46.

Goldfischer, D. (2017) The United States and Its Key Gulf Allies: A New Foundation for Troubled Partnership?, in Almezaini, K.S. and Rickli, J. (eds.) *The Small Gulf States. Foreign and Security Policies before and after the Arab Spring.* London & New York: Routledge, pp. 64–88. DOI:10.4324/9781315619576-5.

Halliday, F. (1980) The Gulf between Two Revolutions: 1958–1979. *MERIP Reports*, 1980(85), pp. 6–15. DOI:10.2307/3010801.

Heard-Bey, F. (1999) The United Arab Emirates: A Quarter Century of Federation, in Hudson, M.C. (ed.) *Middle East Dilemma: The Politics and Economics of Arab Integration.* New York: Columbia University Press, pp. 171–186.

Hellyer, P. (2001) Evolution of UAE Foreign Policy, in Al Abed, I. (eds.) *United Arab Emirates: A New Perspective.* London: Trident Press, pp. 161–178.

Hooglund, E. (1992) Iranian Populism and Political Change in the Gulf. *Middle East Report*, 1992(174), pp. 19–21. DOI:10.2307/3012964.

Hunter, S.T. (1988) Iran and the Spread of Revolutionary Islam. *Third World Quarterly*, 10(2), pp. 730–749. DOI:10.1080/01436598808420079.

Hura, M. et al. (2000) *Interoperability. A Continuing Challenge in Coalition Air Operations.* Rand Corporation, [Online]. Available at: https://www.rand.org/pubs/monograph_reports/MR1235.html. (Accessed 31 January 2021)

Ibrahim, I. (1992) Sovereign States and Borders in the Gulf Region: A Historical Perspective, in Ibrahim, I. (ed.) *The Gulf Crisis. Background and Consequences.* Washington: Georgetown University, pp. 3–17.

Joyce, M. (2012) *Bahrain from the Twentieth Century to the Arab Spring.* New York: Palgrave Macmillan. DOI:10.1057/9781137031792.

Kamrava, M. (2005) *The Modern Middle East. A Political History since the First World War.* London: University of California Press. DOI:10.1525/9780520956858.

Kamrava, M. (2017) Iran–Qatar Relations, in Bahgat, G., Ehteshami, A. and Quilliam, N. (eds.) *Security and Bilateral Issues between Iran and its Arab Neighbours.* London: Palgrave Macmillan, pp. 167–188. DOI:10.1007/978-3-319-43289-2_8.

Karsh, E. (1989) From Ideological Zeal to Geopolitical Realism: The Islamic Republic and the Gulf, in Karsh, E. (ed.) *The Iran–Iraq War. Impact and Implications.* New York: St. Martin's Press, pp. 26–41. DOI:10.1007/978-1-349-20050-4_3.

Katzman, K. (2009) Kuwait: Security, Reform, and U.S. Policy. Congressional Research Service, [Online]. Available at: https://www.everycrsreport.com/files/20090520_RS21513_94dc39c2eb0f46235b92ccf0bbd0cb3e02e16aa2.pdf. (Accessed 31 January 2021)

Katzman, K. (2020) The United Arab Emirates (UAE) Issues for U.S. Policy. Congressional Research Service, [Online]. Available at: https://fas.org/sgp/crs/mid-east/RS21852.pdf (Accessed 31 January 2021)

Kechichian, J.A. (1995) *Oman and the World. The Emergence of an Independent Foreign Policy.* Santa Monica: Rand. DOI:10.7249/mr680.

Kennedy, E.M. (1975) The Persian Gulf: Arms Race of Arms Control? *Foreign Affairs,* 54(1), pp. 14–35. DOI:10.2307/20039552.

Khadduri, M. and Ghareeb, E. (2001) *War in the Gulf, 1990–91. The Iraq–Kuwait Conflict and Its Implications.* Oxford: Oxford University Press.

Kieran, J.A. (1968) The Origins of the Zanzibar Guarantee Treaty of 1862. *Canadian Journal of African Studies,* 2(2), pp. 147–166. DOI:10.2307/484114.

Kinninmont, J. (2011) Bahrain, in Davidson, C. (ed.) *Power and Politics in the Persian Gulf Monarchies.* London: Hurst & Company, pp. 31–62.

Kishk, A.M. (2016) Bahrain and NATO: Essentials of the Partnership and Obstacles, in Akbulut, H. (ed.) *NATO, Cooperative Security, and the Middle East – Status and Prospects.* Austrian Institute for International Affairs, [Online]. Available at: http://www.oiip.ac.at/fileadmin/Unterlagen/Dateien/Publikationen/Report_NATO_WorkshopHP.pdf. (Accessed 31 January 2021), pp. 8–11.

Kostiner, J. (2011) GCC Perceptions of Collective Security in the Post-Saddam Era, in Kamrava, M. (ed.) *International Politics of the Persian Gulf.* New York: Syracuse University Press, pp. 94–119.

Legrenzi, M. (2011) *The GCC and the International Relations of the Gulf. Diplomacy, Security and Economic Coordination in a Changing Middle East.* London & New York: I.B. Tauris. DOI:10.5040/9780755609086.

Louer, L. (2013) Sectarianism and Coup-Proofing Strategies in Bahrain. *Journal of Strategic Studies,* 36(2), pp. 245–260. DOI:10.1080/01402390.2013.790314.

Lucas, R.E. (2014) Monarchies and Protests in the Arab Uprisings: Path Dependencies or Political Opportunities. *Journal of Arabian Studies,* 4(2), pp. 195–213. DOI:10.1080/21534764.2014.971648.

Marschall, C. (2003) *Iran's Persian Gulf Policy. From Khomeini to Khatami.* London: RoutledgeCurzon. DOI:10.4324/9780203417928.

Mason, R. (2018) Breaking the mold of small state classification? The broadening influence of United Arab Emriates foreign policy through effective military and bandwagoning strategies. *Canadian Foreign Policy Journal,* 24(1), pp. 95–112. DOI:10.1080/11926422.2018.1427123.

Matthiesen, T. (2013) *Sectarian Gulf. Bahrain, Saudi Arabia and the Arab Spring that Wasn't.* Stanford: Stanford University Press. DOI:10.1515/9780804787222.

McCourt, D.M. (2009) What Was Britain's "East of Suez Role"? Reassessing the Withdrawal, 1964–1968. *Diplomacy & Statecraft,* 20(3), pp. 453–472. DOI:10.1080/09592290903293787.

Melkumyan, E. (2015) A Political History of Relations between Russia and the Gulf States. *Arab Center for Research & Policy Studies,* [Online]. Available at: https://www.dohainstitute.org/en/lists/ACRPS-PDFDocumentLibrary/A_Political_

History_of_Relations_between_Russia_and_the_Gulf_States_Elena_Melkumyan. pdf (Accessed 31 January 2021).

Ministry of Defence (1966) Defence Review: The Statement on the Defence Estimates, 1966, Part 1, [Online]. Available at: http://filestore.nationalarchives.gov.uk/pdfs/ small/cab-129-124-c-33.pdf (Accessed 31 January 2021)

Naruzzaman, M. (2012) Conflicts between Iran and the Gulf Arab States: An Economic Evaluation. *Strategic Analysis*, 36(4), pp. 542–553. DOI:10.1080/097001 61.2012.689512.

Neubauer, S. (2016) Oman: The Gulf's Go-Between. The Arab Gulf States Institute in Washington, [Online]. Available at: https://agsiw.org/wp-content/uploads/2016/02/ Neubauer_OmanMediator.pdf (Accessed 31 January 2021).

Niethammer, K. (2011) Political Reform and Foreign Policy in the Persian Gulf Monarchies, in Kamrava, M. (ed.) *International Politics of the Persian Gulf*. New York: Syracuse University Press, pp. 234–258.

Okruhlik, G. and Conge, P.J. (1999) The Politics of Border Disputes: On the Arabian Peninsula. *International Journal*, 54(2), pp. 230–248.

Onley, J. (2009) Britain and the Gulf Sheikhdoms, 1820–1971: The Politics of Protection. Georgetown University, [Online]. Available at: https://www.files.ethz. ch/isn/110431/CIRSOccasionalPaper4JamesOnley2009.pdf (Accessed 31 January 2021).

Ostovar, A. (2016) *Vanguard of the Imam. Religion, Politics, and Iran's Revolutionary Guards*. Oxford: Oxford University Press. DOI:10.1093/acprof:oso/9780199387892. 001.0001.

Owen, R.P. (1973) The Rebellion in Dhofar – A Threat to Western Interests in the Gulf. *The World Today*, 29(6), pp. 266–272.

Pakistan Forum (1973) Smaller States of the Arabian Gulf. *Pakistan Forum*, 3(10–11), pp. 37–38.

Pelletiere, S.C. (1992) *The Iran–Iraq War. Chaos in Vacuum*. New York: Praeger.

Peterson, J.E. (2011) Sovereignty and Boundaries in the Gulf States. Setting the Peripheries, in Kamrava, M. (ed.) *International Politics of the Persian Gulf*. New York: Syracuse University Press, pp. 21–50.

Pickering, J. (1998) *Britain's Withdrawal from the East of Suez. The Politics of Retrenchment*. New York: Palgrave. DOI:10.1057/9780333995488.

Pollack, K.M. (2020) Sizing Up Little Sparta. Understanding UAE Military Effectiveness. American Enterprise Institute, [Online]. Available at: https://www. aei.org/research-products/report/sizing-up-little-sparta-understanding-uae-mili- tary-effectiveness/ (Accessed 31 January 2021).

Rickli, J. (2016) New Alliances Dynamics in the Gulf and their Impact on Small GCC States. *Third World Thematics*, 1(1), pp. 1–19. DOI:10.1080/23802014.2016.1188023.

Roberts, D.B. (2011) Punching Above Its Weight. *Foreign Policy*, [Online]. Available at: https://foreignpolicy.com/2011/04/12/punching-above-its-weight-2/ (Accessed 31 January 2021).

Rossiter, A. (2017) Screening the Food from the Flies: Britain, Kuwait, and the Dilemma of Protection, 1961–1971. *Diplomacy & Statecraft*, 28(1), pp. 85–109. DOI:10.1080/09592296.2017.1275514.

N. Rózsa, E. (2020) Deciphering China in the Middle East. *Institute for Security Studies*, [Online]. Available at: https://www.iss.europa.eu/content/deciphering- china-middle-east#_introduction (Accessed 31 January 2021).

Rubin, B. (1989) The Gulf States and the Iran–Iraq War, in Efraim Karsh (ed.) *The Iran–Iraq War. Impact and Implications*. New York: St. Martin's Press, pp. 121–132. DOI:10.1007/978-1-349-20050-4_9.

Saidy, B. (2016) Qatari–US Military Relations: Context, Evolution and Prospects. *Contemporary Arab Affairs*, 10(2), pp. 286–299. DOI:10.1080/17550912.2016.1244902.

Sarbadhikari, P. (1977) The United Arab Emirates in International Relations. *The Indian Journal of Political Science*, 38/2, 143–151.

Schwab, O. (2008) *The Gulf Wars and the United States*. London: Praeger.

Shumilin, A. and Shumilina, I. (2017) Russia as a Gravity Pole of the GCC's New Foreign Policy Pragmatism. *The International Spectator*, 52(2), pp. 115–129. DOI:10.4324/9780203701287-9.

Sieff, M. (2004) Sand in Our Eyes: U.S.–Saudi Relations after Iraq. *National Interest*, [Online]. Available at: https://nationalinterest.org/article/sand-in-our-eyes-us-saudi-relations-after-iraq-664 (Accessed 31 January 2021).

Soubrier, E. (2017) Evolving Foreign and Security Policies: A Comparative Study of Qatar and the United Arab Emirates, in Almezaini, K.S. and Rickli, J. (eds.) *The Small Gulf States. Foreign and Security Policies before and after the Arab Spring*. London & New York: Routledge, pp. 123–143. DOI:10.4324/9781315619576-8.

Smith, S.C. (2002) *Britain's Revival and Fall in the Gulf. Kuwait, Bahrain, Qatar, and the Trucial States, 1950–71*. New York: RoutledgeCurzon. DOI:10.4324/9780203398098.

Sirriyeh, H. (1985) Development of the Iraqi–Iranian Dispute, 1847–1975. *Journal of Contemporary History*, 20(3), pp. 483–492. DOI:10.1177/002200948502000309.

Sreedhar (1982) Uncertainties in the Gulf. *Strategic Analysis*, 6(4), pp. 254–257. DOI:10.1080/09700168209425861.

Strategic Survey (1983) Within the Persian Gulf: Impact of a War. *Strategic Survey*, 84(1), pp. 76–81. DOI:10.1080/04597238308460619.

Theberge, R. (1973) Iran: Ten Years after the "White Revolution". *MERIP Reports*, 1973(18), pp. 3–22.

Trenin, D. (2018) *What is Russia up to in the Middle East?* Cambridge: Polity Press.

Tucker-Jones, A. (2013) *The Iraq War. Operation Iraqi Freedom 2003–2014*. South Yorkshire: Pen & Sword Military.

Ulrichsen, K.C. (2011a) *Insecure Gulf. The End of Certainty and the Transition to the Post-Oil Era*. New York: Columbia University Press.

Ulrichsen, K.C. (2011b) Repositioning the GCC States in the Changing Global Order. *Journal of Arabian Studies*, 1(2), pp. 231–247. DOI:10.1080/21534764.2011.630894.

Valeri, M. (2017) Iran–Oman Relations since the 1970s: A Mutually Beneficial Modus Vivendi, in Bahgat, G., Ehteshami, A. and Quilliam, N. (eds.) *Security and Bilateral Issues between Iran and its Arab Neighbours*. London: Palgrave Macmillan, pp. 149–166. DOI:10.1007/978-3-319-43289-2_7.

Wehrey, F.C. (2014) *Sectarian Politics in the Gulf. From the Iraq War to the Arab Uprisings*. New York: Columbia University Press.

Whitehall Papers (1993) The GCC: Alliance Politics. *Whitehall Papers*, 20(1), pp. 35–50.

Wright, S. (2011a) Qatar, in Davidson, C. (ed.) *Power and Politics in the Persian Gulf Monarchies*. London: Hurst & Company, pp. 113–134.

Wright, L. (2011b) Memories of 1971: A Historical Year in the Emirates. *Asian Affairs*, 42(2), pp. 300–308. DOI:10.1080/03068374.2011.571369.

Wright, S. (2017) Iran's Relations with Bahrain, in Bahgat, G., Anoushiravan, E. and Quilliam, N. (eds.) *Security and Bilateral Issues between Iran and its Arab Neighbours*. London: Palgrave Macmillan, pp. 61–80. DOI:10.1007/978-3-319-43289-2_4.

Yenigun, C. (2016) Oman Security Perspectives and NATO Relations, in Akbulut, H. (ed.) *NATO, Cooperative Security, and the Middle East – Status and Prospects*. Austrian Institute for International Affairs, [Online]. Available at: http://www.oiip.

ac.at/fileadmin/Unterlagen/Dateien/Publikationen/Report_NATO_WorkshopHP. pdf. (Accessed 31 January 2021), pp. 12–19.

Yetiv, S. A. (2008) *The Absence of Grand Strategy. The United States in the Persian Gulf, 1972-2005*. John Hopkins University Press, Baltimore. DOI: 10.5860/ choice.46-1152.

Zabih, S. (1976) Iran's Policy towards the Persian Gulf. *International Journal of Middle East Studies*, 7(3), pp. 345–358. DOI:10.1017/s0020743800025708.

Zahlan, R.S. (1978) *The Origins of the United Arab Emirates. A Political and Social History of the Trucial States*. London: Macmillan Press. DOI:10.1007/978-1-349-03949-4_13.

6 Smaller Gulf states in the age of regional uncertainty (2011–2021)

The last decade brought a serious transformation in the MENA region. The Arab Uprisings (a term that refers to the events taking place between 2010 and 2013), the intensifying Saudi–Iranian rivalry, the spread of transnational networks, and terrorism all changed security calculations in the smaller Gulf states, strengthening the fragmentation process in the subregion. Despite the evolving security challenges, some of the smaller Gulf states managed to increase their influence while also maintaining their regime security. In Chapter 6, these trends will be investigated in four case studies.

Regime stability during the Arab Uprisings (2011–2013)

The Arab Uprisings represent a milestone in the international position of smaller Gulf states, for better and for worse. Their utmost priority was to maintain regime security, while those with a more stable domestic environment – especially Qatar and the UAE – pursued their various interests beyond survival. In the present part, I will focus on how smaller Gulf states tried to achieve regime stability while, in the next one, their intervention will be addressed in terms of armed conflict.

Uprisings in the Gulf in 2011

The Gulf region was not exposed to the series of Arab Uprisings as much as other subregions in the Middle East. In 2011, the number of sizeable anti-government protests[1] did not amount to 10 in Saudi Arabia, the UAE, Oman, Kuwait, and Qatar (the last not experiencing any such demonstrations). On the other hand, Bahrain witnessed more than 30, which was the fourth-largest number in the Middle East (after Syria, Yemen, and Egypt), and even surpassed the number of protests in Tunisia (Lucas, 2014, p. 197).

The reasons behind the relative stability of the Gulf monarchies (except for Bahrain) during the Arab Uprisings can be explained in a variety of ways. First, they performed much better in most socio-economic variables than countries such as Yemen, Syria, or Libya. Several studies[2] suggest that the two most important determinant variables for explaining the different extent of political instability during the early 2010s were commodity price shocks

DOI: 10.4324/9781003158288-7

and youth unemployment rates. From this perspective, smaller Gulf regimes were relatively sheltered (Luciani, 2016) due to their smallness and their economic structure. The rise of commodity food prices in the region was mainly attributed to the rise of oil prices, which was crucial for oil-importers, but also created fiscal leverage for oil-exporters to compensate for economic troubles. They even needed less money to do so due to their small demographic size. Regarding the unemployment rate, smaller Gulf states were divided: Kuwait and Qatar had official unemployment rates of 1–2% prior to 2011, the UAE had 4%, while the Bahraini and Omani had official unemployment rates of 7–8% (Luciani, 2016, p. 194).

Second, some identify the "rentier bargain" as the main reason for the survival of Arab Gulf regimes (Bank, Richter, and Sunik, 2014, p. 165). Through this mechanism, the regime (re)distributes some portion of the profits of hydrocarbon exports among the population in exchange for keeping them excluded from political decision making (Utvik, 2016, p. 2). Most governments in the MENA region have not been able to offer their citizens such a deal. From this perspective, demographic smallness played a positive role – only one demographically small rentier state (Bahrain) went through serious instability, mostly due to mismanaged heterogeneity.

Third, the monarchic political system and a social structure related to the neopatriarchy in the Gulf could also have contributed to domestic stability (Bank, Richter, and Sunik, 2014; Aydin, 2013). Primarily through tribal relations, the regime was able to create a stable environment in which the survival of the political structure will be a shared interest with the co-opted elites. Since their independence, the Gulf monarchies have learned how they can use different sources of legitimacy (Arabism, nationalism, Islam, etc.) in different situations in order to survive.

Despite their relative stability, the domestic order of smaller Gulf states did not remain unaffected. It is worth investigating the four countries, categorised into three groups. The first consists of Qatar and UAE, which remained almost completely untouched by the Arab Uprisings, witnessing no major demonstrations and with some intellectuals calling only for political reform.[3]

The second group is formed by Kuwait and Oman, which witnessed some social movements and protests, but nothing that would threaten their regime's survival. In Oman, the larger cities – Muscat, Salalah, Sohar, and Sur – witnessed huge protests with people demanding more jobs, better salaries, better quality living conditions, less corruption, and the release of political prisoners (Valeri, 2011, pp. 159–160; Okruhlik, 2016, p. 19). More problematically, the demonstration wave reached the Dhofar region as well, and, after a couple of weeks, the taboo of criticising the Sultan himself was broken (Matthiesen, 2013, p. 112).

In Kuwait (Matthiesen, 2013, pp. 93–109), youth movements and other sections of society organised demonstrations heavily in 2011 and 2012, putting huge pressure on the regime. The networks that stood behind these actions are said to have originated from another series of protests in the mid-2000s called the "Orange Movement", which served as the basis for the visual representation of the protests of 2011–2012. Previously, the movement had successfully fought for the voting right of women and the reduction of electoral constituencies. Since 2009, the network of youth organisations and other non-governmental organisations (NGOs) has aimed at forcing the removal of the Prime Minister, Nasser al-Muhammad al-Sabah. Actually, political tensions were high even days before the self-immolation of Muhammad Bouazizi (the symbolical start of the Arab Uprisings). On 8 December 2010, special forces cracked down on an opposition group at a *diwaniya*, assaulting an ex-member of parliament (Jamaan al-Hirbish) and other participants.

This signals that the Kuwaiti events of 2011 and thereafter were not completely connected to regional developments, but were more rooted in the decade-long political crisis (Gharba, 2014 ; Alnajjar and Selvik, 2016). Since the re-establishment of the National Assembly in the 1990s, the political division has become deeper, which is shown by the rising number of interpellations made against members of the government or even the ruling family. Besides social and economic tensions, the political battles were also due to intra-regime competition (see Chapter 4).

The demonstrations in Kuwait took place in two waves. The first started in late 2010 and peaked in November 2011, when youth activists stormed the National Assembly, as a result of which action the Prime Minister was eventually forced to resign. This was the first time that a head of government resigned as a result of public pressure in Kuwait, and, arguably, in the GCC, as well (Gharba, 2014, p. 11). In the same year, *bidoon* tribes also took to the streets to demand equal rights (Barany, 2012, p. 5). Elections were held in February 2012,[4] in which opposition forces were able to form a majority of 35 members of parliament in the 50-seat National Assembly (Gharba, 2014, p. 12). As a result, the Emir dissolved the legislative institution later that year (eight days before it would have been able to pass a bill guaranteeing the independence of the judiciary), giving impetus to the second wave of protests at the end of 2012. These were the most numerous demonstrations in the history of Kuwait and were called the "Dignity of a Nation" (*Karamat Watan*). Due to severe tensions and the harsh actions of the authorities, many people were injured and were jailed. In December 2012, new elections took place; these were boycotted by many opposition forces (including Sunni Islamists and tribes). Finally, the Constitutional Court annulled the results of these elections as well, setting 27 July 2013 as the date for the new elections. This time, the elected National Assembly was in place until 2016.

Bahrain witnessed the most dangerous manifestation of public anger towards the regime in 2011 (Khalaf, 2013; Matthiesen, 2013, pp. 33–49). Demonstrations from both Sunni and Shia backgrounds occupied the Pearl Roundabout in the centre of Manama between 14 February and 18 March 2011, demanding higher salaries and greater political representation. During these weeks, the traditional opposition parties and new organisations (such as the Coalition of the Youth 14 February Movement) rose up to represent the protestors. Two dangerous developments shocked the Bahraini regime and its allies in the Gulf: first, on 7 March, a new umbrella organisation called the *"Coalition for a Republic"* was founded. This organisation pushed not only for limited reforms, but also the abolishment of the monarchy. Second, on 11 March, demonstrations spread to the town of Riffa, which is usually inhabited by the Sunni middle and upper classes.

Demonstrations in Bahrain also coincided with intra-regime struggles (see Chapter 4) (Gengler, 2013). After the death of Emir Isa Al Khalifa in 1999 and the rise of his son, Hamad bin Isa Al Khalifa, to the throne, the *Khawalid* branch of the ruling family – which was centred around Minister of Defence Khalifa bin Ahmed and his brother, the Minister of the Royal Court, Khaled bin Ahmed – and the network constituted by their supporters strengthened considerably. The *Khawalids* are known to despise Shia movements and to have a very strong Sunni identity; therefore, their rise to power is one of the main reasons for the sectarian tools used by the Bahraini state.

Regime survival strategies

Smaller Gulf states reacted to the protests according to the toolkit that they had previously developed. This toolkit consisted mostly of the (re)distribution of decision-making power, economic resources, and norms (Lucas, 2014, pp. 202–210). The main elements of the strategy included a quick rise in economic benefits with limited political reforms, usually enlarging the legislative powers of the consultative bodies. These carrots were supplemented by sticks in the form of firm coercive actions taken by the security and armed forces (Okruhlik, 2016, pp. 21–23).

Regarding the redistribution of norms, the Gulf states did not reinvent new forms of legitimacy but, rather, they framed the events in discourses that would, on the one hand, discredit the demonstrations, but also, on the other, strengthen the role of the regimes. In this regard, two distinct but interconnected discourses emerged among the smaller Gulf states. First, many of the regimes implemented a sectarian narrative regarding the events (Matthiesen, 2013), proclaiming that it was the Iran-backed Shia communities that organised the protests in order to undermine Sunni governments. This represented a new wave of increasing securitisation of Shia identities and groups, depicting them as threats to the stability, development, and peace of the society (Lucas, 2014, p. 209).

Second, several regimes used "geopolitical reasoning" to deflect domestic (and sometimes foreign) criticism about their actions, which means to rhetorically "'spatialise' their foreign (and domestic) policies" to counter the limit of the effects of transnational or regional developments. (Aras and Falk, 2015, p. 328). This strategy is primarily aimed at the domestic environment to legitimise even harsh actions against "international" threats: for example, blaming Iran for playing a revisionist role can easily serve this narrative without referencing sectarian differences. Both narratives were developed by Saudi Arabia and Iran, but smaller Gulf states mirrored their behaviour.

Besides these commonalities, there were substantial differences between the management of domestic developments among smaller Gulf states. Having no major demonstrations, Qatar only implemented certain pre-emptive measures by raising the salaries and social benefits of state employees (Bank, Richter, and Sunik, 2014, p. 175). The wages of public employees were raised by 60%, except for the military personnel, whose income was raised by 120% (Okruhlik, 2016, p. 22).

Despite the small size and weakness of the opposition, the Emirati government was afraid that such developments would contribute to the spread of Islamism and the Muslim Brotherhood network while widening the gap between the poorer and richer Emirates (Forstenlechner, Rutledge and Alnuaimi, 2012; Zaccara, 2013). That is why, in addition to pre-emptive fiscal measures similar to those of Qatar, the government announced projects for infrastructure in the Northern Emirates, and cracked down on intellectuals and Islamists more fiercely. In September, the UAE also held Federal National Council elections (with a nine-month delay); these took place peacefully, though with a very limited turnout (28%). Problematically for the regime, relatively more people came to the polls in the Northern Emirates (especially in Umm al-Quwain, Sharjah, and Ajman, with a turnout of 39–54%) than Abu Dhabi (21%) or Dubai (25%). According to the government, voting behaviour followed tribal patterns, which contributed to the mistrust of the regime in the usefulness of elections.

In Oman, Sultan Qaboos reacted very quickly to the protests (Matthiesen, 2013, pp. 112–113; Okruhlik, 2016, pp. 22–23). After confrontations between demonstrators and the police led to two civilian deaths in Sohar,[5] the Sultan gave the order to the security forces that they should not harm the protesters. He succeeded in breaking up the alliance of unemployed workers and intellectuals by persuading the intellectuals to stay at home and not go out on the streets by means of dismissing several members of the government,[6] announcing 50,000 public sector jobs, and raising the minimum wage by 43%. Once only political demonstrators remained on the street, Sultan Qaboos cracked down on them easily.

Another difference in the Omani approach was the lack of a sectarian narrative in legitimising the actions (Matthiesen, 2013, 113–115). Naturally, this is partly due to the Ibadi majority in the country – a community that mostly stayed away from demonstrations (except for some Ibadis in Muscat); nevertheless, it was also due to the visible internal division at demonstrations. Poorer Shias protested in sympathy with the Bahraini Shias, while some Sunni opposition figures argued that religious minorities (the Shia commercial elite) benefited more from the economic growth than the Sunni middle class. These mixed voices made it unnecessary for the government to implement a sectarian narrative, especially since several members of the Sunni and Shia elite actually supported the Omani regime.

Oman also held orderly elections in 2011. The poll took place on 15 October to elect the members of the Consultative Council, the lower house of the Council of Oman (Zaccara, 2013, pp. 87–92). Of the 655 thousand

potential voters, 518,000 registered, which represents a 52% growth in electoral inquiry since the previous elections in 2007. The high number of candidates were registered from Seeb – one of the main centres of demonstration
– and Nizwa. Elections took place in an orderly manner with a record participation of 76.6% of registered voters. Surprisingly, three organisers of the
previous demonstrations won a seat in the Council (Talib al-Maamari, Salem
al-Ufi, and Salem al-Mashani), who were also jailed for 52 days. After the
elections took place, Sultan Qaboos announced new initiatives to strengthen
the Consultative Council to a limited extent with the right to review the
annual budget, question ministers, and initiate legislative action (Bank,
Richter, and Sunik, 2014, p. 173).

Facing more serious domestic pressure, the Kuwaiti government had to do
considerably more (Barany, 2012, p. 24; Okruhlik, 2016, p. 23). In early 2011,
the government announced a direct transfer of almost 3,600 USD to each
Kuwaiti citizen and basically provided free commodities for 14 months,
including sugar, chicken, rice, and oil. The government also erased many
families' debts. Interestingly, the Kuwaiti state framed these actions as unre-
lated to the Arab Spring but connected to the "50/20" celebrations, which
were to commemorate the independence of the country (1961) and the end of
the Iraqi occupation (1991): nonetheless, *bidoon* tribes were excluded from
the programme. Also in 2011, the government introduced the biggest budget
in its history; the entire planned expenditure amounted to 70 billion USD,
which included increased subsidies and public employee salaries.

Despite the general atmosphere of the Arab Uprisings, the political reforms
of the Kuwaiti regime did not strengthen democratic trends but, rather, used
autocratic tools. Besides dissolving the National Assembly many times, the
Emir issued a "decree of urgency" in October 2012, by which he enabled
himself to change the electoral system unilaterally in order to narrow the
leverage of the opposition.[7] The courts also sentenced a couple of hundred
people indicted with storming the National Assembly, criticising the Emir or
the judiciary, and calling for unlicensed demonstrations (Gharba, 2014, p.
15). On the other hand – possibly due to the fragile political situation –
authorities refrained from excessive use of force.

In the case of Bahrain, the government initially tried to appease the protesters (similar to the steps taken by Oman). The regime promised 2,700 USD
to each family (Barany, 2012, p. 23) and, during February, it showed willingness to engage in negotiations with the opposition parties and other movements (Matthiesen, 2013, p. 48). Nonetheless, following calls for the
abolishment of the monarchy, the Bahrain government started to react more
aggressively. On 14 March 2011, it invited Saudi, Emirati, and Kuwaiti forces
to help restore stability and order in the country. Officially, such forces were
referred to as the Peninsula Shield Force of the GCC but, practically, they
consisted of 2,000 Saudi troops, 600 Emirati policemen (Joyce, 2012, p. 118),
and a faction of Qatari military personnel (Ulrichsen, 2014a, p. 115).

After the arrival of foreign troops, the King announced a state of emergency, which gave security forces wide legal authority to conduct raids,

leading to at least 35 deaths (BICI, 2011, p. 419). Following that, the authorities systemically raided the houses of mostly Shia inhabitants to arrest individuals by the thousand (though many of them were later released), at least 4,500 protesters were fired from their jobs, and at least 500 students were expelled from universities (BICI, 2011, pp. 420–421).

The Saudi-led intervention increased the reliance of Bahrain on Saudi Arabia, but also regionalised the conflict and exposed the country to the political discourse of its neighbours (Wehrey, 2014, pp. 111–113). The action was debated alongside sectarian lines in the Gulf countries. Prominent leaders of both Sunni and Shia communities spoke up supporting or condemning the intervention, including Hezbollah leader Hassan Nasrallah, Grand Ayatollah Ali al-Sistani from Nejef, and political leader Muqdtada al-Sadr of Iraq; and, from the Sunni side, the Qatari based intellectual and religious leader, Yusuf al-Qaradawi. In Kuwait (Wehrey, 2014, pp. 236–238), the National Assembly hosted a debate about the participation of Kuwait in the joint Peninsula Shield Force mission, with Shia members of parliament voicing strong opposition to the whole idea. As a result, the government hesitated at first and, eventually, offered only medical convoys and small naval forces.

In Bahrain, the government tried to frame the protests as being triggered by Iran and attempted to delegitimise opposition groups such as the Wifaq party. On 2 April 2011, the Bahraini government closed down *al-Wasat*, the only newspaper critical of the regime. After the crackdown, the Bahraini government tried to appear to open up for dialogue. In May 2011, the regime announced the National Dialogue Initiative, which was supposed to bring together pro-regime and opposition forces (Wehrey, 2014, p. 120). Nonetheless, only about 8% of the 320 participants were critical of the government. Realising that the dialogue was insincere, the existing opposition parties quickly pulled out of the process. On 1 June, the state of emergency expired (Joyce, 2012, p. 120) and, one month later, the King issued a decree that set up the Bahrain Independent Commission of Inquiry to investigate the events in February and March of 2011 and their implication (BICI, 2011, p. 1). The report attributed responsibility to both the opposition and the government forces regarding the escalation of the events, but not to Iran (BICI, 2011, pp. 413–420). Regardless, the government blamed Tehran for interfering in their domestic affairs, similarly to the Kuwaiti regime (Roberts, 2011a, p. 111).

In addition to national actions, the Gulf states initiated two collective measures at the GCC level. First, King Abdullah of Saudi Arabia initiated a Gulf Union at the annual GCC summit in 2011 (Guzansky, 2015, pp. 25–28). The proposal only served to deepen domestic cleavages in Bahrain[8] and Kuwait.[9] At the next GCC meeting in May 2012, the leaders decided to postpone the decision about the unity, but soon the idea was publicly rejected by Oman (*Arab News*, 2013). The UAE and Qatar also feared that the proposal would lead to a Saudi hegemony (Berger, 2014, 262). The proposal was soon forgotten, proving that the integration dilemma continued to discourage smaller Gulf states from deeper integration.

Second, the GCC also provided financial help to Bahrain and Oman – worth 10 billion USD to each country – to be disbursed during the next decade (Guzansky, 2015, p. 90). This sum was approximately 50% of the yearly GDP of Bahrain and more than 20% of that of Oman (*Reuters*, 2011). The initiative shows the perception by the GCC that the unrest in Oman and Bahrain was more economically motivated, which is, to say the least, questionable (Kinninmont, 2016, p. 120). This financial aid raised the fear that Riyadh wanted to pressure the two small states, especially Oman, to align their foreign policy according to Saudi interests.

Interpreting differences

The management of the events of 2011 by smaller Gulf states follows previously established patterns of regime security behaviour. Consequently, the mistakes and successes of the past were repeated. In the case of Bahrain and Kuwait, the regimes did not manage to completely stabilise their domestic affairs (Goldburt, 2015; Smith, 2016; Katzman, 2020b), mostly due to the harsh sectarian narratives, existing domestic cleavages, and intra-regime strife. Nevertheless, measures were efficient enough to avoid existential crisis, especially due to the loyalty maintained among the traditional Sunni tribal population.

In parallel, Oman managed to tackle the crisis relatively efficiently; even so, economic challenges and historical experiences did not relieve the regime from the possibilities of destabilisation. Qatar and the UAE did not have to face a substantial domestic challenge, although for different reasons (social homogeneity in the case of Qatar, and the efficient federal structure in the UAE). Another commonality between the three more successful Gulf states was the lack of severe sectarian narratives.

During the Arab Uprisings, smallness mostly played a positive role for Gulf states. Their small demographic size was especially beneficial as, coupled with the tribal-neopatriarchal social structure and the rentier bargain, it enabled regimes to allocate financial resources more effectively. Nevertheless, the absolute military smallness of Bahrain became apparent in 2011, after it failed to tackle its domestic challenges. Inviting the Gulf military forces can be seen as a compensatory policy, one that resulted in deepening reliance on Saudi Arabia.

Normative enlargement and omni-balancing after 2011

Considerations of domestic regime stability drove the foreign policy of smaller Gulf states in two ways after 2011. First, their international behaviour should be seen as a continuation – or, rather, an integral part of – regime stability efforts. Through omni-balancing, smaller Gulf states managed both domestic and foreign policy challenges, in the same manner, whether moderate and radical Islamism or Iran.

Second, consequently, the domestic environment shaped their foreign policy leverage to a great extent. Internal problems discouraged Bahrain and Kuwait from taking grand individual initiatives; therefore, they mostly followed the Saudi lead in international affairs (Katzman, 2020a; 2020b), mostly contributing little to maintain the status quo. Enjoying domestic calamity, the Qatari government was able to capitalise on the institutional capacity-building process taking place since 1995 under the leadership of Emir Hamad bin Khalifa Al Thani and his long-time foreign minister Hamad bin Jassim Al Thani (Ulrichsen, 2014b, p. 110). In the UAE, the more assertive foreign policy pursued by the leadership since 2003 was supplemented by intense armament and the strengthening of Abu Dhabi in the federal structure. With its troubled experience and economic challenges, Oman was eager to maintain the status quo from a defensive posture, continuing its tradition of active neutrality.

Besides their diversity, the most interesting observation regarding the activities of smaller Gulf states since 2011 is that some of them over-reached the traditionally assumed limitations of small states (Soubrier, 2017). On the one hand, their adopted aims transcended the narrowly defined interest of survival, and pursued political and economic goals far from their borders, such as in Libya. On the other hand, they implemented various tools, ranging from soft to hard power, using all three faces of power (coercion, agenda-setting, and persuasion).

Authors conceptualised this strategy of Qatar and the UAE in different ways. Babak Mohammadzadeh (2017, pp. 27–31) called it an "aggressive campaign for state branding". According to Lina Khatib (2013, p. 429), such behaviour was conducted to reach the goal of "appealing to and exercising leverage on the international community" and to boost their image. Kristina Kausch (2016) described their role as that of swing states that manage to balance or hedge between great powers. Robert Mason (2020) regarded the two countries as small states seeking "middlepowerhood". Using the vocabulary of Small State Studies, they conducted a virtual enlargement policy to expand their normative size without traditional great power tools, which they did not possess.

Nevertheless, their aims and strategies contradicted each other, necessarily contributing to a more competitive and conflictual relationship between them, especially the UAE and Qatar. As they perceived the status quo differently, their actions were not compatible with each other. While Qatar tried actively to change the regional balance of power by supporting its allies (especially the Muslim Brotherhood), the UAE wanted to strengthen the status quo – and, thus, regional stability – through an assertive foreign policy (Hassan, 2020; Mason, 2020). Similar to the Emirates, Oman also favoured stabilisation efforts, though with different means and with a slightly altered perception of the status quo. The differences between their stance are best observable in two fields: Islamist networks and the Saudi–Iranian rivalry.

Islamist networks and Qatari–Emirati competition

Between 2011 and 2013, it seemed that Islamist movements and the Muslim Brotherhood were able to capitalise on the Arab Uprisings to the greatest extent. The movement, which had been banned in many countries, managed to transform itself into a governmental force in Egypt and Tunisia, and they strengthened their profile in places where they used to be strong (e.g. Syria) and where they had not previously had a presence (e.g. Libya).

For the reasons described in previous sections, smaller Gulf states had a different understanding of the growing influence of the Muslim Brotherhood. Qatar favoured the influence of the Muslim Brotherhood network, which is considered a counter-balance to both Saudi Arabia and Iran. In contrast, Abu Dhabi and the architect of its foreign policy strategy, Crown Prince Mohamed bin Zayed, saw political Islam as the main threat to the stability of the federation. Oman (similarly to Kuwait and Bahrain) had no large stakes in the question, unless threatened with regional instability.

In the years following 2011, Qatar became the strongest proponent of political Islam alongside Turkey. Doha provided arms and financial assistance, network-building, and media support (primarily through the al-Jazeera network) to the "brothers" all over the region (Sultan, 2013). Qatar also used international organisations, including the GCC and the Arab League, to frame developments according to its own goals. Qatar used its military only once (Ulrichsen 2014c, p. 123), but it preferred to use non-state actors to pursue its interests, including the Muslim Brotherhood and other Islamist groups.

In the first years of the Arab Uprisings, the Qatari strategy was quite successful, especially in Egypt, Libya, and Syria. After the fall of Hosni Mubarak in Egypt, Qatar began to subsidise the Muslim Brotherhood-linked Freedom and Justice Party, whose candidate, Mohamed Morsi, won the presidential elections in 2012. Despite Saudi and Emirati reservations, Qatar welcomed Morsi's presidency and provided the new government with financial support worth 7.5 billion USD through aid, loans, and investment (Harb, 2017, p. 81). In Libya, the *Thani* regime was the first to recognise the National Transitional Council as the representative of the Libyan people, the opposition of Moammar al-Qaddafi. In April 2011, it pushed for the endorsement of the Western-led intervention in Libya aimed at creating a no-fly zone and, as had the UAE, contributed to the military action with six fighters. Though they did not participate in any strikes, their presence helped Western states to legitimise the intervention and to avoid the image of a new war between the West and the Arab world (Ulrichsen 2014c, p. 123). Even before the fall of Qaddafi, Qatar began to support the local Muslim Brotherhood network – which did not have a significant social base before 2011 in Libya – and the Tripoli Brigade. Qatar also helped to set up an opposition-led TV network, Libya al-Ahrar (Khatib, 2013, p. 421; Ulrichsen, 2014b, pp. 123–129). In Syria (Ulrichsen, 2014b, pp. 131–144; Nuruzzaman, 2015, pp. 229–230), Qatar severed ties with the *Assad* regime in July 2011 after an attack on the Qatari embassy in Damascus. Since the Muslim Brotherhood had a historical presence in the country, the *Thani* regime had more leverage than it had in Libya to build up its network. Qatar weighed in on behalf of the local Muslim Brotherhood organisation and wanted to dominate the Syrian National

Council and the Free Syrian Army through them. Later, Emir Hamad was the first to give public support for a possible multilateral military intervention against the *Assad* regime. As the political opposition started to lose ground, Qatar gave more support for militias – including, primarily, Ahrar as-Sham.

In contrast, the UAE did not execute a volte-face with regard to foreign policy overnight, but it did become more active in the spring of 2011. By various means, Abu Dhabi tried to stabilise and legitimise the existing regional status quo and support the existing regimes in most countries (Hassan, 2020, p. 194). In Bahrain, it became the strongest proponent of the GCC intervention to support the Khalifa regime. After the fall of Hosni Mubarak in Egypt, the UAE announced it would send a financial package to Egypt worth 3 billion USD, but, unlike Qatar, they did not actually transfer the sum to Cairo as the Muslim Brotherhood took over (Soubrier, 2017, p. 134).

In 2011, the UAE did not fear a radical change in the status quo, therefore it supported the rebels in two crises. In Libya, it provided material and logistical support for the NATO-led intervention and the anti-regime rebels, as well as a place to meet and coordinate their efforts (Ulrichsen, 2012, p. 13). In parallel, the UAE broke relations with Syria and contributed to a financial pool in support of rebels (Katzman, 2020e, pp. 9–10). Emma Soubrier (2017, p. 135) interpreted this policy as a way to strengthen credibility and legitimacy domestically and internationally in an era of youth-inspired transnational mobilisation throughout the region. Moreover, contrary to Mubarak, neither Qaddafi (an unreliable character) nor Assad (an Iranian ally) was a trusted partner of the UAE.

During this period, relations did not deteriorate between the two Gulf states; nevertheless, cracks started to appear following the first momentum of the Arab Uprisings. After the initial success, Qatar's star started to fade, which caused its foreign policy to become more active and, thus, to be viewed more critically. In July 2012, the Qatari-supported Libyan party *al-Watan* (Homeland) failed to succeed in the elections (Ulrichsen, 2014b, p. 130). The newly created Islamist networks did not manage to harvest meaningful social support, and Qatar's aggressive support to them was perceived progressively more harmful and divisive after the death of Qaddafi. Following a transitional period between 2012 and 2014, the country sank into a second civil war between the Western and Eastern tribes, in which Qatar (alongside Turkey) supported the Western tribes due to their alliance with Muslim Brotherhood-linked militias. This "Dawn Coalition" later merged with the Government of National Accord under Fayez al-Sarraj, which became the internationally recognised government, although it remained quite weak and was unable to stabilise the country.

In Syria, despite Qatari efforts, neither Western countries nor Arab states intervened in the Syrian conflict directly, which eventually led to the shrinking territory of Qatari-linked opposition forces. During 2012 and 2013, it became clear that Gulf states supported different factions in the Syrian opposition, with growing enmity between them (Lister, 2015, pp. 84–85).

Similar to the case of Libya, Qatar's image worsened among the Syrian armed forces, as well (Ulrichsen, 2014b, p. 142). The final straw was represented by Egyptian developments when Mohammad Morsi was ousted in 2013, and the armed forces – enjoying Saudi and Emirati support – initiated a brutal crackdown on the local Muslim Brotherhood networks (Berger, 2014, p. 263). Following this, Doha tried to rebrand its efforts as supporting only the Egyptian people rather than a specific political group (Ulrichsen, 2014b, p. 180), but the continuing troubles in Qatari–Egyptian relations showed that they did not succeed.

All these events contributed to the diminishing image of Qatar in the international community. Many juxtaposed the small size of the country with its activism, arguing that it was "punching above its weight" (Roberts, 2011b), or it has an "oversized role" in international affairs (Nuruzzaman, 2015, p. 277). Using the established vocabulary, we can say that the attempt of Qatar to enlarge its normative size caused controversy – not necessarily because of its activities, but because of its strategy. According to David Roberts (2017, pp. 5–6), this can be attributed to two mistakes: underestimating the difficulties in controlling non-state actors, and neglecting the domestic instability of its neighbours and their regime security considerations. Additionally, observers could easily feel a certain change in Qatari foreign policy as, previously, to maintain its mediation capability, Doha had wanted to remain neutral in most conflicts, whereas, after 2011, it sided clearly with Islamist forces, an enemy of many regional actors (Roberts, 2017, pp. 5–6).

In parallel with the growing tensions regarding Qatar, the Emirates became more visible in their activities and their criticism of the Muslim Brotherhood (designating it a terrorist organisation) and other Islamist networks. Regarding Syria, Abu Dhabi criticised the Qatari (and Saudi) policy of supporting more extreme members of the armed opposition. While they did break relations with the *Assad* government, they did not want to overthrow the government at the price of giving more leverage to Islamist groups. Following this, their Syria policy concentrated on providing aid to the Syrian people and, from 2014, participating in the anti-terrorism coalition of the USA (similarly to Qatar) (Ulrichsen, 2014b, p. 141; Sherwood, 2017, p. 156). After the fall of Morsi in Cairo, Abu Dhabi began massive subsidisation of the military leadership and the government of Abdel Fattah Al-Sisi, making available almost 5 billion USD (Almezaini and Rickli, 2017, p. 187).

The post-Islamist Egyptian leadership became a reliable partner of the Emirates in fighting the Muslim Brotherhood network. Since 2014, militarily and politically, the two countries have helped the anti-Islamist forces in Libya, fighting the Qatar-backed groups residing in Tripoli, often without prior consultation with the USA (Sherwood, 2017, p. 150). They trusted Khalifa Haftar, a long-time defector of the *Qaddafi* regime, to fight against the internationally recognised government to whom they gave anti-aircraft missiles and artillery (Heller, 2019).

The UAE has not yet suffered any major drawbacks similar to those of Qatar. It has not angered regional political actors as much as its neighbour, and it has maintained a highly favourable public image. For example, the annual Arab Youth Survey showed that, between 2012 and 2020, the UAE became the most favourable country for young Arabs to live in or to emulate (Asda'a, 2021).[10] These differing perceptions can be explained in various ways: the UAE's pro-stability and status quo policy could be perceived better, its domestic structure allowed a more efficient distribution of labour between hard power (Abu Dhabi) and soft power (Dubai), and, eventually, Qatar sided with the loser side in many cases. Lastly, one could hypothesise that the larger relative size of the UAE made it easier to be accepted normatively as a middle power, contrary to its tiny rival.

In contrast with the two status-seekers, the remaining three smaller Gulf states did not become involved in the struggle over the future of Islamism. As already mentioned, the Muslim Brotherhood was not considered to be a major threat to their regime security; therefore, they only aimed at contributing to stabilisation efforts in the region.[11] Their most important contribution in this regard was their participation in the global coalition against the Islamic State, which they all considered to be a threat to their national security. Of the three countries, Oman showed the most activities in conflicts with a strong Islamist presence, though Muscat mostly continued its tradition of non-interference and facilitation (Aras and Falk, 2015, p. 325). Oman did not intervene in Syria, but tried to keep connections open with the *Assad* regime, which, later in 2015, were used to offer mediation between the government and opposition forces. According to some sources, the Omani government negotiated with Russia about the future of Assad and his family, offering the possibility of relocation to Oman (Neubauer, 2016, p. 1). Actually, Sultan Qaboos offered the same to members of the Libyan Qaddafi family (Katzman, 2020c, p. 15) who entered the country in October 2012. In Egypt, Oman did not side with either the Morsi government or the armed forces, but it criticised the crackdown on the Muslim Brotherhood after 2013.

The intensification of Saudi–Iranian rivalry

One of the major winners of the Arab Uprisings was considered to be Iran. Capitalising on the instability in Syria, Iraq, and Yemen, or the fragile situation in Bahrain, it has enlarged its sphere of influence, and built up its networks using mostly hard power capabilities. Coupled with its alleged nuclear ambitions, the spread of Iranian presence was considered to be a systemic threat for Gulf states. As a reaction, the new leadership in Saudi Arabia tried to formulate a strategic answer after 2015 under the de facto rule of Crown Prince Mohammad bin Salman, which intensified the rivalry between Riyadh and Tehran, especially after Riyadh broke off diplomatic ties with Tehran in 2016. The main proxy battlefield of the rivalry turned out to be Yemen, where Iranians started to support the rebellion of the Shia Houthi movement against the central government of Mansour Hadi. The situation was further aggravated by the Obama administration's decision to engage Iran in the nuclear talks, which led to the signing of the Joint Comprehensive Plan of

Action (JCPOA) in 2015, allowing Tehran to access international markets in exchange for international oversight over its nuclear programme.

Such circumstances constructed a difficult security environment for smaller Gulf states – one in which they faced serious dilemmas. Traditional small state logic and shallow observation would dictate a bandwagoning strategy, according to which weaker entities should have sided with Saudi Arabia and the USA to balance the threat of Tehran, in the same way that they supported Iraq in the 1980s. Moreover, the Iranian threat was more apparent after 2011, especially considering the Bahraini events and the subsequent deepening of the sectarian divide in the Gulf societies (Akbarzadeh, 2017, p. 97). Accordingly, smaller Gulf states' support to the Bahraini or Yemeni governments or (to some extent) the Syrian opposition could be seen as proof of bandwagoning behaviour at first glance.

Nevertheless, in other cases, smaller Gulf states chose different paths and did not side with Saudi Arabia completely, since the situations in the 1980s and the 2010s were markedly different for several reasons. The Iran of the 1980s was seen as much more unpredictable and aggressive than of the 2010s, especially after the election of the moderate Hassan Rouhani in 2013. Moreover, the post-2011 environment was characterised by a series of transnational conflicts, contrary to the traditional interstate war between Iraq and Iran. Smaller Gulf states also learnt from the experience that supporting one great power against another does not necessarily protect them from either one. They also had historical reservations about Saudi expansionism, which caused distrust in bilateral relations, especially with Qatar and Oman.

Consequently, smaller Gulf states' policies differed from each other to a much greater extent than previously in the context of Saudi–Iranian rivalry. The closest to the theoretically assumed behaviour was observable in the case of Bahrain, which feared the Iranian threat the most and had the greatest reliance on Saudi Arabia in terms of security and economy. Bahrain withdrew its ambassador from Tehran in 2015, following signs that Iran wanted to smuggle weapons to the Bahraini Shia opposition (Akbarzadeh, 2017, p. 100). Later, as had the UAE and Saudi Arabia, Bahrain broke off formal diplomatic ties with Tehran (Wright, 2017, p. 77) and followed Riyadh in Yemen to take part in the Saudi-led intervention, as well.

Kuwait also sided with Saudi Arabia in the most pressing questions (Albloshi, 2017, pp. 139–141). One year before the Arab Spring, Kuwait withdrew their Iranian ambassador (though only temporarily) due to the discovery of an alleged Iranian spy cell in the country. The same accusation was also voiced in 2015. They also supported the Yemeni intervention and downgraded relations with Tehran in 2016. Nevertheless, the overall picture is more mixed than in the case of Bahrain: Kuwait refrained from participating in the Bahraini intervention and did publicly support the JCPOA (Katzman, 2020b, pp. 13–14).

The contradictory approach of Kuwait can be attributed to the variables. First, domestic debates are much more to the fore in the emirate about Iran since loyalists, Shia Islamists, and Shias all take part in the public discussion;

consequently, the regime has to balance their needs to some extent (Albloshi, 2017, pp. 139–141). Second, in the Iran portfolio, Kuwait follows the lead not of Saudi Arabia but, rather, the USA; it spoke positively about both the signing of the JCPOA and the American withdrawal (Katzman, 2020b, pp. 13–14). This behaviour is in line with the country's choice of an alliance policy described earlier.

At first glance, the UAE also supported harsh Saudi actions against Iran (Hassan, 2020, p. 195). They vehemently criticised the JCPOA and supported the American withdrawal in 2018. Abu Dhabi supported the Bahraini and the Yemeni interventions, and withdrew its ambassador from Tehran in 2016. Nevertheless, three attributes of the Emirati policy differentiate it from the Saudi–Bahraini line. First, domestically, the Shia community does not pose a major threat to the UAE; it is more like a bridge between the two societies, which has enabled Dubai to become the biggest trading partner of Iran in the region and a gate to accessing information about Iran from the outside world (Sherwood, 2017, p. 148; Katzman, 2020e, pp. 8–9). These ties survived the sanctions regime that has been in place since 2018, as many businessmen have continued trading illegally (Akbarzadeh, 2017, p. 94).

Second, the Emirates prioritise fighting against political Islam over containing Iran; therefore, they are not willing to go as far as Saudi Arabia. That became apparent in the re-establishment of diplomatic relations with the *Assad* regime in 2018 (when Crown Prince Mohamed bin Zayed felt that the opposition was too radical to be an alternative and that Iranian influence could be curbed with Assad in place) and the withdrawal from the Yemeni coalition in 2019 (when Abu Dhabi felt that the investment was not yielding enough).[12] Even before bailing out, the UAE focused on fighting the Yemeni al-Qaeda more than Saudi Arabia had (Heller, 2019).

Third, similarly to Qatar, the Emirati actions during recent years were also driven by broader self-interests, which cannot be solely interpreted as reactions to the Saudi–Iranian rivalry. Under the umbrella of the Saudi-led Yemeni intervention, the UAE has built up its own network focusing on Southern factions which, although supported by the Saudi-backed central government, has its own agenda. In this, the Yemeni adventure of Abu Dhabi is motivated at least partly (if not mostly) by spreading its influence in the broader Red Sea region and the Horn of Africa, an area that is becoming progressively more important in terms of regional competition; a case in point could be the capture of the Islands of Socotra (Heller, 2019).

From the perspective of Qatar, Saudi Arabia is as much of a threat to its independence as Iran; therefore, relations with Iran were not allowed to deteriorate after 2011. Even the fact that Qatar became the most enthusiastic supporter of the Syrian opposition did not undermine this effort – as with the case of the island dispute in the Emirati–Iranian connection, both sides preferred to separate the Syrian question from the framework of general relations (Akbarzadeh, 2017, p. 97). This also shows that, for Doha, subsidising various militias was driven by building up the Muslim Brotherhood-framework and not by countering Iran. Qatar especially needed Iran after

2013, when the Muslim Brotherhood project started to fade, and intra-GCC tensions started to manifest, which is why they even announced new joint projects such as establishing joint free zones (Kamrava, 2017, p. 177). In the subsequent years, Qatar also facilitated indirect talks between Syrian opposition groups and Iranian-backed militias, a move also heavily criticised by Saudi Arabia. On the other hand, Doha has also tried to satisfy certain Saudi security needs: it participated in the Yemeni intervention between 2015 and 2017, albeit only with a few aircraft and a limited contingent, which contributed to the protection of the Saudi–Yemeni border (Katzman, 2020d).

In terms of Qatari logic, balancing between Saudi Arabia and Iran is driven by its survival strategy and is strongly connected to the support of the Muslim Brotherhood. That is why the primary instinct of the Qatari leadership is not to ease tensions between Iran and Saudi Arabia but, rather, to build up its own sphere of influence, which is also a sign that Doha is not satisfied with the pre-2011 status quo.

This distinction is especially important when it comes to the comparison of Qatari and Omani behaviour. Similar to the *Thani* regime, Muscat has refrained from taking sides between Saudi Arabia and Iran but, contrary to Qatar, it does not want actively to reshape the region just to de-escalate tensions. From this perspective, neighbouring Yemen became the most important conflict for Oman, which feared the spill-over effects of the conflict (including refugees and terrorism). Consequently, Sultan Qaboos refrained from joining the Saudi-led coalition, but tried to establish communication between the parties and served as an intermediary between the international community and the Houthi rebels (Colombo, 2017, pp. 63–66). Contrary to Qatar, Muscat's activities have not been seen as problematic in Riyadh and Abu Dhabi, as Sultan Qaboos did not pursue his own agenda but wanted to facilitate discussions (Al-Muslimi, 2017; Lons, 2018). Sultan Qaboos also used his country's traditionally good relations with Iran to ease the tensions between Iran and the Gulf or the West in smaller issues (Guzansky, 2015, p. 102) and to convince everybody that using hard power is not a solution in tackling current challenges, even in the case of Bahrain in 2011. Similar to Dubai and Qatar, Oman also built economic relations (with Iran in the last decade with signing a 60 billion USD gas deal in 2013), which was perceived negatively by Riyadh and Abu Dhabi (Akbarzadeh, 2017, p. 98; Baabood, 2017).

Differences in relations with Iran were reflected in the Qatari and Omani reaction to the signing of the JCPOA. While most Gulf states opposed the agreement (as they considered it an opportunity for Iran to obtain more resources and step up its efforts to build up its regional networks), Doha and Muscat welcomed the deal as a step closer to regional stability (Akbarzadeh, 2017, p. 99). Sultan Qaboos actually took part in the facilitation of the talks between the global powers and Iran to ink the deal (Neubauer, 2016). They both disagreed with the American withdrawal in 2018 and wanted to contribute to the de-escalation of American–Iranian ties in subsequent years.

This review shows how the previously identified differences in foreign and security policy perceptions led to deep divides among smaller Gulf states in the 2010s. In the formation of their omni-balancing strategy, size plays no self-explanatory role. Qatar and the UAE have been driven by their quest to become middle powers and grow their normative size, while Bahrain, Kuwait, and Oman prefer to remain out of the limelight. In this, their historical experiences of weakness, domestic struggles, and spill-over effects of armed conflict play the most significant part.

The Gulf rift and the Qatari survival strategy (2017–2021)

The tensions outlined in the previous sections eventually peaked spectacularly as Bahrain, the UAE, and Saudi Arabia – accompanied by Egypt – decided to counter Qatar's behaviour. On 5 June 2017, the Quartet, together with other states, announced that they would break diplomatic ties with Doha, shut down their airspace and borders with the country, and thus effectively put it under an embargo. Qatari diplomats had 48 hours to leave the four countries, while Qatari citizens had 14 days to do so. The so-called Gulf rift lasted for three-and-a-half years, becoming a symbol of division in the Gulf. The case is quite interesting from a small state perspective as, using a quite nuanced strategy, Qatar managed to withhold pressure and to get out of the crisis quite successfully, despite facing being overpowered.

The causes of the Gulf rift and the motivation of smaller Gulf states

The motivations for why Saudi Arabia and its partners cut ties with Qatar can be attributed to historical tensions outlined in the previous chapters and Qatari foreign policy during the Arab Spring. Al-Jazeera has not only supported the Muslim Brotherhood, but also aired programmes critical of its neighbours. To change the image of Qatar after the failure of the Muslim Brotherhood in Egypt, Emir Hamad decided to abdicate in favour of his son, Tamim bin Hamad Al Thani, while the infamous Hamad bin Jassim Al Thani also resigned. As the two symbolic figures of Qatari foreign policy disappeared from the government, it seemed that Doha was in retreat and became open to changing the course of its foreign policy.

Nonetheless, Emir Tamim did not change the substance of Qatari foreign policy. Consequently, in February 2014 – only eight months after his rise to power – Saudi Arabia, the UAE, and Bahrain withdraw their ambassadors from Doha (Roberts, 2017, p. 7) to send a strong message. [13] At that time, both sides were willing to engage in a negotiation process, which resulted in the Riyadh Agreement[14] (Martini et al., 2016, p. 18). The document has never been made public officially, and there are conflicting narratives about its content (Ibish, 2017). Qatar interpreted it as a general refusal to interfer in each other's internal affairs, while the Saudi-Emirati-Bahraini cohort expected Qatar to stop funding the Muslim Brotherhood network, to expel opposition leaders from its country, and to silence critical voices on its media networks.

Despite unresolved issues, the rift between Qatar and three of its neighbours did not manifest until May 2017. During these two-and-a-half years, domestic and regional developments shaped intra-Gulf relations. In January 2015, King Salman was crowned in Saudi Arabia, which paved the way for his son, Crown Prince Mohammad bin Salman, to centralise power in his own hands. Having no substantial experience in international affairs, Crown Prince Mohammad bin Salman conducted a more active and harsher foreign policy in close cooperation with Crown Prince Mohamed bin Zayed of Abu Dhabi. The attention of Riyadh also shifted from the largely defeated Muslim Brotherhood to countering Iran, while the focus of the UAE remained on Islamist organisations (Al-Akhbar, 2017). In both portfolios, Qatari foreign policy was perceived as dangerous by both states. The election of Donald Trump in 2016 made Riyadh and Abu Dhabi braver in confronting Qatar, as the new American president was quite supportive of their foreign policy (Ulrichsen, 2017).

Similar to regional traditions, the two leaders secured American support before they took actual steps. In the first half of 2017, Crown Prince Mohammad bin Salman and Crown Prince Mohamed bin Zayed both visited President Trump in Washington (*The National*, 2017). On 20–21 May 2017, President Trump visited Riyadh to participate in three summits,[15] where he managed to speak with the leaders of all countries of the Quartet. While there was no official announcement of American support, the approval of the American President manifested itself in a series of tweets published after the announcement of the blockade. With hindsight, the American role in the events building up to the Gulf rift justifies the Qatari ambition to diversify its security relations after 2003.

At the same time, the Quartet also initiated a media campaign against the Qatari regime in May 2017, trying the frame the public discourse both domestically and internationally (ACRPS, 2017a, p. 9). These articles directly attacked the *Thani* regime, trying to undermine its normative membership in the regional Arab, Islamic, and Khaleeji group. For example, descendants of Muhammad ibn Abd al-Wahhab disowned the affiliation to the former Qatari Emir Hamad (Al-Hayat, 2017), while other media reports connected the family to the enemies of Saudi Arabia (*Okaz*, 2017), or personally to Moammar Qaddafi and Ali Abdallah Saleh (Ray al-Yaoum, 2017a). The Ray al-Yaoum media website proclaimed that Qatar left the Gulf flock and is possibly leaving the GCC as well (Ray al-Yaoum, 2017b). In the media campaign, the dissemination of fake news (e.g. *Okaz*, 2017) also played an important role, which made the rift may be the "first international crisis of the "alternative facts'" era" (Ulrichsen, 2017). Such articles included a fake speech by Emir Tamim published by the hacked Qatar News Agency in which he voiced support for Iran, the Hezbollah, and Hamas, or the false information that the Qatari leadership is protected by the Iranian Revolutionary Guards (Al Arabiya, 2017).

The announcements of the Quartet that they would cut ties with Qatar took place in this discursive environment. Shortly after, the four states proclaimed 13 demands for Qatar to meet (ACRPS, 2017b, pp. 113–115), three of which concerned the alleged support of terrorism (the Muslim

Brotherhood), two concerned interference in domestic affairs, two referred to Qatar's media network, and three were connected to Qatari foreign policy in general. These demands pushed Doha to break ties with Iran, terminate Turkish military presence in the country, and to align its foreign policy with the Riyadh Agreement. The last three points included remarks about financial compensation, putting Qatar under financial oversight, and giving Doha 10 days to meet all demands. The 13 demands were later replaced by six principles, two of which concerned the combat against terrorism and extremism; one related to the prohibition of any act that may incite hatred or violence; two were about full commitment to the Riyadh Agreement and the outcome of the May 2017 meeting in Riyadh, and the final demand referred to refraining from interfering in the internal affairs of other states.

Although several regional and global actors proclaimed that they supported a peaceful resolution of the dispute, nobody was able to persuade the two sides to work out their differences. The Kuwaiti Emir Sabah al-Sabah immediately stood up as the mediator in the debate (Schanzer and Koduvayur, 2018). The role came naturally for Kuwait, which engaged in the same activity during the debate between Qatar and the Quartet in 2013–2014 (Rubin, 2014). Both sides trusted the Kuwaiti Emir, who, with his reserved behaviour in the preceding years and his decades of experience, did not alienate either side. While Kuwait has its own issues with Qatar (especially regarding the coverage of Al-Jazeera), it did not join the Quartet due to mistrust of any intention of Saudi Arabia and the UAE to force domestic political change in a neighbouring country (Martin and Cafiero, 2017).

Despite the efforts of Emir Sabah al-Sabah, he was unable to build a bridge between Qatar and the Quartet for years. In September 2017, a phone call took place between Mohammad bin Salman and Emir Tamim, but the process terminated before it could really begin. In December 2017, the annual summit of the Gulf Cooperation Council barely took place, as Saudi Arabia and the UAE announced that they set up a bilateral consultative council that symbolically replaced the GCC on their part. The tension became even more serious during the first anniversary of the blockade when both sides emphasised their narrative in the international public discourse to a much greater extent.

The motivation of smaller Gulf states in the Gulf rift reflected their previously identified security policy priorities. The UAE have been irritated by Qatar's pro-Islamist foreign policy, which, in the view of Abu Dhabi, destabilised the region. The Emirates also considered Qatar an economic competitor in various sectors, which gained importance as diversification attempts unfolded. Bahrain found its place in the Quartet mainly due to historical tensions between the two regimes (Ulrichsen, 2017, p. 181), the island state's growing security reliance on Saudi Arabia, the critical coverage of Al Jazeera about Bahraini domestic developments since 2011, and displeasure regarding the Iranian–Qatari relations.

Kuwait and Oman, on the other hand, were critical of the rift, fearing the destabilising effects of disunity in the GCC (Cafiero and Karasik, 2017). Less dependent on Saudi Arabia than Bahrain, they also feared the formulating of the Saudi–Emirati alliance as a hegemonic attempt in the GCC, something that they had already refused to accept in 2012. Accordingly, Sultan Qaboos remained officially neutral, and tried to contribute diplomatically to the Kuwaiti mediation efforts (Pradhan, 2018, p. 438), playing the role of a "humanitarian facilitator" by contributing to the safe transport of Qatari citizens stuck in the Quartet after the announcement (Al-Muslimi, 2017). In the following years, Oman actually capitalised on the rift as it managed to boost trade with Qatar, becoming its number one destination for the exports of the non-oil sector, while Oman Air also gained a position in the logistics of the region (Schanzer and Koduvayur, 2018).

Qatari survival strategy – transforming a hard power crisis into a soft power one

According to *The Intercept*, the Saudi–Emirati plans did not stop at this point but actually started developing plans for a military attack on Qatar, an idea that spread through rumours in 2014, too (Hearst, 2014). The plan – which was never implemented – supposedly included a ground campaign by the Saudis from the south (with military air support from the UAE), which would have circumvented the American military bases and would have occupied the capital quickly. Nevertheless, the American State Department intervened in the process and discouraged the Saudi leadership from attempting any military solution. Riyadh was more open to compromise even at that time than Abu Dhabi (Emmons, 2018).

In case of a direct military attack, Qatar would have been defeated easily (see Figure 6.1). Actually, according to conventional wisdom, Qatar would have lost the rift due to its relative size. Differences in military size were striking –Qatar's army is slightly larger than that of the smallest Quartet country, Bahrain. Even if we exclude Egypt, the Saudi–Emirati partnership alone would have been able to defeat Qatar in military actions, especially due to its highly vulnerable geopolitical position.

Nevertheless, Qatar avoided a military confrontation, survived the economic fallout of the embargo, and, eventually, the rift ended with Qatar meeting none of the demands. The reason why Doha managed to tackle the crisis was that the policies it had implemented previously made its position stronger for to two reasons (Roberts, 2017, p. 8). First, Qatar relied heavily on the foreign military presence in the country, especially that of the American army and the Turkish army, which set up a base in 2016, following a defence agreement between the two countries in 2014 (Quamar, 2017). The Turkish military contingent – which was enlarged after 2017 – was both a cause for concern for the Saudi–Emirati tandem, and a survival tool for the Qatari regime, forming a traditional alliance dilemma for the country. Second, Qatar tried to use its enlarged normative size and to turn its international political and economic position into a security guarantee. Prior to the crisis, Qatar managed to build interdependences with both of the major players in the

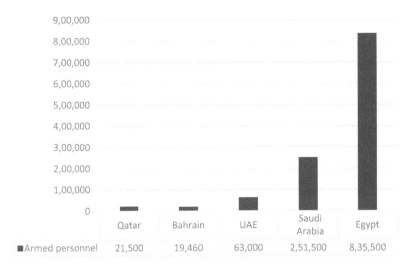

Figure 6.1 Size of armed forces in the Quartet states and Qatar (size of personnel).[16]

international arena in different ways – through liquid natural gas deals (with East Asia), migration cooperation (South Asia), and investments (Europe) (Ulrichsen and Karsik, 2018). The Qatari approach was based on the assumption that members of the international community that had enjoyed cooperation with the emirate would consider its survival to be in their interests. The assumption worked well: when the Quarter urged "all brotherly countries and companies" to cut ties with the country (*The Quint*, 2017), only a handful of states responded.[17]

These measures enabled Qatar to move the GCC rift from the realm of hard power and coercion to that of soft power and persuasion. In this field, relative military smallness did not pose a disadvantage – quite the opposite; one can argue that the relative smallness of Qatar vis-á-vis the economic and military giants of the Quartet was advantageous for the *Thani* leadership, as it was able to frame the events as "David versus Goliath" (e.g. Cole, 2018; Jha, 2017) and thus evoke the positive cognitive perception attached to smallness. More specifically, Qatari diplomatic activities were conducted using a multiple track approach[18] in order to reach different actors in different forums and influence their perception of the events.

Qatar mostly used five methods. First, state-level relations and diplomatic channels were used to spread the Qatari narrative, broaden cooperation, or ask for material help. Doha focused on great powers (such as the United States or Russia) and regional ones (such as Iran, Turkey or Oman). These attempts were crucial for tackling the economic hardship caused by the embargo and tp restructure foreign trade relations (Abu-Siriyya, 2017). In this regard, the re-establishment of diplomatic relations with Iran in August 2017 was crucial (they had been severed in 2016) as Iranian airspace and national waters represented a gateway to connect Qatar with the world (*DW*,

2018). These actions were successful, though they resulted in growing Qatari reliance on Iran. Second, Qatar aimed to strengthen cooperation with international organisations to deepen its embeddedness in multilateral structures. The most important success was signing military cooperation with NATO in January 2018, but Doha managed to get closer to the Shanghai Cooperation Organization as well (NATO, 2018; QMFA, 2017). Meanwhile, the state-led Qatar Charity formalised cooperation with the United Nations High Commissioner for Refugees in October 2017 (UNHCR, 2017).

Third, Qatar turned to supra-national judicial bodies to end certain measures of the Quartet. It submitted individual legal applications at the World Trade Organization (WTO),[19] arguing that their actions were unlawful and violated related international rules. In 2020, the WTO ruled in favour of Qatar against Saudi Arabia on the subject of the protection of intellectual property rights (WTO, 2020). Doha also turned to the International Court of Justice (ICJ, 2018), which called for emergency measures to protect Qatari citizens. In almost four years, the ICJ had not had time to make a final decision, notwithstanding legal means were important to keep the legal perspective on the agenda while projecting Qatar's image as a country committed to peaceful means of dispute settlement (similar to the discourse in the UN Security Council presented in Chapter 4).

Fourth, Qatar used several non-state actors to shape the perception of the members of the international community about the crisis. In the USA, Qatar has worked with about two dozen public relations and lobbying firms (including Blueprint Advisors, Ogilvy Government Relations, Lexington Strategies, and Debevoise & Plimpton), most of which were connected to either President Trump or key Republican figures (Harris, 2018). The aim of the Qatari public relations strategy in Washington was to persuade the American leadership about its narrative. The effort was successful, at least the aim was reached to some extent – on 10 April 2018, President Trump welcomed Emir Tamim Al Thani to Washington and called Qatar an "advocate" of the fight against terrorism (Brookings, 2018).

Fifth, Qatar used international human rights NGOs to support the case of Qatar. Previously, Qatar had had a tense relationship with such organisations as they reported extensively about the inhumane treatment of guest workers (e.g. Amnesty International, 2013). Nonetheless, Qatar realised that, in the right, such actors could be potential allies as the treatment of Qatari citizens raised humanitarian questions. Consequently, Doha invited such international NGOs to investigate individual cases, e.g. Amnesty International visited the country twice during 2017 (*Qatar Living*, 2017). In parallel, Qatar implemented a few measures to better the living standards of foreign workers, many of which hailed by human rights groups (HRW, 2018a, 2018b; Amnesty International, 2017a). Eventually, both Amnesty International (2017b) and Human Rights Watch (HRW, 2017) issued several reports about the Qatari crisis, all of which were critical of the Quartet's actions.

The blockading states responded with an attempt to undermine the rule of the Qatari regime domestically. They calculated that the absolute smallness of Qatar makes it impossible to survive the embargo economically. The blockading countries were responsible for at least one-sixth of the Qatari imports directly and a huge percentage of transit trade (IMF, 2017, p. 8). The embargo also aimed to drive down the value of the Qatari riyal, which would have led to a currency crisis (*Middle East Monitor*, 2017). Politically, the Quartet tried to build up a network of opposition figures in Qatar, mostly from the lineage of the Saudi-friendly previous emir, Khalifa Al Thani, the father of Hamad.[20]

While it was not beyond rationality to expect mounting domestic pressure on the *Thani* regime, the strategy of the Quartet has not produced any tangible results. The embargo had considerable effects on foreign trade, the financial sphere, and tourism (Moody's 2017); however, the Qatari government managed to tackle the economic consequences of the crisis through restructuring, fiscal stimulus, and building up the manufacturing and production industries. By March 2018, the IMF (2018) concluded that the effects of the embargo are "fading", while Qatar's macroeconomic situation remains "resilient". The infrastructural developments to host the 2022 World Cup also continued. On the political side, no opposition forces rose to threaten the rule of the *Thani* regime; moreover, Qatari society engaged in a series of public displays of loyalty towards Emir Tamim bin Hamad Al Thani. The only major defectors in the Qatari society were the members of the Saudi-friendly al-Murra tribe, who were stripped of their citizenship (*The Economist*, 2017).

The conclusion of the Gulf rift in 2021

Signs that the crisis might end shortly started to surface in the second half of 2019 (*Middle East Eye*, 2020), but it was officially resolved only in January 2021, at the 41st Gulf Summit organised in al-Ula. During this process, it became evident that neither a compromise from nor even capitulation of either side would solve the crisis but, rather, changing calculations of Gulf states regarding their relations with other states. During the autumn of 2019, Saudi Arabia began to recalibrate its foreign policy slightly, probably due to its inability to change the tide in Yemen and the drone attack taking place in September on Saudi soil. The incident, which hit oil facilities in Abqaiq and Khurais and was probably conducted by non-state actors with a close connection to the Iranian regime, showed the extant relative military weakness of Saudi Arabia. Subsequently, news began to spread about Crown Prince Mohammad bin Salman favouring a less aggressive and more thought-out strategy. Followed by the Emirati pull-out of Yemen, these actions were seen as the start of a strategic reassessment in the Gulf.

Resolving the Qatari issue at the annual Gulf summit in 2019 may have fit this process, especially since backdoor talks took place between Riyadh and Doha at least since October (Ibish, 2020; *Middle East Eye*, 2020). One month later, Bahrain, the UAE, and Saudi Arabia all delegated their teams for a regional soccer tournament organised by Qatar, which raised expectations about reconciliation. Eventually, the meeting was not attended by

Emir Tamim, and it became evident that the time was not yet right for ending the crisis. Nonetheless, discussions were sustained and, after one year (during which the six Gulf states coordinated their efforts in the fight against the new coronavirus), the Quartet and Qatar managed to end the rift officially. Under American pressure, the four countries announced the re-establishment of diplomatic ties, and the opening up their air space and territory to Qatari nationals.

The reconciliation was welcomed cautiously by observers. First, the fighting ended without any sense of compromise or progress in the specific areas that had caused tension in the first place. Seemingly, Qatar did not accept any of the demands and did not have to give up anything.[21] Relations with Iran would probably be expected to change, but concrete conditions were not seen (Roberts, 2021). Second, the full text of the "Al-Ula statement" or the "solidarity and stability agreement" was not published publicly, as was the case with the 2014 Riyadh agreement (Feierstein, 2021). Third, the main motivation for making peace originated in extra-regional affairs – mostly in the election of Joe Biden as the American president and calculations regarding Iran – and not in intra-Gulf relations. All these factors question the sustainability of Gulf "unity" even in the middle term.

That is why one can make the argument that Qatar won the Gulf rift (Roberts, 2021) due to its strategy of changing the framework of the debate and transferring it from the realm of hard power to soft power. In this, it implicitly managed to rely on existing positive perceptions of small states in the international community. The case also shows that changes in intra-regional relations in the Gulf can often be attributed to calculations regarding extra-regional actors, which again undermines the importance of establishing and maintaining close relations with them for small states.

Besides these general notions, size played two additional roles in the crisis. First, the relatively equal size of Qatar and the UAE, accompanied by similar economic structures and diverse regime security perceptions, sparked competition between them. Contrary to traditional logic, their animosity was deeper than that between Saudi Arabia and Qatar. Second, the case allows us to compare the mediation efforts of a small state (Kuwait) and of a great power (the USA) (Fraihat, 2020). While Kuwait based its activities on legitimacy, the USA used its power as an influencing force. In this case, the USA proved to be the more efficient mediator, a phenomenon that is especially ironic given the mediation experience of Qatar, Kuwait, the UAE, and Oman. Further investigation is needed to understand this trend, which can offer more detail to the general idea about the effectiveness of small state mediation.

Israeli relations and the Abraham Accords (2020)

Traditionally, Israel has not been a significant source of threat for smaller Gulf states. They were far from Israel geographically, and they were not even independent during the first two Arab–Israeli wars. Moreover, in the

1950s–1970s, they feared Arab nationalist republics more, the regimes that advocated Nasserist revolutions in the region. Nevertheless, they did not establish diplomatic relations officially until 2020, when Bahrain and the UAE decided to sign the Abraham Accords, which paves the way for official cooperation.

The case of Israeli relations shows the normative constraints of smaller Gulf states in the international system. Despite their clear interests and intention to move closer to Israel – mostly for economic and security reasons – they have not managed to do so officially for five decades. The reason is the normative obligations deriving from being members of the Arab family, institutionalised in, among others, the Khartoum Resolution of the Arab League in 1967 (Rabi and Mueller, 2017, p. 578). Fighting Israel has basically been a constitutive norm and a social purpose of the Arab identity, making it obligatory for members of the transnational community to avoid relations with Israel.

While bigger states such Egypt were already able to go against the current in the 1970s, this was out of the question for smaller Gulf states, as they relied on the normative protection deriving from membership. They were forced to "downgrade or avoid engagement" (Patrick, 2012, p. 62), but they did not cease relations altogether and pragmatically let them develop when the time was suitable.

History of Gulf-Israeli relations

Smaller Gulf states witnessed the creation of Israel and the first two Arab–Israeli wars as protected states of the British Empire without the ability to conduct independent foreign policy. The most important effect they witnessed derived from the fallout from the British participation in the bombing of Egypt in 1956 alongside Israel and France, which enlarged anti-British feelings in the Gulf societies. This situation was maybe one of the first manifestations of the alliance dilemma described earlier and, while other states valued protection more, Kuwait decided to request independence partly due to avoiding the negative consequences of its patron's Israeli policy.

As the only independent smaller Gulf state, Kuwait did not play any significant role in the Six-Day War in 1967 (Rabi and Mueller, 2017, p. 576); nevertheless, the outcome of the crisis was a positive development for Gulf regimes, as it weakened Arab nationalism and undermined Egyptian hegemonic attempts. Consequently, Saudi Arabia and its allies stepped up to challenge nationalist regimes and tried to take over their place as the defenders of Islamic and Arab causes, especially the Palestinian struggle, with huge money transfers for Arab governments and for the Palestinian people, as well.

Following independence, smaller Gulf states learned to use Palestinian support and the condemnation of Israel politically in several ways. First, they wanted to prove their membership in the Arab interstate society. Second, with such a policy, they maintained regime stability by appeasing domestic sentiments of the issue, especially concerning the approximately half a million Palestinian immigrants (Davidson, 2012, p. 79). Third, they used it as a balancing tool against security threats – on the one hand, to tackle the negative effects of their closeness to Israel's allies and, on the other, indirectly to criticise the Shah's Iran, which maintained a friendly relationship with Israel (until 1979) (Rosman-Stollman, 2004, p. 193).

In practice, they did not mean to do much against Israel; Oman even cooperated with the country in sharing agriculture know-how (especially water desalination and drip irrigation) and military training (Rabi and Mueller, 2017, p. 578). Nevertheless, through harsh boycott policies and participation in the Arab League and Organization of the Petroleum Exporting Countries (OPEC), smaller Gulf states managed to convince others that they play a "reasonably active role in countering Israel" (Davidson, 2012, p. 3). In 1973, they participated in the joint action not to sell oil to Israeli allies, which not only proved to be effective, but also served as a virtual enlargement tool (Rosman-Stollman, 2004, p. 193). Except for Oman – which did not boycott Israel and did not break off relations with Egypt after the Camp David Accords – smaller Gulf states followed the Arab mainstream in the Palestinian question, as the issue was not a priority for them.

The first turning point in relations took place in the early 1990s, for which there were two reasons. First, during the Iraqi invasion of Kuwait, Israeli behaviour was much more beneficial for smaller Gulf states than that of Palestine. To break the coalition of Arab and non-Arab countries condemning the attack and gather support from the region, Saddam Hussein publicly connected the Israeli occupation of the West Bank and Gaza to the Iraqi occupation of Kuwait, saying that it would pull out of the country if Israel did the same over Palestinian territories (Gause, 2010, pp. 106–111). In return, the leadership of the Palestinian Liberation Organisation (PLO) did not support a resolution in the Arab League, which condemned Iraqi actions. Israeli behaviour, on the other hand, was quite beneficial for the Gulf states, not just because of its hostility towards the Hussein regime, but also due to its restraint. Baghdad wanted to pull Israel more into the fight on Kuwait's side in order to undermine the legitimacy of coalition efforts, which is why, in January, it made missile strikes on Israel. Nevertheless, the Jewish state did not retaliate, as Americans asked them not to complicate the issue.

Second, the Madrid and Oslo processes affected Gulf–Israeli relations, too (Rosman-Stollman, 2004, pp. 194–196). Gulf countries took part in the multilateral talks, often as hosts and facilitators in the discussions. Regimes of smaller Gulf states perceived the Palestinian issue as a driving force behind radicalisation, the spread of Islamism, and, ultimately, as something benefiting Iran and its allies (Rabi and Mueller, 2017, p. 583). Contrarily, the peace process contributed to regional stability, of crucial interest to small states.

The publication of the Declaration of Principles in 1993 (which contained the basics of understanding between Israel and Palestine) eased regional tensions enough to break the taboo of cooperating with Israel. It was during this time that Arab unity on the question completely fell apart, leading to diverging state behaviour. This particularly meant that the normative obligation of

Arab states regarding Israel vanished sufficiently to enable trade discussions to take place, especially with Bahrain, Qatar, and Oman. In the following years, Israel opened trade offices in Muscat and Doha (with Kuwaiti plans to follow) – a major breakthrough in Arab–Israeli relations (Al-Khalili, 2009, pp. 113–114). The UAE, following the lead of Saudi Arabia, eased boycott rules against Israel (though mostly because of its obligations as a new member of the WTO), but did not engage in direct talks (Davidson, 2012, p. 176; Rabi and Mueller, 2017, p. 584). The anti-Israeli voices in the Gulf media were turned down to set up the stage for improving relations, even if the public remained adversarial against the Jewish state.

The end of the détente came after 1996 when, after the national elections, Benjamin Netanyahu formed a government that was less open to compromise and basically ended the peace process (Rosman-Stollman, 2004, pp. 194–196). Egypt and Syria put considerable pressure on smaller Gulf states to stop efforts at relations-building. Most of them complied, with Oman leaving its trade office in Tel-Aviv open (although without representation) and Qatar voicing the need for revision of the Arab stance. Nevertheless, both halted their reconciliation attempts, arguing that the Israeli government did not follow the guidelines set previously by the Oslo process (Al-Khalili, 2009, p. 114).

In the years that followed, international attention shifted away from the possible revival of the peace process; however, an important development for smaller Gulf states was the publication of the Saudi-initiated peace plan of 2002 (Rabi and Mueller, 2017, p. 585). The document built on a previous initiative of Riyadh – the Fahd plan of 1982 – and it basically offered Israel recognition in exchange for pulling out of the 1967 territories and Palestinian statehood. While the plan did not materialise, it was embraced by the Arab League and replaced the Khartoum Resolution with a softer normative obligation.

After 2003, smaller Gulf states got occupied with the threat of growing Iranian influence, which eventually led to their growing eagerness and ability to move closer to Israel. Tehran managed to gain influence in the region and wanted to picture itself as the leader of the resistance against "Zionist occupation". The strengthening of Hezbollah in Lebanon and the Palestinian split in 2007[22] contributed to this campaign. As was the case when Nasser dominated the Palestinian question, Gulf states feared that their primary political adversary would stand as the representative of the resistance against Israel.

As a result, the traditional binary setting of Israel versus Arab and Muslim countries fell apart (Rabi and Mueller, 2017, pp. 588–590). In regional politics, differentiation between the "moderate camp" (led by Saudi Arabia) and the "axis of resistance" (led by Iran) also started to show in the Palestinian question (Feuer, 2020). The first tangible sign was the war between Israel and Hezbollah, which undermined the tradition of Arab states unifying against the Jewish state in wartime. The second step was the "war of the summits" (*harb al-qimam*) in 2009, when the two camps organised competing diplomatic talks, both in one of the smaller Gulf states –one in Kuwait and the other in Qatar. This division developed in parallel with the events of the Arab Uprisings and the intensification of the Saudi-Iranian rivalry.

By the 21st century, not just the perception of Israel varied in the Gulf, but also Palestinian relations (Michael and Guzansky, 2020; Turner, 2019). While nominally all smaller Gulf states support the Palestinian people in general, they have different aims and means, especially after the Fatah-controlled West Bank and the Hamas-dominated Gaza Strip became politically independent from each other in 2007. Alongside Saudi Arabia, three of the five smaller Gulf states – Kuwait, Qatar, and the UAE – are among the top donors to the Palestinian territories, as the combined share of the four states reached 90% of all Arab aid. For all of them, supporting Palestine works as a tool to strengthen their soft power and to enlarge their normative size. The most important distinction lies between Qatar, which is the largest donor to the Gaza Strip and favours Hamas, and the rest, which prioritise aid to the West Bank. Doha's intention is attributed to Hamas' ideological similarity to the Muslim Brotherhood network, as well as to the intention of enhancing its own mediation capabilities (between Fatah and Hamas, on the one hand, and between Hamas and Israel, on the other). At the other end of the spectrum, Kuwait and the UAE try to engage with Hamas due to its ideology, its closeness to Iran, and its destabilising activities. This approach is part of their regional stabilisation efforts, even if it limits their leverage on the ground.

The interpretation of the Abraham Accords

Capitalising on the changing normative environment, smaller Gulf states started to ease up their policies towards Israel in the late 2000s (Davidson, 2012, pp. 176–179; Rabi and Mueller, 2017, p. 588). Bahrain closed its boycott office in 2005 and visibly turned down anti-Israeli rhetoric. The UAE quietly unblocked Israeli websites, and rumours started to spread that one member of the Nahyan family flew to Israel for heart surgery. In 2008, Qatar invited the Israeli foreign minister to speak at a conference (where she met with her Omani counterpart). Later, in 2010, Abu Dhabi allowed an Israeli diplomatic delegation to be sent to the country, officially to the International Renewable Energy Agency. In the same year, the Qatar Investment Authority was reported to be forming a new investment fund in cooperation with the Israeli IDB Holdings.

All these activities suggested that sub rosa talks had been taking place over the last decade, paving the way for the announcement of the Abraham Accords in 2020.[23] This communication had mostly been dominated by security cooperation and intelligence-sharing, as well as trade and economic relations (Guzansky and Marshall, 2020, pp. 1–2). These two areas form the basic incentive for deepening ties for both sides – their security perception overlap to a considerable extent (especially in relations with Iran, Islamist networks, and Jihadi organisations), while the level of development in both sides suggests the huge economic potential for cooperation, which helps their efforts to diversify (Stroul, 2020; Solomon, 2021). Making the cooperation visible only decreased the price for the collaboration and made it more efficient.

The timing of the Abraham Accords was mostly down to three factors. First, as already mentioned, the UAE and Saudi Arabia started to recalibrate their foreign policy in 2019; this was driven by their eagerness to balance against Iran more efficiently. Building relations with Israel fits this aim perfectly. Second, the American support provided to the Netanyahu government and the American peace plan published in January 2020 (officially titled "Peace to Prosperity") meant another incentive for Gulf states. The initiative represented Washington turning away from the two-state solution and, coupled with other decisions of the Trump government, a green light for annexing territories in the West Bank. This intention represented an opportunity for the UAE, as it signed the agreement with Israel in exchange for the temporary halt of such activities. Third, Gulf states were also driven by the fear that, should Trump lose the election, Joe Biden would implement a more demanding policy for them and a more friendly approach to Iran (Al Ketbi, 2020).

From the perspective of smaller Gulf states, establishing relations with Israel fits their traditional alliance policy in various ways. First, choosing allies is a matter of balance of threats and interests, not necessarily of (material) power (Feuer, 2020). Iran is still perceived as a revisionist power, while Israel developed to become a status quo force, a potential ally of the moderate camp. Second, in conducting regional affairs, smaller Gulf states have an eye on Washington (Al Ketbi, 2020, p. 7). Making peace with Israel serves as a tool to better relations with the USA, and as a way to prove their value as an ally and, therefore, to obtain access to additional support. In the case of the UAE, this motivation was tangible, as it wanted to be able to purchase the F-35 military jets from the USA (Guzansky and Marshall, 2020, pp. 2–3). On the other hand, diversifying security relations has also been one of the key intents of smaller Gulf states since at least 2003. Third, the political burden brought about by cooperating with Israel (both domestically and internationally) is a threat familiar to smaller Gulf states. They have been dealing with similar alliance dilemmas for centuries, both in the case of Great Britain and the USA.

Both smaller Gulf states had special motivations to join the Abraham Accords (Al Ketbi, 2020; Guzansky and Marshall, 2020; Henderson, 2020). For the Emirates, building relations with Israel was another building block in achieving middle power status in the region. This cooperation and its consequences help the UAE to enlarge its relative military and economic size, as well as its normative size. Polls also indicate that the Emirati population cares more about Iran than the Palestinians; therefore, domestic political costs have so far been low. For Bahrain, the Iranian threat serves as the biggest incentive though, due to its sectarian division, it had to act more carefully than Abu Dhabi (interestingly, both Sunni and Shia circles rejected the agreement). That is probably why it only came second. Also, it is believed that Bahrain had asked for the permission of Riyadh due to its reliance on Saudi

Arabia. From the Saudi perspective, Bahrain can serve as a litmus test for its own opening.

In contrast, the remaining three smaller Gulf states had their own calculations behind avoiding the Abraham Accords (Yaari, 2020; Dazi-Héni, 2020). Oman has been relatively open about cooperating with Israel without the unnecessary fuss surrounding official diplomatic ties (e.g. Netanhayu visited Muscat at the end of 2019). The behind-the-door type of relationship better fits the traditional framework of Omani foreign policy, especially since Muscat tries to keep its normative size small. From a domestic political perspective, the Sultanate just went through a succession process in 2020 while simultaneously coping with the Covid-19 crisis, making the new leader, Sultan Haitham, focus on domestic reforms. Kuwait had similar considerations, especially when it comes to its moderate foreign policy and the transition process taking place after the death of Sabah Al Ahmad Al Sabah in September. Due to its domestic political structure, the anger that would probably follow a decision of normalisation would undermine the regime more than it did in Bahrain, for example. Favouring domestic stability over the potential benefits of becoming closer to Israel continues to hamper any similar diplomatic attempt.

Of the three states, Qatar found itself in the most interesting situation. On the one hand, in a similar way to Oman, it has maintained some level of relationship with Israel since the 1990s but, in the decades that followed, supporting Palestinian organisations played an important role in its foreign policy. Qatari–Israeli de facto cooperation involves the management of the Gaza Strip, where Doha serves as a channel to Hamas and to deliver humanitarian aid (Michael and Guzansky, 2020). On the other hand, Qatar is not in favour of the emergence of the moderate and radical camps as a framework of regional politics, as this would diminish both its security and leverage. As the Abraham Accords preceded the al-Ula Gulf reconciliation summit, Qatar had no opportunity to follow the lead of the UAE, and it is questionable that it would work in the future, especially due to the tense relations between Israel and Qatar's main regional ally, Turkey.

Two regional consequences of the Abraham Accords should also be taken into account, as they affect smaller Gulf states' position. First, by the actions of Bahrain and the UAE, it was proven that the normative obligation for Arab states not to make peace with Israel vanished. The Arab League basically concluded that it considers the Accords as a sovereign decision by its member states, which shows that the Saudi-sponsored Arab Peace Initiative lost its norm-constructing function (Yaari, 2020). Second, such developments contributed to the solidification of the moderate and revisionist blocs (Al Ketbi, 2020; Feuer, 2020). Though they are far from transforming into long-lasting and unified alliances (especially due to the special roles of Turkey, Qatar, and the Muslim Brotherhood), one huge obstacle has been deflected from this process. This suggests the possibility of the transformation of competitive heteropolarity, which probably would shrink the leverage of smaller Gulf states but would elevate their security.

Notes

1 Defined as "any peaceful public gathering of at least 100 people for the primary purpose of displaying or voicing their opposition to government policies or authority, excluding demonstrations of a distinctly anti-foreign nature" (Lucas, 2014, p. 197).

2 Including Al-Shammari and Willoughby (2017); Bjorvatn and Høigilt (2016).

3 In the Emirates, they became famous as the UAE-5 of UAE-7. Barany (2012, p. 8); Forstenlechner, Rutledge and Alnuaimi (2012).

4 Nonetheless, this was the first election in the history of Kuwait during which there was a monitoring mechanism in place led by the Kuwait Transparency Society (Zaccara, 2013, p. 93).

5 Sohar became the centre of the Omani unrest. According to the most widespread narrative, the central role of the city in the demonstrations was due to high local unemployment rates (approximately 15% for the population and 19–20% for the youth on the eve of the Arab Uprisings) and the tensions of the local working class (Worrall, 2012).

6 Reshuffles took place in three waves in February and March of 2011, and February of 2012. The primary victim of these measures was Abd al-Nabi Makki, the Minister of National Economy, who had occupied this position since 1995 (Bank, Richter and Sunik, 2014, p. 172).

7 Since 2005, the elections laws divided the country into five districts, each sending ten representatives to the National Assembly. All voters had four votes to choose between the candidates. This system helped the opposition groups enormously, but the Emir decided to amend it so that each voter would have only one vote. This lowered the threshold for individual candidates, making it easier for pro-government candidates to get in (Gharba, 2014, pp. 14–15).

8 The *Khawalid* branch of the ruling family became the firmest supporter of the initiative, while Shia parties and the youth movements rejected it (Wehrey, 2014, pp. 135–136).

9 In February 2012, the idea was rejected publicly by House Speaker Ahmed al-Saadoon (Al Arabiya, 2013) but the government voiced its support (Arab News, 2013).

10 Qatar popped up as the fifth most preferred country in 2014 and 2015.

11 Besides that, Kuwait supported some members of the Syrian opposition, mostly due to the efforts of the Syrian diaspora living in the emirate to persuade the government to do so (Lister, 2015, p. 70). The Sabah regime also provided financial support for the Saudi–Emirati subsidised Morsi regime in Egypt (Almezaini and Rickli, 2017, p. 188); nevertheless, it was probably motivated by stabilisation rather than ideological strife.

12 For more details, see Katzman (2020e, pp. 9–10), Harb (2019).

13 Similar developments took place in 2002 (Zafirov, 2014, p. 195).

14 Actually, two different documents are called the "Riyadh Agreement": one signed in 2013, and a supplementary agreement attached to it in 2014.

15 A bilateral summit between the USA and Saudi Arabia, a multilateral summit between the GCC and the USA, and a further summit between the USA and other regional states.

16 Compiled by author using data from the World Bank Database, 2021.

17 One year following the eruption of the crisis, in addition to the Quarter, only Chad, the Comoros, the Maldives, Mauritania, Senegal, and Yemen had cut

diplomatic ties with Qatar, while Jordan, Niger, and Djibouti downgraded their relations. In August, Chad re-established relations (*Middle East Eye*, 2018).

18 A term that was used by Lolwah Al-Khater, the spokesperson of the Ministry of Foreign Affairs of the State of Qatar during an interview I conducted with her in Doha on 8 July 2018.

19 See the individual complaints at WTO 2017a, 2017b, 2017c.

20 Such figures include Abdullah bin Ali Al Thani (the brother of Ahmed bin Ali Al Thani, the Emir of Qatar between 1960 and 1971), Sultan bin Suheim Al Thani (the cousin of Khalifa bin Hamad Al Thani, the Emir of Qatar between 1971 and 1995), Fawaz al-Attiya (a Qatari businessman with British citizenship, who was famous for criticising Hamad bin Jassim Al Thani, the former Minister of Foreign Affairs) and Khalid al-Hail (the leader of the so-called Qatari National Democratic Party) (*Middle East Eye*, 2017).

21 Though it tuned down its participation in regional wars (Hassan, 2018).

22 When the moderate Fatah and the Muslim Brotherhood aligned with Hamas broke up the unity government. Since then, Fatah controls the West Bank while the Gaza Strip is under the rule of Hamas.

23 During the 2010s, other smaller-scale signs were observable regarding the possibilities of reconciliation, including the visit of Prime Minister Netanyahu to Oman in 2018, and the arrival of an Israeli judo team in the UAE in the same year. In 2019, Bahrain hosted the economic summit of the coming Trump peace plan (Stroul, 2020; Henderson, 2020).

Bibliography

Abu-Siriyya, J. (2017) Qatar-Iran Economic Relations will Improve, Contrary to Saudi Arabia's Intent. *Foreign Policy Journal*, [Online]. Available at: https://www. foreignpolicyjournal.com/2017/10/27/qatar-iran-economic-relations-will-improve-contrary-to-saudi-arabias-intent/ (Accessed 31 January 2021)

ACRPS (2017a) Crisis in the Gulf Cooperation Council, in Arab Center for Research and Policy Studies: *Crisis in the Gulf Cooperation Council*, [Online]. Available at: https://www.dohainstitute.org/en/Lists/ACRPS-PDFDocumentLibrary/Crisis%20 in%20the%20Gulf%20Cooperation%20Council%20-%20booklet%20by%20ACW. pdf (Accessed 31 January 2021), pp. 7–12.

ACRPS (2017b) Appendix A, in Arab Center for Research and Policy Studies: *Crisis in the Gulf Cooperation Council*, [Online]. Available at: https://www.dohainstitute. org/en/Lists/ACRPS-PDFDocumentLibrary/Crisis%20in%20the%20Gulf%20 Cooperation%20Council%20-%20booklet%20by%20ACW.pdf   (Accessed   31 January 2021), 105–112.

Akbarzadeh, S. (2017) Iran and the Gulf Cooperation Council Sheikhdoms, in Almezaini, K.S. and Rickli, J. (eds.) *The Small Gulf States. Foreign and Security Policies before and after the Arab Spring*. London & New York: Routledge, pp. 89–106. DOI:10.4324/9781315619576-6.

Al Arabiya (2013) Bridging the Gulf: Where Kuwait Stands on the GCC Union. *Al Arabiya*, [Online]. Available at: https://english.alarabiya.net/en/special-reports/ bridging-the-gulf/2013/05/12/Bridging-the-Gulf-where-Kuwait-stands-on-the-GCC-Union.html. (Accessed 31 January 2021)

Al Arabiya (2017) Iran Revolutionary Guards "Protecting Qatar's Sheikh Tamim inside his Palace". *Al Arabiya*, [Online]. Available at: https://english.alarabiya.net/

en/News/gulf/2017/06/07/Iran-s-Revolutionary-Guards-protecting-Qatari-emir-inside-palace-.html (Accessed 31 January 2021)

Al Ketbi, E. (2020) Contemporary Shifts in UAE Foreign Policy: From the Liberation of Kuwait to the Abraham Accords, *Israel Journal of Foreign Affairs*, 14(3), pp. 391–398. DOI:10.1080/23739770.2020.1845067.

Al-Akhbar (2017) Daoula al-Imarat Keqawa Iqlimiya Saida. *Al-Akhbar*, [Online]. Available at: https://www.al-akhbar.com/Opinion/231348 (Accessed 31 January 2021)

Albloshi, H.H. (2017) Iran and Kuwait, in Bahgat, G., Ehteshami, A. and Quilliam, N. (eds.) *Security and Bilateral Issues between Iran and its Arab Neighbours*. London: Palgrave Macmillan, pp. 123–148. DOI:10.1007/978-3-319-43289-2_6.

Al-Hayat (2017) Mufti al-Saudiy: Al-Qararat Didd al-Doha feeha Minfa'a li'Istaqbul al-Qatariyyin. *Al-Hayat*, [Online]. Available at: https://24.ae/article/355239/%D9%85%D9%81%D8%AA%D9%8A-%D8%A7%D9%84%D8%B3%D8%B9%D9%88%D8%AF%D9%8A%D8%A9-%D8%A7%D9%84%D9%82%D8%B1%D8%A7%D8%B1%D8%A7%D8%AA-%D8%B6%D8%AF-%22%D9%86%D8%B8%D8%A7%D9%85-%D8%A7%D9%84%D8%AF%D9%88%D8%AD%D8%A9%22-%D9%81%D9%8A%D9%87%D8%A7-%D9%85%D9%86%D9%81%D8%B9%D8%A9-%D9%84%D9%85%D8%B3%D8%AA%D9%82%D8%A8%D9%84-%D8%A7%D9%84%D9%82%D8%B7%D8%B1%D9%8A%D9%8A%D9%86. (Accessed 31 January 2021)

Al-Khalili, M. (2009) *Oman's Foreign Policy. Foundations and Practice*. London: Praeger Security International. DOI:10.25148/etd.fi13101580.

Almezaini, K.S. and Rickli, J. (2017) The Foreign Policy of the Small Gulf States: An Exception in Small States' Behaviour?, in Almezaini, K.S. and Rickli, J. (eds.) *The Small Gulf States. Foreign and Security Policies before and after the Arab Spring*. London & New York: Routledge, pp. 180–182. DOI:10.4324/9781315619576-11.

Al-Muslimi, F. (2017) Master of the Middle. *Carnegie Middle East Center*, [Online]. Available at: http://carnegie-mec.org/diwan/72715 (Accessed 31 January 2021)

Alnajjar, G. and Selvik, K. (2016) Kuwait – The Politics of Crisis, in Selvik, K. and Utvik, B.O. (eds.) *Oil States in the New Middle East. Uprisings and Stability*. London & New York: Routledge, pp. 113–131.

Al-Shammari, N. and Willoughby, J. (2017) Determinants of Political Instability across Arab Spring Countries. *Mediterranean Politics*, 2017(1), pp. 1–22. DOI:10.1080/13629395.2017.1389349.

Amnesty International (2013): The Dark Side of Migration: Spotlight on Qatar's Construction Sector Ahead of the World Cup. *Amnesty International*, [Online]. Available at: https://www.amnesty.org.uk/files/the_dark_side_of_migration_-_spotlight_on_qatars_construction_sector_ahead_of_the_world_cup.pdf (Accessed 31 January 2021).

Amnesty International (2017a) Qatar/UN: Agreement to tackle migrant labour abuse offers path to reform. *Amnesty International*, [Online]. Available at: https://www.amnesty.org/en/latest/news/2017/10/qatar-un-agreement-to-tackle-migrant-labour-abuse-offers-path-to-reform/. (Accessed 31 January 2021)

Amnesty International (2017b) Gulf dispute: Six months on, individuals still bear brunt of political crisis. *Amnesty International*, [Online]. Available at: https://www.amnesty.org/download/Documents/MDE2276042017ENGLISH.pdf. (Accessed 31 January 2021)

Arab News (2013) Oman Opposes Gulf Union. *Arab News*, [Online]. Available at: http://www.arabnews.com/news/488956 (Accessed 31 January 2021).

Aras, B. and Falk, R. (2015) Authoritarian "Geopolitics' of Survival in the Arab Spring". *Third World Quarterly*, 36(2), pp. 322–336. DOI:10.1080/01436597.2015.1 013307.

Asda'a (2021) Arab Youth Survey Findings. *Asda'a*, [Online]. Available at: https://www.arabyouthsurvey.com/findings.html (Accessed 31 January 2021).

Aydin, A. (2013) Hereditary Oil Monarchies: Why Arab Spring Fails in GCC Arabian States? *Journal of Social Sciences*, 2013(30), pp. 123–138.

Baabood, A. (2017) Oman's Independent Foreign Policy, in Almezaini, K.S. and Rickli, J. (eds.) *The Small Gulf States. Foreign and Security Policies before and after the Arab Spring*. London & New York: Routledge, pp. 107–122. DOI:10.4324/978131 5619576-7.

Bank, A., Richter, T. and Sunik, A. (2014) Durable, Yet Different: Monarchies in the Arab Spring. *Journal of Arabian Studies*, 4(2), pp. 163–179. DOI:10.1080/21534764 .2014.971647.

Barany, Z. (2012) The "Arab Spring" in the Kingdoms Arab Center for Research & Policy Studies, [Online]. Available at: https://www.dohainstitute.org/en/lists/ACRPS-PDFDocumentLibrary/The_Arab_Spring_in_the_Kingdoms.pdf (Accessed 31 January 2021).

Berger, L. (2014) The Gulf Cooperation Council between Unity and Discord towards the Arab Uprisings. *Sicherheit und Frieden*, 32(4), pp. 260–264. DOI:10.5771/0175-274x-2014-4-260.

BICI (2011) Report of the Bahrain Independent Commission of Inquiry. Bahrain Independent Commission of Inquiry, [Online]. Available at: http://www.bici.org.bh/BICIreportEN.pdf. (Accessed 31 January 2021).

Bjorvatn, K. and Høigilt, J. (2016). Youth and the Arab Revolutionsin Selvik, K. and Utvik, B.O. (ed.) *Oil States in the New Middle East: Uprisings and Stability*. New York: Routledge, pp. 39–56.

Brookings (2018) GCC News Roundup: Trump meets with Emir of Qatar, Kuwait says Gulf crisis must end, Houthi political chief killed, (April 1–30). *Brookings*, [Online]. Available at: https://www.brookings.edu/blog/up-front/2018/05/01/gcc-news-roundup-trump-meets-with-emir-of-qatar-kuwait-says-gulf-crisis-must-end-houthi-political-chief-killed-april-1-30/ (Accessed 31 January 2021).

Cafiero, G. and Karasik, T. (2017) Kuwait, Oman, and the Qatar Crisis. Middle East Institute, [Online]. Available at: http://www.mei.edu/content/article/kuwait-oman-and-qatar-crisis (Accessed 31 January 2021).

Cole, J. (2018) David and Goliath: How Qatar Defeated the Saudi and UAE Annexation Plot. *The Nation*, [Online]. Available at: https://www.thenation.com/article/david-and-goliath-how-qatar-defeated-the-saudi-and-uae-annexation-plot/ (Accessed 31 January 2021).

Colombo, S. (2017) Foreign Policy Activism in Saudi Arabia and Oman. Diverging Narratives and Stances towards the Syrian and Yemeni Conflicts. *The International Spectator*, 52(2), pp. 54–70, DOI:10.1080/03932729.2017.1303965.

Davidson, C.M. (2012) *After the Sheikhs. The Coming Collapse of the Gulf Monarchies*. London: Hurst & Co.

Dazi-Héni, F. (2020) The Gulf States and Israel after the Abraham Accords. *Arab Reform Initiative*, [Online]. Available at: https://www.arab-reform.net/publication/the-gulf-states-and-israel-after-the-abraham-accords/ (Accessed 31 January 2021).

DW (2018) Qatar Resumes Full Diplomatic ties with Iran. *Deutsche Welle*, 24 August, https://www.dw.com/en/qatar-resumes-full-diplomatic-ties-with-iran/a-40224340 (Accessed 31 January 2021).

Emmons, A. (2018) Saudi Arabia Planned to Invade Qatar Last Summer. Rex Tillerson's Efforts to Stop it May Have Cost him his Job. *The Intercept*, [Online]. Available at: https://theintercept.com/2018/08/01/rex-tillerson-qatar-saudi-uae/ (Accessed 31 January 2021)

Feierstein, G.M. (2021) The GCC al-Ula Statement: Perhaps a Step, but not a Solution. Middle East Institute, [Online]. Available at: https://www.mei.edu/blog/gcc-al-ula-statement-perhaps-step-not-solution (Accessed 31 January 2021).

Feuer, S. (2020) UAE–Israel Peace is Revealing the Middle East's Faultlines. *The National Interest*, [Online]. Available at: https://nationalinterest.org/blog/middle-east-watch/uae-israel-peace-revealing-middle-easts-faultlines-169689 (Accessed 31 January 2021).

Forstenlechner, I., Rutledge, E. and Alnuaimi, R.S. (2012) The UAE, the "Arab Spring", and Different Types of Dissent. *Middle East Policy*, 19(4), pp. 54–67. DOI:10.1111/j.1475-4967.2012.00559.x.

Fraihat, I. (2020) Superpowers and Small-State Mediation in the Qatar Gulf Crisis. *The International Spectator*, 55(2), pp. 79–91. DOI:10.1080/03932729.2020.1741268.

Gause, G. (2010) *The International Relations of the Persian Gulf*. Cambridge: Cambrdige University Press. DOI:10.1017/cbo9780511818264.

Gengler, J. (2013) Royal Factionalism, the Khawalid, and the Securitization of "the Shi'a Problem" in Bahrain. *Journal of Arabian Studies*, 3(1), pp. 53–79. DOI:10.1080/21534764.2013.802944.

Gharba, S. (2014) Kuwait: At the Crossroads of Change or Political Stagnation. Middle East Institute, [Online]. Available at: https://www.mei.edu/sites/default/files/publications/Ghabra%20Policy%20Paper_0.pdf (Accessed 31 January 2021).

Goldburt, M.W. (2015) The Danger to Kuwait is Authoritarianism. *Carnegie Endowment for International Peace*, [Online]. Available at: http://carnegieendowment.org/sada/60802 (Accessed 31 January 2021).

Guzansky, Y. (2015) *The Arab Gulf States and Reform in the Middle East*. New York: Palgrave Macmillan. DOI:10.1057/9781137467836.

Guzansky, Y. and Marshall, Z.A. (2020) The Abraham Accords: Immediate Significance and Long-Term Implications. *Israel Journal of Foreign Affairs*, 14(3). pp. 379–389. DOI:10.1080/23739770.2020.1831861.

Harb, I.K. (2017) An Economic Explanation for Egypt's Alignment in the GCC Crisis, in *Crisis in the Gulf Cooperation Council* Washington, DC: Arab Center. [Online]. Available at: https://www.dohainstitute.org/en/Lists/ACRPS-PDFDocumentLibrary/Crisis%20in%20the%20Gulf%20Cooperation%20Council%20-%20booklet%20by%20ACW.pdf. (Accessed: 15 September 2018), pp. 77–86.

Harb, I.K. (2019) Why the United Arab Emirates is Abandoning Saudi Arabia in Yemen. *Foreign Policy*, [Online]. Available at: https://foreignpolicy.com/2019/08/01/why-the-united-arab-emirates-is-abandoning-saudi-arabia-in-yemen/ (Accessed 31 January 2021).

Harris, B. (2018) Qatar hires Trump-linked lobbyist ahead of emir's visit. *Al-Monitor*, [Online]. Available at: https://www.al-monitor.com/pulse/originals/2018/04/qatar-hires-trump-linked-lobbyist-emir-visit.html (Accessed 31 January 2021)

Hassan, H. (2018) Qatar Won the Saudi Blockade. *Foreign Policy*, [Online]. Available at: https://foreignpolicy.com/2018/06/04/qatar-won-the-saudi-blockade/ (Accessed 31 January 2021)

Hassan, I. (2020) The UAE: A Small State with Regional Middle Power Aspirations, in Saouli, A. (ed.) *Unfulfilled Aspirations*. Oxford: Oxford University Press, pp. 183–202. DOI:10.1093/oso/9780197521885.003.0010.

Hearst, D. (2014) Saudi Arabia Threatens to Lay Siege to Qatar: Cooperation or Confrontation? *Huffington Post*, [Online]. Available at: https://www.huffington-post.com/david-hearst/saudi-arabia-threatens-to_b_4930518.html (Accessed 31 January 2021).

Heller, C.H. (2019) Little Sparta's Big Ambitions: The Emirati Military Comes of Age. *Real Clear Defence*, [Online]. Available at: https://www.realcleardefense.com/articles/2019/09/17/little_spartas_big_ambitions_the_emirati_military_comes_of_age_114748.html (Accessed 31 January 2021).

Henderson, S. (2020) Bahrain Move toward Israel Risks Domestic Reaction. The Washington Institute, [Online]. Available at: https://www.washingtoninstitute.org/policy-analysis/bahrain-move-toward-israel-risks-domestic-reaction (Accessed 31 January 2021).

HRW (2017) Qatar: Isolation Causing Rights Abuses. Human Rights Watch, [Online]. Available at: https://www.hrw.org/news/2017/07/13/qatar-isolation-causing-rights-abuses (Accessed 31 January 2021).

HRW (2018a) Qatar Joins Core Human Rights Treaties but Rejects Major Protections for Women, Migrant Workers. Human Rights Watch, [Online]. Available at: https://www.hrw.org/news/2018/05/25/qatar-joins-core-human-rights-treaties (Accessed 31 January 2021).

HRW (2018b) Qatar: Year of Crisis Spurred Rights Reforms. Human Rights Watch, [Online]. Available at: https://www.hrw.org/news/2018/01/18/qatar-year-crisis-spurred-rights-reforms (Accessed 31 January 2021).

Ibish, H. (2017) Unfulfilled 2014 Riyadh Agreement Defines Current GCC Rift. The Arab Gulf States Institute in Washington, [Online]. Available at: http://www.agsiw.org/unful-filled-2014-riyadh-agreement-defines-current-gcc-rift/ (Accessed 31 January 2021).

Ibish, H. (2020) A Resolution of Qatar Boycott Looms, but can it last? The Arab Gulf States Institute in Washington, [Online]. Available at: https://agsiw.org/a-res-olution-of-qatar-boycott-looms-but-can-it-last/?fbclid=IwAR3mGaznLKBIKZF gv4kqMzvqT1OaZvRV2exyHBST_qnP6-poBAEHVc766tw (Accessed 31 January 2021).

ICJ (2018) Interpretation and Application of the International Convention on the Elimination of All Forms of Racial Discrimination. *International Court of Justice*, [Online]. Available at: https://www.icj-cij.org/public/files/case-related/172/172-20180611-APP-01-00-EN.pdf (Accessed 31 January 2021).

IMF (2017) Regional Economic Outlook: Middle East and Central Asia, October 2017. International Monetary Fund, [Online]. Available at: https://www.imf.org/en/Publications/REO/MECA/Issues/2017/10/17/mreo1017 (Accessed 31 January 2021).

IMF (2018) Qatar: Staff Concluding Statement for the 2018 Article IV Mission. *International Monetary Fund*, [Online]. Available at: https://www.imf.org/en/News/Articles/2018/03/05/ms030518-qatar-staff-concluding-statement-for-the-2018-ar-ticle-iv-mission (Accessed 31 January 2021).

Jha, A. K. (2017) Widening Gulf: A David vs Goliath Fight between Qatar and Saudi Arabia. *India Today*, [Online]. Available at: https://www.indiatoday.in/magazine/up-front/story/20170703-kingdom-of-saudi-arabia-bahrain-uae-qatar-bihar-indian-workers-986690-2017-06-23 (Accessed 31 January 2021).

Joyce, M. (2012) *Bahrain from the Twentieth Century to the Arab Spring*. New York: Palgrave Macmillan. DOI:10.1057/9781137031792.

Kamrava, M. (2017) Iran–Qatar Relations, in Bahgat, G., Ehteshami, A. and Quilliam, N. (eds.) *Security and Bilateral Issues between Iran and its Arab Neighbours*. London: Palgrave Macmillan, pp. 167–188. DOI:10.1007/978-3-319-43289-2_8.

Katzman, K. (2020a) Bahrain: Reform, Security, and U.S. Policy. Congressional Research Service, [Online]. Available at: https://fas.org/sgp/crs/mideast/95-1013.pdf (Accessed 31 January 2021).

Katzman, K. (2020b) Kuwait: Governance, Security and U.S. Policy. Congressional Research Service, [Online]. Available at: https://fas.org/sgp/crs/mideast/RS21513.pdf (Accessed 31 January 2021).

Katzman, K. (2020c) Oman: Reform, Security, and U.S. Policy. Congressional Research Service, [Online]. Available at: https://fas.org/sgp/crs/mideast/RS21534.pdf (Accessed 31 January 2021).

Katzman, K. (2020d) Qatar: Governance, Security, and U.S. Policy. Congressional Research Service, [Online]. Available at: https://fas.org/sgp/crs/mideast/R44533.pdf (Accessed 31 January 2021).

Katzman, K. (2020e) The United Arab Emirates (UAE) Issues for U.S. Policy. Congressional Research Service, [Online]. Available at: https://fas.org/sgp/crs/mideast/RS21852.pdf (Accessed 31 January 2021).

Kausch, K. (2016) The Promise of Middle Eastern Swing States. *Carnegie Europe*, [Online]. Available at: http://carnegieeurope.eu/2016/05/12/promise-of-middle-eastern-swing-states/iy77?mkt_tok=eyJpIjoiWm1ZME1tVTJNVEl4WVdaaaiIsInQiOiJBNTZUYzBsN1czN0RYXC9DRlVEM0l4c3JQcTJzVDYwKzBTNktcL28rMGN3eG52azZBaWhGZU5mRWs3anhOaG5mG1jMkJSWU9hSXkkakRIVXg0TFVUUlVVdHpllQXl0cVdrS0l6Z2Z0TGNUOUVRRwQjdvPSJ9 (Accessed 31 January 2021).

Khalaf, A. (2013) Squaring the Circle: Bahrain's Pearl Roundabout. *Middle East Critique*, 22(3), pp. 265–280. DOI:10.1080/19436149.2013.822240.

Khatib, L. (2013) Qatar's Foreign Policy: The Limits of Pragmatism. *International Affairs*, 89(2), pp. 417–431. DOI:10.1111/1468-2346.12025.

Kinninmont, J. (2016) Bahrain: Rentierism and Beyond, in Selvik, K. and Utvik, B.O. (eds.) *Oil States in the New Middle East. Uprisings and Stability.* London & New York: Routledge, pp. 113–131.

Lister, C. (2015) *The Syrian Jihad.* Oxford: Oxford University Press.

Lons, C. (2018) Oman: Between Iran and a Hard Place. *European Council of Foreign Relations*, [Online]. Available at: https://www.ecfr.eu/article/commentary_oman_between_iran_and_a_hard_place1 (Accessed 31 January 2021)

Lucas, R.E. (2014) Monarchies and Protests in the Arab Uprisings: Path Dependencies or Political Opportunities. *Journal of Arabian Studies*, 4(2), pp. 195–213. DOI:10.1080/21534764.2014.971648.

Luciani, G. (2016) On the Economic Causes of the Arab Spring and its Possible Developments, in Selvik, K. and Utvik, B.O. (eds.) *Oil States in the New Middle East. Uprisings and Stability.* London & New York: Routledge. pp. 188–204.

Martin, G. and Cafiero, G. (2017) Diplomacy is the Kuwaiti Way. *Middle East Policy Council*, [Online]. Available at: https://www.mepc.org/commentary/diplomacy-kuwaiti-way (Accessed 31 January 2021).

Mason, R. (2020) Small-State Aspirations to Middlepowerhood: The Cases of Qatar, in Saouli, A. (ed.) *Unfulfilled Aspirations.* Oxford: Oxford University Press, pp. 157–182. DOI:10.1093/oso/9780197521885.003.0009.

Matthiesen, T. (2013) *Sectarian Gulf. Bahrain, Saudi Arabia and the Arab Spring that Wasn't.* Stanford: Stanford University Press. DOI:10.1515/9780804787222.

Michael, K. and Guzansky, Y. (2020) Might Qatar Join the Abraham Accords? *INSS*, [Online]. Available at: https://www.inss.org.il/publication/the-abraham-accords-and-qatar/ (Accessed 31 January 2021).

Middle East Eye (2017)"Qatari Opposition Figures to Announce "Government-in-exile": report. *Middle East Eye*, [Online]. Available at: https://www.middleeasteye.net/news/qatari-opposition-figures-announce-government-exile-report (Accessed 31 January 2021).

Middle East Eye (2018) Qatar and Chad Restore Diplomatic Relations. *Middle East Eye*, [Online]. Available at: https://www.middleeasteye.net/news/qatar-and-chad-restore-diplomatic-relations-2058747073 (Accessed 31 January 2021).

Middle East Eye (2020) GCC Summit concludes with no mention of rift between neighbours. *Middle East Eye*, [Online]. Available at: https://www.middleeasteye.net/news/qatar-emir-skips-gcc-summit-amid-speculations-thaw-rift (Accessed 31 January 2021).

Middle East Monitor (2017) Central Banker: Financial War against Qatar is "Mutually Destructive". *Middle East Monitor*, [Online]. Available at: https://www.middleeast-monitor.com/20171127-central-banker-financial-war-against-qatar-is-mutually-destructive/ (Accessed 31 January 2021).

Mohammadzadeh, B. (2017) Status and Foreign Policy Change in Small States: Qatar's Emergence in Perspective. *The International Spectator*, 52(2), pp. 19–36. DOI:10.4324/9780203701287-3.

Moody's (2017) Diplomatic Row is Credit Negative for all GCC Members; Qatar and Bahrain Most Exposed. *Moody's*, [Online]. Available at: https://www.moodys.com/research/Moodys-Diplomatic-row-is-credit-negative-for-all-GCC-members-PR_372581 (Accessed 31 January 2021).

NATO (2018) Qatar Signs Security Agreement with NATO. *North Atlantic Treaty Organization*, [Online]. Available at: https://www.nato.int/cps/en/natohq/news_150794.htm (Accessed 31 January 2021).

Neubauer, S. (2016) Oman: The Gulf's Go-Between. The Arab Gulf States Institute in Washington, [Online]. Available at: https://agsiw.org/wp-content/uploads/2016/02/Neubauer_OmanMediator.pdf (Accessed 31 January 2021).

Nuruzzaman, M. (2015) Qatar and the Arab Spring: Down the Foreign Policy Slope. *Contemporary Arab Affairs*, 8(2), pp. 226–238.

Okaz (2017) Qatar Tasuq Al-Saf... watanahuz liauda al-ama. *Okaz*, [Online]. Available at: https://www.okaz.com.sa/article/1548924/%D8%A7%D9%84%D8%B3%D9%8A%D8%A7%D8%B3%D8%A9/%D9%82%D8%B7%D8%B1-%D8%AA%D8%B4%D9%82-%D8%A7%D9%84%D8%B5%D9%81-%D9%88D8%AA%D9%86%D8%AD%D8%A7%D8%B2-%D9%84%D8%A3%D8%B9%D8%AF%D8%A7%D8%A1-%D8%A7%D9%84%D8%A3%D9%85%D8%A9 (Accessed 31 January 2021)

Okruhlik, G. (2016) Rethinking the Politics of Distributive States: Lessons from the Arab Uprisings, in Selvik, K. and Utvik, B.O. (eds.) *Oil States in the New Middle East. Uprisings and Stability*. London & New York: Routledge, pp. 18–38.

Patrick, N. (2012) Nationalism in the Gulf States, in Held, D. and Ulrichsen, K.C. (eds.) *The Transformation of the Gulf. Politics, Economics and the Global Order*. London & New York: Routledge, pp. 47–65.

Pradhan, P.K. (2018) Qatar Crisis and the Deepening Regional Faultlines. *Strategic Analysis*, 42(4), pp. 437–442. DOI:10.1080/09700161.2018.1482620.

Qatar Living (2017) Amnesty team arrives in Doha to assess impact of illegal blockade on Qatar. *Qatar Living*, [Online]. Available at: https://www.qatarliving.com/forum/news/posts/amnesty-team-arrives-doha-assess-impact-illegal-blockade-qatar (Accessed 31 January 2021).

QMFA (2017) Secretary General of Shanghai Cooperation Organization Meets Qatar's Ambassador. Qatari Ministry of Foreign Affairs, [Online]. Available at: https://www.mofa.gov.qa/en/all-mofa-news/details/2017/09/18/secretary-general-of-shanghai-cooperation-organization-meets-qatar's-ambassador (Accessed 31 January 2021)

Quamar, M. (2017) The Turkish Military Base in Doha: A Step towards Gaining "Strategic Depth" in the Middle East. Institute for Defence Studies and Analyses, [Online]. Available at: https://idsa.in/idsacomments/the-turkish-military-base-in-doha_mmquamar_260917 (Accessed 31 January 2021).

Rabi, U. and Mueller, C. (2017) The Gulf Arab states and Israel since 1967: from "no negotiation" to tacit cooperation. *Journal of Middle Eastern Studies*, 44(4), pp. 576–592. DOI:10.1080/13530194.2017.1360013.

Ray al-Yaoum (2017a) Leyla al-Qabd 'ala Qatar. *Ray al-Yaoum*, [Online]. Available at: https://www.raialyoum.com/?p=680286 (Accessed 31 January 2021).

Ray al-Yaoum (2017b) Akhraj Qatar min al-nisb al-Wahabee.... *Ray al-Yaoum*, [Online]. Available at: https://www.raialyoum.com/?p=682593 (Accessed 31 January 2021).

Reuters (2011) Gulf States Launch $20 Billion Fund for Oman and Bahrain. *Reuters*, [Online]. Available at: https://www.reuters.com/article/us-gulf-fund/gulf-states-launch-20-billion-fund-for-oman-and-bahrain-idUSTRE7294B120110310 (Accessed 31 January 2021).

Roberts, D.B. (2011a) Kuwait, in Davidson, C. (ed.) *Power and Politics in the Persian Gulf Monarchies*. London: Hurst & Company, pp. 89–112.

Roberts, D.B. (2011b) Punching Above Its Weight. *Foreign Policy*, [Online]. Available at: https://foreignpolicy.com/2011/04/12/punching-above-its-weight-2/ (Accessed 31 January 2021).

Roberts, D.B. (2017) Securing the Qatari State. The Arab Gulf States Institute in Washington, [Online]. Available at: http://www.agsiw.org/wp-content/uploads/2017/06/Roberts_Qatar_ONLINE.pdf (Accessed 31 January 2021).

Roberts, D.B. (2021) With New Gulf Agreement, Will Qatar Change? The Arab Gulf States Institute in Washington, [Online]. Available at: https://agsiw.org/with-new-gulf-agreement-will-qatar-change/?fbclid=IwAR0ODINiS0e_cz6pf3W0LZIVMwb-MOOnxDWX7gUmgtIkPn2TClqVIsDHKIgM (Accessed 31 January 2021).

Rosman-Stollman, E. (2004) Balancing Acts: The Gulf States and Israel. *Middle Eastern Studies*, 40(4), pp. 185–204. DOI:10.1080/0026320042000240401.

Rubin, L. (2014) The Riyadh Agreement: A Balancing Act. *Stanford University Press Blog*, [Online]. Available at: https://stanfordpress.typepad.com/blog/2014/05/ideological-seesawing-in-the-middle-east.html (Accessed 31 January 2021).

Schanzer, J. and Koduvayur, V. (2018) Kuwait and Oman Are Stuck in Arab No Man's Land. *Foreign Policy*, [Online]. Available at: https://foreignpolicy.com/2018/06/14/kuwait-and-oman-are-stuck-in-the-arab-no-mans-land/ (Accessed 31 January 2021).

Sherwood, L. (2017) Risk Diversification and the United Arab Emirates' Foreign Policy, in Almezaini, K.S. and Rickli, J. (eds.) *The Small Gulf States. Foreign and Security Policies before and after the Arab Spring*. London & New York: Routledge, pp. 144–167. DOI:10.4324/9781315619576-9.

Smith, B. (2016) Political Reform and Human Rights in Bahrain. House of Commons, [Online]. Available at: http://researchbriefings.files.parliament.uk/documents/CBP-7513/CBP-7513.pdf (Accessed 31 January 2021).

Solomon, J. (2021) Biden Should Build on the Abraham Accords, not Roll Them Back. The Washington Institute, [Online]. Available at: https://www.washingtoninstitute.org/policy-analysis/biden-should-build-abraham-accords-not-roll-them-back (Accessed 31 January 2021).

Soubrier, E. (2017) Evolving Foreign and Security Policies: A Comparative Study of Qatar and the United Arab Emirates, in Almezaini, K.S. and Rickli, J. (eds.) *The Small Gulf States. Foreign and Security Policies before and after the Arab Spring.* London & New York: Routledge, pp. 123–143. DOI:10.4324/9781315619576-8.

Stroul, D. (2020) Diplomacy Built Israeli–Arab Peace. The Private Sector Will Sustain It. The Washington Institute, [Online]. Available at: https://www.washingtoninstitute.org/policy-analysis/diplomacy-built-israeli-arab-peace-private-sector-will-sustain-it (Accessed 31 January 2021).

Sultan, N. (2013) Al Jezeera: Reflections on the Arab Spring. *Journal of Arabian Studies*, 3(2), pp. 249–264. DOI:10.1080/21534764.2013.863821.

The Economist (2017) 55 Members of Al Murrah Tribe Stripped of Citizenship. *The Economist*, [Online]. Available at: http://country.eiu.com/article.aspx?articleid=116 5924500&Country=Qatar&topic=Politics&subtopic=Fo_5 (Accessed 31 January 2021).

The National (2017) Mohammed bin Zayed Visits Trump ahead of US President's Trip to Saudi Arabia. *The National*, [Online]. Available at: https://www.thenational.ae/world/mohammed-bin-zayed-visits-trump-ahead-of-us-president-s-trip-to-saudi-arabia-1.77146 (Accessed 31 January 2021).

The Quint (2017) Qatar Boycott: Arab League Rues Split, MEA Claims India Unaffected. *The Quint*, [Online]. Available at: https://www.thequint.com/news/world/saudi-bahrain-uae-cut-ties-with-qatar (Accessed 31 January 2021).

Turner, M. (2019) "Aid Intervention" in the Occupied Palestinian Territory: Do Gulf Arab Donors Act Differently from Western Donors? *Conflict, Security & Development*, 19(3), pp. 283–288. DOI:10.1080/14678802.2019.1608024.

Ulrichsen, K.C. (2012) Small States with a Big Role: Qatar and the United Arab Emirates in the Wake of the Arab Spring. Durham University, [Online]. Available at: www.dur.ac.uk/resources/alsabah/SmallStateswithaBigRole.pdf (Accessed 31 January 2021).

Ulrichsen, K.C. (2014a) Bahrain's Uprising: Domestic Implications and Regional and International Perspectives, in Gerges, F. (ed.) *The New Middle East. Protest and Revolution in the Arab World.* Cambridge: Cambridge University Press, pp. 332–352.

Ulrichsen, K.C. (2014b) *Qatar and the Arab Spring*. Oxford: Oxford University Press. DOI:10.1093/acprof:oso/9780190210977.001.0001.

Ulrichsen, K.C. (2017) The Qatar Standoff and US Interests. *E-International Relations*, [Online]. Available at: https://www.e-ir.info/2017/08/11/the-qatar-standoff-and-us-interests/ (Accessed 31 January 2021).

Ulrichsen, K.C. and Karsik, T. (2018) How Asian and European Countries Helped Qatar Maintain Sovereignty. *Gulf State Analytics*, [Online]. Available at: https://gulfstateanalytics.com/how-asian-and-european-countries-helped-qatar-maintain-sovereignty/ (Accessed 31 January 2021).

UNHCR (2017) UNHCR and Qatar Charity formalize cooperation agreement to support of global refugee programmes. *United Nations High Commissioner for Refugees*, [Online]. Available at: http://www.unhcr.org/news/press/2017/10/59d37d a24/unhcr-qatar-charity-formalize-cooperation-agreement-support-global-refugee.html (Accessed 31 January 2021).

USDOS (2018), Joint Statement of the Inaugural United States-Qatar Strategic Dialogue. U.S. Department of State, [Online]. Available at: https://www.state.gov/r/pa/prs/ps/2018/01/277776.htm (Accessed 31 January 2021)

Utvik, B.O. (2016) Introduction: The Rentier Bargain at the Trial of the Arab Uprisings, in Selvik, K. and Utvik, B.O. (eds.) *Oil States in the New Middle East. Uprisings and Stability*. London & New York: Routledge, pp. 1–17.

Valeri, M. (2011) Oman, in Davidson, C. (eds.) *Power and Politics in the Persian Gulf Monarchies*. London: Hurst & Co, pp. 135–161.

Wehrey, F.C. (2014) *Sectarian Politics in the Gulf. From the Iraq War to the Arab Uprisings*. New York: Columbia University Press. DOI:10.7312/wehr16512.

World Bank (2021). *World Bank Database*, [Online]. Available at: http://data.worldbank.org (Accessed 31 January 2021).

Worrall, J. (2012) Oman: The "Forgotten" Corner of the Arab Spring. *Middle East Policy*, 19(3), pp. 98–115. DOI:10.1111/j.1475-4967.2012.00550.x.

Wright, S. (2017) Iran's Relations with Bahrain, in: Bahgat, G., Ehteshami, A. and Quilliam, N. (eds.) *Security and Bilateral Issues between Iran and its Arab Neighbours*. London: Palgrave Macmillan, pp. 61–80. DOI:10.1007/978-3-319-43289-2_4.

WTO (2017a) Bahrain – Measures Relating to Trade in Goods and Services, and Trade-related Aspects of Intellectual Property Rights. World Trade Organization, [Online]. Available at: https://docs.wto.org/dol2fe/Pages/FE_Search/FE_S_S006.aspx?Query=(%20@Symbol=%20(wt/ds527/1%20))&Language=ENGLISH&Context=FomerScriptedSearch&languageUIChanged=true# (Accessed 31 January 2021).

WTO (2017b) Saudi Arabia – Measures Relating to Trade in Goods and Services, and Trade-related Aspects of Intellectual Property Rights. *World Trade Organization*, [Online]. Available at: https://docs.wto.org/dol2fe/Pages/FE_Search/FE_S_S006.aspx?Query=(%20@Symbol=%20(wt/ds528/1%20))&Language=ENGLISH&Context=FomerScriptedSearch&languageUIChanged=true# (Accessed 31 January 2021).

WTO (2017c) United Arab Emirates – Measures Relating to Trade in Goods and Services, and Trade-related Aspects of Intellectual Property Rights. World Trade Organization, [Online]. Available at: https://docs.wto.org/dol2fe/Pages/FE_Search/FE_S_S006.aspx?Query=(%20@Symbol=%20(wt/ds526/1%20))&Language=ENGLISH&Context=FomerScriptedSearch&languageUIChanged=true# (Accessed 31 January 2021).

WTO (2020) Saudi Arabia – Measures concerning the protection of intellectual property rights. World Trade Organization, [Online]. Available at: https://www.wto.org/english/tratop_e/dispu_e/567r_e.pdf (Accessed 31 January 2021).

Yaari, E. (2020) The Road Beyond UAE–Israel Normalisation. The Washington Institute, [Online]. Available at: https://www.washingtoninstitute.org/policy-analysis/road-beyond-uae-israel-normalization (Accessed 31 January 2021).

Zaccara, L. (2013) Comparing Elections in Gulf Cooperation Council Countries after the Arab Spring: The United Arab Emirates, Oman, and Kuwait. *Journal of Arabian Studies: Arabia, the Gulf, and the Red Sea*, 3(1), pp. 80–101. DOI:10.1080/21534764.2013.802941.

Zafirov, M. (2014) The Qatar Crisis – Why the Blockade Failed. *Israel Journal of International Affairs*, 11(2), pp. 191–201. DOI:10.1080/23739770.2017.1382072.

Conclusion
Size, power, and regime stability in the Gulf

At first sight, Middle Eastern and North African small states should have found themselves in an unfavourable position by the 21st century. Systemic developments, including worsening instability, intensifying great power rivalry, civil wars and their spill-over effects should, at least theoretically, undermine their security and shrink their leverage. Empirically, nonetheless, this picture is far from precise – as was seen in the last chapters, Qatar, Oman, and the United Arab Emirates have been in the forefront of developments taking place in the Gulf and the broader region. Theoretical expectations fit Bahrain and Kuwait better, but as has been seen, their weakness has been caused only partially by the lack of resources, as mismanaged heterogeneity and domestic problems definitely played a larger role.

Consequently, in spite of their systematically similar position, the five smaller Gulf states play a markedly different role in the region. Tackling the negative consequences of small territorial, demographic, and military size, Bahrain exposed itself to Saudi influence and managed its domestic problems arising from social heterogeneity by forceful measures and by neutralizing Sunni migrant workers. Its domestic challenges, coupled with intra-regime competition (e.g. the rise of the *Khawalid* branch) have limited its foreign policy leverage and drawn attention to domestic affairs, especially since 2011.

Due to its distinct history and identity, Oman was able to develop its own individual security policy, and build up close military relations with Great Britain and the USA without getting too close to them politically, while maintaining a respected, low-key position enabling Muscat to be an effective facilitator. The experience regarding domestic instability and the particularities arising from the Ibadi political culture makes the Omani regime more cautious than its neighbours and more invested in contributing to the peaceful resolution of conflicts.

Due to its particular domestic politics, Kuwait turned inwards and was forced to institutionalise power-sharing among the rival elite groups. Due to its economic and social history, the country has been the most democratic in the region, with a vivid political landscape that includes monarchists, liberals, Islamists, Sunnis, and Shias alike. Kuwait still carries the burdens of the Iraqi invasion, especially in terms of the sensibilities of the regime, which makes the government prioritise domestic issues over international ones. Kuwait

DOI: 10.4324/9781003158288-8

will always be interested in international mediation and peace-making; nevertheless, its toolkit seems more limited than those of its neighbours.

Enjoying domestic stability and conducting a long-term strategy, Qatar managed to enlarge its importance in the international system. Specialising on liquid natural gas exports, cooperating with the Muslim Brotherhood, and using various soft power tools (e.g. mediation), Doha managed to influence political dynamics and secure its place in the interstate society. Qatar's foreign policy success became apparent during the Arab Uprisings when, building on its previously established networks and connections with non-state actors (e.g. the Muslim Brotherhood), it managed to affect political outcomes to a great extent. Besides its geopolitical position, what enabled Doha to conduct such a foreign policy was the lack of serious domestic threats – history tells us that the only serious danger a Qatari emir has to face is intra-regime strife.

Nevertheless, the moment of Qatar has arguably passed. Its allies, especially in Egypt, were pushed out of power, while in other cases – such as in Libya or Syria – have to face extensive competition. The backlash was probably due to moving away too harshly with expected small state behaviour and neutrality, enlarging its normative size, and conducting a locally revisionist strategy with partners of questionable repute. That being said, the failure of Qatar is a relative failure – its image was not shattered to any major extent in the international system and, as the Gulf rift proved, the Qatari regime is resilient to external pressure, and it continues to play an important role in regional affairs, partly due to its unquestionable alliance with the USA.

Decision makers in the UAE definitely learned the lesson from the Qatari experience, even if the federation has been the odd-man-out among the smaller Gulf states. It has a unique domestic political and economic system, a slightly larger material size similar to Israel, the best defence industry, and a staunchly pro-status quo strategy. For Abu Dhabi, maintaining domestic peace and stability is of primary importance, making moderate Islamism the primary threat to the regime. The competition between local elites and tribes (especially between Abu Dhabi and Dubai) is institutionalised through the federative system, which proved to be a fine tool in maintaining stability and avoiding foreign interference. These circumstances, and not necessarily its size, make the UAE a prime candidate for becoming a "middle power".

What differentiates the strategy of Qatar and the UAE can be boiled down to the perception of the status quo. Whereas Qatar tried to change the local and regional balance of power considerably, the UAE mostly supported the stronger side, or had a more limited strategy without the intention of completely undermining regimes and governments.

As we can see from these examples, smallness is far from being the variable that determines power and regime stability in the Middle East. State size is not an objective phenomenon unchangeable by political actors or systemic processes. In practice, state size, power, and stability affect each other constantly, shaping the leverage and survival ability of regimes in direct interaction with each other.

The complex model of size (CMS) has proved to be useful in interpreting this process in various ways. First, differentiating between absolute, relative, perceptual, and normative size enabled us to provide a more nuanced description of their size and position than could have been obtained by just calling them "small." The best example is Qatar, a relative small state that also small in absolute territorial, demographic, and military terms but large in absolute economic terms. On the other hand, smallness does not play a substantive role in the projected identity of Qatar while, normatively, it started to grow considerably in the 2000s. On the other hand, Oman managed to be an influential player without virtually enlarging its normative size in the interstate society. Its intention to engage in facilitation and remain hidden behind the curtains should be seen as a defensive mechanism to avoid attracting undesired attention. These points prove that relative size and systemic position are not the only aspects that determine foreign policy behaviour.

Second, the systemic starting point of the CMS enabled us to investigate Middle Eastern small states in their own regional context. As a result, it was shown that, due to the particularities of the MENA region, small states are better off than one would expect. Due to norm subsidiarity processes related to conflicts, the particularities of statehood, and transnational identities, material smallness should not be seen solely as a cage that deprives states of leverage and security but, rather, one of many attributes which, when tackled correctly, can be used as an advantage as well.

Third, by analysing the effects of smallness not by itself but through interactions with other variables, one can provide a more thorough analysis of how state size affects power and regime stability. In the case of limiting the ability of other actors to interfere in domestic affairs, demographic smallness can be a huge advantage. Small economic and population size, coupled with hydrocarbon resources, leads to fiscal leverage, which can be quite useful in foreign policy.

That leads to how we should update our expectations regarding the foreign policy of small states. In the Introduction, I mentioned two non-traditional ways in which smallness affects states, rather than simply being an insurmountable challenge: incentivising them to conduct compensatory policies, and providing them with a tool in foreign policy (e.g. in mediation or nation branding). The case of smaller Gulf states shows that dealing with the effects of compensatory policies is a bigger issue than dealing with smallness directly. Moreover, for Oman, Qatar, and the UAE, smallness is readily usable to achieve specific aims. Kuwait also projected its smallness after it was attacked by Iraq to gather international support to defend itself.

Concluding the research, I would like to answer two additional questions: What are the potential areas where Gulf studies should evolve? What are the general implications of my investigation on Small State Studies?

As was mentioned previously, a major problem currently in Middle Eastern Studies is the gap between theoretical and empirical studies. The imagined particularity of the region or over-emphasizing the Western nature of IR make only poor excuses not to try to connect international political and economic theories with state- or regional-level analysis. The notions that IR theory is not suitable for the MENA region, or that this geographical area is not a proper case study for IR are used to avoid thorough academic work to make our tools better equipped to be applied in different regional and cultural settings.

Lacking theoretical embeddedness urges scholars to conduct descriptive analysis and to over-emphasize the role of personalities. While it is true that in cases such as Oman, Qatar, the UAE, where foreign policy decision making is loosely institutionalised (at least compared to the Western environment), a leader's personality traits matter to a great extent. Sultan Qaboos, Emir Hamad bin Khalifa Al Thani, and Mohamed bin Zayed thoroughly shaped their country's position in the region. That being said, they are not the sole – and, probably, not the most important – reason why Oman, Qatar, or the UAE has been able to play an important role in the region. A proper way to identify the precise weight of personalities is to analyse succession processes more precisely.

Another aspect in which Gulf studies can develop is putting more emphasis on state and social identities. Naturally, there are many studies focusing on this issue; nevertheless, frequently, their methodological foundation is shaky. The method presented in the book has its limitations but has served as a useful approximation to the phenomenon. Also, more focus could be given to differentiating between the identity of states and societies, as well as the specific mechanisms of identity politics.

When it comes to Small State Studies, the basic ideas of the complex model of size reflect three major implications. First, smallness comes in different forms, which is why scholars of IR should not be satisfied by simplistic notions regarding state size. The picture drawn by Isaac Asimov about smallness being a source of strength and innovation is as valid an interpretation as those that identify smallness with weakness and insecurity.

Second, with its almost sole focus on size, Small State Studies forgot to take into account varieties in state structures and their effect on how smallness plays a role in politics. Without analysing the Middle Eastern state system, one cannot capture the situation of small states precisely. The evolution of regimes, the different dynamics of state-formation, and state-building all give meaning to material smallness. This notion is true whichever region we choose to analyse.

Third, connecting Small State Studies with identity and identity politics should be encouraged. As was described in Chapter 1, many scholars have engaged in such an endeavour, but further work is needed to better understand how smallness affects state identities, national brands, security, and relations between the state and society. In the present research, the investigation of perceptual and normative size is meant to be an added value in this regard.

Naturally, my research has been far from complete. Many subtleties and details have been left out of the analysis due to spatial limitations and for the sake of building an argument. Certain methodological challenges also hampered the investigation, especially in terms of the analysis of identities, norms, and perceptions. The complex model of size helped in eliminating some conceptual and methodological confusion in Small State Studies, but not in all cases.

In IR, size is a complex phenomenon. In order to keep up with the changing international system, we need a complex model to interpret its importance in a thorough manner. The elimination of this blind spot would benefit not just researchers of Middle Eastern or Small State Studies, but also scholars of IR in general. Moreover, foreign policy decision makers could also deepen their understanding of international relations of the 21st century by going beyond their cognitive bias towards size. Large states should not neglect small ones but, rather, learn from them. On the other hand, small states should not deprive themselves of the opportunities that they could enjoy in spite of their smallness – or, perhaps, because of it.

Index

Page numbers in **bold** indicate tables, page numbers in *italic* indicate figures.

Milton Keynes UK
Ingram Content Group UK Ltd.
UKHW022020120124
435953UK00006B/60